BLACK MAJORITY

BLACK MAJORITY

*Negroes in Colonial
South Carolina*

From 1670 through the Stono Rebellion

PETER H. WOOD

W · W · NORTON & COMPANY

New York · London

W. W. Norton & Company, Inc., 500 Fifth Avenue, New York, N.Y. 10110
W. W. Norton & Company Ltd., 37 Great Russell Street, London WC1B 3NU

Books That Live
The Norton imprint on a book means that in the publisher's
estimation it is a book not for a single season but for the years.
W. W. Norton & Company, Inc.

Library of Congress Cataloging in Publication Data
Wood, Peter H   1943-
  Black majority.
  (The Norton library)
  Based on the author's thesis, Harvard, 1972.
  Reprint of the 1st ed. published by Knopf, New York
  Bibliography: p.
  1. Slavery in the United States—South Carolina.
2. South Carolina—History—Colonial period,
ca. 1600-1775. I. Title.
[E445.S7W66   1975]   201.44'93'09757   75-14237

ISBN 0-393-00777-4

Printed in the United States of America

4 5 6 7 8 9 0

*This book is dedicated to
Tyrone Fleet, Matthew Stevens,
and other Americans
younger than myself.*

Take no one's word for anything, including mine
—but trust your experience. Know whence you
came. If you know whence you came, there is
really no limit to where you can go.

I have great respect for that unsung army of
black men and women. . . . I am proud of these
people not because of their color but because
of their intelligence and their spiritual force
and their beauty. The country should be proud
of them, too, but, alas, not many people in this
country even know of their existence. And the
reason for this ignorance is that a knowledge
of the role these people played—and play—in
American life would reveal more about America
to Americans than Americans wish to know.

I am not a ward of America; I am one of the
first Americans to arrive on these shores.

—JAMES BALDWIN, *The Fire Next Time*

✎ Contents ✎

PART FOUR: *A COLONY IN CONFLICT*

LIST OF TABLES

A map showing parish boundaries and population distribution
in 1720 appears on *page* 149.

Acknowledgments

Throughout the course of this work I have received encouragement and assistance from a great number of personal acquaintances and fellow scholars. Most importantly, I have gained from talking and corresponding with a wide range of colleagues, both younger and older than myself. From the start, I have benefitted from the consistent kindness and interest of fellow researchers, and of staff members, in the places where I have worked. Recently, my associates at the Rockefeller Foundation (where such lowland concerns as rice production and the control of malarious mosquitoes are not unknown) have been most helpful, as have friends at Alfred A. Knopf. I am indebted, deeply and in different ways, to all these people. I trust each of them will know, without being named here, how much I value their individual support and counsel.

Among institutions, Harvard's Widener and Houghton libraries and Princeton's Firestone Library gave me full use of their facilities for extended periods. I was a welcome guest at numerous other research centers, especially in South Carolina. The South Carolina Historical Society in Charleston and the South Caroliniana Library in Columbia were particularly gracious. For many months the South Carolina Department of Archives and History, also located in Columbia, served as my second home. These repositories uphold the best traditions of a region where personal kindness and hospitality still mean a great deal, and where history is a vital force demanding study and respect.

Two persons in particular contributed more to this present undertaking than they may realize. Oscar Handlin first introduced me to the vitality of social history. His undergraduate lectures suggested to me something of the diversity and interdependencies that have always characterized American life, and that we have only begun to understand. He later urged me, indirectly, to be both independent and generous in my judgments. Bernard Bailyn communicated to me the excitement, importance, and immediacy of early American history. In his subtlety of approach, depth of research, and clarity of expression, he has followed in a distinguished line of scholars and set an appealing and implausible standard for his students. The congenial and shrewd way in which he offered critical encouragement at every stage of this project has been an important factor in its completion, and I am grateful for his intellectual and personal kindness.

Three other special individuals—Mary Lee Wood, William Barry Wood, and Ann Douglas Wood—each contributed deeply and distinctively to the shaping of this volume and to the unfolding of my life. Both the book and its author are the better for knowing them.

P.H.W.

❧ Introduction ❧

I

I BEGAN this study by wondering at what point, if any, my interests in colonial history and in black history could intersect. I was aware that African slaves, if taken together, were the largest single group of non-English-speaking migrants to enter the North American colonies in the pre-Revolutionary era. Indeed, they were the earliest of any major contingent of ethnic immigrants to reach the continent from across the Atlantic. The proportion of Negroes in the population would never again be so high as it was during the eighteenth century. And yet none of these facts was reflected in the history which I had read.

Traditionally, colonial historians have given the most attention to the northern settlements, where Negro presence was slightest. For those interested in early southern history, Virginia, where blacks were numerous but always in the minority, is often taken to represent—if not constitute—the colonial South. (The idea that several "Souths" may have existed even before the middle of the eighteenth century has not had wide acceptance.) Scholars of black history, on the other hand, while paying great attention to the southern region, have concentrated for the most part on the national period. Where their scholarship deals with slavery it is often organized thematically rather than chronologically, leaving the impression that the institution was a static one and that the records for studying its evolution from the beginnings of settlement do not exist.

Of course a few books provide marked exceptions to each of these generalizations, and their numbers are increasing with time. But for the most part, I had been schooled to believe that the important elements of early American history belonged to the mid-Atlantic and northern colonies and that the verifiable aspects of black history belonged to the nineteenth and twentieth centuries. In spite of such training, or perhaps because of it, I felt a mounting interest in what the Negro author Jean Toomer described as "roots trending away to the Southward." A strong desire grew in me to uncover some of these roots at their earliest and most southerly beginnings. Gradually, such impulses led me to colonial South Carolina.

Black slaves were present in the South Carolina colony from the year of its founding, and by the second generation they constituted a majority of the population. Here was a thin neck in the hourglass of the Afro-American past, a place where individual grains from all along the West African coast had been funneled together, only to be fanned out across the American landscape with the passage of time. Sullivan's Island, the sandy spit on the northeast edge of Charlestown harbor where incoming slaves were briefly quarantined, might well be viewed as the Ellis Island of black Americans. In fact, the colonial ancestors of present-day Afro-Americans are more likely to have first confronted North America at Charlestown than at any other port of entry. It has been estimated that well over 40 per cent of the slaves reaching the British mainland colonies between 1700 and 1775 arrived in South Carolina, while most of the remainder were scattered through the Chesapeake region, and a comparative few (often from the West Indies rather than Africa) entered through northern ports.[1] This being the case, I had found an answer for my initial question and a logical focus for my study.

But this answer posed a more difficult set of questions. What sources—secondary and primary—would be available for such an inquiry? How far back would I be able to press and still find documentary material; how greatly would I need to broaden my boundaries in space and time before I had uncovered the information adequate for a single book? These were not idle questions in the field of black his-

---

[1] Philip D. Curtin, *The Atlantic Slave Trade: A Census* (Madison, 1969), p. 158. The forthcoming book of W. Robert Higgins on the slave trade in colonial South Carolina, coupled with the work of Darold D. Wax and others, will begin to provide the outlines of this eighteenth-century trade. See also Kenneth Winslow Stetson, "A Quantitative Approach to Britain's American Slave Trade, 1700–1773," unpublished M.S. thesis (University of Wisconsin, 1967), p. 48 *ff.*

Roughly ten million people are now thought to have been transported from West Africa to the entire New World during more than three hundred years of active slave trading. From this unprecedented migration a comparatively small number, somewhere in the vicinity of 500,000 individuals, were brought to North America. See Curtin, *passim.*

tory, which, until recently, has had as its controlling and limiting assumption the untested generalization that "although it may be an interesting area, the records for exploring it scarcely exist." Even as I began to come to terms with these uncertainties, I made a number of arbitrary decisions. I would, data permitting, begin at the beginning of the black experience in South Carolina—1670 or earlier. I would refrain from giving direct attention to the transatlantic experience— the African background and the notorious middle passage—not because it seemed remote and insignificant but, on the contrary, because it seemed so varied in itself and so vital to a full understanding of the immigrants I hoped to follow that it must one day become the subject of separate and intensive study. I also decided that I would confine myself geographically to South Carolina, and would proceed forward in time as far as a detailed inquiry permitted. At the outset, I determined that if I could draw forth a meaningful study from one of the least accessible corners of Afro-American history, it would not only be an exciting undertaking in itself, but by implication it would argue the viability of countless other ventures into less remote aspects of black history and culture in the United States.

II

THE HISTORY of colonial South Carolina has not been ignored. Scores of people have given a great deal of attention and thought to this portion of the early American past. All historians are familiar with the pleasing sense that comes from feeling engaged in a joint enterprise with many who have surveyed similar territory at a previous time. I have had my full share of this pleasurable feeling over the last several years, reading through a fascinating range of historical work. Yet the sum of all the secondary scholarship now available concerning early South Carolina hardly adds up to a total picture, for the majority of the colony's population remains in comparative anonymity. In 1935 David Duncan Wallace, the author of a four-volume history of the region, outlined "Some Unexploited Fields in South Carolina History."[2] It is striking that while he raised questions about Indians, poor whites, and indentured servants, he made no mention whatsoever of

---

[2] S.C. Hist. Assoc., *Proceedings, 1935* (Columbia, 1936), pp. 26–35.

Negro slaves. A generation later, much of this unawareness still continues.[3] As a result, most Americans would find it hard to conceive that the population of one of the thirteen original colonies was well over half black at the time the nation's independence was declared.

This is not to say that historians have totally neglected South Carolina's black majority. Since as long ago as 1895 occasional articles have attempted to define aspects of their situation.[4] One of the earliest publications of the historian U. B. Phillips was a lengthy piece on slave labor in the vicinity of Charleston (known as Charlestown before its incorporation in 1783).[5] While Phillips' opening assertion about the primacy of "the low-lying coast region of South Carolina and Georgia" in the study of black history still rings true, much of what followed is extremely dated. A longer study by Frank J. Klingberg made a similar claim for the significance of the lowland region. "No other area of the American continent," he wrote, "is more rewarding for the study of the relationship between the Negro and white man, than that embraced under the term, colonial South Carolina."[6] But Klingberg's book, although titled *An Appraisal of the Negro in Colonial South Carolina,* is devoted to a small group of Anglican missionaries and their efforts to convert a very limited number of slaves. Such studies, some of which professed to have exhausted documentary evidence, only helped spur me to search out primary materials for myself.

This search was not always simple, and like any historian I can admit to occasional frustration in pursuing my concerns. How else could one feel coming across a letter such as the following? "I had something to say of the Negroes here," wrote an Anglican minister to the Society for the Propagation of the Gospel in 1710, "but cannot now; having scarce time to recommend my Eldest Son, whom I send

[3] While working in the South Carolina Archives I noticed that one of the newest grade-school histories of the region contains two references to Negroes in its hundred-page treatment of the colonial period. A white graduate student working there in American history once asked me, "Did they have slaves in those days?"

[4] E.g., Edward McCrady, "Slavery in the Province of South Carolina, 1670–1770," Amer. Hist. Assoc., *Report, 1895* (Washington, D.C., 1896), 629–73; Albert H. Stoddard, "Origin, Dialect, Beliefs, and Characteristics of the Negroes of the South Carolina and Georgia Coasts," *GHQ,* XXVIII (1944), 186–95. Of greater usefulness is M. Eugene Sirmans, "The Legal Status of the Slave in South Carolina, 1670–1740," *JSH,* XXVIII (1962), 462–73.

[5] Ulrich B. Phillips, "The Slave Labor Problem in the Charleston District," *Political Science Quarterly,* XXII (1907), 416–39.

[6] Klingberg, *Appraisal,* p. 1.

to London, in hopes the Venble Society may do something for him and take care of him."[7]

Yet if some curtains remained closed forever, others could be partially or wholly drawn aside. On balance, the greatest source of pleasure from my research was the realization which gradually emerged that primary resources for my proposed undertaking were more than ample. Where I had first thought it might be possible or necessary to bridge 150 years, I soon limited myself to half that span. Consideration of the detailed materials from the Revolutionary era would have to await a separate study. Whether I could even do justice to the materials for the early generations became the central question. My task would not be so much to "wrap them up," as one New England professor advised me, but rather to "open them up" for continuing exploration by others with similar or separate interests. I hope it will be clear from the text which follows that in the particular field I have chosen to cultivate, and in those adjacent to it, a great deal of intensive work still lies ahead.

III

As I IMMERSED myself in the relevant primary sources, several impressions emerged. Information concerning Negroes within the colony, once sought, could not only be found but could hardly be avoided. Often a volume of records which had no reference to "Negroes" or "Slaves" in its index would still contain pertinent material in the actual text. As one might expect, it became increasingly clear that the role of the black majority was major rather than minor, active rather than passive. Negro slaves played a significant and often determinative part in the evolution of the colony.

It appeared that the transition to an African work force at the start of the eighteenth century, due to the interweaving of variables which are widely familiar, may also have depended in part upon several factors explored here in detail for the first time. A number of Africans possessed prior familiarity with rice cultivation, which could have greatly enhanced the value of all blacks as workers, particularly in the years when this commodity was first being established. Further-

[7] *Johnston*, p. 61.

more, West Africans, like Sicilians and others who have lived in malarious climates for centuries, had retained a high incidence of sickle-cell trait, a genetic characteristic the negative effects of which were balanced by its positive contribution: the ability to inhibit malaria among humans constantly exposed to infectious mosquitoes. Whatever the importance of these hypotheses, Africans brought with them distinctive strengths and skills that suited them to life in the Carolina lowlands, and that, ironically but understandably, contributed to the gradual evolution of their status as chattel slaves in the frontier province.

I have been impressed from the start by the potential for comparisons existing in the materials I have used. In the first place, the relationship between the Negroes in early South Carolina and those in other mainland and Caribbean colonies awaits further consideration. Secondly, factors linking the experience of black people in the seventeenth and eighteenth centuries with the better-known experience of the nineteenth and twentieth centuries are both more complicated and more direct than has yet been seen. In addition, comparisons and contrasts between the lives of enslaved immigrants arriving in the southern colonies and European workers reaching the North in later times have hardly begun to be explored. I have refrained from pursuing any of these comparisons actively in the present study, believing that their eventual development depends in part upon the soundness of the specific observations which can be made about the lives of blacks in the Carolina colony itself.

The fact that such observations emerged primarily from documents written by white hands is for me a source of interest rather than dismay. Historians must make intelligent use of all materials at their disposal, and although I believe that "black history" has not yet focused nearly directly enough upon the lives and experiences of black Americans, I am not averse to analyzing "white" sources in pursuit of this end. While I have not limited my sources racially, I have made an effort to confine them chronologically. Too often Afro-American history has been read backward, with nineteenth-century evidence being used to support generalizations about eighteenth-century life. To avoid the distortions which come from looking through the wrong end of a telescope, I have tried to proceed forward through time. The chapters of this study, although semitopical, are arranged chronologically, and only in isolated instances have I used materials from the post-Revolutionary period. In fact, I have tried to refrain from using most sources dating after the era of the Stono Rebellion in 1739.

Finally, in my desire to show in some detail the rough terrain of a human landscape that has often been perceived from the distance as flat, it appeared advantageous to follow an interdisciplinary route. I have pursued such a course, bringing rudimentary medical science, statistics, and linguistics into this study where it seemed appropriate. Others might have drawn upon different disciplines with equal or greater relevance. I am convinced that any weaknesses which arise in my work from adopting this approach do not come from venturing too far, but rather from failing to proceed far enough. I remain a firm believer in R. G. Collingwood's observation that

The enlargement of historical knowledge comes about mainly through finding how to use as evidence this or that kind of perceived facts which historians have hitherto thought useless to them. The whole perceptible world, then, is potentially and in principle evidence to the historian. It becomes actual evidence in so far as he can use it.[8]

The dedication of this book to Americans younger than myself represents a simple, personal, and deeply felt reaffirmation.

P. H. W.

August 1973

[8] R. G. Collingwood, *The Idea of History* (Oxford, 1946), p. 247.

Notes on the Text
and a List of Footnote
Abbreviations

ANDREW JACKSON once observed that he had little respect for anyone who could think of only one way to spell a word. Judging from the sources I have used, Jackson's respect for many of his South Carolina forebears must have been enormous in this regard. In utilizing direct quotations from original sources, I have retained not only creative spelling, but also creative grammar and punctuation as well. Obtrusive brackets and the patronizing term "sic" appear as little as possible. Untypable signs, such as that once used for "per," have been translated, and the more random usages of italics have been omitted.

Though we are by no means as liberal with capital letters as our ancestors, I have chosen to capitalize a number of terms, such as New World, Assembly, and Proprietor. Except where quoting older sources, I have capitalized the word "Negro," a practice which did not become standard in this country until President Franklin Roosevelt made it a matter of official policy. I have not capitalized such terms as "black," "white," "mustee," or "mulatto," whether used as nouns or adjectives. The South Carolina port of Charlestown did not become known as Charleston until the end of the American Revolution (although the shift in pronunciation no doubt preceded the shift in spelling), so I have utilized the colonial spelling. I have brought colonial dates into conformity with a calendar year beginning January 1, and I have abbreviated the publication dates for weekly newspapers to a single day. (Thus the *South Carolina Gazette* for Feb. 8–15, 1734/5, is cited as appearing Feb. 15, 1735.)

An earlier version of this work, slightly longer, clumsier, and more heavily documented, was accepted as a doctoral dissertation in American history at Harvard in 1972. A bound copy is available in the Harvard University Archives to any curious scholar. That work, with the same title as this volume, is cited here where necessary as: Wood, "Black Majority." The statistical parts of Chapter V, along with a segment of Chapter XI and Appendix C, appear in a demographic essay published in a volume edited by Stanley L. Engerman and Eugene D. Genovese entitled *Race and Slavery in the Western Hemisphere: Quantitative Studies* (Princeton, 1974). Since these figures have never been given direct consideration before, it is hoped that their inclusion here will prove more instructive than confusing. With regard to the numerous footnotes accompanying the text, they are not intended to weight it down, but simply to strengthen it. They provide a tangible roadbed over which others may find it useful to travel. If any fellow scholar takes encouragement or guidance from them, their presence will be justified. Nevertheless, the general reader must not be deterred by these academic cobblestones and is urged to proceed across them fearlessly at a comfortable pace. To help smooth the way slightly, I have made use of the following abbreviations. (Certain volumes cited frequently in a shortened form are listed fully in the Bibliographical Note at the back of this book.)

AHR: American Historical Review.

AJTM: American Journal of Tropical Medicine.

BPRO Trans.: Records in the British Public Record Office Relating to South Carolina, 1663–1782. These thirty-six handwritten volumes were compiled in 1895 under the direction of W. Noel Sainsbury and are known as the Sainsbury Transcripts; they are available in the South Carolina Department of Archives and History. The first five volumes have been published in a facsimile form (Atlanta and Columbia, 1928–47) and are cited here as BPRO *Trans.*

Coll.: South Carolina Historical Society, *Collections.*

CRNC: William L. Saunders, ed., *The Colonial Records of North Carolina,* 10 vols. (Raleigh, 1886–90).

CRSG: Allan D. Candler and Lucien L. Knight, eds., *The Colonial Records of the State of Georgia,* 26 vols. (Atlanta, 1904–16).

DRNY: E. B. O'Callaghan, *et al.,* eds., *Documents Relative to the Colonial History of the State of New York,* 15 vols. (Albany, 1855–83).

GHQ: Georgia Historical Quarterly.

Guerard Letterbook: The Letterbook of John Guerard, 1752–54, SCHS.

JNH: Journal of Negro History.

JSH: Journal of Southern History.

mfm: microfilm.

MR: Miscellaneous Records, SCDAH.

msv: manuscript volume.

NYHS: New-York Historical Society.

Parish Trans.: Parish Transcripts, NYHS. (Mr. Parish and his colleagues transcribed all they could find in the British Public Records which pertained to Negroes and slaves in the North American colonies.)

Pringle Letterbook: The Letterbook of Robert Pringle, 1737–45, SCHS. Walter B. Edgar has edited a two-volume set of this letterbook (Columbia, 1972).

rpt.: reprinted.

RRP: Records of the Register of the Province, SCDAH.

RSP: Records of the Secretary of the Province, SCDAH.

SCCH: South Carolina Commons House, the journals of which are in the SCDAH. References to these manuscript journals are given as SCCHJ.

SCCHJ: South Carolina Commons House Journals: Alexander S. Salley, ed., *Journal of the Commons House of Assembly,* 21 vols. (Columbia, 1907–46); and J. H. Easterby and Ruth S. Green, eds., *The Colonial Records of South Carolina,* 1st ser.: *The Journal of the Commons House of Assembly, 1736–1750,* 9 vols. (Columbia, 1951–62).

SCDAH: South Carolina Department of Archives and History, Columbia, S.C.

SCG: South Carolina Gazette.

SCHGM: South Carolina Historical and Genealogical Magazine (called the *South Carolina Historical Magazine* since 1952, but cited here as *SCHGM* throughout).

SCHS: South Carolina Historical Society, Charleston, S.C.

SCL: South Caroliniana Library at the University of South Carolina, Columbia.

SCUHJ: Journals of the South Carolina Upper House in the SCDAH.

SRNC: Walter Clark, ed., *State Records of North Carolina,* 26 vols. (Winston, Goldsboro, N.C., 1895–1914).

Statutes: Thomas Cooper and David J. McCord, eds., *The Statutes at Large of South Carolina,* 10 vols. (Columbia, 1836–41).

Warrants: Alexander S. Salley, ed., *Warrants for Land in South Carolina (1672–1711),* 3 vols. (Columbia, 1910–15).

WIMR: Wills, Inventories, and Miscellaneous Records, Works Progress Administration typescript, SCDAH.

WMQ: William and Mary Quarterly.

WMR: Wills and Miscellaneous Records, SCDAH.

BLACK MAJORITY

⊷ Prologue ⊶

Small Beginnings

I

ALONG the coastal plain of the North American continent there is a broad wedge of land which stretches from the hazy base of the Appalachian Mountains to the uneven rim of the Atlantic Ocean. This low triangle of green and brown, spread out like a fan between the Savannah River and the sea, has been known for the past three centuries as "South Carolina." Earlier, for a far longer period, it was called by a series of distinctive titles belonging to the local Indian groups, who proved the first and most enduring residents of the area. Long before the region of Carolina was named for an English king, and generations before any English subject set foot there, people from West Africa were walking its sandy shoreline.

The first Africans came in 1526 as members of a sizable Spanish expedition from the West Indies. This venture for reconnaissance and settlement, organized by an aging Spanish functionary named Lucas Vásquez de Ayllón, involved some five hundred people who had crowded aboard six ships and a tender in the port of La Plata on the north coast of Hispaniola in midsummer after several years of planning and delay. Weeks later, in the vicinity of Cape Fear, they approached the continent which would eventually be called America, after the Florentine navigator who had sailed these waters thirty years before. To the Spanish-speaking Indians, Africans, and Europeans on shipboard, however, the region was "Tierra del licenciado Ayllón," an extensive realm of nineteen provinces which Charles V had "licensed" to their commander three years earlier.

Spanish explorations had recently revealed that the expanse of water southwest of the Florida peninsula was a landlocked gulf, and the attention of competing European states was now being directed briefly toward the coastline north of Florida. Ayllón's men (like those of Verrazano in 1524 and Gómez and Quexos in 1525) complied with royal instructions by scanning these shores for a passage to the Orient. But they were as unsuccessful in this search as in their effort to establish a permanent foothold near Cape Fear. After a discouraging summer the entire company moved off along the coast by land and water toward the southwest, where scouts reported a more suitable spot for habitation. Entering what would one day be South Carolina, the party attempted in early fall to establish the settlement of San Miguel de Guadalupe beside a broad river, apparently the Peedee. But circumstances did not improve. Although fish were plentiful in the shallow marshes, the colonists were too numerous to be fed easily, and Indian assistance became less accessible when their own native translators deserted them. By mid-October the colony had been reduced to misery by inadequate food and inclement weather, and its commander lay dangerously sick.

Even then, the venture might have survived to make Carolina a Catholic domain named for a Spanish-speaking King Charles, had not Ayllón chosen as his successor for governor a nephew in far-off Puerto Rico. The result was that when Ayllón died on October 18, tension developed immediately among his lieutenants over the right to command. The logical successor was quickly overthrown and confined by several would-be leaders who exerted an arbitrary control over the dwindling settlement. Their tyranny fell most heavily upon the slave contingent, and before long the Negroes struck back, setting fire to the usurpers' hut at night (an act of slave arson which would mark the beginning of a lengthy tradition). In the struggle which followed, the junta was deposed, but the settlement project itself lost whatever impetus remained. Soon most of the survivors, black and white, decamped for Santo Domingo, although there is speculation that some of the rebel slaves remained behind to cast their lot with the Indians.[1]

The involvement of these Negroes in Ayllón's expedition was not surprising, for West Africans had been resident in the Spanish Indies for several decades. Their presence in the New World before, and

[1] Woodbury Lowery, *The Spanish Settlements Within the Present Limits of the United States, 1513–1561* (New York, 1901), pp. 161–68, 447–52; Joseph C. Carroll, *Slave Insurrections in the United States, 1800–1865* (Boston, 1938), p. 13, speculates that Indians instigated the revolt. Aptheker, *Slave Revolts,* p. 163, asserts that the Negroes numbered one hundred and that some of them stayed in North America permanently.

during, the initial journey of Columbus in 1492 remains a matter of conjecture, but there is clear evidence of their growing numbers within a decade after his initial landfall. Many of the early arrivals, such as "Diego el Negro," who served on Columbus' flagship during his final voyage, were personal servants born or brought up in Spain. But as the local population of the Indies declined catastrophically— decimated by novel disease, consumed by incessant labor, starved to make way for the crop-destroying cattle and hogs of the Spanish—the invaders turned increasingly to Africa for manpower.[2] Since Spain had no trading factory there, an exclusive license was granted to Genoese agents in 1517 to transport Negroes to the West Indies for four years. This belated effort to forestall the genocide of the native "Indios" marked the start in earnest of a mass traffic in laborers from Africa which would not abate for more than three hundred years. Negroes were soon accompanying Balboa and Cortés, Narváez and Coronado; and when the conquistadors entered South America, blacks marched in the armies of Almagro, Pizarro, Alvarado, and Valdivia.[3]

As gold turned the attention of such armies increasingly toward the southern hemisphere, the Carolina region saw little of these mixed bands of foreigners. In the spring of 1540 Hernando De Soto's expedition, including Negroes brought from Cuba, wandered northward briefly through Cherokee country, but De Soto never took advantage of the permission he had been granted by the crown to settle an extensive tract with fifty Africans.[4] Only an occasional shipwreck brought strangers during the next two decades, and the contingent of Europeans and Africans who visited Santa Elena (Port Royal Sound) under Angel de Villafane in May 1561 proved unwilling or unable to remain.[5]

Over the next hundred years French and Spanish settlers battled intermittently against the Indians, the elements, and each other in

[2] On the complex demographic, cultural, and environmental balances of this period, see Carl O. Sauer, *The Early Spanish Main* (Berkeley, Calif., 1966) and Alfred W. Crosby, Jr., *The Columbian Exchange: Biological and Cultural Consequences of 1492* (Westport, Conn., 1972).

[3] J. F. Rippy, "The Negro and Spanish Pioneers in the New World," *JNH*, VI (1921), 183–85. Pre-Columbian contact received its most extensive consideration from a Harvard Slavic professor: Leo Wiener, *Africa and the Discovery of America*, 3 vols. (Philadelphia, 1920–22). The 1970 transatlantic voyage of Thor Heyerdahl on the African-built *Ra II* offered grounds for renewed speculation.

[4] Lowery, *Spanish Settlements*, pp. 215, 218. One third of the slaves were to be women; all were to be imported free of duty.

[5] On Sept. 23, 1561, Philip II proclaimed an end to official Spanish colonization efforts in this region. *Ibid.*, pp. 352–53, 374, 376.

efforts to sustain outposts along the north Florida coast. Negroes were
drawn into the service of each nation at times, and both blacks and
whites were known to have taken up residence among adjacent Indian
tribes upon occasion.[6] Even before the traditional date of 1619, when
the first group of slaves was sold in Virginia by a Dutch trader, it
seems likely that there was already a small scattering of Africans resident on the southern mainland. When Englishmen on an "excursion
into Carolina" from the North in 1653 encountered a Tuscarora chief-
tain, he invited the company "to go to his chief town, where he told
them was one Spaniard residing, who had been seven years with them,
a man very rich, having about thirty in family, seven whereof are
negroes; and he had one more negro leiger [resident] with a great
nation called the Newxes."[7] But while a few individuals—both African
and European—mingled with the Indians over the years, no overseas
visitors were able to sustain a separate settlement upon South Carolina shores until 1670. In large measure, the permanent settlement
which emerged at that date stemmed initially from the English colony
of Barbados in the West Indies, unlike the other North American
settlements which grew more directly from European sources. This
Caribbean background contributed to the colony's distinctive mixture
of African and European elements at an early stage and helped to
differentiate it markedly from older and more northerly mainland
colonies.

II

BARBADOS had first been settled in 1627, when several dozen individuals were set down on its uninhabited shore by the English ship
William and John.[8] Roughly one man out of every four in this

---

[6] For evidence of Negro presence in the late sixteenth century, see Mary Ross,
"French Intrusions and Indian Uprisings in Georgia and South Carolina, 1577–1580,"
GHQ, VII (1923), 272.

[7] Salley, *Narratives*, p. 27.

[8] An Englishman had been cast ashore on Bermuda as early as 1583; others
touched at St. Lucia in 1605 and Grenada in 1609, but despite the increasing number
of English ships "below the line" no island settlement was achieved until 1623, when
some colonists settled on St. Christopher. From there they soon spread out over what
would later be called the Leeward Islands. At the same time, under separate auspices,
settlement began farther south on Barbados. This most "windward" of all the Indies
had been set apart by geography, and for the English its possession was a prize.

company was a Negro, and these hands, supplemented by several dozen Indians from the South American mainland, commenced the work of clearing the heavily wooded island. English interest in the colony was immediate, and within two years well over a thousand white persons had been sent out as tenants.[9] Africans were by no means numerous in the early settlement; small numbers of slaves were purchased from Dutch ships or brought from Spanish colonies to supplement the considerable flow of indentured labor from England. But within little more than a decade the situation began to change.[10] The introduction of sugar technology to Barbados, its promise of rapid success heightened by the decline of Brazilian works, demanded new forms of power at every stage. Horses were imported to turn the mills; wood was cut to feed the fires; and at one point, with roads still inadequate for carts, camels were brought from Africa to carry the heavy leather sacks of sugar along dry stream beds to the coastal docks.[11]

But it was the demand for manpower which rose most sharply. Profits from sales in England, along with credit from Dutch traders, were rapidly invested in those laborers who could be obtained in the

---

Barbados had a more serviceable harbor than St. Christopher, and its southerly location had strategic as well as climatic value. It had more fresh water than Antigua, fewer peaks than Nevis, broader fields than Montserrat and, though less than 170 square miles in area, was considerably larger than any of these other English possessions. Henry C. Wilkinson, *The Adventurers of Bermuda* (London, 1933; 2nd edn., 1958), p. 30; James A. Williamson, *The Caribbee Islands under the Proprietary Patents* (London, 1926), pp. 13–23; Charles M. Andrews, *The Colonial Period of American History*, 4 vols. (New Haven, Conn., 1934–38), II, 243–45; C. S. S. Higham, *The Development of the Leeward Islands under the Restoration, 1660–1688* (Cambridge, England, 1921), pp. xiii–xiv.

[9] Williamson, *Caribbee Islands*, pp. 36–38; Vincent T. Harlow, ed., *Colonising Expeditions to the West Indies and Guiana, 1623–1667* (*Hakluyt Society Publications*, 2nd ser., no. LVI, London, 1925), pp. 30–41.

[10] Dutch sugar planters in coastal Brazil, under increasing duress from Portugal after the restoration of that monarchy in 1640, began to disperse through the Caribbean. Aggressive Dutch traders not only sold islanders the elaborate milling and boiling machinery of sugar refining, but they offered to transport additional labor from Africa and carry the commodity to Europe. Vincent T. Harlow, *A History of Barbados, 1625–1685* (Oxford, 1926; rpt. 1969), p. 42. See also Richard S. Dunn, *Sugar and Slaves: The Rise of the Planter Class in the English West Indies, 1624–1713* (Chapel Hill, N.C., 1972), and the forthcoming studies by Richard B. Sheridan and Jerome S. Handler.

[11] Adelaide Berta Helwig, "The Early History of Barbados and Her Influence upon the Development of South Carolina," unpublished Ph.D. thesis (University of California, Berkeley, 1931), pp. 107–8. Richard Ligon's 1657 map showing camels and a black driver is reprinted in the front of Harlow, *Barbados*. A century later, camels were considered for use in South Carolina. See *Laurens*, II, 513.

largest numbers on the most regular basis, from the nearest possible
points and for the longest possible service. Such involuntary recruits
came from West Africa. As patterns of production altered, therefore,
patterns of population also shifted. Where whites had predominated
during the first generation of settlement, blacks became a majority
during the second, and their numerical dominance in Barbados continued to grow. Moreover, the European population declined substan-
tially in absolute terms as economies of scale in the production of
sugar allowed rich settlers to force poorer Europeans off the land.[12] As
big planters engrossed the island's limited acreage during these years,
the mass of the white population could cling to small holdings, cultivate marginal lands, or indenture themselves to the service of others,
but their prospects for social and economic advancement grew increasingly bleak. Given these conditions, it is remarkable how many
remained in Barbados, unwilling or unable to risk a new start elsewhere. But when it is recalled that during the third quarter of the
seventeenth century there were more people on this single teardrop of
an island than in any one of England's older and more sprawling mainland colonies, it is not surprising to find a substantial stream of emigrants from Barbados during these years.

At first, officials accepted these departures as inevitable overflow, but concern increased as numbers mounted. In 1670 two thousand people were said to have quit the island in the previous year.
While some of these émigrés may have intended to return, their total
departures in a single year represented roughly 4 per cent of a population estimated at thirty thousand blacks and twenty thousand whites.
A law was soon passed to prevent plantation owners from further en-
larging their estates.[13] But such engrossment of land was not the only
centrifugal force at work; natural calamities contributed as well. An
onslaught of crop failures, epidemics, fires, and hurricanes during the
1660s and 1670s damaged the colony's precarious economic and social

[12] During the 1660s and 1670s, 175 white planters (less than 7 per cent of
Barbadian landowners) expanded their holdings to include control over more than half
of the slaves, servants, and land on the island. By 1680, there were only 365 landlords
(among more than 2,500 titleholders) who possessed the twenty slaves considered
necessary for a moderate sugar plantation. Harlow, *Barbados,* pp. 338–40; Richard S.
Dunn, "The Barbados Census of 1680: Profile of the Richest Colony in English
America," *WMQ,* 3rd ser., XXVI (1969), 7, 11, 12, 16, 17.

[13] Richard S. Dunn, "The English Sugar Islands and the Founding of South
Carolina," *SCHGM,* LXXII (1971), 82–83; Harlow, *Barbados,* pp. 307, 340.

well-being.[14] These natural devastations, when combined with land scarcity, foreign competition, and the disruptions caused by the warfare of European seapowers, affected all elements of the population. Some substantial planters found cause to join and even lead new ventures. Younger sons of established families, for whom no land remained, often took their inheritance in slaves and servants, and boarded ship. Small landholders who had been squeezed from their holdings departed, as did bond-servants who could obtain no property when their terms expired. Political exiles, of whom Barbados had received a large share, joined the exodus after the English Restoration; debtors and criminals were occasionally allowed, even encouraged, to depart. And almost invariably, enslaved Africans were a part of each outgoing contingent.

Some migrants, like the buccaneer Henry Morgan, resorted to the high seas, but most had specific destinations in mind. The chosen locations varied with time: Surinam and Jamaica in the 1650s, Antigua and Montserrat in the 1660s, Tobago and the northern mainland in the 1670s.[15] By 1680 Gov. Atkins could write to the Lords of Trade: "People no longer come to Barbados, many having departed to Carolina, Jamaica, and the Leeward Islands in hope of settling the land which they cannot obtain here."[16] Although the fraction of this wider migration that embarked for Carolina was never large, those who traveled to that coast from Barbados—both blacks and whites—were to make up a significant segment of the first permanent colony in that region after 1670. And even during the preceding decade, the activities of a group of Barbadian Adventurers helped lay out the terms under which the Carolina coast would eventually be colonized.

[14] Caterpillars destroyed crops in 1663; insect blight and severe drought caused similar damage a decade later. Large fires broke out in Bridgetown in 1666 and 1673 and in St. Michaelstown in 1668 and 1672. The island was hard hit by tropical storms in 1669 and 1675, and epidemic diseases brought intermittent destruction. Helwig, "Barbados and Her Influence," pp. 144–46, 160.

[15] *Ibid.*, pp. vii, 140–41, 148–49.

[16] Oct. 26, 1680, quoted in Harlow, *Barbados,* p. 308 n.

PART ONE

African Workers in the Carolina Lowlands

The Colony of a Colony

I

NOT long after King Charles II was restored to the English throne in the spring of 1660, a Barbadian planter named John Colleton arrived in London, along with scores of other hopeful subjects from the provinces, to seek rewards for past loyalty to the displaced monarch. Colleton promptly joined with other loyal gentry to seek a royal charter for the American region directly south of Virginia. Although a prior grant in 1629 had bestowed the territory upon Sir Robert Heath, the company of Huguenots dispatched under that patent in the early 1630s never reached their destination. And in 1663, to remove any lingering doubts about previous rights, the Restoration Privy Council declared that "such Letters Patent (if any were) are become voyd." With that decision, Colleton and seven other gentlemen at the English court assumed the status of "Proprietors" over a transcontinental domain which extended through five degrees of latitude, and which was expanded two years later, in an act of diplomatic audacity, so that its southern boundary stretched well below the Spanish settlement at St. Augustine.[1]

The Proprietors' motives were frankly commercial. By capitalizing on the migrations then underway between the various American colonies it might be possible, without ever sending out a ship from England, to relocate experienced settlers in a subtropical climate and gather in not only rents upon the land but also proceeds from a whole new range of commodities. Theoretically the investment would be negligible and the profits would be quick. But actual plans were uncertain at first, and colonists were sought from such differing quarters as New England, Bermuda, and Barbados. Even before promotional

[1] Andrews, *Colonial Period*, III, 183–84, 189–90. The declaration of Aug. 12, 1663, is in *CRNC*, I, 42.

efforts began, a group of New England husbandmen had transported their livestock to the Cape Fear region, but details of their experience are obscure, and their tenure was brief. A few Virginia farmers, perhaps employing black as well as white labor, had taken up lands on the north shore of Albemarle Sound. But the coastline farther south (with the exception of some English sailors recently shipwrecked near St. Helena's) was inhabited by several thousand Indians and a small scattering of Spaniards when, in the summer of 1663, the eight Proprietors began to press their claim.[2]

Not surprisingly, the most direct initiative for colonization came from crowded Barbados. Peter Colleton (Sir John's son) and his influential relative, Sir Thomas Modyford, returned there from London to promote the proprietary scheme, and they soon found two hundred people ("amongst them many persons of good quallity") with enough interest in the prospect to unite as the Barbadian Adventurers. On the strength of a brief visit to the coast by a Barbadian captain, William Hilton, members of this group subscribed one thousand pounds of sugar each to underwrite the plan, in exchange for five hundred-acre portions of the initial settlement. The two organizers sent off a letter pressing for concrete assurance of a tract of land, which the subscribers desired "may be called the Corporation of Barbados Adventures." Colleton and Modyford went on to inform the Proprietors, with some exaggeration, that "many hundreds of noble famillyes" were among those "willing and ready to remove spedily theither to begin a setlement," and they stressed "the aptnes of . . . persons heare ingaged to further such a work as well for their experienced planters as for the number of there Negros and other servants fitt for such labor as wilbe there required."[3]

The Barbadians' reference to "Negros and other servants" illustrates that the lines between limited servitude and lifelong slavery were not yet totally clear in England's expanding empire. Mention of Africans, however, could not have failed to catch the attention of the eight Carolina Proprietors, each of whom was familiar with the prac-

[2] Wesley Frank Craven, *The Southern Colonies in the Seventeenth Century, 1607–1689* (Wendell Holmes Stephenson and E. Merton Coulter, eds., *A History of the South*, I [Baton Rouge, La., 1949]), pp. 317–20, 323–24; Andrews, *Colonial Period*, III, 193–96.

[3] T. Modyford and P. Colleton to Proprietors, Aug. 12, 1663, *Coll.*, V, 10–11. They reported Capt. Hilton had been immediately reengaged to sail in his ship *Adventure* with her crew of twenty-two "for discovery of that coast southwards from Cape Faire as far as 31 degrees."

tice of enslaving blacks.[4] For these men in London, a slave colony in Carolina might dovetail nicely with other interests, and upon receiving word of the Barbadian plan they expressed their intent to encourage it "by all wayse and meanes." Only days earlier they had published their own "Declaration and Proposals to all that will Plant in Carolina," suggesting a system of "headrights" for allotting acreage to the heads of every household in proportion to the numbers of people they brought with them. A copy of the proprietary document was immediately forwarded to the Adventurers in Barbados.[5]

II

THE PROPRIETORS REALIZED that Barbados could provide seasoned settlers from a short distance at a minimal cost. With sugar production intensifying and slave imports increasing, the white population had begun to decline in relative and absolute terms, and emigration was already common.[6] Given the fact that the Spanish had been present in Florida for a century, the Proprietors felt that some of these uprooted Barbadians might understand the profits and dangers of contacts with Spain in ways which could strengthen a mainland colony being settled, as one migrant would put it, "in the very chaps of the Spaniard." The Adventurers for their part must have sensed in the suggested headright system an ideal opportunity for turning the island's over-

[4] Sir John Colleton had been a considerable planter in Barbados for a decade, and Sir Anthony Ashley Cooper, who was more experienced in colonial affairs and more deeply interested in Carolina than any of his older colleagues, had become part owner of a plantation in St. George's Parish on Barbados in the late 1640s. (The failure of this venture in 1655 may have made Ashley forever ambivalent about the profitability, if not the justice, of Negro slavery.) The Duke of Albemarle had correspondents in Barbados, as did the Earl of Clarendon, himself a property owner in Jamaica. Andrews, *Colonial Period*, III, 183–87. The Berkeleys were equally familiar with slavery. Sir William, twice governor of Virginia, would see the Negro population of that colony grow from fewer than two hundred at the start of his first term (1641) to well over two thousand by the end of his second (1677). His brother, Lord John Berkeley, along with Ashley, Colleton, and the two other Proprietors, Sir George Carteret and the Earl of Craven, was an active entrepreneur in the growing English trade in black laborers. Craven, *Southern Colonies*, pp. 152, 214, 390, 400–401, 323. Berkeley, Carteret, and Colleton were members of the short-lived Company of Royal Adventurers to Africa organized by the Duke of York in 1660. McCrady, *Proprietary Govt.*, p. 357. Ashley, Carteret, Craven, and young Peter Colleton were involved in the subsequent Royal African Company.

[5] Coll., V, 15; *CRNC*, I, 43–46, 58.

[6] See Prologue, notes 12–16, above.

abundance of people into that which white Barbadians had grown to covet most—land.[7]

Since the Proprietors' initial headright proposal had simply specified the portions of land to be given those who transported "men-servants" and "woman-servants," the Barbadians devised, in Modyford and Colleton's alternate proposals of 1664, three significant adjustments that neatly served their purposes. Where the Proprietors had specified "that there be always one man armed and provided . . . in the colony, for every fifty acres which we shall grant," the Adventurers agreed only that within the next five years, for each *one hundred* acres received in Carolina, they would "have one Person white or black, young or old, transported at their Charge." Conscious that the prospect of land would interest numerous whites in Barbados who were too poor to pay their way, the Adventurers also expanded considerably the size of tracts promised to indentured servants. And finally, since many of the white Barbadians had invested heavily in African labor and were suspicious of the construction placed on the general word "servant" by the Proprietors, a clause was inserted in the proposal to guarantee returns in real estate upon any blacks they could transport:

Item, To the Owner of every Negro-Man or Slave, brought thither to settle within the first year, twenty acres; and for every Woman-Negro or Slave, ten acres of Land; and all Men-Negro's, or slaves after that time, and within the first five years, ten acres, and for every Woman-Negro or slave, five acres.[8]

By January of the following year, when Maj. William Yeamans, representing at least eighty-five of the now somewhat divided Adventurers, set his hand to the elaborate and aptly named "Concessions . . . of the Lords Propryators" in London, the drift of all these Barbadian proposals had been accepted. Negro involvement was recognized specifically in the distinction made between adult European men-servants, relied upon to bear arms, and a secondary category of "weaker" servants (contributing less to the strength of the outpost) which included "woemen and children" on one hand and "slaves above

[7] Sept. 9, 1670, *Coll.,* V, 183. Works linking early Carolina and the Caribbean include John P. Thomas, Jr., "The Barbadians in Early South Carolina," *SCHGM,* XXXI (1930), 75–92; Helwig, "Barbados and Her Influence"; Sirmans, *Colonial S.C.,* part 1; and Dunn, "The English Sugar Islands," pp. 81–93; but the connection has still not been fully explored.

[8] Salley, *Narratives,* p. 58.

yᵉ age of fowerteene yeares" on the other. Members of the former category would now bring eighty, not fifty, acres to their importers, and forty acres would be allotted for any "weaker" servant. Land grants for freed servants were raised from ten to forty acres.[9]

Months before this agreement, however, and only weeks after the return of Hilton from his successful reconnaissance, a party of impatient Barbadians had already set out for Cape Fear. Their fleet, like several later ones, fell under the command of Maj. Yeamans' father, the prominent and somewhat erratic Barbados planter John Yeamans. Entering the Cape Fear River in late May, they proceeded upstream more than twenty miles and began clearing land for the first, and least successful, "Charles Town."[10]

Nor was that the only project. Within eighteen months, Yeamans, now armed with a knighthood, a governor's commission, and the Proprietary Agreement negotiated by his son, had brought another contingent from Barbados to Cape Fear, in the expectation of leading them south to begin a settlement at Port Royal. Such a plan, several years in the making, was never realized. Disasters compounded on sea and land to bring the survival of the Charles Town colony itself into jeopardy. By the summer of 1666 the prominent men who composed the Assembly there were willing to concede their "ill suckses," and before the end of the following year the settlement had entirely disbanded.[11]

In 1666 a London pamphleteer, taking certain promotional liberties, put the population of the enterprise at "about 800 people," but it is unclear what size this short-lived settlement attained. It is also uncertain what percentage of the participants were Negroes. There can be little question, however, about the general significance of West Africans in the schemes of white Barbadians at this time. In a memorial dated September 29, 1666, and signed by John Yeamans, Jr., among others, the lieutenant governor and council of the island addressed their king on these matters with deference and conviction: "least wee should presume too farr wee shall only say that thes Setlements have beene made and upheld by Negroes and without constant supplies of them cannot subsist. . . ."[12]

---

[9] *CRNC*, I, 75–93, esp. 86, 87. (Europeans did not regard all Negroes as slaves as yet; however, almost all whom they classed as slaves were Negroes.)

[10] Salley, *Narratives*, p. 67; Craven, *Southern Colonies*, p. 330.

[11] *CRNC*, I, 148.

[12] Salley, *Narratives*, p. 67; *CRNC*, I, 150.

III

IT MAY HAVE BEEN the failure of the first Barbadian efforts, or it may have been the increasing predominance of Sir Anthony Ashley Cooper (soon to be named the first Earl of Shaftesbury), which redirected the thoughts of the remaining Proprietors toward a new colonization effort in 1669. In any case, after six years of sporadic interest, minimal investment, and nonexistent returns, they determined to send out the nucleus of a colony from London. The purchase of three secondhand vessels alone exceeded their entire previous outlay,[13] and it implied for the first time a proprietary decision to assume the major long-term expenses and risks for establishing a settlement in Carolina. But while new money and initiative flowed from London, the Proprietors continued to rely on existing colonies for further manpower, as evidenced by the offer of a liberalized headright of 150 acres for each new arrival. Barbados naturally remained a focus for proprietary expectations. It was made clear that prior grants to Barbadians would be honored, and the ships *Carolina, Port Royal,* and *Albemarle* were instructed to sail by way of the sugar island. In August over one hundred people departed from England for Barbados and Carolina.

These colonists took with them a blank commission for Sir John Yeamans in Barbados entitling him, or someone of his choosing, to become governor of the expedition. They also carried a draft of the Fundamental Constitutions, an elaborate proprietary statement of method and purpose which had not yet reached final form.[14] The finished document, sent out the following spring, was a bizarre mixture of political theory and specific instructions. Although it never fully governed the colony's development, it did contain, along with incongruous references to "landgraves" and "leet men," important observations upon the subject of Negro slavery. The Constitutions formally extended religious toleration to slaves,[15] but it was made explicit that any slave

---

[13] Craven, *Southern Colonies,* pp. 333, 335, 338.

[14] *Coll.,* V, 119–23, 164; Wesley Frank Craven, *The Colonies in Transition, 1660–1713* (New York, 1968), p. 99.

[15] The ideas of religious toleration evolving in the mind of John Locke, who as secretary to Ashley and the Proprietors probably drafted the document (*ibid.,* p. 102 *n*), may lie behind the statement: "Since charity obliges us to wish well to yͤ Souls of all

converting to a Christian denomination remained, during his worldly life, "in ye same State and Condition he was in before." And the document went on to offer explicit assurance to whites that "Every Freeman of Carolina, shall have absolute power and authority over Negro Slaves, of what opinion or Religion soever."[16]

Despite clauses that acknowledged and even gave indirect encouragement to the use of black slaves in the projected settlement, the Fundamental Constitutions remained unclear on the specific question of whether the Proprietors would grant the importer of an enslaved Negro, as they granted the importer of an indentured European, a headright of 150 acres. Uncertainty about the headrights on black laborers may have limited their presence in the initial fleet of 1669, though it is possible that at least one Negro was aboard the three ships when they departed from London.[17] The *Three Brothers*, a local sloop hired by Sir John Yeamans after the *Albemarle* was driven aground in a November gale, may well have added other Negroes before it left Barbados. Yeamans himself went back to Barbados before the fleet of which he had taken command finally reached Carolina in the spring of 1670, and since he owned numerous slaves it is possible that lingering confusion over the headright system prompted this return. At any rate, a letter sent to him by several Proprietors about this time sought to set the matter straight. "Sir," it began:

Your letters of the 28th of November we have received, by which we perceive the effectual paines you have taken in our Port Royall designe for which we give you many thanks, We find you are mistaken in our Concessions that wee have not made provision of Land for negroes by saying that we grant 150 acres of land for every able man servant in that we mean

---

men, and Religion ought to alter nothing in a mans Civill Estate or right it shall be Lawful for Slaves as well as others, to enter themselves and be of what Church or profession any of them shall think best and thereof be as fully members as any freemen." BPRO *Trans.*, I, 203.

16 BPRO *Trans.*, I, 204. This may represent a further confirmation of the servile legal status of Christian Negroes, or it could be a specific come-on to West Indian planters who regarded their dominion over Negro laborers as complete. Alternatively, however, it can be seen as an intimation that in a wilderness colony employing black slaves white dominance was likely to be far from "absolute" in actual fact.

17 There is a curious entry in the accounts of John Rivers, Ashley's kinsman and personal agent, who sailed from England aboard the *Carolina*. Just before settling his final lodging bill and going aboard ship in late July 1669, Rivers paid 19 *s.* "to Mr Miller for a boy" and 11 *s.* "to Mr Wote for bringing to me a bricklaier and a Blackmore." *Coll.*, V, 132.

negroes as well as Christians And the same in other proportions which you may cause to be laid out to those who carry negroes.[18]

THIS TURNABOUT is noteworthy. In their official instructions sent out aboard the *Carolina* the Proprietors had made no mention of Negroes or slaves when explaining the newest headright system.[19] They spoke only of "men-servants" and "women-servants" and thereby repeated, whether consciously or inadvertently, the form of their initial "Proposals" published six years before. In 1664 they had responded to a Barbadian counterproposal by conceding black adults a status in the headright system equivalent to white women and children. Now, however, apparently in response to a pointed query from Yeamans, the Proprietors acknowledged total equality between unfree white and black migrants in terms of the amount of acreage they commanded as a headright for their importer. Such a construction represented a substantial victory for those Barbadians whose major holdings were in slaves. Sir John Yeamans himself was among the first to take advantage of this means for increasing landholdings in Carolina, and the Proprietors' interpretation must have influenced the actions of other slaveholders as well. The net result was an increase in the number of Negroes who would be transported involuntarily to Carolina during the early years.

IV

THE *Carolina*, under Capt. Henry Brayne, reached the coast in late March 1670, ahead of her sister ships. Making land at Seewee Bay, the settlers were directed by hospitable Indians to a sheltered site on the west bank of a nearby river which they renamed the Ashley. They accepted this location, whether through satisfaction or exhaustion, as a substitute for the intended destination of Port Royal, and by the end of May the remainder of the company had joined them there. Brayne had already been dispatched to Virginia for more men and supplies when Gov. William Sayle, the elderly Bermudian whom Yeamans had named as his substitute, addressed a report to the Proprietors in late June. "Though we are (att present) under some straight for want

[18] *Coll.*, V, 164. The mixture of racial and religious designations shown here was commonplace at the time.
[19] *Coll.*, V, 119–23.

of provision," wrote Sayle; "yet we doubt not (through the goodness of God) of recruits from sundry places." Capt. Brayne was a propertied Barbadian with settlement ambitions of his own, and when he returned from Virginia with livestock and supplies on August 23, he also imported for his own advancement "one lusty negro man 3. cristian servants and a oversear."[20]

The fact that this first fully documented Negro arrival reached the colony alongside Europeans is indicative of a pattern of black and white imports which was to predominate for several decades. Three slaves who arrived several weeks later represent two other patterns which would be frequent in the early years. In the first place, they appear to have been united by kinship ties, and secondly, they were imported by leaders of the settlement, in this case the Sayle family. Capt. Nathaniel Sayle had ventured to Bermuda in the *Three Brothers* in June, and when he returned in September 1670 he brought back to his father, the governor, three white servants and three Negroes. The latter were listed as John Sr., Elizabeth, and John Jr.[21] This small black family from Bermuda constituted the first group of Negro arrivals to be recorded by name, and they were among the last people considered technically to have arrived with the "first fleet" (a distinction which held benefits for their white master). In the same month Joseph Dalton could write to Ashley, "The Collony is indeed safely setled and . . . there only remaines the preservation of it."

For Dalton as for others, preservation seemed to depend first of all upon "a speedy peopling of this place." Therefore, despite the hurricane season, Capt. Brayne was dispatched for Barbados, where he arrived safely at the end of October. Immediately promoters of the Carolina venture circulated a proclamation throughout the island: "Now for the better Expedition in settling of the said province and encouragement of all manner of people that have a desire to tranceport themselves servants negroes or utensils the Lords proprietors of the province of Carrolina hath provided the Carrolina friggott . . . for the tranceportation of the said people."[22] In less than three weeks Thomas Colleton reported that "wee have gotten more peoples Harttes

[20] Joseph I. Waring, *The First Voyage and Settlement at Charles Town, 1670–1680* (Columbia, 1970), pp. 24–25; *Coll.*, V, 171, 215, 227.

[21] *Warrants*, I, 52. Cf. *Coll.*, V, 280 *n.* I have spelled slave names as they appear in the records and have not put any of them in quotation marks, but it must be kept in mind that many names had been imposed by masters rather than bestowed by parents. For further discussion, see Chapter VI.

[22] *Coll.*, V, 211. For Dalton's remarks, see *Coll.*, V, 182.

then you can immaggen," and the next month more than one hundred people set out aboard two vessels, reaching Ashley River in February 1671.[23]

The number of Negroes in this contingent remains uncertain. The "Barbados Proclamation," having mentioned Negroes specifically at one point, omitted all further direct reference. It distinguished only between men-servants, women-servants, and boys under sixteen, and it spoke simply of people "minded to transport themselves servants or goodes for the said province." Capt. Brayne had reported to the Proprietors in November that Sir John Yeamans was sending "his oversear with 10. able men; the most part Carpinters and Sa[w]yers; M͏ʳ Stroud the marchant and Justice Harvy is sending downe his sonn with 10. or more hands with hime."[24] Most such able hands were probably black.

A few of the Negroes arriving that winter are recorded explicitly. In February a man named Yackae was imported by Capt. John Robinson, later a member of the council, and a woman named Grace was brought by Mrs. Jane Robinson (presumably the captain's wife). John Norton, another man with the title of Captain although a "joyner" or simple carpenter by trade, imported a Negro called Emanuell. They lived on Oyster Point, the wooded peninsula which lay across the Ashley from the initial settlement at Albemarle Point and which would become the colony's center and the enduring site of Charlestown by 1680.[25] In less than two years they had cleared enough land so that Norton could identify himself as a "Planter," but he was so heavily in debt that both Emanuell and the would-be "plantacon" were destined to be seized by officials. A similar fate must have befallen Crow, a slave who came from Barbados in the same month. His owner, Surveyor General John Culpepper, became engaged in some disorders along with John Robinson and Yeamans' overseer, Thomas Gray, and the three fled the colony so hastily in 1673 that each probably left slaves behind. Several weeks after the arrival of Crow, a captain bringing provisions from Jamaica via Bermuda is known to have

[23] *Coll.*, V, 243, 267.

[24] *Coll.*, V, 211, 212, 229. Brayne and others use the phrase "send down" because for ships relying on the prevailing Northeast Trades Carolina was somewhat downwind from Barbados.

[25] *Warrants*, I, 54; Agnes Leland Baldwin, *First Settlers of South Carolina, 1670–1680* (Columbia, 1969), n.p. Culpepper's 1671 map, reproduced from the Shaftesbury Papers in Waring, *First Voyage*, p. 33, shows a single house among the trees on the Cooper River side of Oyster Point.

brought "Richard Hanke (a Quaker) his wife, 9 children & one negro man."[26]

Gov. Sayle died in March 1671, and in June Sir John Yeamans arrived from Barbados, bringing eight black servants, and fully expecting to resume the governorship which he had delegated away. "Sir Jo Yeamans intends to stay all the winter," noted John Locke in London, summarizing a letter from Carolina for his proprietary employers; "[he] brought negroes and expects more." Historians whose interests lay elsewhere have occasionally noted these Negroes as the "first" to reach Carolina.[27] The designation is mistaken, but Yeamans' slaves do have special interest as early black frontiersmen. When Joseph West refused to hand over the governorship, Landgrave Yeamans promptly "retyred himselfe to his Countrey house," a rude and isolated "barony" created by his slaves. After the governor's title had been restored to him, Yeamans returned to Albemarle Point in June 1672 because attacks from the neighboring Spanish and their Indian allies were feared, but with the exception of a few personal servants, his slave force remained behind, several dozen in number and well armed.[28] Later the same month the council (after making detailed arrangements for Carolina's defense which described where certain men in outlying regions were to report in case of alarm) ended by ordering that all other inhabitants were to "repaire to Charles Towne with their Armes and Ammunicon . . . (except the Negroes in the Governo[rs] plantacon who are there left to defend the same being an outward place)."[29]

Although Yeamans died in 1674, there were still twenty-six slaves listed as part of the estate which his widow, herself the owner of slaves, contested several years later.[30] Nor were Gov. Yeamans

[26] A. S. Salley, ed., *Journal of the Grand Council of South Carolina, April 25, 1671–June, 24, 1680* (Columbia, 1907), p. 65; *Warrants*, I, 53; *Coll.*, V, 222 *n*, 424 *n*, 476; cf. *Warrants*, I, 279, 281.

[27] *Coll.*, V, 349; Rivers, *Sketch*, p. 109; McCrady, *Proprietary Govt.*, p. 151.

[28] *Coll.*, V, 337; *Journal of the Grand Council, 1671–1680*, p. 81. The grand council voted at this time (*ibid.*, p. 33) that the governor must live in town for "the better safety" of the settlement.

[29] *Ibid.*, pp. 36–37. Even in Barbados, Negroes occasionally bore arms at this time. Harlow, *Barbados*, pp. 214–15.

[30] Lady Margaret Yeamans had received from her husband "old Hannah & hir children Jupeter little Tony & Joane" as part of a bequest before he left Barbados in 1671. She transported all of these slaves except Tony to Carolina the following year, along with five more "of her own proper Negroes namely . . . Rentee, Gilbert, Resom, Jossee & Simon, and one man servant John: Hopkins arriveing in August 1672, and ffebruary 1674." *SCHGM*, XI (1910), 112–13; *Warrants*, I, 112.

and his wife the only ones to transport unfree labor on a significant scale. Simon Berringer, for example, acquired extensive land by importing dozens of "Servants and Negroes," apparently from Barbados, in 1671 and 1672. But the capital for such large investments was uncommon, and less wealthy immigrants had to be content with importing occasional hired hands from the sugar island. By the second summer of settlement almost half of the whites and considerably more than half of the blacks in the colony had come from Barbados. "The Barbadians," John Locke noted from London, "endeavour to rule all."[31]

Partly to offset this Caribbean faction and partly to augment the colony as a whole, migrants were actively sought from other quarters. In the fall of 1671 the proprietary laws and concessions were circulated in New England and Virginia, and vessels trading for provisions in New Jersey and New York actively solicited settlers. Several hundred New Yorkers who were discouraged by high taxes and hard winters expressed such interest that their government had to institute a passport system to prevent the departure of any debtors. A list of the passes issued for more than forty people removing to Carolina in late November includes seventeen Negro servants. Not all of these persons took passage on the three ships provided, but other New Yorkers may well have followed later. Those who did migrate undertook a new settlement called Jamestown on James Island Creek,[32] and although the town itself soon vanished, the newcomers, both black and white, were absorbed into the Carolina colony. By 1674 an eager London pamphleteer could claim to be "credibly inform'd . . . that divers are gone, and going," to Carolina not only from the West Indies and the British Isles, but also from Bermuda, the Bahamas, New England, New York, New Jersey, and the entire Chesapeake region.[33]

V

DESPITE THE VARIED ORIGINS of this early population, the settlement on the west bank of the Ashley can be sketched in terms of its rough size and its initial struggle for subsistence. The first summary of migration

---

[31] *Warrants*, I, 84; *Coll.*, V, 347.
[32] *Coll.*, V, 351, 352, 388; *DRNY*, XIV, 658–59; Waring, *First Voyage*, p. 37.
[33] Gascoyne, *True Description*, pp. 1–2.

data was submitted to Ashley by Secretary Dalton during the second winter of settlement. By then the arrival of 337 adults and 62 children below the age of sixteen had been recorded. Of these 399, according to his figures, at least 16 were absent and three times that many (or 12 per cent) had died. Grown men appear to have outnumbered women and children by more than two to one. But Dalton's report is flawed by an error of addition or transcription, and he gives no indication whether he has included Negroes or counted them separately.[34] Ironically, therefore, the best hints of the size and racial composition of the colony in the early 1670s must be drawn from the records of watchful Spanish officials at St. Augustine.

According to a deposition dated August 1, 1671, an Indian messenger from a tribe dwelling near the English outpost alerted the Spanish governor "that the settlement grows, that the castle is getting bigger, [and] that many Negroes have come to work." During the following summer a Spanish soldier named Antonio Camunas visited briefly at the Albemarle Point settlement. Camunas reported that by then there were several communal buildings and roughly ninety private dwellings spread out between the vegetable gardens in the neighborhood of the fortifications. He put the number of men able to bear arms at 250, with 100 Negroes suited to fight if necessary, but he may not have included men clearing land in the outlying areas. An Irishman named Brian Fitzpatrick who fled to St. Augustine later in 1672 claimed there were 800 English and 300 Negroes in the Carolina colony. Fitzpatrick's totals are higher than others gathered by Spanish officials during the first half of the decade, but the proportion of blacks which he suggests (27 per cent) is quite similar to the percentage (30 per cent) implied by Camunas' earlier estimate.[35]

It seems evident, therefore, that even in the earliest years, between one fourth and one third of the colony's newcomers were Negroes. Among these first several hundred black Carolinians at least three out of every four were men. A sample of two dozen Negro immigrants arriving during the first three years whose names and/or sex can be ascertained suggests men outnumbering women by three to one, and a larger such sample of recorded black arrivals stretching over the first twenty-five years shows a ratio of more than two to one overall. Among African migrants, therefore, as among Europeans, the

34 *Coll.*, V, 381–82.
35 Childs, *Colonization*, pp. 132–35. Cf. Chapter III, note 11, below.

numerical predominance of men was greatest at the outset, declining gradually but remaining considerable even after several decades.[36]

Even though the initial contingent was small and made up predominantly of adult men, an immediate problem was created in the Carolina settlement by the lack of adequate provisions. The advance publicity which had helped attract a number of the first settlers predicted a bountiful natural setting, but as was often the case during European colonization, those people most willing to migrate were not always those best equipped to subsist. "The first Planters," observed a newcomer in the 1680s, "were most of them tradesmen, poor and wholy ignorant of husbandry . . . their whole business was to clear a little ground to get Bread for their Familyes." Even those Englishmen with farming experience were notably less familiar with the agricultural peculiarities of a southern Atlantic coastal climate than their Indian neighbors or their West African and Caribbean slaves. In the first summer of settlement Gov. Sayle reported that daily rations had been reduced to a pint of peas per person: "wee have but 7 weekes provision left . . . the Country affording us nothing, wch makes it goe very hard with us and wee cannot Employ our servants as wee would because wee have no victualls for them." In September a prominent settler informed Lord Ashley that he had brought only two servants from England and none from Barbados "consideringe ye scarcetie of provision wch would betide us," and Joseph West protested the following spring that servants transported upon Ashley's account "wilbe a great charge to the plantation, wee haveing nothing as yet but what is brought."[37]

The demand for provisions and the continuing expense to which it put the Proprietors prompted an adjustment in their philosophy of

[36] For samples, see Wood, "Black Majority," pp. 85–87. Although the seventeenth-century demographic data are thin for Europeans and non-Europeans alike, it seems clear that by 1695 some two thousand Negroes resided in the province. (Such an estimate excludes the Albemarle settlement to the north, which had only a few hundred blacks and was under a separate deputy by then.) This figure was scarcely half the number present in Maryland and hardly a quarter the number in Virginia, where there had been blacks for three times as many years. Even New York still contained roughly as many slaves as the southernmost colony. But the European contingent in South Carolina remained far smaller—between two thousand and four thousand—than in any of the settlements farther north, so that in proportional terms the community's black population was distinctly more significant by 1695 than in any other mainland colony. The best recent summary of population data for this period is Craven, *Colonies in Transition,* pp. 288–93.

[37] Salley, *Narratives,* p. 184; *Coll.,* V, 171, 202, 267.

settlement. People of substance had been an important element in the colony's design from the start, but as the cost of supplying dependent settlers grew, emphasis upon the presence of propertied men increased.[38] The letters of Lord Ashley late in 1671 illustrate this altered outlook. He wrote Yeamans on December 15:

I am glad to hear soe many considerable men come from Barbadoes for wee find by deare Experience that noe other are able to make a Plantation but such as are in a Condition to stock and furnish themselves, the rest serve onely to fill up Numbers and live upon us and therefore now wee have a competent Number until wee are better stocked with Provisions[.] I am not very fond of more Company unlesse they be substantiall Men.[39]

Such a policy, combined with aid from local Indians and increasing cultivation, allowed the colonists to report by March 1673 that they had "quite mastered the want of victuals."[40] Later the same year Joseph West advised the Proprietors that if they now sent out more men and tools the colony could turn to "English Husbandry" and "quickly be a very plentiful place."[41]

The Proprietors, however, were already looking beyond mere subsistence to the production of some lucrative staple. Almost from the outset, therefore, efforts for simple survival were coupled with experimentation. Englishmen planted diverse seeds in the unfamiliar soil and dispatched sample cargoes to probe uncertain markets. Cotton, indigo, ginger, grapes, and olives were among the crops urged by the Proprietors as potential staples but tested by the settlers without notable success. Rice—if only a bushel of it—was also tried and all but discarded.[42] Tobacco cultivation was undertaken more widely, but

---

[38] *CRNC*, I, 100; Craven, *Southern Colonies*, p. 339. (The prevalent political theories of James Harrington in England lent strength to this property consideration.)

[39] *Coll.*, V, 361. The next day (p. 364) Ashley wrote to Mathias Halsted, one of the captains engaged in procuring settlers:

I would have you in all places where you shall touch to encourage men of Estates to remove into Carolina. But forbeare to invite the poorer sort yet a while, for wee finde our selves mightily mistaken in endeavouring to gett a great Number of poore People there it being substantial men and theire Familyes, that must make the Plantation which will stock the country with Negroes, Cattle and other Necessarys, whereas others relye and eate upon us.

[40] Quoted in Waring, *First Voyage*, p. 32. At the same time, however, no one could spare enough to provision an Indian being detained in prison. *Coll.*, V, 422.

[41] *Coll.*, V, 425.

[42] *Coll.*, V, 125, 267, 377 n. Sir Peter Colleton tried to remind his fellow Proprietors at one point that even Barbados had had slow and uncertain beginnings, but

competition with established producers closer to Europe proved difficult. Wood products, including staves and tar, were exported to nearby
colonies, but at the start quantity was limited by the numbers of laborers available.[43] Greater profits derived from the rapidly expanding commerce in furs, but proprietary guardedness on the one hand
and troubled Indian relations on the other combined to keep this
speculative trade in the hands of a few. For a greater number the
simplest production and readiest market were found in the raising of
livestock.

VI

CATTLE HAD FIGURED in English schemes for Carolina from the beginning. As early as 1650 a writer had cited the availability of stock from
Virginia as one of the advantages of the region, and in 1663 Hilton
recorded that the unhappy Massachusetts migrants who had recently
sojourned near Cape Fear had abandoned their cattle to the local
Indians. An early visitor to Charlestown quipped that the initial settlement lacked only "cattle, company and good liquor."[44] To supplement
the population's scanty diet at first, barreled beef had to be imported,
and most of the incoming livestock had to be butchered.[45] The Proprietors willingly replaced these animals, trusting that gradually Carolina
would adopt the rudimentary European pattern of husbandry whereby

---

such a comparison must only have whetted proprietary appetites, especially when
Colleton stated that "if wee hould our ground . . . Carolina will excell all other
English plantations." *Coll.,* V, 423.

[43] *SCHGM,* XXXVII (1936), 139–40; *Charleston Yearbook, 1883* (Charleston,
1884), p. 394; *Coll.,* V, 387.

[44] Salley, *Narratives,* pp. 6, 53; Waring, *First Voyage,* p. 34.

[45] *Coll.,* V, 146, 178, 319, 350. Although the six sows and a boar which West was
advised to transport from Barbados with the first fleet may never have arrived, livestock for provision was purchased promptly and dearly from Virginia. *Coll.,* V, 126,
127. The families migrating from New York in 1671 were asked to "give ⅓ of their
cattle for transporting the rest." *Coll.,* V, 347. And a caller at Bermuda in the next
decade noted that captains there "frequently Export Cattle, Swine and Turkies for the
Carribies, and Carolina." John Crafford (Crawford), *A New and Most Exact Account
of the . . . Famous Colony of Carolina . . .* (Dublin, 1683), p. 4. In May 1682
Thomas Newe wrote that few settlers at first had the "wherewithall to purchase a
Cow, the first stock whereof they were furnished with, from Burmudas and New
England." Salley, *Narratives,* p. 184.

cows were generally confined in pastures (to utilize manure), milked regularly, and slaughtered annually, with only a few being maintained through the winter to replenish the herd.[46]

A far different pattern actually emerged. The settlement was so sparse and the land so abundant that animals could be allowed to graze freely, requiring almost no time from the limited labor force. Furthermore, the climate proved mild enough and the forage plentiful enough so that there was no necessity for annual butchering. As a result, livestock multiplied at an unanticipated and unprecedented rate while demanding minimal attention from the owners. This situation was so unfamiliar for Englishmen that it aroused concern among the Proprietors. It has been "our designe," they stated indignantly, "to have Planters there and not Graziers."[47]

Despite this initial resentment of expanding herds, the Proprietors gradually came around, probably through Shaftesbury's mediation, to several notable concessions. They acknowledged, first of all, the logic and profit of early settlers raising enough stock to provision later arrivals, as the Puritans had done in New England a generation earlier.[48] By 1674, one source stated that, "where Beef two years since was sold at 12 s. a 100, and Pork at the rate of 16 s. . . . Cattel . . . begins to be plentiful, and Hoggs of a prodigious encrease."[49] "Severall in the Country have great stocks of Cattle," wrote Thomas Newe from Charlestown in 1682, "and they sell so well to new comers that they care not for killing, which is the reason provision is so dear in the Town."[50] In 1687 an official went so far as to report the "Cheif sub-

[46] See instructions given to West in 1669, *Coll.*, V, 126.

[47] *Coll.*, V, 437–38. In a letter of Sept. 20, 1683, a newly arrived Huguenot named Louis Thibou described the conditions which he found. (A copy of the original French letter and a typescript translation are in the SCL.) Thibou wrote: "the cattle feed themselves perfectly well at no cost whatever; . . . and they give you a calf every year, which is a good profit costing no more to feed a lot than a few; you feed them by their thousands in the woods."

. [48] Bernard Bailyn, *The New England Merchants in the Seventeenth Century* (Cambridge, Mass., 1955), pp. 32, 47. Lord Shaftesbury proposed a separate livestock barony of his own in Carolina at an early date. He envisioned (but never established) a plantation with three hundred or four hundred head of cattle, "whereby Wee could Offer encouragm^t to rich men, to come amongst us, who might be sure there from us to have catle at a certaine and cheap rate, and advice, and assistance in planting." *Coll.*, V, 447; cf. Andrews, *Colonial Period*, III, 200 n.

[49] Gascoyne, *True Description*, pp. 2–3. Lady Yeamans was said to have five hundred turkeys and four hundred hogs.

[50] Salley, *Narratives*, p. 182. Newe added that "they in the Country are furnisht with Venison, fish and fowle by the Indians for trifles."

sistance of the first Settlers being by Hoggs, & Cattle they sell to the New-Comers, and with which they purchase Cloathes, and Tooles from them."[51] And by the 1690s Gov. Archdale could write, "The New Settlers have now great Advantage over the first Planters, being they can be furnish'd with Stocks of Cattle and Corn . . . at reasonable Rates."[52]

While white settlers felt uneasy about open grazing at first, numerous black newcomers understood this practice. In Africa, although domesticated cattle were absent from the area near the Congo due to the presence of the tsetse fly, such animals were common across much of the western region, and many of the slaves entering South Carolina after 1670 may have had experience in tending large herds. People from along the Gambia River, a location for which South Carolina slave dealers came to hold a steady preference, were expert horsemen and herders. English visitors expressed high admiration for their standards of cleanliness with respect to dairy products, and contemporary descriptions of local animal husbandry bear a striking resemblance to what would later appear in Carolina. Gambian herds grazed on the savannahs bordering the river and in the low-lying paddy fields when the rice crop was off; at night they were tethered within a cattlefold and guarded by several armed men.[53] African stock was even traded for export occasionally during the seventeenth century.[54]

As early as the 1670s there is evidence of absentee investors relying upon Negro slaves to develop herds of cattle in Carolina. In 1673, for example, Edmund Lister of Northumberland County, Virginia, bought one hundred acres of land along the Ashley River on Oyster Point from an illiterate laborer named John Gardner. Lister sent three men south ahead of him to prepare the land (not an unusual practice), but he died in the following year before reaching South Carolina. One

[51] Quoted in Verner W. Crane, *The Southern Frontier, 1670–1732* (Ann Arbor, 1929), p. 110 *n*; cf. *SCHGM*, XXX (1929), 4.

[52] Salley, *Narratives*, p. 291.

[53] John J. McKelvey, Jr., *Man Against Tsetse: Struggle for Africa* (Ithaca, N.Y., 1973), notes that the presence of the tsetse precluded cattle in certain areas, but he goes on to show that Africans learned to herd away from the tsetse fly and to use the bile of infected cattle as a disease inhibitor. Also see Melville J. Herskovits, "The Culture Areas of Africa," *Africa*, III (1930), 67, 72, 73; Douglas Grant, *The Fortunate Slave, An Illustration of African Slavery in the Early Eighteenth Century* (London, 1968), pp. 24–25.

[54] In 1651, for example, the English Guinea Company, precursor of the Royal African Company, instructed a captain to barter liquor at the Gambia River for a "Cargo of negers or Cattel" to be carried to Barbados. Donnan, *Documents*, I, 129.

of those he had sent ahead was an indentured servant with only several months left to serve, but the others were apparently black slaves experienced with livestock, for in 1676 Lister's widow stated in a bill of sale that her "Dec^d Housband, did formerly Transport Severall Negros, out of this Colony of Virginia, into Carolina and did there Settle them upon a Plantacon, together wth Some Cattle."[55]

Even when the white owners lived within the province, the care of their livestock often fell to a black. The slave would build a small "cowpen" in some remote region, attend the calves, and guard the grazing stock at night. When Denys Omahone sold a fifty-acre tract (still inhabited by Indians) to a new white arrival in the 1680s, the property contained four calves, three steers, five sows, one boar, and a "Negro man by name Cato."[56] Upon the death in 1692 of Bernard Schenckingh, a well-to-do Barbadian migrant with four estates, the appraisers of his James Island holdings reported that "In sight and by account apeareth 134 head of Cattle [and] one negro man." Half a century later, the estate of Robert Beath at Ponpon included, "a Stock of Cattle . . . said to be from Five Hundred to One Thousand Head. . . . Also a Man used to a Cow Pen and of a good Character."[57] It is even possible that the very word "cowboy" originated through this set of circumstances.[58]

---

[55] The holding may have been considerable, for the widow received ten thousand pounds of good tobacco for the land, Negroes, and stock from a Virginia gentleman who was himself an absentee owner of slaves in Carolina. RSP (1675–95), pp. 39–41; cf. A. S. Salley, ed., *Records of the Secretary of the Province and the Register of the Province of South Carolina, 1671–1675* (Columbia, 1944), pp. 59, 66–69. It was long ago suggested that the particularly numerous slaves in the Narragansett country of Rhode Island played an important role on the renowned stock farms of that region. Edward Channing, "The Narragansett Planters," *Johns Hopkins University Studies in Historical and Political Science*, 4th ser., no. 3 (Baltimore, 1886), pp. 9–10.

[56] MR "A" (1682–90), pp. 318–19. This pattern continued. In 1690 Seth Sothell gave his father-in-law one of several large landholdings along with "thirty head of Cattle belonging to ye Said Plantation and one Negr^o Man." Archdale Papers, mfm, SCDAH, item 26, Jan. 25, 1690, copy of will. Cf. Gary S. Dunbar, "Colonial Carolina Cowpens," *Agricultural History*, XXXV (1961), 125–30.

[57] RSP (1692–1700), p. 38; *SCG*, March 19, 1741.

[58] Might not the continued predominance of "cowboy" over alternative terms such as "cattleman" represent a strange holdover reflective of early and persistent black involvement in the American cattle trade? This most American of words was already applied during the colonial period to men stationed at cowpens with herding responsibilities. Gray, *Agriculture*, I, 147. During the Revolution the word was used with a derogatory connotation (cf. "house-boy") to describe American Tories who made organized raids on the cattle of Whig farmers. Marshall W. Fishwick, "The Cowboy: America's Contribution to the World's Mythology," *Western Folklore*, XI (1952), 78. As late as

The raising of livestock, fostered in different ways by whites and blacks, could not have developed into a source of livelihood without pressure from an external market. Barbados and other Caribbean islands which were turning to the intensive cultivation of sugar presented just such insistent demands. New Englanders had prepared to ship beef and pork to the West Indies as early as the 1640s, and in 1666 the English king had been warned that "Barbados and yᵉ rest of yᵉ Caribee Islands . . . have not food to fill their bellies."[59] It appears that much of the interest in Carolina settlement among prominent Barbadians derived from hopes for developing an economy which could complement their own. Almost immediately Carolina began providing the island with food for the labor force, wood for the cane-boiling fires, and staves for the shipment of molasses sugar. As early as 1674 the Carolina Proprietors complained to the governor and council that Yeamans and his followers seemed to want the mainland colony "soe ordered that . . . itt might arive att no other pitch then to be Subservient in Provisions and Timbʳ to the Interest of Barbados."[60]

Such subservience to West Indian interests developed rapidly. By 1678 Barbadians were shipping nearly ten thousand pounds of sugar to Carolina[61] and in return were receiving beef, pork, and lumber products. A letter from Carolina in 1682 reported, "they do send a great deal of Pork, Corn and Cedar to Barbados, besides the victualling of severall Vessels that come in here. . . . Now each family hath got a stock of Hogs and Cows," the writer continued, "which when once a little more encreased, they may send of[f] to the Islands cheaper then any other place can, by reason of its propinquity, which trade alone will make it far more considerable than . . . those other places to the North of us."[62]

Newcomers, released servants, and petty traders continued to invest their first earnings in stock to take advantage of cheap land. But

---

1865 young Negroes with livestock responsibilities were still being designated as "cow boys" (two words) in the plantation records of the Southeast. U. B. Phillips and J. D. Glunt, eds., *Florida Plantation Records* (St. Louis, 1927), pp. 566, 568, 570.

[59] Mass. Hist. Soc., *Collections*, 4th ser., VI, 538; Francis Lord Willoughby, in Harlow, *Barbados*, p. 283.

[60] *Coll.*, V, 436.

[61] Higham, *Leeward Islands*, p. 210. This was only a fraction of what Barbados sent directly to England and to the older American colonies.

[62] Salley, *Narratives*, p. 184. By 1690 John Stewart could ask rhetorically, "In more southerly setlements Can our easy rear'd-up flocks of great Cattell or . . . Hogs and hams be rejected?" *SCHGM*, XXXII (1931), 82.

at the same time others were beginning to convert livestock profits into investments in labor. This process is typified by Thomas Stanyearne, who came to the colony in May 1675 with his wife and children. His will, made out in 1682, orders that his debts be paid off if possible with the cattle which constituted the major portion of his holdings, and that the grazing tract of more than a thousand acres on Wando River "be sold & negroes bought wth the produce thereof & such negroes . . . be equally divided Amongst my foure sons."[63] The will of a Berkeley County cooper named Edward Paty tells a similar story. Paty arrived in the early 1680s and tended the cattle of his prosperous father-in-law, Thomas Gibbes, who had come out from Barbados. Paty eventually became the owner of several tracts himself, and he ordered that at his death "one of my Plantations be sould . . . , and the Effects . . . laid out to purchase Young Negroes."[64]

Thus the raising of livestock for the Caribbean had initial advantages for the white settlers. It freed manpower for clearing the land while still providing a source of food. Cattle-grazing offered a method for buying time and a means of acquiring capital. But this enterprise simply marked an initial stage in the colony's economic growth, and few viewed it as a satisfactory end in itself. Instead, the prevailing philosophy was that foretold in a note from Sir John Colleton in 1665. He reported an attempt to purchase a large quantity of sows for the settlement at Albemarle, "whereby we may have a quantity of Hoggs flesh, wch will soonest come to bare to send to Barbados wch will pduce us Neagroes & Sarv^ts: to rayse a plantacon."[65]

This economic link with Barbados continued throughout the first generation and remained strong enough so that even after 1700 English documents occasionally referred to "Carolina in ye West Indies."[66] Partly through circumstance and partly through design, the

[63] RSP (1675–95), pp. 144–45; cf. pp. 74, 460.

[64] *Ibid.*, pp. 333–34, 369–71.

[65] William S. Powell, ed., *Y^e Countie of Albemarle in Carolina: A Collection of Documents, 1664–1675* (Raleigh, 1958), p. 7 (cf. note 39 above). Samuel Wilson made an almost identical observation in 1682 (Salley, *Narratives*, p. 172; cf. p. 174):

> Hogs increase in Carolina abundantly, and in a manner without any charge or trouble to the Planter. . . . there are many Planters that are single and have never a Servant, that have two or three hundred Hogs, of which they make great profit: Barbados, Jamaica, and New-England, affording a constant good price for their Pork; by which means they get wherewithal to build them more convenient Houses and to purchase Servants, and Negro-slaves.

[66] RSP (1694–1705), p. 345.

initial settlement literally "served" the Caribbean plantations, and this subservient status was not lost upon ambitious colonists. A Carolina minister living in the remote vicinity of Albemarle after 1700 could still write, "the planter here is but a slave to raise a provision for other Colonies."[67] By then conditions in the lowlands farther south had already begun to change markedly, but during the early decades of its establishment, the South Carolina settlement had been little more than the dependent servant of an island master—in short, the colony of a colony.

[67] The Rev. John Urmston, July 7, 1711, *CRNC*, I, 764. (North Carolina was not fully recognized as a distinct colony until the appointment of a separate governor there in 1712.)

Black Labor—White Rice

I

NO development had greater impact upon the course of South Carolina history than the successful introduction of rice. The plant itself, shallow-rooted and delicate, is now rare on the landscape it once dominated, but its historical place in the expansion of the colony and state is deep-seated and secure, hedged round by a tangle of tradition and lore almost as impenetrable as the wilderness swamps near which it was first grown for profit. Despite its eventual prominence, the mastery of this grain took more than a generation, for rice was a crop about which Englishmen, even those who had lived in the Caribbean, knew nothing at all. White immigrants from elsewhere in northern Europe were equally ignorant at first, and local Indians, who gathered small quantities of wild rice, had little to teach them. But gradually, after discouraging initial efforts, rice emerged as the mainstay of the lowland economy during the first fifty years of settlement, and the cultivation of this grain for export came to dominate Carolina life during the major part of the eighteenth century. "The only Commodity of Consequence produced in South Carolina is Rice," commented James Glen in 1761, "and they reckon it as much their staple Commodity, as Sugar is to Barbadoes and Jamaica, or Tobacco to Virginia and Maryland."[1]

Throughout the eighteenth century white Carolinians marveled at their own industry and good fortune in having conjured this impressive trade from a single bushel of rice, and they debated which Englishman should wear the laurels for introducing the first successful bag of seed. In 1726 a Swiss correspondent stated that "it was by a

[1] Glen, *Description*, p. 95. See Gray, *Agriculture*, II, 1021–23.

woman that Rice was transplanted into Carolina,"[2] and occasional mention was made of the idea that the first seeds came aboard a slaving ship from Africa. "Opinions differ about the manner in which rice hath been naturalized in Carolina," wrote the Abbé Raynal at the end of the eighteenth century. "But whether the province may have acquired it by a shipwreck, or whether it may have been carried there with slaves, or whether it be sent from England, it is certain that the soil is favourable for it."[3]

Since rice cultivation had a halting beginning which stretched over several decades, numerous bags of imported seed could have contributed to its growth. Documentary evidence is scanty, and it therefore seems likely that minor issues of individual precedence may never be fully resolved. One fact which can be clearly documented, however, and which may have considerably greater significance, is that during precisely those two decades after 1695 when rice production took permanent hold in South Carolina, the African portion of the population drew equal to, and then surpassed, the European portion.[4] Black inhabitants probably did not actually outnumber whites until roughly 1708.[5] But whatever the exact year in which a black majority was established, the development was unprecedented within England's North American colonies and was fully acknowledged long before the English crown took control of the proprietary settlement in 1720.

The fact that the mastery of rice paralleled closely in time the emergence of a black majority in the colony's population has not been lost upon scholars of the early South. But while few have failed to note it, none can be said to have explained it adequately. What could either be a mere coincidence on the one hand, or a crucial interrelation on the other, has been bypassed with short passages carefully phrased. One author observed that in 1700 "The transition from mixed farming and cattle raising to rice culture was just beginning, and with it the

[2] This claim, unnoticed by historians, is contained in a letter of Nov. 4, 1726, from Jean Watt in Neufchatel to M. le Col. de Valogne in London. BPRO Trans., XII, 156–57. For other claims, see BPRO Trans., XVII, 165; *Gentleman's Magazine*, XXXVI (1766), 287; Gray, *Agriculture*, I, 277.

[3] Abbé Raynal, *Philosophical and Political History of the Possessions and Trade of Europeans in the Two Indies*, 6 vols. (2nd edn., London, 1798), VI, 59. (The first edition in 1772 offered only the shipwreck theory.)

[4] Cf. Chapter V, notes 45 and 46, below.

[5] See Chapter V, Table I, below.

development of negro slavery."[6] Another stated that "South Carolina's especially heavy commitment to the use of Negro labor coincided closely with the development of rice as a new and profitable staple."[7] Similarly, a third scholar concluded that despite an earlier preference for Negro labor, white "South Carolinians did not import Negroes in large numbers until after the introduction of rice in the 1690's."[8] In short, there appears to be an ongoing consensus among the leading southernists that somehow "rice culture turned planters increasingly to slave labor,"[9] but the causal relationships suggested, or perhaps skirted, by such observations have received little analysis.

Were Negro slaves simply the cheapest and most numerous individuals available to a young colony in need of labor? Or were there other variables involved in determining the composition of the Carolina work force? In exploring such questions it is first necessary to examine the different sorts of potential labor—red, white, and black— which existed in the early years. It will then be possible, by focusing on the process of rice cultivation at the end of this chapter and on matters of health in the next, to suggest two separate factors which may have contributed far more than has been acknowledged in fostering the employment of African slaves.

II

ALTHOUGH PERSONS FROM AFRICA had been enmeshed in New World colonization for more than a century and a half before the founding of Carolina, alternative sources of labor were very real possibilities during the early years of the lowland settlement. The option closest at hand was that presented by the numerous Indian tribes which had inhabited the area for centuries. Their interaction with white and

---

[6] Crane, *Southern Frontier*, p. 22.

[7] Craven, *Colonies in Transition*, p. 292. Craven continued, "Although experiments with rice date from very early in the colony's history, success apparently came only in the last decade of the century, when new channels for the supply of Negro labor to the North American colonies also opened."

[8] Sirmans, *Colonial S.C.*, p. 24; cf. Appendix A.

[9] Aubrey C. Land, ed., *Bases of the Plantation Society* (paperback edn., New York, 1969), p. 206. Cf. Frank Robert Hawkins, "Legislation Governing the Institution of Slavery in Colonial South Carolina," unpublished master's thesis (University of Wisconsin, 1968), p. 1.

black foreigners during the colonial era constitutes a separate story, but it is clear that they provided some much-needed support in the early years. English trade goods could be used to purchase their services cheaply, and no expensive importation costs were incurred. Difficulties in verbal communication were offset by the Indians' impressive knowledge of the land; they could provide ready food, suitable medicine, and safe passage in a semitropical wilderness environment which was unfamiliar to Europeans. Several neighboring tribes, with a pragmatic eye upon English firearms and woolens, were quick in coming forward to assist the new colonists, offering "to fish, and hunt their Game for a Trifle; to fell Tim[ber, to plant] Corn, and to gather in their Crop: as also to Pilot, and convey them from on[e place] to another."[10]

Settlers were greedy for involuntary as well as voluntary Indian labor, despite obvious disadvantages.[11] Acts of enslavement were risky, since any provocations in the earliest years contained the danger of retaliation.[12] In later decades, as the colony became slightly more secure, local slaving ventures presented a threat to the growing Indian trade. Moreover, women and children were more likely than men to be

[10] Gascoyne, *True Description*, p. 3. Louis Thibou's letter of Sept. 20, 1683, SCL, described the European settler's situation:

> If he wishes to hunt or to have an Indian hunt for him there is no lack of venison or game. An Indian will provide a family of 30 with enough game and venison, as much as they can eat, all the year round for 4 crowns. . . . We have 15 or 16 nations of Indians round us who are very friendly and the English get on well with them; the largest number is not more than 500 strong. They bring them a great quantity of deer skins and furs.

[11] Southeastern Indians had long accepted a pattern of forced servitude for criminals, debtors, and war prisoners, but it appeared to Europeans that "Their Slaves are not over-burden'd with Work." Lawson, *New Voyage*, p. 240; cf. p. 210. The standard work on Indian slavery is Almon W. Lauber, *Indian Slavery in Colonial Times within the Present Limits of the United States* (*Columbia University Studies in History, Economics and Public Law*, LIV, no. 3, New York, 1913). See also Crane, *Southern Frontier;* John T. Juricek, "Indian Policy in Proprietary South Carolina: 1670–1693," unpublished M.A. thesis (University of Chicago, 1962); and the following unpublished Ph.D. dissertations: Lawrence Foster, "Negro-Indian Relationships in the Southeast" (University of Pennsylvania, 1935); William Robert Snell, "Indian Slavery in Colonial South Carolina, 1671–1795" (University of Alabama, 1972).

[12] One disadvantage of unfettered livestock was the antagonism they aroused among the Indians. Wandering herds damaged Indian crops as they had done in the Caribbean during the previous century and in New England more recently. Local tribes occasionally stole troublesome stock, and recriminations were constant. The Europeans, however, were not above turning these annoyances to advantage. The disappearance of several hogs could offer a helpful pretext for slaving raids like those made among the Coosas (Kussos) in 1671 and the Westoes in 1672. See BPRO *Trans.*, I, 174; Crane, *Southern Frontier*, p. 123; Waring, *First Voyage*, pp. 38, 46–47.

taken alive during intertribal wars and sold to the colonists. Even when white traders promoted intertribal conflicts to obtain cheap slaves, the likelihood of later escape by the captives reduced their value in the vicinity.[13]

But when Indians were sold to an unfamiliar region where they were less likely to run away, their value as slaves went up. Therefore a small commerce developed in exchanging Indian captives abroad for more tractable white or black labor,[14] or for additional livestock which would encroach further upon Indian land. During the late seventeenth century, in fact, Carolina was more active than any other English colony in the export of Indian slaves. In 1679, for example, the Carolina bark *Mary* carried "goods and slaves" to Virginia to exchange for several mares and a hold full of neat cattle.[15] At the Proprietors' insistence, a system of permits was established to regulate these deportations. It provided that no slave was to be exported "without his owne consent," but among the victims fear of their Indian captors and ignorance of their white purchasers seems to have made this consent readily obtainable.[16]

Although the Proprietors had few scruples about slavery as an institution, they protested strenuously against the "evill men" who "made a trade of enslaving & sending away the pore Indians."[17] In part they were fearful of prompting hostilities with local tribes or the nearby Spanish (fears realized when a combined force of Spaniards, Indians, and Negroes attacked the settlement in 1686), and in part they were anxious to protect their peaceful trade in deerskins, which provided the colony's first source of direct revenue to England.[18] With the opening up of this lucrative Indian trade to more people in the 1690s, the European settlers themselves became increasingly willing to curtail their limited reliance upon native American labor. Although

13 See Lauber, *Indian Slavery*, p. 288.

14 Edward McCrady, "Slavery in the Province of S.C.," p. 641, points out that this process was familiar elsewhere: "In 1650, Indians who failed to make satisfaction for injuries in Connecticut were ordered to be seized and delivered to the injured party, 'either to serve or to be shipped out and exchanged for negroes, as the case will justly bear.'"

15 RSP (1675–95), pp. 36–37. Maurice Mathews and James Moore, who undertook the venture, were both associated with Indian trading.

16 *Coll.*, V, 367; *Journal of the Grand Council, 1671–1680*, p. 80.

17 BPRO *Trans.*, I, 289; II, 59–60.

18 BPRO *Trans.*, II, 184; McCrady, *Proprietary Govt.*, p. 190. Cf. Louis R. Smith, "South Carolina Indian Trade Regulations, 1670–1756," unpublished M.A. thesis (University of North Carolina, 1968).

enslavement of Indians continued on into the settlement's second generation, any thought of utilizing such laborers as the core of the colonial work force had dissipated well before the end of the seventeenth
century.

The alternative of a white labor force presented a different set
of variables. Simple reasons of custom, language, and religion naturally made Europeans prefer to have other Europeans working with
and under them. But it was one thing to promote independent migration from Europe and another to contract serviceable labor from there.
Some of the difficulties became apparent with the first fleet that
paused at Kinsale in Ireland to obtain several dozen servants. The
attempt failed totally, and Robert Southwell wrote to Lord Ashley
that the Irish there had been so "terrified with the ill practice" of
being shipped to the Caribbean islands "where they were sold as
slaves that as yet they will hardly give credence to any other usage."[19]
Not even offers of brief service and generous land grants could offset
this negative publicity entirely.[20]

For the overall availability of white labor in the colony, the
number of Europeans recruited was less important than the terms of
indenture under which they came. Individual contracts varied widely.
Some whites may have signed on as servants for the outward passage
in order to help someone else obtain land through the headright system, only to be released upon arrival to take up lands of their own.[21]
Others worked until the cost of their passage was paid. It was not un-
heard-of for elderly people to indent themselves for life, but generally
a specific term of service was set. Among colonies competing for European labor such terms of service had to be roughly comparable, and

[19] *Coll.*, V, 153. Southwell's credibility as an agent was enhanced "because they
know I never had anything to doe with the West India trade, but have ransómed
many of them that have beene snatched up and privately conveyed on board the ship
bound that way." Yet even this was not enough.

[20] If previous abuses complicated the recruitment process in England, so did
efforts to regulate the system of "voluntary servitude" there. In 1682 the king and
council issued an order, renewed in 1686, calling for all English indentures to be recorded before a magistrate and to be cleared with a guardian wherever minors were
involved. The fact that the Navigation Laws prohibited direct trade by the American
colonies with Ireland and Scotland added further to the difficulty of procuring labor
from those two sources.

[21] *Warrants*, II, 81. Hugh Carteret received a warrant for 325 acres on March 20,
1683, which included "70 acres for his wife arrieving a ser^t: upon his acco^{tt}: in August
1671 [and] 70 acres allowed his wife at the expiracon of her servitude." Cf. *Warrants*,
I, 61.

they tended to decrease through time. The usual term in Barbados dropped from five to seven years before the Restoration to three to five years after, with bargains for as little as one year's labor being struck in certain instances.[22] Carolina contracts diminished similarly: in an indenture surviving from 1682 a London sawyer promised to serve for two years in the Charlestown settlement.[23]

Such brief contracts resulted in a rapid turnover in the dependent white work force, and Gov. Archdale, addressing the commons in 1695, was not the first to complain of the "Servants that Dayley become free."[24] More important, even a steady flow of indentured servants failed to increase the available pool of unfree manpower beyond a certain fixed point; it merely replenished the small supply of persons serving work-terms, while the overall population continued to grow.[25] To maintain even this supply it was necessary for the colony to avoid the risk of adverse rumors about extended servitude. In 1687, therefore, a statute was passed which set maximum limits upon terms of service for new white arrivals according to their age. The same act imposed a further expense upon the employer by requiring him to provide each servant at the end of his term with "one suite of Apparell, one barrel of Indian Corne, one Axe and one Hoe."[26]

Even before their terms expired, English servants who sensed their value in a labor-scarce economy could often better their lot. One man appealed successfully to the grand council for a change of household, since his current master "could not at present maintaine him with convenient & necessary provisions, and clothes."[27] And many who could not bargain for their well-being must have stolen instead, for "Servants purloyning their masters goods" became an early topic of

22 Harlow, *Barbados*, pp. 190 *n*, 301 *n*.

23 MR "A" (1682–90), p. 7.

24 *SCCHJ*, 1695, p. 7.

25 Cf. Thomas J. Wertenbaker, *The Old South* (New York, 1942), p. 308 *n*.

26 *Statutes*, II, 30–31. These "freedom dues," like terms of service, had to be competitive between colonies seeking indentured labor. North Carolina's promise of "Corne & Cloathes" is mentioned in *CRNC*, I, 579. For laws elsewhere, see Gray, *Agriculture*, I, 365–66.

27 *Journal of the Grand Council, 1671–1680*, p. 52; cf. *Coll.*, V, 318. McCrady, "Slavery in the Province of S.C.," p. 633, cites the case of a woman named Elizabeth Linning who was taken up at the dockside in Glasgow. A captain transporting thirty-two political prisoners who had been banished to the colonies sold Linning into service in May 1684, but she was able to petition successfully for her liberty within the same year.

concern.[28] Occasional disappearances and acts of flagrant disobedience were other matters of common anxiety. Severe penalties deterred most, though by no means all, white servants from attempting to flee the colony altogether, but many shared the disposition of Philip Orrill, who was sentenced to twenty-one lashes for threatening his mistress, tossing his rations to the dogs, "and divers other Gross abuses and destructive practices."[29]

General lethargy and laziness constituted one further vice which seemed prevalent among whites (and which was by no means confined to servants). Whether the Europeans were simply diverted from their Protestant ethic of work by the mild climate or instead actually sacrificed some measure of their physical health is a topic to be touched upon in the next chapter, but the observation was commonplace. "Inhabitants toil not in summer to accommodate themselves with Winter's Provision," wrote Gascoyne, and Archdale observed bluntly that the "natural Fertility and easy Manurement, is apt to make the People incline to Sloth."[30] Thus in quality, as well as in quantity, white indentured labor clearly left something to be desired.

---

[28] *Coll.,* V, 358. How many white servants had been convicted of similar crimes elsewhere and then deported to Carolina has always been a matter of debate, but there is little doubt that some who arrived on indentures had criminal records. A memorandum in the British Public Record Office (BPRO *Trans.,* III, 204) dated July 2, 1697, reads: "This day a Letter was writ to Mr Thornburgh about some Women Convicts now lying in Newgate [prison] for transportation proposed to be sent to Carolina."

[29] *Journal of the Grand Council, 1671–1680,* pp. 33–34; cf. 14, 22–23, 25, 47, 54–55, 63–64; also see Sirmans, *Colonial S.C.,* pp. 21–22. Masters felt the odds for such ill behavior to be stronger among certain groups than among others. Joseph West, for example, having complained openly about the first servants drawn from England, held those from Barbados in even lower repute. He wrote the Proprietors in 1671:

> I hope yor Honnrs are thinking of sending a supply of Servts from England, for some of these wilbe out of their time the next yeare, and wee find that one of our Servts we brought out of England is worth 2 of ye Barbadians, for they are soe much addicted to Rum yt they will doe little but whilst the bottle is at their nose.

Coll., V, 299; cf. 387, 436–37. A "Drinker's Dictionary" which appeared in *SCG,* May 7, 1737, listed "Been at Barbados" as one local expression for being drunk or hung over.

[30] Gascoyne, *True Description,* p. 2; Salley, *Narratives,* p. 290. A general consideration of this theme appears in David Bertelson, *The Lazy South* (New York, 1967), esp. Chapter III.

III

THE ALTERNATIVE of African labor was a plausible one from the out-set. It appeared natural to colonizers from the West Indies and in-triguing to those from western Europe, and it afforded certain advantages to both. Since Africans came from a distance, their exploi-tation did not present the serious diplomatic and strategic questions posed by Indian labor, yet their Caribbean sources were closer and their transportation costs lower than those of white workers. Unlike white servants, Negroes could be held for unlimited terms, and there was no means by which word of harsh or arbitrary treatment could reach their homelands or affect the further flow of slaves. Moreover, Africans had long had the reputation of being able to fend for them-selves more readily than Europeans in the subtropical southern At-lantic climate—a valuable asset when provisions were scarce.[31]

The barriers posed by language were scarcely more formidable for Africans than for other non-English-speakers and had often been reduced through time spent in the West Indies. The useful effects of this Caribbean "seasoning" are noted in a letter of 1688. Edmund White wrote from London to Joseph Morton, two-time governor of the Carolina colony, offering the chance for investment in a slave ship which was sailing directly to the Guinea Coast, but acknowledging that Morton might rather venture his capital on Negroes already in the West Indies. If that were the case, White went on to recommend that Morton contact one Col. Johnson in Barbados, asking whether, "when any bargaine of negroes is to be had, he would buy them for you and keep them upon his plantation till he can send them." This, White assured Morton, "he can doe with much care & the negroes will be the better after they have been ashore for sometime and their work will be worth their keeping."[32] It is notable that White added, "let y^r

---

[31] For example, a century earlier (June 4, 1580) the Council of the Indies in Madrid, in urging that thirty slaves be sent out from Havana to work on the fortifica-tions at St. Augustine, remarked that, "With regard to their food, they will display diligence as they seek it in the country, without any cost to the royal treasury." Jeannette Thurber Conner, trans. and ed., *Colonial Records of Spanish Florida* (De Land, Fla., 1930), II, 315.

[32] *SCHGM*, XXX (1929), 3. (The term "seasoning" was used in different ways to cover the process of adjustment—physical and psychological—faced by Europeans and Africans entering the plantation colonies of the New World.)

negroes be taught to be smiths shoemakers & carpenters & bricklayers: they are capable of learning anything & I find when they are kindly used & have their belly full of victualls and [possess suitable] clothes, they are the truest servants."[33]

The actual methods of obtaining black labor were quite varied at first, and many of the colony's earliest Negro slaves, like certain European and Indian workers, were secured by dubious means. Piracy was at its height in the Caribbean during the period of Carolina's settlement, and there is little doubt that colonists occasionally offered shelter and provision to buccaneers in exchange for portions of their spoils.[34] In 1684 the governor of Jamaica, protesting the increase of piracy to the Lords of Trade and Plantations, "represented to them the great damage that does arise in His Majesty's service by harbouring and encouraging of Pirates in Carolina."[35] A year later the Proprietors wrote their colony concerning some accused pirates, transported from Charlestown to London for trial, who reportedly "had negroes gould and other things which were seized in Carolina," all of which would fall to the Proprietors if the men were found guilty.[36] A large pirate fleet had plundered Vera Cruz in 1683, and according to the depositions made by several runaway English servants at St. Augustine in January 1686, South Carolina obtained roughly two hundred Negroes from this and other raids.[37] (The appearance of Spanish names among early slaves supports such testimony.) Raiding parties carried off Negroes from New Providence, the nearest English slave island in the Bahamas, twice during 1684, and again in 1703.[38]

A few Negroes no doubt came to Carolina through the practice of "salvaging" for resale slaves who had been abandoned to their own

[33] *Ibid.*, pp. 3–4. (See Appendix A.) Of course few Europeans in the seventeenth century were likely to concede—or even suspect—that such Negro skills with metal, leather, wood, and masonry could well be the result of prior familiarity. Still, it was soon granted among whites that, by one means or another, blacks seemed to "understand most handycrafts." The Rev. John Urmston, July 7, 1711, *CRNC*, I, 764.

[34] *Journal of the Grand Council, April–Sept., 1692*, pp. 54, 60. *SCHGM*, XVII (1916), 15, 16; IX (1908), 187.

[35] *CRNC*, I, 347.

[36] BPRO *Trans.*, II, 31.

[37] Cited in Childs, *Colonization*, p. 207. The date is misprinted there as Jan. 11, 1696.

[38] *Ibid.*, pp. 195–96, 207; Mass. Hist. Soc., *Collections*, 5th ser., VI, 88 *n.* Cf. Shirley Carter Hughson, "The Carolina Pirates and Colonial Commerce, 1670–1740," *Johns Hopkins University Studies in Historical and Political Science*, 12th ser. (Baltimore, 1894).

devices in the Caribbean as a result of natural disasters or shipboard rebellions.[39] Other blacks were imported to Carolina from as far away as England upon occasion.[40] As for imports directly from Africa, it is possible that interlopers in the slave trade who were turned away from Barbados by the Royal African Company might have traveled as far as Carolina, but this seems unlikely, for the colony's economy would not reach a scale capable of absorbing and paying for a large ship-load of slaves on short notice until well after the turn of the century. One or two small vessels from Charlestown may have risked an At-lantic crossing to seek a cargo of African workers before 1700, but any such efforts were exceptional during the colony's first generation.[41]

Throughout the first twenty-five years the documentary evi-dence suggests that most Negroes arriving in Carolina were brought in small numbers, by specific owners, from points in the western hemi-sphere. For example, in 1683 the ship *Betty*, "rideing att Anchor in the Roade of Barbadoes & bound for Ashley River in Carolina," took aboard six Negroes, along with two half-barrels of flour and two bar-rels of rum, for delivery "unto Bernard Schenckingh or to his Assignes." Upon their arrival, Schenckingh was to pay what must have been the standard shipping charge of fifty shillings per head for the group of slaves, which included four men (June, Meningo, Walle, Bache), one young woman (Cumboe), and a boy (Popler).[42] Because of the direc-tion of Carolina's mercantile ties and the broader patterns of the English slave trade, Barbados served as the main source for this small-scale commerce in Negro labor. Due to the increased exertions of the

[39] It was a common practice aboard slave vessels in distress to nail down the hatches over the "live cargo." See "Life of Equiano," pp. 99, 113. For a description of the salvage of slaves from a wrecked Dutch ship, see E. B. O'Callaghan, ed., *Voyages of the Slavers St. John and Arms of Amsterdam* (*New York Colonial Tracts*, no. 3, Albany, 1867). Some abandoned Negroes were able to protect their independence. The Black Caribs who inhabited the island of St. Vincent before any Europeans were the survivors from a slave ship which sank near Bequia in 1675. Ebenezer Duncan, *A Brief History of St. Vincent* (Kingstown, St. Vincent, W.I., 1941; 4th edn., 1967), p. 2.

[40] RSP (1675–95), pp. 239–41, 260, 272. Conceivably, a few of the black slaves removed from Mediterranean galleys and transported to the French West Indies during this period could have ended up in the Ashley River colony. Paul W. Bamford, "Slaves for the Galleys of France, 1665 to 1700," in John Parker, ed., *Merchants and Scholars: Essays in the History of Exploration and Trade* (Minneapolis, 1965), pp. 180–84.

[41] See Chapter IV, note 16, below.

[42] RSP (1675–95), p. 128. In the next decade the master of the ketch *Mary* out of Boston was instructed to travel between Carolina and New Providence "or elsewhere with pork and beef and mind that he purchase three or four good negroes." Records of the Court of Ordinary (1692–1700), p. 26, cited in *SCHGM*, VIII (1907), 171.

Royal African Company and the growing number of separate traders, that island entrepot received more than seventy thousand slaves between 1670 and 1695.[43] Barbadian disdain for Irish labor ("commonly very idle") was expressed to the Lords of Trade and Plantations in 1676 by Sir Jonathan Atkins, who claimed that sugar planters had found by experience that black slaves worked better at one third the cost. In 1680 he observed that "since people have found out the convenience and cheapness of slave labour they no longer keep white men, who formerly did all the work on the Plantations."[44]

The preferences of the Caribbean landlords, although geared to a very different economy, must have been widely known to their Carolina cousins. Carolina's reliance upon Barbados for what slaves its white colonists could afford served to strengthen further the existing ties to the sugar island, and these bonds—in a circular fashion—helped predispose would-be planters in the mainland colony to black labor. Since little social hierarchy was possible at first in the southern wilderness, slave ownership quickly became a means for Englishmen to establish status distinctions in the mainland settlement. Their food, clothing, and shelter became more similar with migration; the destitute lived somewhat better, and the well-to-do somewhat worse, than they had before. At Bridgetown in Barbados, where more than 90 per cent of white householders owned Negroes—almost twice the percentage that possessed white labor[45]—the pattern counted for little, but in Charlestown, where white servants represented a smaller, safer, and more common investment than black, the possession of Negroes assumed additional social connotations.

Since an African retinue, however forlorn, served to distinguish and to reinforce authority patterns among whites, it is not surprising that at first local officials were among the largest individual importers of slaves. Among the early governors, Sayle brought several slaves despite his brief tenure; Yeamans and Morton owned dozens between them. James Colleton employed black laborers on his extensive barony and probably left most of them there when he returned to Barbados; while Seth Sothell possessed at least ten slaves even before he replaced

[43] In the last quarter of the seventeenth century Barbados accounted for almost 40 per cent of the British slave trade, a trade which itself still represented less than 30 per cent of the entire Atlantic commerce in Africans during the period. Curtin, *Atlantic Slave Trade*, pp. 55, 119, 122, 124, 129.

[44] Harlow, *Barbados*, pp. 309, 308 n.

[45] Dunn, "The Barbados Census of 1680," 23.

Colleton.[46] Sir Nathaniel Johnson, who would become governor in 1702, had imported over several decades more than one hundred "Servants & Negroes at Sundry times on his account in this parte of the province," and when the Rev. Samuel Thomas visited Johnson's Cooper River estate of "Silk Hope," he noted that "his family is very large many servants and slaves."[47]

Such status-seeking had certain implications for the slaves purchased to fill symbolic roles. Several hundred Negroes must have belonged to the handful of whites who each owned more than a dozen black workers before 1695. These slaves apparently lived upon large tracts in remote areas, where contacts with other Africans were limited but where the nucleus of a social unit larger than a family could already exist. Supervision was partial and activities varied, for new crops were being tried and new land cleared annually. (It is misleading to glorify—or damnify—any of these isolated seventeenth-century holdings as "plantations.") For slaves who had served on sugar plantations the uncertainties of the frontier must have posed a welcome contrast to the harsh routine of the islands, and for those who were dressed handsomely and employed superficially in ways calculated to enhance their master's stature, there were the small gratifications which the patronizing and the patronized always share. But labor was too scarce for any but the most highly placed to restrict Negroes to symbolic or genteel functions as yet. If certain masters purchased blacks to announce their social arrival, most employed them to better their economic well-being. In general, therefore, slaves simply shared the calling of the white household to which they were annexed, participating fully in the colony's growing number of specialized trades.[48]

[46] On Colleton, see *SCHGM*, XII (1911), 43–52; *SCHGM*, XXXII (1931), 21–22. On Sothell, see BPRO *Trans.*, I, 208.

[47] *Warrants*, II, 215; cf. 107, 116, 212, and *SCHGM*, XVIII (1917), 12–13; *SCHGM*, IV (1903), 226.

[48] Some prosperous craftsmen owned whole black families, more than one member of which may well have been employed in the business. Stephen Fox, a tanner from Barbados, brought four men, four women, and four children with him aboard the *Mary* in May 1679; the extensive estate left by James Beamer, a "joyner," in 1694 included three men, three women, and six children; a carpenter named Thomas Gunstone owned two men, two women, and four children who were sold together in 1698. *Warrants*, II, 56; WIMR (1692–93), p. 208; RRP (1696–1703), pp. 100–101.

IV

THERE WERE, however, numerous impediments to the use of African labor in Carolina, and widespread enslavement of Negroes was by no means a foregone conclusion from the start. An inexperienced Huguenot settler claimed that "any man who has a couple of negroes, a ready-made plantation, [and] a maid-servant . . . can live very happily . . . in this country at small outlay,"[49] but in fact the outlay required for black labor was by no means small. Indeed, it was their price, more than anything else, that limited the viability of slave laborers at first. If African labor was recognized in the Caribbean as potentially more profitable than European labor over the long run, it still entailed a larger initial investment, and many early settlers in Carolina who could not afford to bring slaves brought indentured servants instead. A Negro purchased outright for an unlimited period could be worked harder, maintained more cheaply, and retained longer than a white servant under a limited indenture, but only after several years of steady labor would these comparative advantages begin to carry weight.[50] The additional cost and responsibility of such a purchase had limited appeal in a frontier colony where money was scarce, risks were high, and the future nature of the economy was still uncertain.

Whenever slave labor could be purchased cheaply, it usually represented an excessive gamble. The Canteys, an Irish family of small means who reached Carolina by way of Barbados in the 1670s, acquired along the way a slave named Marea and her infant son, Jacke. This "Sicke Dropsecall diseased Negro woman" was later appraised at two pounds and could hardly have been a valuable asset.[51] Moreover, even white Carolinians with sufficient capital to import healthy Negro labor could not always find sound investments at hand. Barbadian planters, who reckoned the mortality of their bondsmen at one in twenty annually, had prior call upon their island's expanding supply

---

[49] Letter of Louis Thibou, Sept. 20, 1683, SCL. Cf. notes 47 and 50 in Chapter I, and also note 10 above, where Thibou refers expansively to "a family of 30."

[50] Some suggestion of comparative monetary values can be gotten from the inventory reproduced in Appendix B.

[51] RSP (1675–95), pp. 61, 69.

of imported slaves. As a result, other settlements, as close to Barbados as Nevis, complained about the price and quality of Negroes available through re-export. In the more distant and less wealthy mainland colony these problems were still greater.[52]

Foreign competition compounded these difficulties. Not only were the English colonies in the Caribbean, to which Jamaica had been added in 1655, exploiting Africans in growing numbers, but the mainland colonies of Spain were obtaining an increasing percentage of their slaves through British merchants. Although the Navigation Acts of 1661 excluded foreign ships from trading with English colonies, several thousand of the Royal African Company's slaves were annually diverted into "assientist" vessels, and in 1685 the Lords of Trade officially exempted from seizure "Spanish ships that are come to buy negroes"[53] at English ports in the Caribbean. Since the Spaniards could generally pay high prices in hard coin without requesting credit, they received priority over English planters and pushed the cost of Company Negroes upward. When the planters resorted to interlopers to supply their own demand, the expense of procuring slaves in Africa was also increased. Overall slave prices among the English appear to have risen more than 20 per cent during the 1680s.[54] Therefore, advantages related to employing Negroes in Carolina were largely offset by increasing demands for their services elsewhere.

And indeed, in Carolina itself the attraction of foreign demand was felt. Although the re-export of slaves from Charlestown for profit would not prove generally feasible for another three quarters of a century, the first generation of white settlers were never free from the thought of exchanging valuable Negro labor for Spanish bullion. Lord Shaftesbury, himself associated with the Royal African Company, had commerce with the Florida Catholic settlement in mind when he con-

[52] Donnan, *Documents*, I, 205; Higham, *Leeward Islands*, p. 161.

[53] Lords of Trade to colonial governors, April 10, 1685, *Calendar of State Papers, America and West Indies, 1685–1688*, p. 28. Jamaica, as the westernmost island of the English, became the logical center for this commerce, and by the first decade of the eighteenth century it had swept past Barbados as a slave entrepot and consumer of British goods. In the late 1600s, however, it remained common for Spanish sloops to roam as far east as Barbados to acquire Negroes and cloth. Curtis Nettels, "England and the Spanish-American Trade, 1680–1715," *Journal of Modern History*, III (1931), 3 n, 28; Harlow, *Barbados*, p. 311 n.

[54] Nettels, "England and the Spanish-American Trade," pp. 5, 7, 11. At times interlopers were carrying as much as a third of the trade. Curtin, *Atlantic Slave Trade*, p. 125.

sidered establishing his barony in Carolina. "You are to endeavour," he instructed Andrew Percivall in 1674, "to begin a Trade with the Spaniards for Negroes, Clothes or other Commodyties they want."[55] In the 1680s when eleven blacks (members of a larger contingent of "diverse negroe slaves" which had run away from South Carolina) appeared at St. Augustine, embraced Catholicism, and sought permanent asylum there, Maj. William Dunlop negotiated to sell them to the Spanish for sixteen hundred pieces of eight.[56] After the Spanish raid of 1686, in which thirteen of Landgrave Morton's slaves were carried off, his brother-in-law killed, and "great desolation . . . made in the South part of this Settlem^t,"[57] Gov. Colleton reopened trading relations so quickly that eyebrows were raised.[58] "The truth is," confirmed a later report, "there was a design on foot to carry on a Trade with the Spaniard."[59] Strategic considerations finally outweighed commercial interests, however, and no regular profits came to the English from selling slaves to their nearby Spanish rivals.

Next to the high initial cost, it was the frequency of disappearances which presented the greatest drawback to employing black labor, and these two factors were of course related. The unlimited term which raised the price of the slave also increased his motivation to escape; unlike the indentured servant's his situation contained no prospect of predictable improvement. Since settlement conditions were harsh and means of social control superficial, disappearances were frequent for all varieties of unfree labor in the new province, but the departure of a servant with several years left to serve was less costly to his white master than the absence of a lifetime slave.[60] Some

[55] *Coll.*, V, 442.

[56] *SCHGM*, XXXIV (1933), 24. There were two women and a three-year-old child, along with eight men, listed as Conano, Jesse, Jaque (Jack), Gran Domingo, Cambo, Mingo (suspected of killing an Englishman), Dique (Dick), and Robi.

[57] Quoted in Rivers, *Sketch*, p. 425. Two of the slaves escaped and returned. Salley, *Narratives*, p. 205. The others included eight men named Peter, Scipio, Doctor, Cushi, Arro, Emo, Caesar, and Sambo, plus three women listed as ffrank, Bess, and Mammy. *SCHGM*, XXXIV (1933), 4. The eleven remained in St. Augustine and were rumored to be "actually imployed in buildinge a Fort." Rivers, *Sketch*, p. 425.

[58] Assemblymen informed Seth Sothell when he arrived to replace Colleton in 1690: "wee are of oppinion wee ought not to be angry at a trade with the Spaniards, but as Englishmen . . . [we wonder] y^t soe exercrable a barbarity . . . should be buryed in silence for the hopes of a little filthy lucre." Rivers, *Sketch*, p. 425.

[59] Edward Randolph to the Board of Trade, June 28, 1699, BPRO *Trans.*, IV, 90.

[60] The difficulties posed to English Carolinians by black runaways had already been felt in older colonies. As far back as 1648 a traveler touching at Barbados had noted that there were "many hundreds of Rebell negro slaves in the woods." Force,

newcomers were undoubtedly deterred from running away by ignorance of local geography, but many were knowledgeable and realistic about the prospects for escape, if only because of the regulations which forbade it. The likely refuge of St. Augustine was a constant subject of public discussion in early years, and the appearance of Carolina slaves and servants there gives evidence that its whereabouts was not overlooked.[61] Although more distant and less inviting, Virginia was also known, particularly to those laborers who had been brought from that direction. As early as 1671, when Yeamans sent Dr. Henry Woodward on a secret overland journey to the north, Gov. West had expressed concern to Lord Ashley that "if he arrives safe in Virginia, there is a way laid for o^r Serv^{ts} to range in, wee have lost two allready."[62]

Similar concerns are borne out in the colony's first legislation devoted entirely to slavery, an "Act for the Better Ordering of Slaves" passed by the Assembly in 1690 and quickly disallowed by the Proprietors for political reasons.[63] This statute represented little more than a

---

Tracts, II, no. 7, p. 5. Yet the Caribbean experience was not entirely analogous. Island runaways were ultimately circumscribed in a way which may have made them more united, resourceful, and desperate at times but which limited their alternatives for escape. Mainland servants, on the other hand, had no absolute natural barrier, and both black and white took advantage of the coastal passages and overland trails that stretched beyond the edges of the colony. Regulations controlling shipboard departures, comparable to those passed in Barbados in 1670, could not have the same effect they had in the island settlement. *Journal of the Grand Council, 1671–1680,* pp. 20, 32–33; *Coll.,* V, 222.

[61] By 1689 the red, white, and black populations of the Spanish settlement totaled almost fifteen thousand, and outside St. Augustine there already existed the makings of a distinct Negro community which would grow with time. Charles W. Arnade, *The Siege of St. Augustine in 1702* (Gainesville, Fla., 1959), pp. 9–11; "Dispatches of Spanish Officials Bearing on the Free Negro Settlement of Garcia Real de Santa Teresa de Mose, Florida," *JNH,* IX (1924), 144 ff.; translation of a letter in Spanish from Don La Reano de Torres, governor of St. Augustine, to John Archdale, Jan. 24, 1696, Archdale Papers, mfm, SCDAH, item 13.

[62] *Coll.,* V, 338.

[63] The first act to mention slaves in its title had been ratified Sept. 25, 1682, and was similar to subsequent acts passed in 1687, 1692, and 1696. All were aimed at "inhibiting the Trading with Servants and Slaves" and reflected the difficulty of imposing strict controls in a wilderness environment. *Statutes,* II, v–viii, acts 7, 34, 81, 135.

The tendency to associate "Servants" and "Slaves" together in these statutes may derive from the loose structure of the labor system in early Carolina, or it may stem from the fact that "all negroes and slaves" were accounted as freehold property rather than chattel property. This meant that, contradictory to the Fundamental Constitutions, a master owned the right to a slave's services but not to his person, and could not transfer or dispose of him at will. Such a legal nicety was by no means thoroughly

reworking by the local West Indian faction of a strict law drawn up by whites in Barbados after a suspected Negro plot in 1688.[64] Significantly, the law initiated a system of tickets for slaves sent on errands, despite the absence of any effectual means of enforcement, and it sanctioned such brutal corporal punishments as branding, nose-slitting, and emasculation at a time when very few slaveowners in the wilderness colony were yet in a secure enough position to resort to punishments more severe than whipping.[65] Patterns among runaways will be traced more thoroughly in Chapter IX, but since piracy was so rampant during this first generation it is worth noting here that pirates occasionally conspired with Negroes to mutual advantage.[66] Having benefited in some instances from the slaves' arrival, the buccaneers were not above profiting from their escape, and more than one black was transported away to be sold again elsewhere or retained as a crewman. Nor was the line between pirate and non-pirate particularly clear in this turbulent era. The French pirate ship *La Trompeuse*, which included Negroes and Indians as well as Europeans among its crew, served briefly as an official man-of-war in 1684.[67] On the other hand, H.M.S. *Drake*, although assigned to protect the Carolina coast, engaged in this illegal traffic on the side. A letter of 1690 denounces her commander as a "Piraticall villain" who "seases carys abroad and receaves of Negros Runing

---

recognized in daily practice, but it does reflect Carolina's affinity with the Caribbean, where the freehold definition of slavery was commonplace. Sirmans, "Legal Status of the Slave in S.C., 1670–1740," 465; *Statutes*, VII, 344.

[64] Richard Hall, comp., *Acts Passed in the Island of Barbados, from 1643, to 1762, Inclusive* (London, 1764), act no. 82; John Poyer, *The History of Barbados, from the First Discovery of the Island, in the Year 1605, till the Accession of Lord Seaforth, 1801* (London, 1808), pp. 128–44. Slave uprisings had already been undertaken on the island in 1649 and 1675 and rumored in 1683. When a larger conspiracy was uncovered there in 1692 (Poyer, pp. 155–57), assemblymen in Charlestown considered prohibiting importation "of such slaves as have been Conserned in any plott in Barbados." *SCCHJ, 1693*, p. 15.

[65] Section V of the law required masters to search regularly for weapons in "all their slaves houses" at a time when it is likely that few Carolina Negroes yet lived in such separate and solid dwellings. Other portions of the act, however, pertained more closely to the local situation: masters were ordered to issue every slave a convenient set of clothes annually and to refrain from giving slaves Saturday afternoons free as had been the custom in Carolina until that time.

[66] There is even an instance on record of a Negro and an Indian helping a captured pirate to escape. McCrady, *Proprietary Govt.*, p. 609.

[67] Violet Barbour, "Privateers and Pirates of the West Indies," *AHR*, XVI (1911), 564.

from their Masters 2000 lib [pounds] worth to the ruining [of] many famalies."[68]

The attitudes of neighboring Indians, more than the activities of pirate groups, were crucial to the retention of black labor during this first generation. Local tribes could assist runaway Negroes or else capture and return them, depending upon a variety of factors. It quickly became apparent to white colonists that the nature of this response would in large measure determine the frequency and success of slave departures, and efforts were undertaken to have the surrounding native population assume, in effect, the confining function performed by the sea in the West Indies.[69] The Proprietors, through selfish concern for the growing fur trade, offered constant reminders that without good Indian relations "you can never get in yor Negroes that run away."[70] By the 1690s, as Negro numbers expanded and the trade in furs opened up, the white colonists took concrete steps to set black and red at cross purposes. Gov. Thomas Smith reported to the commons at the start of its fall session 1693 that he had "by the Advice of the Councill Sumond all yᵉ neighbouring Indians to Receive Some Comands from yᵉ Councill relateing to Runaway slaves." Yet despite such dealings, Indian relations with the white slavemasters remained ambiguous, and the disappearance of black servants from the isolated colony continued. An inventory compiled the following spring for an extensive Charlestown estate includes, at a value of twenty-nine pounds, "one negro man named will now rund away."[71]

Despite these various drawbacks, hundreds of Negroes were brought to Carolina to supplement labor from other sources. Frequently during the first generation black and white workers were im-

[68] John Stewart to Maj. William Dunlop, April 27, 1690, *SCHGM*, XXXII (1931), 25.

[69] The fact "that the Indians will be of great Use to yᵉ Inhabitants of our province for the fetching in againe of such Negro Slaves as shall Runn away from their masters" (BPRO *Trans.*, I, 174) was regarded by the Proprietors as grounds for improving relations with the Indians and curtailing their enslavement. A proprietary letter of 1683 hints that many would-be migrants "cannot see how in a large Contingent yor negroes when Run away shall bee brought in againe, unless yᵉ Indians be preserved." BPRO *Trans.*, I, 260. (The reference to "a large Contingent" of runaways is significant. Even if a clerical error altered what should have read, "a large Continent," as is possible, the passage would still be a notable commentary on the complications of mainland slavery.)

[70] BPRO *Trans.*, II, 293.

[71] *SCCHJ*, 1693, p. 27; RSP (1692–1700), p. 164.

ported on the same boat by the same planter, as was the case with "Tom: Samboe: Betty & Peter," who arrived at Charlestown in September 1682 alongside their master and his six European servants.[72] Already it was generally understood that indentured servants were white and their terms were short, while nonwhite laborers served for life; but anomalies remained common. A European could be bound to a life term;[73] an Indian could obtain an indenture.[74] And regardless of formal status, the actual conditions of life and labor did not yet vary greatly between servant and slave, free and unfree. The fact that few new residents were so well stationed as to be exempt from hardship, or so insignificant as to be expendable, is underscored by the letter of a young Huguenot girl who arrived in 1685. Judith Giton wrote to her brother in Europe, *"J'ai bien été dans ce pais six mois sans avoir gouté de pain, et que je travaillois à la terre comme une esclave."*[75]

Where white migrants "worked like slaves," black arrivals labored in many respects like hired hands, and there were numerous households in which captured Indians, indentured Europeans, and enslaved Africans worked side by side during these first years. For example, the estate of John Smyth, who died in 1682, included nine

[72] RSP (1675–95), p. 116. A sample of 45 Negroes imported during the 1670s shows that at least 40 belonged to persons who transported white labor as well.

[73] *Ibid.*, p. 123. In 1682 one Mathew English, who had arrived as a servant from Barbados in 1671 and risen to be provost marshal, got a laborer named Robert Midling to agree in writing to work "in all or any manner of Service . . . dureing the whole terme and time of his Naturall life, for which . . . Mathew English doth covenant . . . to finde him . . . Sufficient meat drinke Washing lodgeing and apparrell."

[74] *Ibid.*, p. 188. The 1683 will of William Jackson, a farmer who had come from London in 1673 and whose holdings after ten years were primarily in hogs and cattle, reads in part: "I give unto my two serv^ts one breeding sow per piece & I doe moreover Acquitt them from any service they bringing the crop well into the house & my Indian Dan serveing time as per Indenture & my Indian boy serveing seaven yeares unto . . . Milleson Jackson & then to be ffree."

[75] Charles W. Baird, *History of the Huguenot Emigration to America*, 2 vols. (New York, 1885), II, 297. A portion of Baird's translation of the Giton letter (II, 182–83) reads:

After our arrival in Carolina we suffered all sorts of evils. Our eldest brother died of a fever, eighteen months after coming here, being unaccustomed to the hard work we were subjected to. We ourselves have been exposed, since leaving France, to all kinds of afflictions, in the forms of sickness, pestilence, famine, poverty, and the roughest labor. I have been for six months at a time in this country without tasting bread, laboring meanwhile like a slave in tilling the ground. Indeed, I have spent three or four years without knowing what it was to eat bread whenever I wanted it.

Negroes, four Indians, and three whites.[76] Even though such depen-
dents were not all engaged in the same tasks or accorded equal status,
they must have fulfilled complementary functions at close quarters.
In the final balance, therefore, no one form of labor seemed sufficiently
cheap or superior or plentiful to preclude the others.

V

JUST AS NO SINGLE TYPE of manpower predominated within the colony
at first, no single economic activity preoccupied the varied work force
of the early years. Given this context, the large-scale transitions to a
slave labor force and to a rice-growing economy during the second
generation take on particular interest. Both changes depended upon a
great number of separate variables, and it is certainly conceivable
that these parallel developments, so thoroughly intertwined in later
years, had little causal relation at the outset. Every colony was in
search of a staple, and South Carolina's commitment to rice developed
only gradually; as late as 1720 there was probably more labor engaged
in the production of meat exports and naval stores than in the growing
of rice. Likewise every colony was in search of labor, and if each obtained from the nearest source workers who were accustomed to the
prevailing climate, it was natural that the northern colonies would
draw servants from Europe while the southern colonies were taking
slaves from the West Indies and Africa. In South Carolina, there were
logical reasons for the appearance of black laborers irrespective of the
tasks intended for them. More than any mainland colony, its roots of
settlement and early commercial ties stretched toward Barbados and
the other islands of the English Caribbean. African labor was already
in steady supply there, and English colonists from the West Indies
who were economically unable to bring Negroes with them at least
brought along the social aspiration of slave ownership. Laborers from
the British Isles were in shorter supply during the period of South

---

[76] RSP (1675–95), pp. 21–22. Smyth was a merchant-planter who had brought
five Negroes and several servants with him from New York in 1671. He eventually
became a member of the grand council and a Lord Proprietor's Deputy. (The inventory for his estate is reprinted in Appendix B.) Even after 1700 the employment of
Negro men and Indian women was being commended to would-be planters as "profitable
advice." See Crane, *Southern Frontier*, p. 113 n.

Carolina's early settlement than they had been during the initial years of the Virginia or Maryland colonies, and after the end of the government monopoly on the slave trade in 1699, the mainland colony closest to the Caribbean stood to benefit most from the participation of private English traders in the traffic in unfree labor.

Even reduced to briefest form, these points are logical enough, and in themselves they suggest little more than a temporal association between the development of rice and slavery. But one possible link has never been fully explored. Scholars have traditionally implied that African laborers were generally "unskilled" and that this characteristic was particularly appropriate to the tedious work of rice cultivation. It may well be that something closer to the reverse was true early in South Carolina's development. Needless to say, most of the work for all colonists was what one Scotsman characterized as simple "labor and toyl of the body,"[77] but if highly specialized workers were not required, at the same time there was hardly a premium on being unskilled. It seems safe to venture that if Africans had shown much less competence in, or aptitude for, such basic frontier skills as managing boats, clearing land, herding cattle, working wood, and cultivating fields, their importation would not have continued to grow. Competence in such areas will be considered elsewhere, but it is worthwhile to suggest here that with respect to rice cultivation, particular know-how, rather than lack of it, was one factor which made black labor attractive to the English colonists.

Though England consumed comparatively little rice before the eighteenth century, the cheap white grain had become a dietary staple in parts of southern Europe by 1670, and Carolina's Proprietors were anticipating a profit from this crop even before the settlement began.[78] The colonists sent out from London in 1669 did not possess rice among their experimental samples, although an enticing pamphlet for the Cape Fear settlement several years earlier had suggested that "The meadows are very proper for Rice."[79] Nevertheless, a single bushel or

[77] John Stewart to William Dunlop, April 27, 1690, *SCHGM*, XXXII (1931), 7.

[78] Most of what little rice northern Europeans had seen came from the Mediterranean basin at this time, and Carolina, as her promoters enjoyed emphasizing, stood in roughly the same latitude as Jerusalem. The Duke of Albemarle must have spoken for all the Proprietors when he wrote to the governor of Barbados in 1663 that their new domain might be expected to produce "wine, oyle, reasons, currents, rice, silke &c; . . . as well as . . . beefe and poorke." *Coll.*, V, 15.

[79] Salley, *Narratives*, p. 69 and note 2.

barrel of rice was shipped by the Proprietors along with other supplies aboard the *William & Ralph* early in 1672. This quantity may have been planted rather than eaten, for one of several servants who defected to St. Augustine two years later told the Spanish governor that the new colony produced "some rice" along with barrel staves and tobacco.[80] But by 1677 the colonists still had little to show for their experimental efforts, and their sponsors wrote impatiently from London: "wee are Layinge out in Severall places of ye world for plants & Seeds proper for yor Country and for persons that are Skill'd in plantinge & producinge . . . Rice oyles & Wines." There is no direct evidence, however, that the Proprietors followed through on this promise, or that they responded helpfully to later requests for guidance.[81]

During the 1680s, perhaps after the arrival of a better strain of rice seed from Madagascar, the colonists renewed their rice-growing efforts.[82] The mysteries of cultivation were not unraveled quickly, however, as is shown by several letters from John Stewart in 1690.[83] Stewart had been managing Gov. James Colleton's "Wadboo Barony" and was taking an active part in rice experimentation.[84] He claimed

[80] *Coll.*, V, 389–90; Childs, *Colonization*, p. 137.

[81] BPRO *Trans.*, I, 59; cf. note 88 below.

[82] Evidence left by white Carolinians concerning the start of rice production can be found in A. S. Salley, *The Introduction of Rice Culture into South Carolina* (*Bulletins of the Historical Commission of South Carolina*, no. 6, Columbia, 1919); Gray, *Agriculture*, I, 277 ff.; Clowse, *Ec. Beginnings*, pp. 123–32. The Madagascar tradition has been popularized in Duncan C. Heyward, *Seed from Madagascar* (Chapel Hill, N.C., 1937). On slaves from that region, see Virginia B. Platt, "The East India Company and the Madagascar Slave Trade," *WMQ*, 3rd ser., XXVI (1969), 548–77. St. Julien R. Childs, long familiar with these matters, suggests in a letter to the author (June 14, 1973) "that about 1693–1696, two and possibly more 'privateers' came into Charlestown from Madagascar, bringing booty captured from ships along the east coast of Africa. They probably also brought Madagascar rice and Negroes. It is even possible that some of the men who came on these vessels had engaged in growing rice in Madagascar."

[83] For the two letters to William Dunlop quoted in this paragraph, see *SCHGM*, XXXII (1931). The extraordinary Stewart was a Scottish frontiersman possessed of boundless energy, supreme vanity, and an outrageously florid prose style, who sought credit for such things as the introduction of silk culture and the initiation of trade with the Upper Creek Indians. (See BPRO *Trans.*, II, 248; Crane, *Southern Frontier*, p. 46 n.) He professed expertise and optimism about every possible resource from buffalo to caviar, and he once listed all his "experiments projections and Rationale for Inriching the Inhabitants . . . wherein yow'l sie 51 projects, all holding test to reason and truth." *SCHGM*, XXXII (1931), 86.

[84] For "Wadboo Barony" at the head of the western branch of Cooper River, see *SCHGM*, XII (1911), 43 ff. With respect to rice, Stewart's suggestions included draining swamps, manuring with swamp-mud, and planting the seeds more thickly than had been customary. "The Governor," he noted in his letter (p. 86), "both in Sevanoh and

to have cultivated the crop in twenty-two different places in one season to ascertain the best location and spacing of the plant. Stewart boasted, perhaps truthfully, that already "Our Ryce is esteem'd of in Jamaica," but even this arch promoter did not yet speak of the grain as a logical export staple. Instead he proposed that rice could be used for the distilling of beer and ale ("from what I observ'd in Russia"), and he went on to suggest that planters "throw by Indian corne to feed slaves with rice as cheaper."

The processing as well as the planting of rice involved obstacles for the Europeans, which may explain why they had discarded the crop initially. "The people being unacquainted with the manner of cultivating rice," recalled an Englishman during the eighteenth century, "many difficulties attended the first planting and preparing it, as a vendable commodity, so that little progress was made for the first nine or ten years, when the quantity produced was not sufficient for home consumption."[85] Similarly, Gov. Glen would later claim that even after experimenters had begun to achieve plausible yields from their renewed efforts around 1690, they still remained "ignorant for some Years how to clean it."[86]

By 1695 Carolina was not yet one of the sources from which England drew her moderate supply of rice, and the colonial legislature was still urging diversity of output as it cast about for a suitable economic base.[87] In 1698 the Assembly was seeking information on such possible activities as whale fishing and the raising of Smyrna currants. Although a request was also made that the Proprietors "Procure and

---

swamp sow'd his Rice thin aftr the Gooscreek philosophers' old measurs." Stewart asserted (p. 17) that both Colleton and Sir Nathaniel Johnson were converted to his design for using at least "3 bushels Ryce sowen on an acre . . . and all our neighborhood follow'd."

[85] *Gentleman's Magazine*, XXXVI (1766), 278–79. Thomas Lamboll recalled how in 1704, as a ten-year-old boy walking to school near Charlestown, "he took notice of some planters, who were essaying to make rice grow."

[86] *Description*, p. 94. In 1691 a Frenchman named Peter Jacob Guerard received a two-year patent on "a Pendulum Engine, which doth much better, and in lesse time and labour, huske rice; than any other [that] heretofore hath been used within this Province," but there is no indication that the device itself succeeded, or that it helped to spur further invention as hoped. *Statutes*, II, 63. Guerard came to South Carolina in April 1680 aboard the *Richmond* with a group of French Huguenots. He was a goldsmith by trade and served as collector of the port in 1696. *SCHGM*, XLIII (1942), 9–11. His pendulum device may have been nothing more than a pestle attached to the limb of a tree so that it would swing back up after each stroke into the mortar below.

[87] *SCCHJ*, Nov., 1695, pp. 12, 13, 15.

Send . . . by yᵉ: first oppertunity a moddell of a Rice mill,"[88] it is doubtful that any such thing was ever found or sent. More than a decade later, Thomas Nairne mentioned the practice of cleaning rice in mills turned by oxen or horses, but no such labor-saving machines came into common use. It is notable that Nairne, like many others in South Carolina at the start of the eighteenth century, continued to view rice in large part as an adjunct to the livestock economy. " 'Tis very much sow'd here," he wrote in 1710, "not only because it is a vendible Commodity, but thriving best in low moist Lands, it inclines People to improve that Sort of Ground, which being planted a few Years with Rice, and then laid by, turns to the best Pasturage."[89]

In contrast to Europeans, Negroes from the West Coast of Africa were widely familiar with rice planting. Ancient speakers of a proto-Bantu language in the sub-Sahara region are known to have cultivated the crop. An indigenous variety (*Oryza glaberrima*) was a staple in the western rain-forest regions long before Portuguese and French navigators introduced Asian and American varieties of *O. sativa* in the 1500s.[90] By the seventeenth and eighteenth centuries, West Africans were selling rice to slave traders to provision their ships. The northernmost English factory on the coast, James Fort in the Gambia River, was in a region where rice was grown in paddies along the riverbanks. In the Congo–Angola region, which was the southernmost area of call for English slavers, a white explorer once noted rice to be so plentiful that it brought almost no price.[91]

The most significant rice region, however, was the "Windward Coast," the area upwind or westward from the major Gold Coast trading station of Elmina in present-day Ghana. Through most of the slaving era a central part of this broad stretch was designated as the Grain Coast, and a portion of this in turn was sometimes labeled more explicitly as the Rice Coast. An Englishman who spent time on the Windward Coast (Sierra Leone) at the end of the eighteenth century

[88] *SCCHJ, 1698,* p. 36.

[89] Nairne, *Letter from S.C.,* p. 11.

[90] Daniel F. McCall, *Africa in Time-Perspective* (Boston, 1964), p. 69. See the articles on the history of sub-Saharan food crops by J. Desmond Clark, H. G. Baker, and W. B. Morgan in the *Journal of African History,* III (1962), 211–39. (The *Journal* gives data on the detailed research on African rice by R. Portères on pp. 237–38.)

[91] Grant, *Fortunate Slave,* pp. 24–25. Lydia Parrish, *Slave Songs of the Georgia Sea Islands* (New York, 1942), p. 227 *n.* Parrish is one of the few writers to have hinted that African people may have known what to do with rice seeds in Carolina.

claimed that rice "forms the chief part of the African's sustenance." He went on to observe, "The rice-fields or *luqars* are prepared during the dry season, and the seed sown in the tornado season, requiring about four or five months growth to bring it to perfection."[92] Throughout the era of slave importation into South Carolina references can be found concerning African familiarity with rice. Ads in the local papers occasionally made note of slaves from rice-growing areas,[93] and a notice from the *Evening Gazette,* July 11, 1785, announced the arrival aboard a Danish ship of "a choice cargo of windward and gold coast negroes, who have been accustomed to the planting of rice."[94]

Needless to say, by no means every slave entering South Caro-

[92] Joseph Corry, *Observations upon the Windward Coast of Africa* (London, 1807; rpt. in London, 1968), p. 37. Cf. Christopher Fyfe, *Sierra Leone Inheritance* (London, 1964), pp. 20, 29, 77.

[93] Donnan, *Documents,* I, 375, 377–80, 413, 428, 438, 442. An ad for the arrival in Charlestown of 250 Negroes "from the Windward & Rice Coast" is reprinted in Daniel P. Mannix and Malcolm Cowley, *Black Cargoes: A History of the Atlantic Slave Trade, 1518–1865* (New York, 1962), plates following p. 146. The caption observes that these slaves were "valued for their knowledge of rice culture."

[94] The most dramatic evidence of experience with rice among enslaved Africans comes from the famous rebels aboard the *Amistad* in the nineteenth century. Thirty-six slaves from the Sierra Leone region were shipped illegally from Lomboko to Cuba, and in the wake of their successful shipboard uprising they eventually found themselves imprisoned in New Haven, Conn. There they were interrogated separately, and excerpts from the interviews drive home this familiarity with rice in personal terms. John W. Barber, *A History of the Amistad Captives* (New Haven, 1840; rpt. in New York, 1969), pp. 9–15:

> He was a blacksmith in his native village, and made hoes, axes and knives; he also planted rice.

> There are high mountains in his country, rice is cultivated, people have guns; has seen elephants.

> He was caught in the bush by four men as he was going to plant rice; his left hand was tied to his neck; was ten days going to Lomboko.

> He was seized by four men when in a rice field, and was two weeks in traveling to Lomboko.

> He is a planter of rice.

> His parents are dead, and he lived with his brother, a planter of rice.

> He was seized by two men as he was going to plant rice.

> 5 ft. 1 in. high, body tattoed, teeth filed, was born at Fe-baw, in Sando, between Mendi and Konno. His mother's brother sold him for a coat. He was taken in the night, and sold to Garlobá, who had four wives. He staid with this man two years, and was employed in cultivating rice. His master's wives and children were employed in the same manner, and no distinction made in regard to labor.

lina had been drawn from an African rice field, and many, perhaps even a great majority, had never seen a rice plant. But it is important to consider the fact that literally hundreds of black immigrants were more familiar with the planting, hoeing, processing, and cooking of rice than were the European settlers who purchased them. Those slaves who were accustomed to growing rice on one side of the Atlantic, and who eventually found themselves raising the same crop on the other side, did not markedly alter their annual routine. When New World slaves planted rice in the spring by pressing a hole with the heel and covering the seeds with the foot, the motion used was demonstrably similar to that employed in West Africa.[95] In summer, when Carolina blacks moved through the rice fields in a row, hoeing in unison to work songs, the pattern of cultivation was not one imposed by European owners but rather one retained from West African forebears.[96] And in October when the threshed grain was "fanned" in the wind, the wide, flat winnowing baskets were made by black hands after an African design.[97]

Those familiar with growing and harvesting rice must also have known how to process it, so it is interesting to speculate about the origins of the mortar-and-pestle technique which became the accepted method for removing rice grains from their husks. Efforts by Europeans to develop alternative "engines" proved of no avail, and this process remained the most efficient way to "clean" the rice crop throughout the colonial period. Since some form of the mortar and pestle is familiar to agricultural peoples throughout the world, a variety of possible (and impossible) sources has been suggested for this

[95] Melville J. Herskovits, *Life in a Haitian Valley* (New York, 1937), illustrations opposite p. 100; William R. Bascom, "Acculturation among the Gullah Negroes," *American Anthropologist*, XLIII (1941), 49.

[96] Bascom, "Acculturation," p. 45; Henry Glassie, *Pattern in the Material Folk Culture of the Eastern United States* (*University of Pennsylvania Monographs in Folklore and Folklife*, no. 1, Philadelphia, 1968), p. 117.

[97] Nathan I. Huggins, Martin Kilson, Daniel M. Fox, eds., *Key Issues in the Afro-American Experience*, 2 vols. (New York, 1971), I, illustrations opposite p. 128; Melville J. Herskovits, *The Myth of the Negro Past* (2nd edn.; Boston, 1958), p. 147. Much of this work had been done by women in Africa, though by no means all of it, as note 94 above makes clear. Female involvement with rice culture could help explain why men and women were more nearly equal in numbers and in money value in South Carolina than in the West Indies. It is also possible (as Paul Wrobel has pointed out to me) that certain African men, such as the Mende from Sierra Leone, may have found forced involvement in the cultivation of swamp rice to be particularly demeaning by their own values.

device.[98] But the most logical origin for this technique is the coast of Africa, for there was a strikingly close resemblance between the traditional West African means of pounding rice and the process used by slaves in South Carolina. Several Negroes, usually women, cleaned the grain a small amount at a time by putting it in a wooden mortar which was hollowed from the upright trunk of a pine or cypress. It was beaten with long wooden pestles which had a sharp edge at one end for removing the husks and a flat tip at the other for whitening the grains. Even the songs sung by the slaves who threshed and pounded the rice may have retained African elements.[99]

In the establishment of rice cultivation, as in numerous other areas, historians have ignored the possibility that Afro-Americans could have contributed anything more than menial labor to South Carolina's early development. Yet Negro slaves, faced with limited food supplies before 1700 and encouraged to raise their own subsistence, could readily have succeeded in nurturing rice where their masters had failed. It would not have taken many such incidents to demonstrate to the anxious English that rice was a potential staple and that Africans were its most logical cultivators and processors. Some such chain of events appears entirely possible. If so, it could well have provided the background for Edward Randolph's comment of 1700, in his report to the Lords of Trade, that Englishmen in Carolina had "now found out the true way of raising and husking Rice."[100]

[98] Glassie, *Pattern in the Material Folk Culture*, pp. 116–17, even suggests a Russian derivation, citing Dimitry Zelenin, *Russische (Ostslavische) Volkskunde* (Berlin and Leipzig, 1927), pp. 84–86.

[99] Herskovits, *Myth*, p. 147; Parrish, *Slave Songs*, pp. 13, 225–33, and plates 7 and 8. In 1969 the linguist David Dalby observed (London *Times*, July 19): "The verb 'sock,' in the sense of 'to strike,' especially with something, has recently been popularized in the black American phrase 'sock it to me' (with an obscene connotation), and is reminiscent of a similar-sounding verb in Wolof meaning 'to beat with a pestle.'"

[100] BPRO *Trans.*, IV, 189–90.

"The Soveraign Ray
of Health"

I

COULD certain physical advantages have helped determine the Negro's primary role in the development of the rice-growing economy in colonial South Carolina during the late seventeenth and early eighteenth centuries? Comparative susceptibility to disease is a subject scientists have only recently begun to understand. It is worth reviewing the historical evidence in the wake of their findings to see whether one significant factor in the utilization of black labor may not have been widespread partial immunity to certain lowland diseases. Needless to say, a variety of nonmedical factors were also at work, but it is useful to devote separate attention to exploring this postulated difference in health between Africans and Europeans.

During the century in which South Carolina existed as an English colony, a good deal was written about the changing conditions of health which prevailed among the settlers, for the physical well-being of individuals and the condition of the provincial body politic as a whole were directly related. At the start, despite the customary hardships of colonization, the outlook was generally optimistic. "Our people (God be praised) doe continue very well in health," wrote Joseph West to Lord Ashley during the first autumn, "and the country seemes to be very healthfull and delightsome."[1] In England, the author of *A True Description of Carolina* included a rhapsodic account of the new settlement's "salubrious Air" in 1674. "The Heavens shine upon this famous Country the soveraign Ray of health; and has blest it with a serene Air, and a lofty Skie, that defends it from noxious In-

[1] *Coll.*, V, 203.

fection." Partly to encourage English migration, but also to reflect early reports, he continued, "nor is there any known Distemper incident to the Inhabitant whereby to terrify and affright him; who for the most part lives by the Law of Plenty, extended to the utmost limits of Sanity."[2]

Despite such disclaimers, English newcomers found they experienced with increasing frequency an initial illness similar to the seasoning which was commonplace in the West Indies, but they continued to minimize its impact. Thomas Newe wrote after his arrival in 1682: "one thing I understand (to my sorrow) that I knew not before, . . . most have a seasoning but few dye of it."[3] Of greater concern to Christian immigrants during these early years seems to have been the incredible rattlesnake. If the presence of this unknown serpent heightened the similarity between Carolina and Eden, rumors of its venomous wiles actually became a discouragement to potential settlers, as suggested by this reassuring letter from Louis Thibou in 1683:

As for the rattle-snake, of which there has been so much talk in England, you can easily kill it for it does not move more than a tuft of grass; a child could kill one with a switch. It is true that a few people have been bitten by accident, but there is a good remedy for that here and no one has ever died of their bite.[4]

But even as Thibou wrote, the colony's sanguine reputation was being called into question from a different quarter. With the relocation of the townsite to Oyster Point and the increase in newcomers—both white and black—after 1680, there was a simultaneous increase in complaints about "fever and ague," the contemporary phrase for malaria. Attention shifted from swamp-dwelling reptiles to the lowland swamps themselves. In 1671 John Locke, secretary to the Proprietors in London, had made special note of an early report that "The rivers generally run through marshes which are not unhealthy."[5] But a decade later it had to be acknowledged, even by an author favorably impressed with the region, that colonists "who in this Country have

---

[2] Gascoyne, *True Description*, pp. 1–2.

[3] Salley, *Narratives*, p. 183. Young Newe, who wrote this letter on May 29, was dead before the year was out.

[4] Thibou's letter (in the SCL) was intended to encourage prospective migrants; he dismissed the alligator as a harmless reptile and noted that snakes were no more common than in France.

[5] *Coll.*, V, 386.

seated themselves near great marshes are subject to Agues."[6] In 1682 the Proprietors, dissatisfied over reports of Charlestown's new location, sent instructions that any further towns in the adjacent counties were to be located "if possible farr from Marshe swamps or standing waters."[7] When word of increasing illness during certain seasons reached them several years later, they wrote smugly to the colonists, "Wee are very sorry for y[e] great Sickness you have been troubled wth w[ch] wee Impute cheefly to the unhealthy Scituation of Charles towne." The Proprietors regretted the fact that country dwellers had been brought to town for guard duty during "the unhealthy months," and they even ordered adjournment of the council and other courts between June 10 and October 10 so "that men might not be Compelled to come in y[e] sickly months into that unhealthy place."[8]

Unlike rural settlers, new migrants from Europe were not so able to avoid the infected village. The Scottish contingent that arrived aboard the *Carolina Merchant* in October 1684 provides a case in point. According to a report sent to Sir Peter Colleton the following spring, their group of 148 persons, intending to start a settlement at Port Royal, reached Charlestown intact after ten weeks at sea. "We found the place so extraordinarie sicklie," wrote the two leaders, Lord Cardross and William Dunlop, "that sickness quickley seased many of our number and took away great many . . . and discoraged others, insomuch that they desarted us." The two reported that many "sold ther servants" and refused to proceed to Port Royal, "the number of those who fixedly resolved to adhere to us, . . . being bot 51." The move to a new and slightly higher location was undertaken promptly. "We came here the beginning of November; sicklie as we wer. . . . We setled ourselves altogether in a verie convenient place . . . , free of swamps and marishes, a high bloffe land excellently weell watered, of such wholesome air as many of us quickly recovered." The two spokesmen, both of whom had suffered from fever and ague before reaching Port Royal, concluded that "none have contracted sicknes since we came tho many died of the sicknes they contracted in Charlestoun at our first arrivell."[9]

[6] Samuel Wilson, *An Account of the Province of Carolina* (London, 1682), reprinted in Bartholomew R. Carroll, ed., *Historical Collections of South Carolina*, 2 vols. (New York, 1836), II, 19–35.

[7] Rivers, *Sketch*, appendix, p. 400.

[8] BPRO *Trans.*, II, 35.

[9] March 27, 1685, *SCHGM*, XXX (1929), 72–73.

By the mid-1680s disenchantment had reached wide enough proportions to jeopardize the colony's development. "We are by all people informed," wrote the Proprietors in 1684, "that Charles Towne is no healthy situation . . . and all people that come to the province and landing there and the most falling sick it brings a Disreputation upon the whole Country." Colonial leaders could only respond, two years later, by urging the Proprietors to give "all possible incourajement to people that are here already to continue and to all others (especially to Englishmen) to transport themselves hither since for these eighteen Months last past aboundantly more English have gone off than have come on[,] a thing of itselfe very discouraging to all that remaine."[10] As early as 1671 the council had passed a law, patterned on a Barbados statute, prohibiting inhabitants from leaving the colony without a special license, but disillusioned migrants still slipped away.[11] In the spring of 1687 this statute prohibiting unlicensed departures from South Carolina was reenacted, but by then word of the unhealthy conditions which prevailed in the colony had become common knowledge throughout the empire.[12] A nobleman in England

[10] BPRO *Trans.*, I, 293; *SCHGM*, XXX (1929), 86.

[11] *Coll.*, V, 369–70. José Miguel Gallardo, "The Spaniards and the English Settlement in Charles Town," *SCHGM*, XXXVII (1936), 133, repeats the following account of testimony given to officials in St. Augustine on Oct. 25, 1679, by a twenty-two-year-old English Protestant named John Hash:

> He said that in England he had heard glowing tales about the said settlement of Carolina, and he left his country in order to improve his future. Discovering this to be impossible, and in view of the want and suffering he had had to endure, he and his three companions decided to take a launch to go to a place where they might find passage to England. . . . He said he thought there were in the said province about four hundred men.

Months earlier the Proprietors had dismissed such behavior with the complaint that many who left, after failing to make ends meet through their own idleness, later excused themselves by putting "the blame on the Countrey . . . to the Discouragement of others." May 19, 1679, BPRO *Trans.*, I, 83–84.

[12] A vessel which left Gravesend in May 1686 contained twenty-seven servants destined to be sold in Carolina and eight English merchants and their families heading for Charlestown of their own volition. A Huguenot refugee named Durand was also aboard, having heard excellent things of the climate. As they neared the American coast they met a Barbados vessel carrying sugar and slaves to Maryland. According to Durand's account, the captain of this vessel informed them concerning Carolina, "that two years ago he had carried there thirty-two persons from Plymouth, all very vigorous, that he went back there eleven months later and that he did not find but two alive, and that there was not an acre of good land in all the south of Carolina." At this the English freemen and Durand begged space aboard the slaver, which transported them to the Chesapeake, leaving the Carolina-bound servants and crew to their fate. See Childs, *Colonization*, pp. 244–45. Gilbert Chinard edited Durand's account as *Un Français en Virginie* (Baltimore, 1932) and made an English translation in 1934.

used what may have been a popular phrase when, in expressing his determination never to return to Ireland, he declared he would "rather live and die in Carolina."[13]

Nor was negative commentary confined to English-speakers. A pamphlet appeared in Europe with the express purpose of refuting a tract which encouraged migration. The author sought to dissuade Huguenot refugees from sailing to the religiously tolerant but physically enervating colony of Carolina, declaring Charlestown to be the "great charnel house of the country."[14] Many of those who disregarded this warning died soon after landing, a fact which explains why numerous French names that appear on the rolls of early Huguenot arrivals then vanish abruptly. The disappearance of other French names can be explained by the fact that some persons reembarked hastily when they discovered their mistake.[15] A narrative written in 1687 by an anonymous Frenchman living in Boston contains the following doleful passage:

Two young men have just arrived from Carolina, who give some account of the country. In the first place, they say, they have never before seen so miserable a country, nor an atmosphere so unhealthy. Fevers prevail all the year, from which those who are attacked seldom recover; and if some escape, their complexion becomes tawny [*ilz deviennent tout bazannés*],[16] like that of the two who have arrived here, and who are pitiable to behold. Moreover, the heat is so intense as to be almost unendurable, and as to infect the water, consequently producing sickness, as they have no other beverage. They bring us also tidings that before their departure a ship had

[13] Childs, *Colonization,* p. 243.

[14] "Remarques Sur La Nouvelle Rélation de la Caroline Par Un Gentilhomme Français." Copies of this pamphlet no longer exist, but William Gilmore Simms apparently possessed one as part of his extensive collection of Caroliniana, for he wrote in the first volume of *Magnolia,* a monthly which appeared in 1842, that the work "has for its purpose to deter the French refugees from settling in South Carolina, and exposes the inaccuracies in the 'New Account of Carolina.' " See Huguenot Soc. of S.C., *Transactions, 1897,* V, 88–90.

[15] Childs, *Colonization,* pp. 247–52.

[16] The effects of living in South Carolina were often said to be written on the faces of Europeans. For example, a visitor to Charlestown before the Revolution found most of the women there to have "Pale Sickish Languid complexions." "Charlestown in 1774 as Described by an English Traveler," *SCHGM,* XLVII (1946), 180. Whether due merely to avoidance of the sun or to some internal disorder, this appearance seems to have become synonymous with Carolina's ill-health for Englishmen in the northern colonies. Massachusetts Gov. Thomas Hutchinson once wrote that a prominent inhabitant of Boston "has changed in one evening a tolerably healthy Nova Scotia countenance for the pale, sickly complexion of South Carolina." Letter of Oct. 31, 1771, in the Mass. Archives, XVII, 249–50.

arrived from London, with one hundred and thirty persons on board, including the crew; of whom one hundred and fifteen died as soon as they landed, all from malignant fevers which spread among them. Some eighty persons are coming from Carolina to settle here, or in New York.[17]

In the following years white Carolinians of all stations continued to remove themselves to other English colonies.[18] New migrants entering the settlement may well have been uninformed or fatalistic.[19] One Massachusetts document from the 1690s illustrates the trepidation with which a group of serious-minded New Englanders approached a move to Carolina. A group of families from Essex County sailing for the South, ahead of others who had also signed a compact to go, received a paper drawn up by the Rev. Jonathan Wise entitled "Instructions for Emigrants . . . to South Carolina, 1697." They were to report back accurately as to whether the climate was not perhaps "so disord^{r}ly that Nature may faile mens hopes." In Wise's mind, only a question about the spiritual state of the province came ahead of this inquiry into problems of health in the region: "We would have you Curious in informing y^{r}selves how ye Countrie is for Health: and whether ye Climate does Agree well wth the Bodyes of o^r N-Eng^d People." The minister noted that, "To think any Countrie on this side Heaven should have a Writ of Ease, and Securitie against Diseases or Death is but a vanitie," but he still urged the migrants to consider "whether that Countrie ma'nt be more Incident to Sicknesse, and the Decrease of ye Inhabitants than ours."[20]

[17] Baird, *Huguenot Emigration*, II, 393.

[18] For example, a joiner named Thomas Barker, who owned several slaves, elected to return to Jamaica. RSP (1694–1705), p. 148. Another slaveowner named John Clapp sold his estate on the east side of Stono River and emigrated to Long Island. RSP (1675–95), pp. 275, 312, 399. Gabriel Thibou, son of the Charlestown vintner quoted earlier, also removed to New York before 1700. *SCHGM*, XLIII (1942), 2, 4, 14–16.

[19] Elder William Pratt, a New England churchman who had visited South Carolina in 1695, returned early in 1697 with his family and some parishioners to found the settlement of Dorchester, named for the Massachusetts town they had left. Pratt's journal shows that he purchased a Negro woman from Capt. Rhett for £25 and that he survived the scourges of 1698—an outbreak of smallpox, an earthquake, and a severe fire in Charlestown—all of which he interpreted as signs of God's judgment. Soon after that, the "climate not agreeing with him," he returned to Massachusetts, perhaps in the wake of the yellow fever epidemic of 1699. *Charleston Yearbook, 1897* (Charleston, 1898), p. 509 ff.; Salley, *Narratives*, pp. 199–200. That same epidemic took the life of John Cotton, Jr., the uncle of Cotton Mather who came to Charlestown late in 1698 to serve as minister to the English and Scottish dissenters there and died the following September. John Duffy, "Yellow Fever in Colonial Charleston," *SCHGM*, LII (1951), 191; cf. *SCHGM*, XII (1911), 27.

[20] *Charleston Yearbook, 1899* (Charleston, 1900), appendix, pp. 149–54.

At the end of the seventeenth century and the beginning of the eighteenth, the white population of South Carolina may even have declined slightly. Some gave military dangers as a reason for emigration; others cited political tyranny to explain why "good people . . . are going from us."[21] But by now sickness was also an acknowledged factor in population decline. The Anglican Commissary in Charlestown discovered for himself that the warm air and fertile soil were offset by "poverty and diseases," and John Lawson ventured the unorthodox suggestion that Christian immigrants "of a mean Fortune" would do better to marry Indian women (and presumably move inland) "than to suffer the Hardships of four or five years Servitude, in which they meet with Sickness and Seasonings amidst a Crowd of other Afflictions." Far into the eighteenth century newcomers from Europe remained of two minds about the region, and many must have shared the sentiments expressed by an immigrant in 1737: "I herewith wish to have everybody warned that he should not hanker to come into this country, for diseases here have too much sway, and people have died in masses."[22]

As in the previous century, such discouraging reports were counterbalanced by one-sided promotional literature. But when a glowing statement drew fresh recruits, it led eventually to further disillusionment, and such a vicious circle was of little benefit to the image of the colony. The only way to break this circle was that suggested by James Glen in 1748. Anxious to attract displaced Protestants from Europe, Glen expressed his wish, "that some honest plain account of Carolina was printed and sent over to be dispersed in Germany avoiding all false and flattering descriptions which always do hurt and make those that are so unhappy as to be deluded by them, think themselves trepanned when they do not find the Paradise that had been painted to them."[23]

[21] Edward Randolph, June 28, 1699, BPRO *Trans.*, IV, 90; Daniel Defoe, "Party-Tyranny" (1705), in Salley, *Narratives*, p. 245.

[22] *Johnston*, pp. 60–61; Lawson, *New Voyage*, p. 246; Samuel Dyssli, Dec. 3, 1737, *SCHGM*, XXIII (1922), 89. Cf. Chapter IV, note 137, and Chapter V, note 50, below.

[23] Oct. 10, 1748, BPRO Trans., XXIII, 233.

II

SOUTH CAROLINA'S REPUTATION for ill-health, which in part offset its obvious attractions, was not based upon general hearsay but upon the observation of specific disorders. Predominant among these diseases was the intermittent fever, often cited as "fever and ague," which we now know as malaria. This illness can range from a slight inconvenience to a mortal sickness. The mosquito-borne malaria parasite destroys red corpuscles in the human bloodstream, putting a continual strain on the parts of the body which create blood. The parasites take hold first in the liver, where they grow and divide for ten days before breaking out into the blood. The spleen, the organ which normally filters the system, becomes enlarged in its effort to function efficiently in sifting malaria parasites out of the bloodstream. Normally covered by the lower ribs on the left side of the body, it now extends down into the stomach region and becomes easily "palpable." At the same time, increased activity among white blood cells, which capture the malaria parasites and digest them, sets off a basic biological mechanism which causes sharp chills and high fever. These primary symptoms, accompanied by severe headaches, occur at intervals and are accompanied by fatigue and sometimes total loss of strength. All such outward signs were well known to inhabitants of the Carolina coast.

Some of the earliest and most detailed firsthand accounts of the disease occur in the letters of missionaries from the Society for the Propagation of the Gospel in Foreign Parts, who served in the region after 1700.[24] The majority of this small group seems to have suffered

[24] Two of these missionaries wrote copious letters that have been edited in separate volumes by Frank J. Klingberg, and each man is revealed as a sufferer from chronic malaria. Gideon Johnston arrived in 1708 to be the minister of St. Philip's Parish, Charlestown, ranking over the other missionaries as Commissary to the Bishop of London. Klingberg states (*Johnston*, p. 8) that "Johnston's own suffering makes his letters a clinical report on the menaces of health to a Briton. . . . The problems of health, as revealed in his letters, show that there is a wholly new chapter in American medical history yet to be written." Commissary Johnston was beset by illness within his first year and only with the approach of colder weather the next November did he sense signs of improvement. "I now begin to recover a little health," he wrote (p. 31), "but am still deprived of the use of my hands, and know not how long I may continue in this condition." The next July he spoke (pp. 35, 37) of "my continual sickness, which has been a great disadvantage to me," and added that his whole family had been "equally Exercised this way," but still he continued with his preaching and

from the disease, and there is little reason why they cannot be regarded as representative of the white population to which they ministered. In 1706 William Dunn, the minister to St. Paul's Parish, who resigned his post after a year, was reported by a colleague to be "afflicted with the Feaver and Ague, and as he was on the recovery is fall'n sick again."[25] Robert Maule, assigned to St. John's Parish the following year, reported to the S.P.G. secretary in 1709:

I had my health indifferently well from my arrival into this Country, till about the latter end of this Summer; but then I was Seized with a very severe fit of Sickness; being held for near three Months together of a fever and Ague which at length concluded in a most Violent Belly Ache; so vio-

---

catechising as well as "visiting the sick, of which there is always Numbers here; and . . . burying the dead." Six months later Johnston stated (p. 77) that it was difficult even to enumerate his communicants due to "the continued change of Inhabitants, in a place of such Concourse & Mortality." He complained (p. 76) that "It is no pleasing task to fflesh & blood, to be Ministering to Sick or dying Persons, & to be exposed to all the ffilth & Nauseous Smells & Ghostly Sights." He noted of his own condition (p. 69): "My want of health loudly calls for a little respite at least, if not for a total Manumission from this dangerous and difficult Warfare; for I am still forced to write with both hands, which shows the weakness of my Body, not to say anything of the ffevers and Spasms I am continually subject to." Johnston's hint for replacement was ignored, and he served on until 1716, when he drowned in Charlestown harbor after his boat upset during a public occasion.

The papers of Dr. Francis Le Jau, a minister in nearby Goose Creek Parish, are equally telling. Le Jau arrived in 1706 and stated (in spite of "The Sickness wch was still raging in Town") that "this is the finest Climate I ever saw." (*Le Jau*, p. 18.) But a year or two later it was rumored in London that he was dead (p. 49), and in October 1709 he reported of his "Temporal State" (p. 61):

my seasoning is hardly over yet, I did linger for some Months this Summer and had at last a severe visitation, but short, thro' divine mercy; It was a fever and ague for a fortnight I feel a Continual pain in the head these two Years and above with short Intervals of not above three days. I am satisfyed to do the Will of God, and do confess I deserve to suffer a great deal more.

When a fall epidemic that may have included several diseases got under way in 1711, Le Jau wrote (p. 97) that "The Country is . . . sickly and most of us are often out of order," but he continued his labors. In 1716 he was confined to bed from August onward (pp. 182, 188) "with the most dangerous fitt of sickness I Ever had; it was an Inflammation of stomach with continual feaver," and by November he despaired for his life. In a mournful letter to the Society's secretary, he hinted that transfer to Barbados might help and added: "in Ten years time I have had I really believe by computation Six years or more Sickness." (Barbados, where the S.P.G. owned a plantation, remained free of malaria throughout the eighteenth century.) After half a dozen relapses Le Jau's intermittent illness improved the next spring (p. 202), but his frame remained "worn out with labour in this sickly and desolate country," and he died the following fall. (Cf. Chapter V, note 11, below.)

25 Francis Le Jau, Dec. 2, 1706, S.P.G. mfm I, SCDAH.

lent indeed that I verely believed it wu'd have ended my days; but I thank
God I am now pretty well recover'd again.[26]

Even in an unscientific age, people suffering from such a widespread and unpleasant disorder were observant of its circumstances.
They could not fail, first of all, to take in the seasonal nature of the
disease. In 1723 an S.P.G. minister sent from Charlestown to North
Carolina wrote, "I and my little family have laboured under a severe
fitt of Sickness the Feaver and Ague commonly known by the name of
the Seasonings incident to all new Comers here." In terms which were
quite familiar to London authorities by then, he described the illness as "holding one from the beginning of August to the latter end
of December."[27] Visitors to the region later in the eighteenth century
frequently repeated similar observations concerning "intermittent
fevers."[28] Johann Schoepf, for example, noted that the "numerous
fevers which every summer and autumn so generally prevail, sparing
but few, are enough in themselves to ruin by their reputation the
strongest constitutions."[29] The famous minister Henry Muhlenberg
noted in his journal on September 12, 1774, "My friends said that in
Carolina and Georgia September was the most dangerous month of
the year for epidemical sicknesses and deaths." Muhlenberg, who had
arrived from Pennsylvania only four days earlier, went on to relate a
report "that one English doctor had declared that at the present time
he alone had about six hundred patients suffering from acute fever
and other complaints."[30]

[26] Robert Maule, March 6, 1709, S.P.G. mfm I, SCDAH. When Maule died late
in 1716, "after 3 years Sickness which brought him to a Consumption and Lingering
feaver," he was the fourth missionary to die in eighteen months. *Le Jau*, p. 191. A fifth
minister was planning to quit his cure in Charlestown, which involved particularly
heavy duty, especially "in a time of Sickness very frequent here." *Ibid.*, p. 196.

[27] Thomas Newman, May 9, 1723, quoted in Joseph I. Waring, *A History of
Medicine in South Carolina, 1670–1825* (Columbia, 1964), p. 2. Another minister, the
Rev. Richard Ludlam of Goose Creek, succumbed after five years of ill-health during
the particularly sickly fall of 1728. His wife had died two weeks earlier. See St. Julien
R. Childs, "Kitchen Physick: Medical and Surgical Care of Slaves on an Eighteenth
Century Rice Plantation," *Mississippi Valley Historical Review*, XX (1934), 549–50.

[28] Frank W. Ryan, Jr., "Travelers in South Carolina in the Eighteenth Century,"
unpublished M.A. thesis (University of North Carolina, 1943), p. 116.

[29] Johann David Schoepf, *Travels in the Confederation* (translated and edited
by Alfred J. Morrison, Philadelphia, 1911), part 2, p. 217.

[30] *Muhlenberg*, II, 567. Within days both he and his wife were stricken with
fever, headaches, and other symptoms which lasted through the fall. "Many persons die
here of this type of flux," wrote Muhlenberg, "and it is said to keep on and gradually
waste the system." See *ibid.*, pp. 568, 570, 576, 577.

Settlers were equally aware that intermittent fevers varied with the location as well as with the month. At first, as we have seen, the low-lying port of Charlestown seemed the focus for disease. According to a 1704 statute designed to regulate sanitary conditions in the small but crowded town, "The air is greatly infected and many maladies and other intolerable diseases daily happen."[31] Charlestown, with its growing populace and steady influx of newcomers, continued to be most subject to epidemic contagions such as yellow fever, a disease which was often confused with malaria throughout this era, but the prevalence of "fevers and ague" shifted away from the city as the century progressed. A Charlestown doctor who described the province in 1763 observed:

The Summer Diseases begin commonly in *July*, and disappear about *Christmas*. In *Charles-town*, these Diseases are proportionably less frequent, and milder than in the Country; for we are pretty clear of Trees, have a large Opening to the Sea, a Kind of Ventilation in the Streets, besides a Thousand culinary Fires in the hottest Season to dry the Air: In the Country they have none of those Advantages.[32]

Before the Revolution, and for more than a century after, intermittent fevers were commonly known in South Carolina as "country fevers," in part perhaps because they were endemic to the locality as a whole, but primarily because they were most prevalent in the countryside.

Furthermore, it was observed that not all parts of the country were equally affected. Low-lying regions somewhat set off from the sea were sensed to be the worst areas in this regard; and since inland swamps were the earliest location of rice cultivation, planters raising this crop soon learned to spend the summer and fall near the shore when possible.[33] In the mid-1700s wealthy whites even developed a common routine of removing their families to Newport, Rhode Island, during that portion of every year. But the sea voyage was costly and occasionally dangerous, and a simpler solution was eventually recognized.[34] From the beginning of the century, Englishmen visiting the

---

[31] Cited in Waring, *History of Medicine*, p. 15.

[32] Milligen, *Short Description*, pp. 154–55.

[33] In Jamaica the breeze from the sea, which became associated with healthy times, was known by 1740 as "the doctor." Frederic G. Cassidy, *Jamaica Talk: Three Hundred Years of English Language in Jamaica* (London, 1961), p. 111.

[34] Carl Bridenbaugh, "Charlestonians at Newport, 1767–1775," *SCHGM*, XLI (1940), 43–47; cf. "Colonial Newport as a Summer Resort," R.I. Hist. Soc., *Collections*,

back-country had been aware of its distinctive geography,[35] and as non-rice growers established themselves in slightly higher and less damp locations, they boasted increasingly of the superior inland climate. Rivalry between the lowland and the back-country, or simple disbelief, seems to have slowed acceptance of such claims, but by the eve of the Revolution a visitor to Charlestown could report that "Fellows, especially those who live in the Interior parts of the Province, know the further you go back the healthier it is."[36]

Country fevers had long been associated with swamps and standing water, both by ancient tradition and steady observation. Prior to the Revolution an Anglican minister named Charles Woodmason attributed the mortality among the clergy to "The Situation of the Parsonage Houses—most of which are built in the Old Style, on Edge of Swamps, in a damp moist situation, which quickly kills all Europeans, not season'd to the Clime." He went on to explain that "The Old Planters us'd this Method in order to view from their Rooms, their Negroes at Work in the Rice Fields—But this Method," Woodmason reported, "now is banish'd—The[y] find the bad Effects—and are all removing their Houses back into the High and dry Lands, remote from the Swamps."[37] Not long before, George Milligen had given a similar explanation for illness among the planters. "In the Country," he wrote, "the Inhabitants in general (being more careful to acquire

---

XXVI (1933), 1–23. Compare the comment of a minister traveling in the back-country in the decade before the Revolution:

> The Gentry us'd annually to go off to some of the Northern Colonies for Change of Air—But they find it now rather too Expensive. One of our Dons (Benj. Smith Esq.) was last Year cast away, he and family in going to Rhode Island—and many have left their Bones in these Places—They are therefore now thinking of their own poor despised Back Country, and are now flocking up where I am, to build Summer Seats, and Hunting Boxes. Lands, not valu'd at a Shilling P acre three Years past, now sells for a Guinea—and is rising—And the Back Inhabitants, are (at last) carrying the Points they've so long labour'd for.

Charles Woodmason, *The Carolina Backcountry on the Eve of the Revolution, The Journal and Other Writings of Charles Woodmason, Anglican Itinerant*, edited with an introduction by Richard J. Hooker (Chapel Hill, N.C., 1953), pp. 195–96.

[35] Lawson, *New Voyage*, p. 89, states:

> Towards the Sea, we have the Conveniency of Trade, Transportation, and other Helps the Water affords, but oftentimes, those Advantages are attended with indifferent Land, a thick Air, and other Inconveniences; when backwards, near the Mountains, you meet with the richest Soil, [and] a sweet, thin Air. . . . One part of this Country affords what the other is wholly a Stranger to.

[36] "Charlestown in 1774 as Described by an English Traveler," 180.

[37] These statements are from the letter quoted in note 34 above.

splendid Fortunes, than to preserve their Healths) build their Houses near their Rice-Fields, or Indigo-dams, where they must always keep stagnating water."[38]

The introduction of floodgates to enhance the cultivation of rice in the second half of the century increased the amount of standing water at times. Likewise, production of indigo, which increased after the 1740s to reach a height of more than one million pounds (over one third of South Carolina's total exports) by 1775, necessitated large amounts of water steeping in vats and stagnating behind dams. An astute military engineer from Holland, who had charge of improving Charlestown's fortifications in the 1750s and who became familiar with all the construction practices in the province, claimed to see a direct and unfortunate relationship between these methods of agricultural improvement and the worsening health of the colonists. David Ramsey, South Carolina's patriot-physician, made a similar observation in 1796, linking the cutting of trees and building of millponds to the creation of miasmas thought to produce "bilious and intermitting fevers in the country."[39]

Ramsey and his contemporaries were also aware of a connection between rainfall and these diseases.[40] As early as 1717, a year of several severe hurricanes, a relationship had been observed between the "Wett Summer" and the "Sickly Fall," and 1728 was likewise noted as a year of severe storms and a considerable epidemic.[41] In 1739, another season of ill health, the merchant Robert Pringle remarked in late August: "great Quantitys of Rain, & the wett weather still Continues." He added, "It is likewise very Sickly here at present both in Town, & Countrey, a great many people being affected with Fevers[,] & Fevers & Agues."[42]

Frequent comment was also made upon the seasonal invasion of mosquitoes, though little significance was attached to their presence. Eliza Lucas Pinckney, renowned for her encouragement of indigo culture, observed that despite South Carolina's generally pleasing cli-

[38] Milligen, *Short Description*, pp. 154–55.

[39] G. Terry Sharrer, "Indigo in Carolina, 1671–1796," *SCHGM*, LXXII (1971), 97; John William Gerard De Brahm, in Weston, *Documents*, p. 179; Ramsey, *Sketch of the Soil, Climate, Weather, and Diseases of South Carolina* (1796), quoted in Waring, *History of Medicine*, p. 291.

[40] David Ramsey, *The History of South Carolina from its First Settlement in 1670 to the Year 1808*, 2 vols. (Charleston, 1809), II, 539.

[41] See Waring, *History of Medicine*, pp. 27, 35.

[42] Pringle Letterbook, Aug. 29, 1739.

mate, "4 months in the year is extreamly disagreeable, excessive hott, much thunder and lightening, and muskatoes and sand flies in abundance."[43] Logically but ironically, these biting insects came to rival the rattler as the natural enemy which most detracted from the colony's reputation in the eighteenth century. A traveler in the 1740s explained to London readers, "Muskettos are long sharp Flies, whose Venom, I believe, according to their Bulk, is as baleful as that of a Rattle Snake."[44] He explained that while mosquito netting was still considered effeminate in the struggling new colony of Georgia, its use had become commonplace in Jamaica and Carolina among those who could afford it.

Such netting made sleeping easier, but there was little sense that it might contribute to good health. On the other hand, one partial remedy against the effects of country fever was widely acknowledged. Cinchona bark, from a South American tree, which contained a substance similar to quinine, had been recognized by the Spanish as an effective inhibitor of the specific symptoms of malaria for some time. This item entered the English pharmacopoeia late in the seventeenth century, and despite its cost, colonists in South Carolina bought increasing quantities of it under such various names as "Peruvian bark," "Spanish bark," "Jesuit bark," and "China bark."[45] A visitor in 1783 remarked upon how widely this medicine was consumed: "Many of the residents here are attacked almost every year by intermittent fevers, and others escape them only by the quantity of China-bark which they take as a preventive. It has become almost the mode to be always chewing China-bark during the fever months or at least to swallow daily several doses of it."[46]

III

ONE FURTHER SET of observations emerges from contemporary sources on health in the South Carolina colony, and it concerns the comparative susceptibility of Africans and Europeans to certain diseases. The

---

[43] Elise Pinckney, ed., *The Letterbook of Eliza Lucas Pinckney, 1739–1762* (Chapel Hill, N.C., 1972), p. 40. Her husband, Charles, died of malaria, and she herself had suffered (p. 14) from the same disease.

[44] Ga. Hist. Soc., *Collections*, IV (1878), 13.

[45] Childs, *Colonization*, pp. 92, 262–63.

[46] Schoepf, *Travels in the Confederation*, part 2, p. 217.

view of this complicated issue was inevitably hazy in an era when medical diagnosis was unrefined and statistics were occasional at best. Moreover, one epidemic could often overlap with others, as in the dismal autumn of 1711. "Nver was there a more sickly or fatall season than this," wrote Commissary Johnston, "for the small Pox, Pestilential ffeavers, Pleurisies, and fflex's have destroyed great numbers here of all Sorts, both Whites, Blacks and Indians,—and these distempers still rage to an uncommon degree."[47] That winter Francis Le Jau estimated that nearly two hundred whites and between three hundred and four hundred slaves had been carried off by disease. Since Africans outnumbered Europeans by something less than two to one at that point, the percentage of Negro deaths was roughly equal to the proportion of blacks in the total population.[48]

Where the cause of sickness was clear, there were often no obvious differences for rates of morbidity and mortality between Africans and Europeans. Lionel Chalmers, a Charlestown physician who gave serious attention to such matters, wrote in the 1770s, "There are many more negroes than white people in this town and province, and these of African descent, are as susceptible of all sorts of diseases as those of the other colour. . . ."[49] For example, smallpox, which swept through the colony half a dozen times, took a heavy toll among both races, and slaves from Africa, like servants from Europe, were considered safer investments and drew higher prices when facial pockmarks testified that they had endured the disease on the other side of the Atlantic.[50] When epidemics fell close together, as in 1760 and 1762, slaves logically bore the brunt of the second onslaught, since thousands of black newcomers had been imported in the intervening years.[51]

Having stated the similarities with respect to disease, Chalmers cited the observed differences. It was generally agreed that slaves

[47] *Johnston,* p. 99.

[48] *Le Jau,* p. 108.

[49] Lionel Chalmers, *An Account of the Weather and Diseases of South Carolina* (London, 1776), p. 32.

[50] It was native Indians who had the highest mortality rate from smallpox, and awareness of this fact no doubt decreased their value as workers in the colonial labor force.

[51] See Joseph I. Waring, "James Killpatrick and Smallpox Inoculation in Charlestown," *Annals of Medical History,* new ser., X (1938), 301–8. Killpatrick and others kept tables of deaths from smallpox among inoculated and non-inoculated citizens, both black and white, but the racial variations in the colony's subjection to smallpox have not been unraveled.

were "liable to particular complaints, which seem peculiar to negroes only."[52] Certain illnesses were transported from Africa to Carolina. (Filariasis, for example, had an endemic focus in the Charlestown region that remained unique on the entire continent until its disappearance within this century.[53]) But black susceptibility was most marked for the variety of pleurisies and lung diseases that included influenza, pneumonia, and tuberculosis. Whenever respiratory ailments were infectious, they seemed to occur among slaves in epidemic form. There were several such visitations in the 1720s, and in 1748 Gov. Glen acknowledged that planters who invested in Negroes ran the possible risk of having them "swept off" by pleurisies if not by smallpox.[54]

Even when they were not epidemic, respiratory sicknesses among Africans transported to America (or Europe) were frequent enough to arouse note.[55] One consideration was certainly cold weather. Early in the eighteenth century it became an axiom of the slave trade to the mainland colonies that new Negroes should .not be disembarked during the winter months for fear of sickness. Therefore, South Carolina's almost Caribbean climate posed a distinct advantage to slaveowners that was recognized at an early stage and may have been too thoroughly dismissed by modern commentators. "Negroes," wrote Samuel Wilson in 1682, "By Reason of the mildness of the Winter thrive and stand much better, than in any of the more Northern Collonys, and require less clothes, which is a great charge sav'd."[56] Inadequate supplies of clothing, however, or a sharp change in the weather could bring on such infections even in the lowlands. David Ramsey commented, "To colds, fevers, and such complaints as result from a variable climate they are rather more liable than white people." The doctor went on to claim, "They are incorrigibly careless and wantonly expose themselves to the dangers which result from sudden changes of the weather."[57]

[52] Chalmers, *Account of the Weather and Diseases*, p. 32.

[53] Waring, *History of Medicine*, p. 19.

[54] Oct. 10, 1748, BPRO Trans., XXIII, 229. Henry Laurens wrote to Gedney Clarke concerning a shipment of slaves in 1756: "Another grand impediment to the Sale was a Parapneumonia breaking out in many parts of the Province and sweeping off great numbers of Negroes." Donnan, *Documents*, IV, 343; cf. Lawson, *New Voyage*, p. 270.

[55] Philip D. Curtin, "Epidemiology and the Slave Trade," *Political Science Quarterly*, LXXXIII (1968), 210.

[56] Salley, *Narratives*, p. 172.

[57] Ramsey, *History of S.C.*, II, 92–93. Cf. Childs, "Kitchen Physick," pp. 551–53.

Overwork, far more than carelessness, appears to have been an inducement to such illnesses, especially late in the year when masters pressed their slaves into pounding the rice crop to prepare it for market, just as the days grew shorter and the nights cooler. The designer of a rice-cleaning machine tried to argue in 1733 that "the Pounding of Rice by Negroes, hath been of very great Damage to the Planters of this Province, by the excessive hard Labours that is required to Pound the said Rice which has killed a large Number of Negroes."[58] In 1755 Alexander Garden (the observant South Carolina doctor and naturalist after whom Linnaeus named the gardenia) sent to the Royal Society of Arts in England a sympathetic description of the exertions demanded from the Negroes who raised rice:

Our Staple Commodity for some years has been Rice and Tilling, planting, Hoeing, Reaping, Threshing, Pounding have all been done merely by the poor Slaves here. Labour and the Loss of many of their Lives testified the Fatigue they Underwent, in Satiating the Inexpressible Avarice of their Masters. You may easily guess what a Tedious, Laborious, and slow Method it is of Cultivating Lands to Till it all by Hand, and then to plant 100, 120 Acres of Land by the Hand, but the worst comes last for after the Rice is threshed, they beat it all in the hand in large Wooden Mortars to clean it from the Husk, which is a very hard and severe operation as each Slave is tasked at Seven Mortars for One Day, and each Mortar Contains three pecks of Rice. Some task their slaves at more, but often pay . . . dear for their Barbarity, by the Loss of many . . . Valuable Negroes, and how can it well be otherwise, the poor Wretches are Obliged to Labour hard to Compleat their Task, and often overheat themselves, then Exposing themselves to the bad Air, or Drinking Cold Water, are immediately . . . Seized with dangerous Pleurisies and peripneumonies . . which soon rid them of Cruel Masters, or more Cruel Overseers, and End their Wretched Being here.[59]

IV

WHILE IT IS CLEAR that Negroes were especially susceptible to certain illnesses, and that the evolving routine for rice cultivation was hardly conducive to good health among blacks, it is also clear that offsetting

[58] *SCG,* July 17, 1733.
[59] "Correspondence Between Alexander Garden, M.D., and the Royal Society of Arts," *SCHGM,* LXIV (1963), 16–17.

variables were at work. Much of the evidence already given would imply that the health of black Carolinians was hardly as good as that of their white owners, and yet contemporaries were aware that in point of fact certain key sicknesses often seized the master and spared the slave. Chalmers himself expressed the common belief that this was notably true with respect to "yellow or malignant fever."[60] As has been mentioned, yellow fever and malaria, the bilious and intermittent fevers of the eighteenth century, were consistently confused, but together these two "fevers" constituted the greatest health hazard confronted by Europeans settling in the subtropical southern Atlantic region.[61] Whites in Carolina seeking labor would not have been likely to overlook any marked differences in susceptibility to these major diseases, and the contention that Africans seemed to hold a comparative advantage is borne out by the evidence which follows.

Yellow fever, bringing high mortality within a brief time span, was the more readily observed of the two. It became prevalent in the West Indies during the second half of the seventeenth century, reaching Bermuda in 1692, where it took the lives of 640 whites and 120 slaves.[62] It was present in Barbados the same year, but it did not touch the southern colonies of the mainland until the end of the century.[63] It

[60] Chalmers, *Account of the Weather and Diseases*, p. 32. Colonial historian Gary B. Nash points out, in "Slaves and Slaveowners in Colonial Philadelphia," *WMQ*, 3rd ser., XXX (1973), 241, note 46, that "Slave mortality rates are badly in need of investigation." He cites the preliminary comments of Potter, "Growth of Population in America," in D. V. Glass and D. E. C. Eversley, eds., *Population in History: Essays in Historical Demography* (London, 1965), pp. 568–659. Nash also adds: "Robert R. Kuczynski, a pioneering student of demographic trends in the British colonies, concluded on the basis of unstated evidence that the mortality rate of whites in North America was greater than that of slaves. See Kuczynski, *Population Movements* (Oxford, 1936), 17."

[61] Curtin, "Epidemiology and the Slave Trade," p. 209. Although yellow fever was more epidemical, more devastating, and more thoroughly confined to urban areas, both diseases occurred seasonally, varied with the weather, and produced chills, aches, and high fever. Both were known to be prevalent in the West Indies and especially in coastal Africa, where they were often thought to have originated. Therefore, even though it was frequently possible to distinguish between these two sicknesses, it was also logical to relate them.

[62] Henry C. Wilkinson, *Bermuda in the Old Empire* (London, 1950), p. 145. Despite recently imposed restrictions on new slave imports, it seems likely that Negroes made up more than one fifth of Bermuda's population. Therefore, even allowing for underrecording, these death figures suggest that the island's blacks fared comparatively well.

[63] Cf. Wyndham B. Blanton, "Epidemics, Real and Imaginary, and Other Factors Influencing Seventeenth Century Virginia's Population," *Bulletin of the History of Medicine*, XXXI (1957), 459.

reached South Carolina with a vengeance in 1699. A survivor named Hugh Adams wrote to Samuel Sewell of Massachusetts, "It is hard to describe the terrible Tempest of Mortality in our Charlestown; which began towards the latter end of August, and continued to the middle of November." He backed this up with the striking testimony that during this time "there died in Charlestown, 125, English of all sorts; high and low, old and young, 37, French, 16, Indians, and 1 Negro."[64]

If Adams' figures are even vaguely correct, Charlestown's Negroes (by this time nearly equal to the whites in number) survived the 1699 epidemic with astonishing success. Adams claimed to have "read the Catalogue of the dead," and it is not so easy to assume that slave deaths were simply overlooked as it would be if no Negroes or Indians were cited. Moreover, since the town's growing percentage of Africans showed a lower rate of mortality, it is logical to suspect that they had a lower rate of morbidity as well. The same presumptions arise with the return of yellow fever seven years later. In the epidemic of 1706, "a pestilential Fever very mortal especially to fresh Europeans," 140 white colonists lost their lives.[65]

As yellow fever recurred during the eighteenth century, medical men made repeated observations as to whom it touched most severely. James Killpatrick observed that in 1739, "Charles Town, the unfortunate Capital of this Province, was visited . . . with a bilious Fever, which was probably imported from Africa, or the Caribbee-Islands." "I am very apt to think," the doctor continued, that it "is the same Disease that seems to be endemic with them, and is so fatal to Europeans arriving there."[66] In mid-October of the same year, as the

[64] Mass. Hist. Soc., *Collections*, 5th ser., VI, 11–12. Adams continued:

the Distemper raged, and the destroying Angel slaughtered so furiously with his revenging Sword of Pestilence, . . . that the dead were carried in carts, being heaped up one upon another Worse by far than the great Plague of London, considering the smallness of the Town. Shops shut up for 5 weeks; nothing but carrying Medicines, digging graves, carting the dead; to the great astonishment of all beholders.

[65] Thomas Hassell, Sept. 6, 1707, quoted in Waring, *History of Medicine*, p. 23. In an optimistic description of the province printed in 1707, former governor John Archdale conceded the degree to which "the late Pestilential Feaver . . . weakened and thined the People." Salley, *Narratives*, p. 304. Cf. Chapter V below.

[66] Killpatrick noted that the sickness "destroyed many, who had got thro' the Small-pox" of the previous year. "The Patients generally burst into Haemorrhages from different Parts, and, a praemature Jaundice appearing, died the third, fourth or fifth Day." *An Essay on Inoculation Occasioned by the Small-Pox being brought into South Carolina in the Year 1738* (London, 1743), p. 56.

epidemic began to abate with the arrival of cooler weather, Robert Pringle wrote: "We have been Afflicted with very great Sickness & Mortality in this Town for some time Past, & has been very fatal to Strangers & Europeans especially."[67]

The yellow fever epidemic of 1745 became the subject of an inaugural dissertation by the Carolinian John Moultrie, Jr., when he went to study medicine in Edinburgh. Africans, he told his Scottish examiners, were among those least likely to contract the disease.[68] A more prominent Charlestown doctor made similar observations concerning Negroes during the outbreak of 1748. "The subjects which were susceptible of this fever," wrote John Lining, "were both sexes of the white colour, especially strangers lately arrived from cold climates. Indians, Missees [Mustees], Mulattoes of all ages, excepting young children, and of those only such as had formerly escaped the infection."[69] Lining's essay, although written in 1753, received publication in 1799 in Philadelphia, several years after that city's famous yellow fever outbreak.[70]

In the same year that Lining's account finally appeared, yellow fever returned to the southern port city, where whites and blacks by this time each numbered well over eight thousand.[71] Dr. David Ramsey paid careful attention to "the extent of the mortality in Charles-

[67] Pringle Letterbook, Oct. 16, 1739. Cf. Sept. 26, 1739.

[68] Waring, *History of Medicine*, p. 51. Moultrie's treatise was first published in Latin, *De Febre Maligna Biliosa Americae* (Edinburgh, 1749), and later it was translated into French by M. Aulagnier, *Traité de la Fièvre Jaune* (Paris, 1805).

[69] *A Description of the American Yellow Fever* (Philadelphia, 1799), quoted in Waring, *History of Medicine*, p. 57 (cf. pp. 257–58). See also *SCHGM*, XXX (1929), 209.

[70] At the start of Philadelphia's yellow fever epidemic in 1793, Dr. Benjamin Rush and others expressed (somewhat too categorically) convictions about black immunity which may have had their roots in Lining's observations about South Carolina. Leaders of the city's Negro community felt assured "that people of our colour were not liable to take the infection," and the Free African Society undertook to nurse the sick and cart the dead. Absalom Jones and Richard Allen, *A Narrative of the Proceedings of the Black People, during the Late Awful Calamity in Philadelphia in the Year 1793* (Philadelphia, 1794), p. 3. At first the illness did "not seem to be so prevalent . . . among the negroes." Letter of Isaac Heston, Sept. 19, 1793, Hist. Soc. of Pa. But later, enough Negroes became sick and died to force both Rush and the blacks to adjust their optimistic idea of complete racial immunity. (I am indebted to Josephine M. Ober for the contents of this note.)

[71] According to the U.S. Bureau of the Census, *First Return of the Whole Number of Persons within the Several Districts of the United States* (1790), Charleston had a total population in 1790 of 16,359 people, with 7,684 slaves among slightly more than 8,000 Negroes.

ton in the four most sickly months of 1799." According to his account, "the whole number of persons (inclusive of both white and black) interred in the different burial grounds of this city in the months of July, August, September and October, was 544, and of these 123 were negroes."[72] Although this ratio of 3.42 white deaths for every black death does not begin to compare with the ratio of more than one hundred to one suggested by Adams' data for the epidemic a century earlier, it does indicate that Carolinians must still have had a thorough awareness that variations by race in susceptibility to yellow fever persisted as late as 1799.

While yellow fever was South Carolina's most formidable contagion over the years (until replaced by cholera in the nineteenth century), the single most consistently prevalent major disease among the colonists was undoubtedly malaria. The number of those affected was great, the mortality was low, and the symptoms, which varied in their intensity, could be suppressed somewhat with Jesuit bark. For these reasons no simple statistics exist that might give the relative impact of this disease on Africans and Europeans. In the absence of such direct local documentation, it is worth quoting excerpts from a treatise on diseases among Negroes by a doctor in Jamaica. James Thompson cited the rarity of intermittent fever among slaves and reported a fellow physician at Rio Bueno as saying of Negroes, "I have not met among them with a pure tertian intermittent in the whole of my practice, and those of forty years' experience mention it as a rare occurence, confined to mulattoes and house-negroes."[73]

Thompson conceded that this immunity was not absolute, noting the presence during the fall of mild attacks of fever among the Negroes which were "speedily cured by a few doses of bark and bitterwood combined."[74] But he emphasized the comparative difference between white and black, supporting his argument with anatomical evidence. Europeans entering more tropical regions and contracting malaria were known to suffer liver conditions. Thompson, who continued to equate hot weather and malaria, as was customary, wrote on the basis of numerous dissections: "Arguing falsely from the effects of

[72] Quoted in Waring, *History of Medicine*, p. 293.
[73] James Thompson, *A Treatise on the Diseases of Negroes* (Kingston, Jamaica, 1820), p. 14.
[74] *Ibid.* Thompson mentioned one black woman (pp. 153–54) who "had been subject to an intermittent fever for six months, which she attributed to the situation of her house being extremely low and swampy."

heat on our own system, we imagine that the liver should be found vitiated in structure in the negro: The very reverse is the case in every examination that has come under my consideration: No overflow of bile is to be found, and the fact is well worthy of attention of those who practise amongst them."[75] Distinctions noted in Jamaica had long been apparent in Carolina as well. Africans, the white colonists repeatedly observed, could labor through the entire rice-growing season, "being better able," as John Brickell put it, "to undergo fatigues in the extremity of the hot Weather than any *Europeans*."[76]

In 1735 the trustees for the colony of Georgia sent to Samuel Eveleigh in Charlestown a list of their reasons for preferring white to Negro labor. It included the point that "A new arrived Negro is more ignorant than a new arrived white man [that is to say, the African is less likely to understand the language and customs of the English], therefore for the first year, the ignorance of the one may be set against the Danger of the sickness of the other." Eveleigh, on the basis of first-hand experience in Carolina, did not consider this balance to be equal and ventured his own opinion that "without Negroes Georgia can never be a Colony of any great Consequence." He went on to state: "I observed, whilst at Georgia great Quantity's of Choice good Land for Rice, And am positive that that Commodity can't (in any great quantity's) be produced by white people. Because the Work is too laborious, the heat very intent, and the Whites can't work in the wett at that Season of the year as Neg[rs] do to weed the Rice."[77]

This interpretation remained a standard one throughout the eighteenth century.[78] In 1769 Lord Montagu sent a memorandum to the Earl of Hillsborough from Charlestown, detailing South Carolina's major staples ("Rice Indico and Naval Stores and lately Hemp"). "These kinds of produce," wrote Montagu, "cannot be raised and ex-

---

[75] *Ibid.*, p. 7. Cf. William D. Postell, *The Health of Slaves on Southern Plantations* (Baton Rouge, La., 1951), pp. 74–76.

[76] Brickell, *Natural History*, p. 276.

[77] Parish Trans., box marked "Md. and other cols.," folder 169, pp. 13–14. Cf. Chapter IV, note 35, below.

[78] The outlook of European colonists in the rice-producing region receives a suitable summary in Gray, *Agriculture*, I, 283:

> It was the prevailing belief in the colonial period that white men could not endure the conditions of labor required by the industry—the necessity of working continually in the hot, pestilential swamps, the laborious processes of clearing land, digging and cleaning ditches, preparing and cultivating land entirely by hand labor, and harvesting, threshing, and pounding rice.

tended but by the labour of Slaves supplied by the African Trade."[79]
According to Alexander Hewatt, a local historian who wrote in 1779:
"During the summer months the climate is so sultry, the air so poisoned by marshy swamps, that no European without hazard, can en-
dure the fatigues of labouring in the air."[80]

During the nineteenth century this tenet was exaggerated dubi-
ously as an element in the justification of the slave system. Recent
generations of historians have therefore had to labor steadily to un-
ravel elaborate arguments for the "predestined" or "natural" causes of
American race slavery. They have soundly and rightly refuted the
claims that Africans were somehow "racially suited" to servile status.
As several have stated, "it is hardly proper to load nature with responsibility for human institutions," yet it is equally improper for historians
to ignore relevant advances in scientific understanding to quite the
degree that they have in the past.[81] For the various pieces of historical
data already presented only gain their full significance and meaning
when they are seen in the light of several current perceptions in the
world of medical science.

V

As AMERICAN DISEASE PATTERNS become less dramatic and more uniform, it grows increasingly hard to recollect the importance of sickness
as a critical variable in previous centuries.[82] On the other hand, expansion of world travel in recent generations has heightened awareness
of the idea of "epidemiologic regionalism." This is no more than the
historical concept that different geographical areas have had distinctive disease patterns, and that for any migrating individual or group,

[79] *SRNC*, XI, 225.

[80] Alexander Hewatt, *An Historical Account of the Rise and Progress of the
Colonies of South Carolina and Georgia*, 2 vols. (London, 1779), rpt. in Bartholo-
mew R. Carroll, ed., *Historical Collections of South Carolina*, 2 vols. (New York, 1836),
I, 110.

[81] Oscar and Mary F. Handlin, "Origins of the Southern Labor System," *WMQ*
(1950), rpt. as Chapter I of Oscar Handlin, *Race and Nationality in American Life*
(Boston, 1957), p. 3. For an attempt to view human history in genetic terms, see
C. D. Darlington, *The Evolution of Man and Society* (New York, 1969).

[82] Consider the first sentence of William L. Langer's 1957 presidential address to
the American Historical Association, *AHR*, LXIII (1958), 283: "Perhaps I may begin
by recalling Freud's observation that contemporary man, living in a scientific age in
which epidemic disease is understood and to a large extent controlled, is apt to lose
appreciation of the enormous, uncomprehended losses of life in past generations."

the greater the variance between the region left and the region entered, the higher the probability of contracting novel illnesses. Differences in susceptibility are generally most pronounced at the time of initial migration—the first years for a new individual, the first generations for a strange group. Philip D. Curtin's study of the epidemiology of the slave trade has underscored the possible significance of this disease-region concept for Afro-American history.[83]

The concept has particular applicability for early Carolina. European settlers promptly became aware that this portion of the southern coast presented not only distinctive weather and wildlife, but new varieties of sickness as well. After three years in South Carolina one eighteenth-century British doctor reported to a colleague that he had so far "proceeded with much caution," finding himself "in a Country where the diseases are a little different from those of Britain." Not surprisingly, this doctor's list of the illnesses most frequently encountered in the lowland region began with "the different kinds of the remittents, called here the Fall Fever."[84] While such physicians became all too familiar with the symptoms of malaria, they were unable to decipher what caused it or how it spread. Indeed, it was not until late in the nineteenth century that scientists began to perceive that the disease is prompted by a microscopic parasite, transmitted from the bloodstream of one human to that of another by certain varieties of the female anopheline mosquito.[85]

We now realize that *Anopheles quadrimaculatus*, one of the breeds of mosquito which can serve as a vector or carrier for the parasite, was present in the freshwater marshes when the first settlers arrived.[86] If earlier explorers had not already brought malaria, some

[83] Curtin, "Epidemiology and the Slave Trade," p. 216. Curtin devotes considerable attention to the West Indies, where Africans arriving from a similar climate are shown to have once been noticeably less susceptible to the "fevers" of the Caribbean than whites arriving from England. He goes on to comment that "North America was certainly different in this respect," and indeed it was, if taken as a whole. But modern political boundaries must not be allowed to obscure the fact that climatically lowland South Carolina has more in common with the West Indies than with much of the Atlantic seaboard. Cf. Chapter I, note 66, above.

[84] Samuel Miller to William Cullen, Oct. 6, 1789 (Cullen Mss., University of Edinburgh), quoted in Waring, *History of Medicine*, p. 108.

[85] There is an extensive amount of scientific and historical literature on malaria. One of the clearest recent discussions is Michael Colbourne, *Malaria in Africa* (London, 1966).

[86] M. D. Young, *et al.*, "The Infectivity of Native Malarias in South Carolina to *Anopheles Quadrimaculatus*," *AJTM*, XXVIII (1948), 303–11.

of these immigrants no doubt carried the disease from Europe, where it was present in a mild form,[87] and mosquitoes feeding on their blood could promptly have spread the parasite. Stephen Bull wrote to Lord Ashley in September 1670: "there is some p'souns that have had the feaver and Ague butt we observe little Mortality in the distemper neither is the distemper neere soe high as is vsuall in other Places."[88]

Optimism about comparative good health was short-lived,[89] for by the early 1680s the mild type of malaria plasmodium (*vivax*) appears to have been supplemented by one of the more dangerous strains, known as *falciparum*. It seems likely that this new variety of malaria parasite reached the colony via an English sailor or a West Indian slave who had previously been in West Africa.[90] Annual recurrences of this sickness quickly produced the dubious reputation already described, prompting some whites to leave the colony and others to avoid it. Malaria could even have contributed to a low birthrate, since it is capable of causing pregnant women to abort.[91] Continuous construction work, coupled with the commencement of rice cultivation, may have made the disease endemic before 1700, for these activities put the colonists in close proximity to a population of vector mosquitoes which increased in proportion to the amount of stagnant fresh water in which the *Anopheles quadrimaculatus* could breed.[92] In February 1709 the Rev. Le Jau at Goose Creek, where rice planting had begun in earnest, wrote that "The Climate dos visibly alter here for the worse," and three years later he reported, "The Surgeons

---

[87] Childs, *Colonization*, pp. 109–10, 186. The absence of malaria from pre-Columbian America is argued in F. L. Dunn, "On the Antiquity of Malaria in the Western Hemisphere," *Human Biology*, XXXVII (1965), 385–93.

[88] *Coll.*, V, 193; cf. Salley, *Narratives*, p. 138.

[89] An increase in malaria contributed to disillusionment with an initial marshy site of settlement in more than one English mainland colony. Richard H. Shryock, *Medicine and Society in America: 1660–1860* (Ithaca, N.Y., 1960), p. 86.

[90] Childs, *Colonization*, p. 208. Cf. Mark F. Boyd, *et al.*, "On the Relative Susceptibility of Anopheles Quadrimaculatus to Plasmodium Vivax and Plasmodium Falciparum," *AJTM*, XV (1935), 485–95.

[91] Greer Williams, *The Plague Killers* (New York, 1969), p. 111. (This book describes the pioneering efforts of an American foundation to combat hookworm, malaria, and yellow fever.) Cf. H. M. Giles, *et al.*, "Malaria, Anaemia and Pregnancy," *Annals of Tropical Medicine and Parasitology*, LXIII (1969), 245–63.

[92] At the end of the eighteenth century David Ramsey wrote (*History of S.C.*, II, 75): "Every carolinian who plants a field—builds a house—fills a pond—or drains a bog, deserves well of his country. From the operation of these causes a change for the better has already taken place to a certain extent. . . . Bilious remitting autumnal fevers, have for some time past evidently decreased."

are of opinion that the Aire has been infected these 14 Yeares."[93] There is no doubt that by this time much of the early white population was suffering from chronic malaria.[94]

From the beginning, Africans proved less likely to suffer from this prevalent disease. The immunity among slaves was partial, but it was also heritable, passing from one generation of Negroes to the next. These interesting distinctions are now understood in terms of the genetic concept of "balanced polymorphisms," which suggests that a genetic trait which might otherwise disappear will persist as long as its disadvantages are balanced by offsetting advantages.[95] The so-called "sickle-cell trait" is the best known of these genetic polymorphisms. Although not detrimental in itself, this inherited hemoglobin characteristic, if present in both parents, can produce offspring who suffer from sickle-cell anemia and are likely to die in childhood. The gene which controls this characteristic would only survive in a population if it offered some countervailing asset, and in the case of sickle-cell trait this asset has now been discovered to be a heightened resistance against malaria.[96]

In contrast to current popular understanding, sickle-cell trait is by no means a "racial" characteristic of Negroes. It is found among numerous non-Negroid populations that have lived in a malarious environment (Sicily provides one example), and it is absent among certain Negroid groups. However, since *falciparum* malaria, carried by the *Anopheles gambiae* mosquito, has for centuries been endemic throughout much of West Africa, it is not surprising to find S-hemoglobin (sickle-cell trait) persisting among many of the peoples in this

[93] *Le Jau*, Feb. 18, 1709, p. 53; Feb. 20, 1712, p. 108. During the ten weeks before the second letter was written, seventy-two whites had died in St. Philip's Parish (Charlestown) alone. See Frank J. Klingberg, "Commissary Johnston's Notitia Parochialis," *SCHGM*, XLVIII (1947), 26–34.

[94] The symptoms described by the missionaries in note 24 above can be compared with those presented in N. E. Wilks, *et al.*, "Chronic Ill-Health from Unrecognized Malaria," *East African Medical Journal*, XLII (1965), 580–83.

[95] See T. R. Dublin and B. S. Blumberg, "An Epidemiologic Approach to Inherited Disease Susceptibility," *Public Health Reports*, LXXVI (1961), 499–505; B. S. Blumberg, ed., *Genetic Polymorphisms and Geographic Variations in Disease* (New York, 1961).

[96] The actual reasons why a blood system which contains cells shaped like a sickle or crescent as well as the normal circular red blood cells proves less susceptible to attacks of the malaria parasite are only now becoming understood. L. Luzzato, E. S. Nwashuku-Jarrett, and S. Reddy, "Increased Sickling of Parasitized Erythrocytes as Mechanism of Resistance against Malaria in the Sickle-Cell Trait," *The Lancet*, Feb. 14, 1970, pp. 319–22.

region.[97] Inevitably, there was a high incidence of this trait among slaves brought to the New World, and those reaching the lowlands of South Carolina would have perpetuated this genetic characteristic as long as it served a function in a highly malarious region.[98]

Even in the present generation, judging from studies begun in the 1950s, the incidence of sickle-cell trait among Gullah Negroes in coastal South Carolina remains above the general norm for American blacks and approximates the level familiar among West African populations. There seems little doubt about the observation of an anthropologist that "Values for abnormal hemoglobin in the Charleston sample are close to African ones and may have been maintained at this high level through the action of falciparum malaria."[99] But the eradication of malaria in the Southeast over the past half century has negated the importance of S-hemoglobin, and this genetic trait will eventually recede among Carolina Negroes as it has among Afro-Americans who have lived for more generations in nonmalarious areas.[100] The clear and ironic implication, therefore, is that sickle-cell trait, the negative consequences of which are only now being studied seriously, may in the seventeenth and eighteenth centuries have had a positive influence in warding off malaria which gave its bearers an obvious if highly dubious advantage in the cultivation of rice.[101]

[97] Jean Henri Pierre Jonxis, ed., *Abnormal Haemoglobins in Africa* (Oxford, 1965). Cf. Jordan, *White Over Black,* pp. 583–85, "Note on the Concept of Race." Also, see the article of Stephen L. Wiesenfeld, "Sickle-Cell Trait in Human Biological and Cultural Evolution," *Science,* CLVII (Sept. 8, 1967), 1134–40, examining the relationship between sickle-cell trait, malaria, and patterns of agriculture in Africa. (In his useful notes, Wiesenfeld states that "what has been called *Anopheles gambiae* is now thought to be a complex of five or more sibling species.")

[98] Cf. Frank B. Livingstone, "Anthropological Implications of Sickle Cell Gene Distribution in West Africa," *American Anthropologist,* LX (1958), 533–62.

[99] W. S. Pollitzer, "The Negroes of Charleston (S.C.); A Study of Hemoglobin Types, Serology, and Morphology," *American Journal of Physical Anthropology,* new ser., XVI (1958), 258. Cf. P. K. Switzer, "The Incidence of the Sickle Cell Trait in Negroes from the Sea Island Area of South Carolina," *Southern Medical Journal,* XLIII (1950), 48–49; W. S. Pollitzer, *et al.,* "Blood Factors and Morphology of Negroes of James Island, Charleston, S.C.," *American Journal of Physical Anthropology,* XXII (1964), 393–98; Edwin Boyle, Jr., *et al.,* "Prevalence of the Sickle Cell Trait in Adults of Charleston County, S.C., An Epidemiological Study," *Archives of Environmental Health,* XVII (1968), 891–98.

[100] Cf. M. Siniscalco, *et al.,* "Population Genetics of Haemoglobin Variants," World Health Org., *Bulletin,* XXXIV (1966), 379–93; Mark F. Boyd, "An Historical Sketch of the Prevalence of Malaria in North America," *AJTM,* XXI (1941), 223–44.

[101] This point has not been made directly anywhere in the current spate of literature concerning sickle-cell disease. For the beginnings of present scientific activity,

Besides this inherited advantage, a partial and less significant pattern of "acquired" immunity was also at work. The body responds to frequent attacks of numerous illnesses by producing substances called antibodies which circulate in the bloodstream and destroy the invading parasite. Such resistance is not passed on genetically, but depends instead upon the transfer of antibodies from an immune mother to an unborn child.[102] Such protection only lasts for a few months until an infant can begin to develop its own resistance in response to malaria attacks. Where the disease is prevalent for part or all of every year, as in much of West Africa, these children build up enough immunity so that in adult life their bodies can deal with most of the malaria parasites with which they are continually infected.[103] Such acquired resistance varies greatly with individuals and lapses when exposure to infection disappears.

As for yellow fever, we again have a clearer picture of the reasons for African resistance than we once did. Like malaria, it is a mosquito-borne illness, but immunity to it depends entirely upon acquired rather than inherited resistance. Persons who survive yellow fever once are generally safe thereafter, and since the disease is least fatal to infants and small children, the more constant its presence among a population the more widespread their immunity and the lower their mortality. Such a pattern tended to perpetuate itself. The antibodies to yellow fever virus which were in an African mother's

---

see Robert D. Scott, "Health Care Priority and Sickle Cell Anemia," American Med. Assoc., *Journal*, CCXIV (1970), 731–34 (also editorial, 749).

[102] Colbourne, *Malaria in Africa*, p. 30:

In most parts of Africa practically every child is born free from malaria, even though the mother may be infected and there may actually be malaria parasites in the mother's womb. Although the mother does not pass on any of the malaria parasites in her body to her child, she does pass on some of her immunity and this protects the child at birth and for the first months of its life.

[103] *Ibid.*, p. 36. Writing of the present, Colbourne states that "East and West Africa show differences: the malaria in the west is widespread and intense; that in the east shows much more variation," and he continues:

In Ghana, although transmission takes place in the south all through the year and in the north for only about five months, there is no great difference between the amount of malaria in the two parts of the country. Most of the children are infected before they are one year old; they pass through several years of heavy infection and are frequently sick until the age of about four years. During school life the amount of sickness is reduced, although there are still many malaria parasites in the blood, and the children's spleens remain enlarged. In adult life this immunity stays fairly constant and the spleen reduces in size.

bloodstream would cross the placenta and "passively immunize" the child in utero, so that when born, it was protected through early infancy. There was high likelihood that infants living in endemic areas would be exposed to yellow fever during their first year. This exposure would cause only a mild sickness, since the infant still possessed the mother's antibodies, and it would stimulate the child's system to produce its own antibodies in order to provide protection in later life.

Thus people coming from West Africa, where yellow fever was endemic along much of the coast, were more likely to resist the disease in Charlestown, where it recurred at intervals, than were those European newcomers who had had no previous exposure. Given the distribution patterns of yellow fever, which occurred in Carolina with more frequency than in Europe but with less frequency than in West Africa, it was inevitable that over time immunity would build slightly among the free Caucasians and decline slowly among the slaves. As a result, the differential in resistance between white and black would have been most pronounced before 1740, when the proportion of African-born slaves in Carolina's Negro population was highest, but the overall difference would not disappear until well after the closing of the slave trade.[104]

Because of the unusual importance of disease as a significant social variable at times of large-scale rapid migration, such epidemiological advantages as these cannot be taken lightly with regard to the creation, or analysis, of a colonial labor force. Just as the Europeans took advantage of the fact that certain Africans had a technical knowledge in raising and processing rice, they also capitalized upon the physical resistances of people from a semitropical "disease region" which bore a closer resemblance to coastal Carolina than did most parts of Europe. Even where an awareness of this variable was not explicitly stated, its effects must have done a great deal to reinforce the expanding rationale behind the enslavement of Africans.

[104] This explains the different statistics cited for notes 64 and 65 above. Curtin, "Epidemiology and the Slave Trade," pp. 196–97; Duffy, "Yellow Fever in Colonial Charlestown." Cf. Foster M. Farley, "Stranger's Fever," *South Carolina History Illustrated,* I (1970), 54–61, and Farley's forthcoming book on yellow fever in South Carolina.

PART TWO

The Changing Frontier

❧ IV ❧

Black Pioneers

I

DURING the American Revolution the hundreds of black slaves who were requisitioned to fortify and provision the colonial army in the South were known officially as "pioneers." Their essential tasks, such as driving teams of oxen, herding cattle, and squaring cypress logs, had by that time grown less commonplace as the routine on large plantations became more regular and the frontier receded into the upland wilderness. But a half century earlier, well before the term "pioneers" was first applied to companies of black workers,[1] the fundamental (though by no means simple) skills of pioneer existence were being shared almost universally among South Carolinians. The period stretching from the successful introduction of rice in the 1690s to the overthrow of the proprietorship and the appointment of the first royal governor in 1720, a quarter century which includes roughly the second generation of settlement, represents in many ways the high-water mark of diversified Negro involvement in the colony's growth. During these years some fifteen thousand blacks came to make up the majority of the lowland population, and to a degree unique in American history they participated in—and in some ways dominated—the evolution of that particular social and geographical frontier.

These black pioneers constitute the region's first real "Afro-Americans." Probably a greater proportion of them were born in Carolina than the generation of blacks which preceded them or than any which followed until the time of the American Revolution. Also, absenteeism among slaveowners (with the social distancing it implies) was less frequent than it had been in the earliest years or than it would

[1] Negroes "engaged in the public service" and earning money for their masters on wartime task forces were first described as "pioneers" during Gen. Oglethorpe's Florida expedition in 1740. *De Bow's Review*, XXIX (1860), 580.

be in later decades. On the whole, despite a growing and sometimes brutal enforcement of distinctions along racial lines, servants and masters shared the crude and egalitarian intimacies inevitable on a frontier.

In a colony which remained the most exposed outpost on the English-speaking mainland, external dangers provided a strong unifying force. Hostilities with the Spaniards toward the south continued during these years, and equivocal relations with neighboring Indians came gradually to an impasse. Fear of the French rose rapidly with the establishment of their outpost at Mobile,[2] and even the Atlantic pirates, who had retreated from the Caribbean to the Bahamas and the mainland coast for a last stand at the beginning of the eighteenth century, became steadily more resented as Carolina's overseas traffic spread.[3]

Within the colony, rising inflation and widespread debt exerted leveling influences.[4] The same could apparently be said for rum and politics upon occasion. An ordinance of 1693, patterned on an act passed in Barbados, deplored the ease with which Negroes were able to participate in Charlestown's expanding trade in strong liquors.[5] John Ash protested that in the elections for the Assembly in 1701, "Strangers, Servants, Aliens, nay Malatoes and Negroes were Polled, and Returns made."[6] Several years later, ministers described a "headstrong and Giddy populace," prone to factional "broils . . . , for as to the Common sort of people they'l do any thing for a Glass of Liquor."[7]

The general concern for daily provisions served as another common denominator on the frontier. According to the naturalist John Lawson, "A poor Labourer, that is Master of his Gun . . . hath as good a Claim to Delicacies . . . as he that is Master of a greater Purse." Put another way, this meant that almost everyone's diet was meager at times. The Anglican Commissary in Charlestown com-

---

[2] Crane, *Southern Frontier*, pp. 72–73; BPRO Trans., VII, 304.

[3] Barbour, "Privateers and Pirates of the West Indies," pp. 565–66. *Le Jau*, p. 189.

[4] *Johnston*, p. 7; *Le Jau*, p. 138.

[5] *SCHGM*, VIII (1907), 200–201. An order of the governor and council, dated April 10, 1693, observed that:

Great numbers of negros Knowing they can have drink in Charles towne for mony or what else they bring without: being Examined how they come by it, are thereby Incouraged in great numbers to Resort to Charles Towne—Especially on Sundays to ye: prjudice of theire masters & mrses & apparent hazard of ye: peace & safety of ye: whole Contery.

[6] Salley, *Narratives*, p. 271, cf. p. 239.

[7] *Johnston*, p. 20; *Le Jau*, p. 30, cf. pp. 29, 47.

plained, "the Water about the Town is so Brackish, that it is scarcely potable unless mixed with . . . Liquors," and Francis Le Jau, the minister in the well-settled Goose Creek district, reported that his family, which included several slaves, ate nothing but Indian corn. "I must own," he commented, "the more I am acquainted with Every persons Circumstances I find the more that the best of them Labour under great difficulties . . . few Excepted."[8]

One difficulty from which no one was yet exempt at the start of the eighteenth century was the threat posed to livestock by wild animals. Negroes, as well as Indians and Europeans, shared fully in hunting beasts of prey, though rewards earned by slaves were kept by their masters. An act of 1703 declared that "whatsoever white person by himselfe or slave shall destroy and kill [a] wolfe, tyger [panther] or beare, shall have tenn shillings; and for every wild catt, five shillings." By the same token, when creek channels were to be cut or bridges built to improve transportation during these years, "all the male Inhabittants" in the vicinity were expected to participate.[9] Thus common hardships and the continuing shortage of hands put the different races, as well as the separate sexes, upon a more equal footing than they would see in subsequent generations. An excellent illustration comes from the case of a Huguenot named Elias Horry who fled Paris at the time of the Edict of Nantes. He took up land among other French refugees near the Santee River in 1697 and "worked many days with a Negro man at the Whip saw." While these two men could easily face each other on opposite sides of the same log, their descendants a century later would live in different worlds. The European's grandson was Gen. Peter Horry, a wealthy rice planter near Winyaw Bay; the African's grandchildren were undoubtedly slaves on plantations in the same area.[10]

II

THE RUDE PRACTICALITY which minimized social barriers on the early coastal frontier is nowhere more apparent than in the personal alliances of Carolinians. Since the population was predominantly non-

---

[8] Lawson, *New Voyage,* p. 20, cf. p. 19; *Johnston,* p. 62; *Le Jau,* pp. 146, 114.

[9] *Statutes,* II, 216; *SCCHJ, 1702,* pp. 12–13.

[10] Alexander S. Salley, ed., "Journal of General Peter Horry," *SCHGM,* XXXVIII (1937), 51–52.

European and the first official emissaries of the Christian faith were just beginning to arrive, the formal doctrine of "marriage" as evolved in Europe was still of only limited relevance. Freed from old pressures and surrounded by new ones, men and women from three continents forged intimate relationships based upon diverse traditions and precarious circumstances. The Anglican missionaries (described in the next chapter) were as struck by white mores as by black and red. Gideon Johnston, for example, reported "Poligamy and incestuary Marriages are often countenanced for want of Care," an assertion made vivid by the fact that at one point he had "turn'd out for Polygamy" the clerk responsible for registering marriages in his parish. The naturalist John Lawson had several children by a woman named Hannah Smith whom he never married, and when he was killed by the Tuscarora Indians in 1711, she became the executrix of his will. Francis Le Jau claimed that even the Assembly included "Notorious Adulterers," and he sought advice from London on a series of white alliances which illustrate the disruption of European precedent. One man married his brother's wife; another eloped with an orphan girl of fourteen without her guardian's consent; a third, who had a wife living in Barbados, was wedded to a local woman as well.[11]

Such ad hoc relationships were more openly, and perhaps more frequently, interracial than in later years. Several documents suggest the range of acknowledged intimacy existent between free white men and Negro, Indian, or mulatto women. In 1692, for example, a white woman petitioned the grand council to force her French husband to return to her promptly or else make settlement with her for the Negro woman with whom he was living (perhaps her own slave) and undertake monthly alimony payments. A white Indian trader, making out his will in 1707, granted freedom to an Indian woman by whom he had several daughters and left her with two Indian slaves, a woman and a girl.[12] James Gilbertson, a Colleton County planter and assemblyman who had been in the colony more than thirty years, made notable provisions for a mulatto slave and her children in 1720:

My will is that my mulatto woman Ruth shall be free immediately after my Decease, & also my will is that her three female children Betty, Molly, and

11 *Johnston*, pp. 126, 77; Lawson, *New Voyage*, p. xxxvii; *Le Jau*, pp. 27, 56–57, 150–51.
12 *Journal of the Grand Council, 1692* (Columbia, 1907), pp. 16–17; *SCHGM*, XIII (1912), 86.

Keatty shall be free at the age of one and Twenty years, my will is also that Ruth have the feather bed W:ch the Indians did Cutt up, also a pot and her maintenance upon my plantation during her natural life.[13]

At the same time, black men had relationships with white servants and free women, and it was not until 1717 that racial anxieties reached a level sufficient for legislative action. An act passed in that year "for the better governing and regulating white servants" made clear that "any white woman, whether free or a servant, that shall suffer herself to be got with child by a negro or other slave or free negro, . . . shall become a servant for . . . seven years." If the woman was a servant, she had seven years added to her term, and if the begetter was a free Negro, he was made a servant for seven years. Moreover, according to the act, "the issues or children of such unnatural and inordinate copulation shall be servants until they arrive at the age of the male twenty one years and the females eighteen years."[14]

Whether or not the order was enforced, its existence implies the frequency of these associations by which a growing number of mulattoes became mingled through the population, only to have their descendants sifted back into the ever more arbitrary and rigid "black" and "white" categories of later times. Similarly, although of less concern to white legislators, a considerable amount of miscegenation occurred between Negroes and Indians during this period. The term "mustee" came to be used in South Carolina to distinguish those who were part Indian, and the remainder of their ancestry was often African. Even after 1720 black and red Carolinians continued to share slave quarters, though at a steadily decreasing rate, but in the proprietary era wills like that of 1718, referring to "all my Slaves, whether Negroes, Indians, Mustees, Or Molattoes," remain commonplace.[15]

[13] Quoted in E. Horace Fitchett, "The Traditions of the Free Negro in Charleston, South Carolina," *JNH*, XXV (1940), 140.

[14] *Statutes*, III, 20. The act added that "any white man that shall beget any negro woman with child, whether free or servant, shall undergo the same penalties as white women."

[15] WMR (1711–18), p. 100. On the decline in the numbers and values of Indian slaves, see Chapter V below. A law of 1719 (*Statutes*, III, 77) assessed a tax on slaves regardless of sex, age, and other distinctions,

> save that an Indian slave being reputed of much less value than a negroe, all persons possessed of Indian slaves shall pay for each Indian in proportion to half the value of what shall be rated and imposed for each negroe, and no more. And for preventing all doubts and scruples that may arise what ought to be rated on mustees, mulattoes, &c. all such slaves as are not entirely Indian shall be accounted as negroe.

The close interaction between slave and nonslave sometimes led toward the establishment of legal equality in individual cases, but never so fully or frequently as has sometimes been suggested. From the beginning of settlement, freedom had occasionally been purchased by some few slaves or given to others for a variety of specific reasons. For example, a Negro named Will, belonging to Nicholas Trott, was offered his freedom if he would sail on a Guinea voyage under William Rhett aboard the frigate *Providence* in 1696. The slave completed the trip and received his manumission in 1699.[16] In general, however, interracial intimacy appears to have figured more frequently in manumissions than loyal service or frugal savings, and a high proportion of those few obtaining liberty were the black women or mulatto children claimed by white men. A scholar who has considered this matter writes, "the miscegenous nature of South Carolina society is nowhere better revealed than by the fact that one-third of all the recorded colonial manumissions were mulatto children and three-fourths of all adult manumissions were females."[17] Thus Billy, the mulatto son of a Negro servant woman, was manumitted by a Berkeley County widow in 1737, and a mulatto girl named Rachel received her freedom and an endowment of £100 upon the death of her mistress in 1745.[18]

A few of the free persons of color with some European ancestry passed over into the ranks of the white society, as in the thoroughly documented case of Gideon Gibson and his descendants. Gibson was a free Negro carpenter from Virginia who took up settlement along the

[16] WMR (1694–1704), p. 192. (Will may have been employed as a "linguist"; see Chapter VI, note 19, below.) This is the earliest evidence of a slave voyage to Africa from South Carolina. For the next several decades Rhett and Trott played significant roles in the small local traffic. Cf. Peter H. Wood, "Luck of the *Fly*," *Sand-lapper, The Magazine of South Carolina* (Dec. 1971), 56–57.

[17] John D. Duncan, "Slave Emancipation in Colonial South Carolina," *American Chronicle, A Magazine of History*, I (1972), 66. Duncan adds:

> Infrequently a master openly acknowledged his bastard children in a certificate of manumission as did John Williams in freeing his mulatto daughters Sabrina and Molly in 1754. In another case twenty years later the executors of a St. Paul's Parish planter freed Maria and Amy, *mulatto* children of a *Negro* slave named Maria and also Jack, the *mulatto* child of a *Negro* slave named Nancy, "there being reason to believe that they are his Issue." Later the son of the deceased man also freed Nancy thus giving his half-brother Jack a free mother.

[18] Documents signed by Sarah Somerville (Aug. 15, 1737) and Elizabeth Cheesman (Aug. 13, 1745), in Charleston County MR (1736–40), WPA Typescript, vol. 109, n.p., SCDAH. In the case of Rachel, both the girl and her endowment were to be looked after by the owner's brother, who was also to receive "the child when it shall be born that my Negro Woman Grace is now with Child with."

Santee River "for the better support of his Family."[19] Some members of this family were summoned before the governor and council in 1731 to explain their presence. The Virginian's father had also been free, it appeared, and since he came from an older colony with a longer tradition of miscegenation, it is likely that Gibson's non-African heritage went back several generations. Moreover, the carpenter's wife and children were classified as "white," and Gibson proved to be the possessor of seven slaves in his own right. Within a generation his family owned considerable land and was active in the white politics of Craven County.

Such worldly success, however, was hardly the rule for free mulattoes in the colony. They were far more likely to see their legal inheritance diminish or disappear. The children of Parthena, a Negro woman, were bequeathed an Ashley River estate by their white father, Joseph Pendarvis. In his will of 1735 Pendarvis devised the valuable property on Charlestown Neck to Childermas Croft and John Hyrne as trustees for the children, but Croft appropriated the land to himself and the rightful inheritors fell back into obscurity, and perhaps servitude.[20] The lifelong struggle to maintain the status of nonslave was shared by hundreds during the colonial period and is typified in the career of Johnny Holmes, a free Negro wheelwright and carpenter. Although well known in the region of Charlestown and Goose Creek, he found it so difficult to acquire a living that he indentured himself to the venerable Nicholas Trott. Judge Trott in turn sold his services to a resident of Savannah Town, from whom he ran away in 1736.[21] The penalty for such departures was an extension of servitude, and Holmes may never again have been his own master.

The complications of "free" status were compounded by the fact that manumissions were often less than total, being hedged around with various qualifications. A Negro woman named Mall, who received her freedom from a Charlestown cooper in 1744 for "several good and faithful peices of Services," paid a token price of five shil-

[19] Parish Trans., S.C., Box I, folder 4, pp. 24–25. Gibson's story is traced in Jordan, *White Over Black*, pp. 171–73.

[20] *SCHGM*, XIX (1918), 35.

[21] *SCG*, Nov. 13, 1736. A mulatto girl named Phillis, sold by Jacob Martin, physician, to Elisha Poinsett, victualer, May 15, 1745, may have been in a similar situation, for she still had twelve years remaining on an indenture. Charleston County MR (1736–40), WPA Typescript, vol. 108, p. 429, SCDAH. A firsthand comment on the hardships accompanying freedom at this time is in "Life of Equiano," p. 90.

lings,[22] but others who could not buy their liberty outright were subject to long-term obligations. One pattern was for a black to receive a promise of freedom at some future time upon the condition of obedient behavior: an early example of this involved a slave named Tickey who was guaranteed his release in four years' time *unless* convicted of any insubordination toward his mistress in the interim.[23] Another condition of manumission could be a lifetime tax: an illiterate planter from Edisto Island dictated into his will of 1724: "I give my Negro Man named John his freedom at my death . . . paying or Causeᵍ to be paid every year after he is free during his Life twenty Shillings to my Son in Law Joseph Russell or his heirs."[24]

Beyond the terms of manumission arranged between individual masters and servants, the government gradually imposed constraints of its own. Colonies which relied increasingly upon black slaves looked with growing disfavor upon free Negroes. In 1723 Virginia deprived them of the right to vote or possess firearms and imposed a discriminatory tax.[25] Likewise, in South Carolina, where free Negroes had occasionally voted, directions for electing representatives to the Assembly made it explicit in 1721 that only "free White men" meeting the age and property qualifications could participate. The Negro Act passed the following year required that any freed slaves must leave the province within twelve months of receiving manumission or else forfeit their freedom, and a similar statute in 1735 added the provision that slaves manumitted "for any particular merit or service" who should

[22] Manumission by John Townsend, Sept. 25, 1744, Charleston County MR (1736–40), WPA Typescript, vol. 107, n.p., SCDAH.

[23] Manumission by Ame Williamson, widow of Samuel Williamson, vintner, May 11, 1702, WMR (1694–1704), p. 426, SCDAH. Cf. Duncan, "Slave Emancipation," p. 66:

> The case of Richard Dun Lawerence, "Gentleman" of Goose Creek, was a case in point in 1754. After purchasing a *Negro* woman named Phebe and her *mulatto* son named Samuel, Lawerence for "good causes & considerations" manumitted Phebe, "Reserving nevertheless to myself full power to order & direct the said Negro Wench Phebe as long as I shall continue a Batchelor or until my day of Death which ever first happen[s]." For the same "good causes & considerations" Lawerence freed Samuel, "Reserving nevertheless to myself until the said Samuel shall arrive to the age of Twenty one Years full Power to order & direct the said Samuel in such manner with regard to his living services & Education as I shall think proper."

[24] Will of Henry Bower, planter of Edisto Island, July 24, 1724, WIMR (1722–26), p. 408.

[25] John H. Russell, *The Free Negro in Virginia, 1619–1865* (Baltimore, 1913), p. 52.

return to the colony within seven years would also lose their free-dom.[26]

The major Negro Act passed in 1740 after the Stono Rebellion relegated all criminal cases against free Negroes to the same second-class judicial process designed for slaves. It also made clear that any further manumissions were to depend upon a special act of the Assembly.[27] Although this policy may not have been perfectly observed, individual grants of freedom remained scarce until the Revolutionary era, so that Negroes of free status do not appear ever to have exceeded 1 per cent of the black population during the half century when South Carolina was a royal colony. (During the 1760s, for example, there were never as many as two hundred free Negroes registered in the entire region.[28]) Under the proprietorship before 1720 the few legally free blacks may have represented a slightly larger proportion of the Negro population, but their daily existence in the frontier colony could not have been dramatically different in many ways from that of their slave brothers.

III

WITHIN THE SLAVE POPULATION ITSELF, it was not always easy to dis-tinguish separate categories as yet. Charlestown was still too small and the majority of lowland estates were still too modest to generate those clear distinctions in Negro life-styles between city and country which became familiar in the nineteenth century. By that later era a whole class of blacks had been mired in the work of the rice fields for generations, isolated from a smaller and largely hereditary grouping

[26] BPRO Trans., XI, 385–86; *Statutes,* VII, 384, 396. Cf. Brickell, *Natural History,* p. 276:

> The Planters at their Death used to make some of their favourite Negroes free, but there is now an established Law (especially in Virginia) that if they do not quit the Province in about Eleven Days after their Freedom, whoever takes them they become his Property; but before the expiration of that time they either go to another Province or sell themselves to the Christians. The Planters seeing the Inconveniences that might attend these kind of Priviledges to the Negroes, have this and all other Laws against them continually put in practice, to prevent all Opportunities they might lay hold of to make themselves formidable.

[27] *Statutes,* VII, 402.

[28] Public Treasurer Recs., Gen. Tax Receipts (1761–69), msv, SCDAH. See also Marina Wikramanayake, *A World in Shadow: The Free Black in Antebellum South Carolina* (Columbia, S.C., 1973).

of tradesmen and house slaves. But in the first half of the eighteenth century Negroes in South Carolina were more unified by the common ground of Old World ancestry and recent migration than they were set apart by contrasting routines. On the one hand, a great many plantation slaves had spent time in Charlestown, at least when they arrived from overseas; on the other hand, few urban slaves were totally exempt from some measure of agricultural routine, if only at planting and harvest time.

Advertisements for slaves in the *South Carolina Gazette*, which began publication in the 1730s, make it apparent that even then no sharp line yet separated those in livery from those in work clothes, and the number of persons with diverse talents reflects the fact that jacks-of-all-trades were still at a premium in the widening settlement. Hercules, the slave of a Goose Creek lawyer-planter, "used to wait on his Master in Charlestown, & is now by trade a Cooper"; Peter, auctioned by John Simmons in 1733, was experienced as "a Bricklayer, Plaisterer and White-washer."[29] Subsequent notices included such descriptions as: "has serv'd his time to a Barber, and is a good Cook," "used to a Boat, and something experienced in the Butcher's Trade," "his chief Time has been spent in the Kitchen, Stable, Garden and playing for the Dancing-School," "can work at the Shoemaker and Carpenter's Trades."[30] In 1739 a Charlestown master put up for sale "a Negro Man who is a very good Cook, makes Soap and Candles very well, has had the Small Pox, is healthy and strong, speaks good English, and is fit for a Boat."[31] Few were more versatile than Tartar, a slave auctioned the following year and acknowledged to be "a good Groom, waiting Man, Cook, Drummer, Coachman, and hacks Deer Skins very well."[32]

The demand for diverse kinds of labor continued to be obvious to European arrivals. "Artificers are so scarce at present," reported the founder of Purrysburg in 1731, "that all sorts of Work is very dear."[33]

[29] *SCG*, Oct. 28, 1732; Feb. 17, 1733.

[30] *SCG*, Sept. 28, 1734; Feb. 15, 1735; Sept. 6, 1742; Aug. 29, 1743.

[31] "Also a Negro Woman, understands all manner of House Work, she washes very well, and is likewise fit for a Plantation." *SCG*, Feb. 29, 1739.

[32] *SCG*, April 11, 1740.

[33] John Peter Purry, "A Description of the Province of South Carolina, Drawn up at Charles Town, in September, 1731," rpt. in Force, *Tracts*, II, 7. William Bellinger, in charge of the construction of Palachacolas Fort on the Savannah River, wrote to Gov. Nicholson from Beaufort, Aug. 31, 1723: "am in great want of a Carpenter not having one man Capable of doing the Carpenters work which hath Caused me the more Vexation and my own Labour but hope to go through it in good time." BPRO Trans., X, 142.

Not simply in the expanding rice fields, but in numerous other places as well, white employers showed a widespread preference for Negro slaves in filling their labor needs. Brickell noted that numerous slaves were active in trades "and prove good Artists in many of them." He added: "Others are bred to no Trades, but are very industrious and laborious in improving their Plantations, planting abundance of Corn, Rice, and Tobacco, and making vast Quantities of Turpentine, Tar and Pitch, being better able to undergo fatigues in the extremity of the hot Weather than any Europeans."[34]

A discouraged Swiss arrival in the late 1730s observed that "the land which is distant from the rivers and which is distributed to the new-comers, is hot beyond all measure, and if one wishes to plant anything at all on it, especially in the beginning when it must be cleared, it requires strong hand-work." He went on to note the presence of "very many negroes who are sold thither as slaves. These people are worth a high price, because they are much more able to do the work and much cheaper to keep in food and drink than the Europeans."[35]

Basic considerations of health and cost were supplemented in certain ways by the existence of appropriate skills among the Africans, and it is only from the more closed society of later times, which placed a high premium upon fostering ignorance and dependence within the servile labor force, that white Americans have derived the false notion that black slaves were initially accepted, and even sought, as being totally "unskilled." The actual conditions of the colonial frontier meant that workers who were merely obedient and submissive would have been a useless luxury. The white slaveholders, whose descendants could impose a pattern of mannered outward docility upon their Negroes, were themselves dependent upon a pioneer pattern of versatility and competence among their workers during these early years.

For example, the raising of livestock, though comparatively labor-free, remained a significant feature of the colony's economy, with slaves continuing their dominant role. Occasionally near town the task of herding cattle was demeaned,[36] but in rural areas it involved considerable responsibility. (In 1741 the estate of Robert

[34] Brickell, *Natural History*, pp. 275–76.

[35] Hans Wernhard Trachsler, "Brief Description of a Journey to the Province of Carolina, Situated in the West Indies" (translated from German), *SCHGM*, XXI (1920), 101.

[36] "Any Lad or old Negro fit for nothing else, can easily drive up, and bring back all the Cattle Night and morning." *SCG*, Sept. 9, 1732.

Beath at Ponpon included, "a Stock of Cattle . . . said to be from Five Hundred to One Thousand Head . . . Also a Man used to a Cow Pen and of a good Character."[37]) Moreover, slaves fenced off necks of land for pastures, built pens for calves, and erected shelters for hogs; they branded new animals, hunted for strays, and ferried stock to and from the numerous island preserves. There was employment in butchering, barrel-making, and salt-gathering, and in packing and loading the meat for export. Occasionally a long winter or a sudden hurricane upset this process briefly,[38] and there was sometimes talk of being overstocked or fear of sickness among the animals, but in general the enterprise flourished and expanded. Observers raised in Europe marveled at this growth, attributing it primarily to the ease of winter grazing. "These Creatures have mightily increas'd since the first settling of the Colony, about 40 Years ago," wrote Nairne in 1710. "It was then reckon'd a great deal to have three or four Cows, but now some People have 1000 Head, [and] for one man to have 200 is very common." Similarly, Lawson noted "such a wonderful Increase, that many of our Planters, from very mean Beginnings, have rais'd themselves, and are now Masters of hundreds of fat Beeves, and other Cattle."[39]

Despite such successes, most of those who took up "plantations" in the early 1700s were actually frontier farmers seeking a stable agricultural existence through the employment of a few black slaves. These Negroes, far more than their descendants, were still sharing a common undertaking as members of an interracial family unit. "A Planter," explained Nairne, "is a common Denomination for those who live by their own and their Servants Industry, improve their Estates, follow Tillage or Grasing, and make those Commodities which are [exported]."[40] He estimated that by this definition fully 70 per cent of all whites (and no doubt an even larger percentage of blacks) were engaged in some form of planting.

Nairne went on to offer the following useful description of a typical undertaking:

If any one designs to make a Plantation, in this Province, out of the Woods, the first thing to be done is, after having cutt down a few Trees, to split

---

[37] *SCG,* March 19, 1741.
[38] *Le Jau,* pp. 38, 137.
[39] Nairne, *Letter from S.C.,* p. 13; Lawson, *New Voyage,* pp. 87–88.
[40] Nairne, *Letter from S.C.,* p. 43.

Palissades, or Clapboards, and therewith make small Houses or Huts, to shelter the Slaves. After that, whilst some Servants are clearing the Land, others are to be employed in squaring or sawing Wall-plats, Posts, Rafters, Boards and Shingles, for a small House for the Family, which usually serves for a Kitchin afterwards, when they are in better Circumstances to build a larger. During the Time of this Preparation, the Master Overseer, or white Servants, go every Evening to the next Neighbour's House, where they are lodg'd and entertain'd kindly, without any Charges. And if the Person have any Wife or Children, they are commonly left in some Friend's House, till a suitable dwelling Place and Conveniences are provided, fit for them to live decently.

The properest Time to begin a Settlement is in September, or, at farthest, before the first of December. The Time between that and the first of March is spent in cutting down and burning the Trees, out of the Ground, design'd to be sowed that Year, splitting Rails, and making Fences round the Corn Ground, and Pasture. The smallest Computation usually made is, that each labouring Person will in this Time, clear three Acres fit for Sowing.[41]

This summary of common practice goes on to make plain that Negro men and women could be purchased in roughly equal numbers, at not dissimilar prices, and expected to perform comparable tasks. While noting that European women participated little in the most rugged stages of planting, Nairne suggests that their African counterparts, equipped with the appropriate "Hoes, Hatchets, Broad Axes, . . . and other necessary Tools," were each expected, like black and white men, to clear and cultivate the equivalent of three acres annually.[42]

Rice was frequently the first crop tried in these new fields, sometimes being sown among the fallen trees even before stumps and logs had been removed. The chronic shortage of labor and the initial absence of know-how imposed constraints upon production of this commodity which have already been discussed. A less obvious but equally significant limiting factor at first was the scarcity of seed. As rice cultivation spread, planters withheld considerable amounts of grain to expand their own acreage or to sell to new growers. The generous sowing ideas of the 1690s, intended to reduce hoeing costs, intensified this scarcity.[43] The swing back to thinner planting in the next decade may reflect an effort to improve the crucial seed/yield ratio through continued experimentation. Soon it was usual to sow the grain in furrows

[41] *Ibid.*, pp. 49–50.
[42] *Ibid.*, pp. 52, 53, 59.
[43] See Chapter II, note 84, above.

eighteen inches apart, using as little as a peck of seed per acre.[44] Seed
scarcities must have been compounded at times by the dense flocks of
grosbeaks, which had already become known as "rice birds" from
their menacing fondness for the crop.[45]

But the greatest constraint on rice production came from England, where in 1704 Queen Anne's government proclaimed it one of
the "enumerated commodities" which could not be shipped directly
from an English colony to a foreign port. Since rice was a cheap and
bulky grain for which shipping expenses formed a critical part of the
final cost, this mercantilist policy damaged Carolina's competitive
position. England, where all rice was to be carried, had scarcely any
taste for the grain as yet, and the ports of northern Europe to which
it could be most easily reexported were little better. The steadiest
European rice consumers, the people of the Iberian peninsula south
of Cape Finisterre, would continue to draw most of their supply
from the Mediterranean until the Carolinians, after years of dicker-
ing in London, were finally allowed direct access to that market in
1731. Earlier in the century, the colony's steadily rising production
of rice stood in constant danger of overburdening its arbitrarily limited market.[46]

IV

WHILE RICE WOULD DOMINATE the colony's later economy even more
than livestock had shaped the earliest phase, it was the so-called forest
industries which particularly characterized Carolina in the early eighteenth century. The same trees which posed an obstacle to planting
proved a valued resource, and the necessary process of clearing land
became a lucrative enterprise in its own right, demanding more labor
than cattle-grazing but less capital than rice-planting. This natural
frontier pursuit took numerous forms, based on the diversity of the
coastal forests and the varied demands of consumers; wood was needed
by Charlestown carpenters for new houses, by Bermuda shipwrights
for their vessels, and by Caribbean planters for the fires which boiled

[44] Gray, *History of Agriculture,* I, 280.

[45] *SCCHJ, 1701,* pp. 6, 13; Lawson, *New Voyage,* p. 141. A bounty was placed
on rice birds by an act of 1701. *Statutes,* II, 179.

[46] McCrady, *Proprietary Govt.,* p. 687; *CRNC,* II, 423–25. See the recent discussion in Clowse, *Ec. Beginnings,* pp. 122–32, 220–22, 233–44.

their sugar cane. According to Thomas Lowndes, an agent for the colony in the 1720s: "a diligent and provident planter very near defrays the expense of clearing the Land by due Management of the Timber and Wood felled and grubbed up. Hence Barbados Nevis and Antegoa are furnished with fuel and for many years last past a considerable Lumber Trade has from hence been carried on to Jamaica and Great Britain."[47]

The very word "lumber" had assumed a new and positive meaning under these conditions. In England the term applied, and still applies, to any kind of discarded or superfluous material. On the colonial frontier, however, where settlers lived surrounded by standing and fallen trees, "lumber" quickly became synonymous with "wood," first as a cumbersome obstruction but soon as a marketable commodity.[48]

Obviously timber could be exported more easily and profitably if it were cut up before it left the province, and as early as 1696 a bill was prepared "to Prohibitt the Transporting of Sead^r Timber in the Logg."[49] This increased the demand for skilled sawyers (already at a premium) and a degree of labor friction was inevitable; later that same year it became necessary to appoint an officer "for the Measureing of ffatt and Cube worke betweene buyer and Seller, and workemen and their Imployers, for the prevention of Strife and Differences."[50] William Privat, a Charlestown mariner regularly at sea during these years, put more than half his worldly earnings into two African men whom he must have lent out steadily as a team of sawyers, for his other possessions included two wheelbarrows, two axes, two wedges, and a saw.[51] Many Negroes from this generation, usually working in pairs, spent most of their lives chopping and sawing timber, and very few slaves would not at some point have used a wedge to split fence rails, a froe to slice shingles, or an adze to square beams.[52]

[47] BPRO Trans., XIII, 211.

[48] Frederic G. Cassidy, "Language on the American Frontier," in Walker D. Wyman and Clifton B. Kroeber, eds., *The Frontier in Perspective* (Madison, Wis., 1957), p. 195.

[49] *SCCHJ, 1696*, p. 19.

[50] *Ibid.*, pp. 47–48.

[51] RSP (1692–1700), p. 143. Cf. *SCCHJ, 1725*, p. 56. March 19, 1725: "The Petition of John Goodbee setting forth that one of his negroes was killed by the fall of a Tree whilst working on the roads was read & rejected."

[52] Cf. D. E. Huger Smith, "A Plantation Boyhood," in Alice R. Huger Smith, *A Carolina Rice Plantation of the Fifties* (New York, 1936), pp. 66, 69. The author de-

Negroes shared and even dominated the cooper's art in South Carolina almost from its beginning. Well before the turn of the century they were shaping staves for export to older colonies which had diminished wood supplies and well-established staples, and as the local economy expanded, this production necessarily increased. Saplings were cut steadily to provide the coopers with sufficient hoops, and in 1714 an act was passed to impose uniform dimensions upon the thousands of barrels being made for beef, pork, rice, and naval stores.[53]

It was this last category, including tar, pitch, rosin, and turpentine, which formed the heart of South Carolina's forest industry and even of its whole economy during the early eighteenth century. Edward Randolph listed various naval stores ahead of rice as rising commodities when he visited the colony in 1699,[54] and unlike rice, their production received encouragement from Great Britain in the next quarter century. The resinous products (as well as the masts and spars) which England used in maintaining her ships were drawn primarily from the Baltic in the late seventeenth century, and this crucial trade had been worsening since 1689, when the Stockholm Tar Company obtained a monopoly. During the next decade England renewed costly hostilities with France, and her naval needs increased. At the same time, English merchants saw the price of Swedish tar double, their share of the carrying trade dwindle, and the drain of specie to the Baltic rise dramatically. The outbreak of the Great Northern War

---

scribes nineteenth-century activities around the saw pit at Smithfield Plantation on the Cumbahee River, which must have closely resembled work being done commonly in the colonial era:

> A tall pine tree would be cut down in the woods and there trimmed. . . . Then three or four or more yokes of oxen would slowly draw the heavy weight to the pit. Here expert axmen with broad axes would square the timber, cutting off the bark and sap wood. The saw pit was a broad ditch over which on posts was a frame work of beams, making a parallelogram. Upon this the timber was hoisted and the head-carpenter carefully marked on it the lines of the cuts. A carpenter mounted on the frame and another below pulled the long course saw up and down. . . .

> Such carpenters do not exist now; from cutting down the pine-trees to hanging the window blinds they built the great house and the barns and the mill and all the other houses.

[53] *Statutes*, II, 615–17; cf. 178, 216, 264, 298.

[54] "They are set upon making Pitch Tarr and Turpentine and planting Rice and can send over great quantities yearly if they had encouragement from England to make it having about 5000 slaves to be employed in that service upon occasion." BPRO *Trans.*, IV, 92.

between Sweden and Russia, which lasted from 1699 to 1721, brought on a crisis in London dockyards; Englishmen were entirely excluded from the Baltic trade, and the flow of tar and pitch from that region fell off by four fifths. In 1705, therefore, Parliament passed an act to encourage the production of naval stores in the colonies, offering bounties of £4 per ton (eight barrels) on tar and pitch and £3 per ton on rosin and turpentine. Despite American inexperience and hazardous shipping conditions during the War of Spanish Succession, the Naval Stores Act drew an increasing amount of shipwrights' materials to England, and in 1713 the bounties were extended for another twelve years. By 1715 America was producing almost half of England's tar and pitch, and over the next eight years the colonies contributed four fifths of the needed supply, or more than sixty thousand barrels per year.[55]

Somewhat to the surprise of English theorists, Carolina rapidly outstripped the northern colonies in this production, and even some of the naval stores recorded as arriving from New England during this period were actually shipped originally from Charlestown. Edward Randolph reported to the Lords of Trade in 1699 concerning prospects for pitch and tar:

since my arrivall here I find I am come into the only place for such Commodities upon the Continent of America. . . . The season for making these Commodities in this province being six months longer than in Virginia and more Northern plantations a planter can make more Tarr in one year here with 50 slaves than they can do with double the number in those places their slaves living here at very easy rates and few clothes.[56]

Land in the thinly settled southern colony was as yet comparatively cheap, and this had considerable importance for an industry where as much as five hundred acres was considered necessary for every ten Negroes engaged.[57] Moreover, tracts of pitch-pine remained within easy access of the network of coastal rivers which still afforded the primary means of transport. After 1725, with the bounties curtailed and the pine forests receding from the cheapest water routes,[58] the production of naval stores would fall increasingly to North Carolin-

[55] Justin Williams, "English Mercantilism and Carolina Naval Stores, 1705–1776," *JSH*, I (1935), 171–75.

[56] BPRO *Trans.*, IV, 93.

[57] Lawson, *New Voyage*, p. 87; BPRO Trans., XIV, 90–91.

[58] BPRO Trans., XVII, 180–82.

ians, and more and more lowland whites would invest profits from tar and pitch in laborers capable of planting their newly cleared acreage in rice. But in the first two decades of the century it was oozing black tar, fully as much as dusty white rice, which occupied the energies of South Carolina's Negro population.

Turpentine, the resinous substance tapped from the living pitch-pine, was less valuable than other naval stores, but its extraction paved the way for producing tar and pitch. (Rosin, obtained in small amounts by the troublesome process of boiling turpentine with water, was only occasionally distilled for export.) A tall person would chop channels in a standing pine so that they converged at its base, where several boards were fixed to catch the liquid as it drained down the trunk and hardened. "The Channels," Nairne explained, "are cut as high as one can reach with an Axe, and the Bark is peeled off from all those parts of the Tree that are expos'd to the Sun, that the Heat of it may the more easily force out the Terpentine."[59] A variation was called boxing the tree: "The Planters make their Servants or Negroes cut large Cavities on each side of the Pitch-Pine Tree . . . wherein the Turpentine runs, and the Negroes with Ladles take it out and put it into Barrels."[60] Such grooving, peeling, and hollowing demanded considerable skill, and it was regarded as wasteful for seasoned axemen to assume the simpler chore of felling trees; instead the pines were often allowed to drain and dry for several years, after which time a strong wind would bring them down. Slaves were set to work, especially in winter, gathering this so-called lightwood and splitting it into billets several feet in length. Negroes also constructed the actual tar kilns into which these sticks were placed.[61]

Once fired, a kiln burned down slowly with a flameless heat over several days (depending upon the amount of wood it contained) and demanded vigilant attention. Slaves attended the wooden drain day and night to see that the hot tar which trickled forth was caught and

[59] Nairne, *Letter from S.C.*, pp. 11–12.

[60] Brickell, *Natural History*, p. 265.

[61] This was done by leveling off part of a rise of ground to create a circular clay floor inclined slightly downward toward the middle. From that central point a wooden pipe was laid, the lower end of which extended outside the circumference over a hollowed spot where a bucket or barrel could be placed to catch the tar. The sticks of lightwood were then stacked in a circular fashion, ends sloping toward the center of the kiln, and the pile was sealed around the sides and top within a thick layer of earth or sod. An opening was left in the top through which to kindle the wood, but after it began to burn even that was covered over.

ladled into barrels. Another man, whose task required a skill and intuition comparable to that of the highly respected boilers on sugar plantations,[62] was responsible for tempering the internal heat by thrusting a stick through the sod to regulate the flow of air. A well-burned kiln yielded considerably more and better tar than one which was poorly attended. Nor were such tasks without danger. According to the naturalist John Brickell: "It sometimes happens through ill management, and especially in too dry Weather that these Kilns are blown up as if a train of Gun-powder had been laid under them by which Accident their Negroes have been very much burnt or scalded."[63]

Pitch could be created "either by boiling Tar in large Iron Kettles, set in Furnaces, or by burning it in round Clay-holes, made in the Earth."[64] This process may have sometimes been done by different men, for a document from 1713 lists William Canty, Jr., of Berkeley County, strictly as a "Pitch Boyler." He owed a debt at 10 per cent annual interest to landgrave Thomas Smith, which he intended to pay off with two hundred barrels of pitch per year, and in the meantime Smith had the right to claim any of the thirteen slaves who were working with Canty.[65]

The Yamasee War affected local forest industries to such an extent that Richard Splatt, one of the colony's early wholesalers in slaves, had to order timber from the North for a ship he was building in 1715, but during the last two years of the decade more than thirty thousand barrels of pitch and over forty thousand barrels of tar were sent to Great Britain, and another twenty thousand barrels of these products were shipped to other colonies.[66] (Rice exports, although considerably smaller, were rising sharply: nine thousand barrels in 1718 and thirteen thousand in 1719.) A statement by the Assembly at this time in response to an official query concerning St. Augustine suggests the important role blacks regularly played in the production of naval stores. The Spanish post, reported the legislature, "is a Garrison containing 300 sory Soldiers being mostly Banditti and undisciplined [men]" with almost no trade or enterprise, "Except lately they make

[62] Cf. Orlando Patterson, *The Sociology of Slavery, An Analysis of the Origins, Development and Structure of Negro Slave Society in Jamaica* (London, 1967), pp. 55, 62.

[63] Brickell, *Natural History*, p. 266.

[64] Nairne, *Letter from S.C.*, p. 13.

[65] RRP and RSP (1711–15), pp. 325–26.

[66] BPRO Trans., VII, 269–70.

some Pitch & Tarr with the help of the Negro Slaves plundered by their Indians from our ffrontier Settlements."[67] Other such slaves may have been instrumental in the beginning of similar production several years later near the French outpost at Mobile. Judge Blakeway of the Vice Admiralty Court in South Carolina passed on reports from there in 1724 that members of the Mississippi Company "have fallen on a Method of Making Naval Stores and that for three years last past they have made Pitch and Tar, . . . and have already settled four Plantations with fifty Negroes on each to carry on that Work."[68]

V

CLEARING FORESTS and providing timber products were by no means the only pioneering tasks in which Afro-Americans shared, as is apparent from an examination of the fur trade. During the first fifteen years of the century, England imported annually from Carolina an average of fifty thousand deerskins plus other assorted pelts.[69] While most of the hunting and trapping was done by Indians and the procurement and export was managed by whites, Negroes were active in most intermediate stages of the trade. Given the open and inviting nature of the colony's border at the turn of the century and the danger inherent to owners through any contact between their unfree labor and free outsiders, a legislative committee proposed in 1701 "that no Contracted Servant or Slave, Shall Go or be Sent among yᵉ Indjans to Trade." But such laborers were essential enough to the commerce for the Assembly to alter the resolution, providing merely "That no Servant or Slave be sent beyond . . . Savana Town."[70]

It is not clear how much of this provision was carried into law, for Negroes were among those who regularly rowed up the Savannah

[67] "Answer to the Queries sent by the Honᵇˡᵉ the Lords Commissioners of trade and plantations relateing to the State of South Carolina," Jan. 29, 1719, The Coe Papers, SCHS.

[68] BPRO Trans., XI, 138–39. Blakeway added: "of what Consequence this may in time be to Great Britain is humbly submitted to their Lordships Consideration."

[69] Crane, *Southern Frontier*, p. 111. "Deer-Skins are one of the best Commodities Carolina affords, to ship off for England, provided they be large." Lawson, *New Voyage*, p. 129; cf. 93.

[70] *SCCHJ, 1701*, pp. 7, 8.

River, which Col. John Barnwell described as "the ordinary thor-owfare to the Westward Indians," and returned downstream with boatloads of skins. Other slaves in Port Royal and Charlestown were engaged in trimming, weighing, and packing these skins for ship-ment.[71] Robin, a Negro man owned by Barnwell, earned £4 per month for his master through "doing the Work and Labour of the Storehouse and Trade in Charles Town" in the spring of 1717.[72]

Later in the same year Robert Graham organized a pack train of twenty-two horses to carry nearly £1,000 in trade goods to the factors at Savannah Town and beyond. Among the six men he hired for the overland trek were two slaves, including a Negro owned by Col. Alexander Mackey "named Timboe, who was imployed in the said Trade . . . to tend the Pack-Horses [and] . . . to serve as Interpre-ter." Timboe's presence was so clearly essential to the success of this major venture that his owner drove a hard bargain. In late December, several days before the pack train's departure, Mackey extorted from Graham a promise to supplement Timboe's high monthly earnings of £10, 10 shillings with £2 more taken from his own monthly wages. When the party returned safely from among the Creeks the following May, Mackey was able to collect more than £60 from the Commis-sioners of the Indian Trade "in Consideration of his said Negro's ex-traordinary Service, and being Linguist."[73]

Timboe's role as a highly valued interpreter is emblematic of the intriguing intermediary position occupied by all Negro slaves during these years. African newcomers found themselves in close proximity not only to Europeans but to Indians as well, for during the proprie-tary era several thousand Indian slaves still shared the same tasks and the same quarters with Africans from overseas, and their numbers were small compared to the tribes of free Indians which continued to

[71] BPRO Trans., XIII, 78–79. The following ads appeared in *SCG*, May 4, 1734; Nov. 23, 1734:

To be sold a Negro Man, a Leather-Dresser by Trade, by Mrs. *Collin's* over against the French Church.

To be Sold A Negro man named *Moon,* by Trade a Skin-packer (and Screws). . . . Enquire of Mrs. SARAH SOMERVILLE in *Charleston.*

[72] William L. McDowell, Jr., ed., *Journals of the Commissioners of the Indian Trade, September 20, 1710–August 28, 1718* (Columbia, 1955), p. 172; cf. pp. 194, 217, 243.

[73] *Ibid.,* pp. 248, 252, 287. Compare the references to Abraham, a well-known Negro interpreter to the Florida Indians during the Second Seminole War, in Frederick Marryat, *A Diary in America,* 3 vols. (London, 1839), III, part 2, 238, 250.

live in semi-autonomy within the region of English settlement. In fact Thomas Nairne estimated in 1710 that while black slaves outnumbered whites in the colony, they were themselves greatly outnumbered by Indian subjects.[74] Negroes, therefore, encountered Indians not merely through trading ventures and escape attempts at the periphery of English settlement, but also in the course of daily life within the colony itself.

After the Yamasee War, with Indians growing more desperate and Negroes more numerous, official efforts to preclude intimate contact between these two groups increased.[75] By 1721 most Indians were denied entry to the English settlement, but strict regulations concerning Negro participation in the Indian trade did not come for another decade. In 1731 an act proclaimed: "if any person . . . shall . . . employ . . . any negro or other slave, in the Indian country, or in rowing up or down any boat or perriagoe, to or from any of our garrisons, or to or from their respective trading houses, such person . . . shall forfeit the sum of one hundred pounds."[76]

Toward the end of the century, when the proclaimed boundaries again became porous, increased numbers of runaway slaves would cast their lots with the remaining Indian tribes and transmit elements of white culture in the process.[77] But conversely, it appears that at the beginning of the century Africans may have served as important agents in absorbing aspects of red culture and conveying them to the displaced Europeans.

It is worth observing that Negroes and Indians, despite natural differences and white efforts to generate further antagonisms, had in common comparable personal and ancestral experiences in the subtropical coastlands of the southern Atlantic. Their ability to cope with this particular natural world was demonstrated, and reinforced, by the reliance Europeans put upon them to fend for themselves and others. Early forms of Indian assistance and black self-sufficiency made a lasting impression upon less well-acclimated whites, and as late as 1775

[74] Nairne, *Letter from S.C.*, p. 44.

[75] For a discussion of this triangular relationship, see William S. Willis, "Divide and Rule: Red, White, and Black in the Southeast," *JNH*, XLVIII (1963), 157–76. Cf. Wesley Frank Craven, *White, Red, and Black: The Seventeenth-Century Virginian* (Charlottesville, Va., 1971). Also see the references in Chapter II, note 11, above.

[76] *Statutes*, III, 332.

[77] William S. Willis, "Anthropology and Negroes on the Southern Colonial Frontier," in James C. Curtis and Lewis L. Gould, eds., *The Black Experience in America* (Austin, 1970), p. 47.

we find an influential English text repeating the doctrine that in Carolina "The common idea . . . is, that one Indian, or dextrous negroe, will, with his gun and netts, get as much game and fish as five families can eat; and the slaves support themselves in provisions, besides raising . . . staples."[78]

Moreover, not only were West Africans and Indians more accustomed to the flora and fauna of a subtropical climate generally, but both possessed an orientation toward the kinds of "extreme familiarity with their biological environment, the passionate attention . . . to it and . . . precise knowledge of it"[79] which Europeans in Africa and America have in turn admired, belittled, and ignored. Lawson expressed the thought that if white Carolinians "would be so curious as to make nice Observations of the Soil, and other remarkable Accidents, they would soon be acquainted with the Nature of the Earth and Climate, and be better qualified to manage their Agriculture to more Certainty." But he went on to confess, as would Jefferson and others after him, that Europeans seemed to become less careful and observant rather than more so in the unfamiliar verdancy of the American South.[80]

Both their background and their subservient status put foreign slaves in a better position to profit from contact with Indians than their equally foreign masters. As the number of Indians declined and their once-formidable know-how dissipated, it was the Negroes who assimilated the largest share of their lore and who increasingly took over their responsibilities as "pathfinders" in the southern wilderness. Slaves were, of course, responsible for transporting goods to market by land and water. But an even more striking index of white reliance upon black knowledge is the fact that the primary means of direct communication between masters was through letters carried by slaves. Charlestown set up a local post office at the beginning of the eighteenth century, and by 1740 there was a weekly mail going south toward Georgia and a monthly post overland to the north via Georgetown and Cape Fear,[81] but with the exception of these minimal ser-

---

[78] *American Husbandry* (London, 1775), rpt. in Land, *Bases of the Plantation Society*, p. 67.

[79] Claude Lévi-Strauss, *The Savage Mind* (English edn.; London, 1966), p. 5. Cf. Chapter I, "The Science of the Concrete," *passim*.

[80] Lawson, *New Voyage*, pp. 80, 81.

[81] *Statutes*, II, 188–89; *SCG*, Sept. 17, 1737; Dec. 1, 1737; May 3, 1739; Nov. 20, 1740.

vices, local letters were entrusted entirely to Negro boatmen and runners throughout the colonial period.[82]

Obliged to transport passengers, messages, and goods, slaves naturally became guides as well as carriers. Lawson, traveling from the Ashley to the Santee by canoe at the turn of the century, relates that at one point a local doctor "sent his Negro to guide us over the Head of a large Swamp." The young naturalist records that it was "the most difficult Way I ever saw, occasion'd by Reason of the multitude of Creeks lying along the Main, keeping their Course thro' the Marshes, turning and winding like a Labyrinth," with rapid and unpredictable changes in the tide. In 1727 Maurice Harvey, the provost marshal, was accused of seeing a local debtor named Henry Simmons and failing to seize any of his Negroes as collateral, even though Harvey "Had at the same time a horse & slave boy of Sim'on's to Show him the way to Dʳ: Corbinesses."[83]

In October 1745 a white traveler coming from Philadelphia recorded in his journal: "had a Negro to guide us the Road being Intricate,"[84] and in the same month an S.P.G. minister wrote from St. Bartholomew's Parish:

As soon [as] I arrived in the Parish several Parishioners persuaded me to buy Negroes. [After protesting] . . . I consented . . . not knowing full well the ways and management of country affair. Therefore I bought a Negroe man with his wife and daughter, and was obliged also by extream necessity to buy 3 horses with bridles and saddles, one for me, another for my wife, and the other for a Boy servant, for it would be impossible for me to go through the Parish between the woods without a Guide.[85]

In 1770 William De Brahm would observe that slaves, besides being stationed at their masters' gates to offer hospitality to white travelers, were often sent with departing guests "to cut down small trees in the way of carriages, to forward and guide through unfrequented forrests,

---

[82] For example, John Stewart referred (April 27, 1690) to several local letters which had been carried "by 2 Negroes." *SCHGM*, XXXII (1931), 26. Later William Richardson, writing from Bloom Hill Plantation on the Wateree River to his wife in Charlestown, stated: "this is intended to go by bob to whom I shall give strict charge [torn] to remain in town but one day. therefore my good Girl do dispatch him for if he disobeys my orders I most certainly shall make him repent it." *SCHGM*, XLVII (1946), 11.

[83] Lawson, *New Voyage*, pp. 20–21; *SCCHJ, 1726–1727*, p. 119.

[84] James Pemberton, Diary of a trip to S.C., 1745, entry for Oct. 17, on mfm in SCL.

[85] Charles Boschi, Oct. 30, 1745. *SCHGM*, L (Oct. 1949), 185.

. . . [and] to set them over streams, rivers and creeks."[86] It is not an unrelated fact that ever since colonial times Negroes have commonly served as guides to white sportsmen in the Sea Islands and throughout the coastal South.[87]

VI

IN COPING WITH their new environment, it is clear that Negroes not only drew upon their associations with Indians but also brought to bear numerous aspects of their varied African experience. The term "carryover" (which anthropologists have applied to objects as tangible as the banjo and to beliefs as vague as spiritualism) fits a range of techniques and insights which were probably retained in the eighteenth century and which will only be fully explored as we learn more about the parent cultures from which these slaves were taken. Unlike the local Indians, for example, numerous Negroes possessed a familiarity, as already noted, with the herding of stock and the cultivation of rice. Nor would indigo and cotton be strange plants to many Africans in later years, as they were to most European and American workers.[88]

Certain crops besides rice may actually have been introduced from Africa, although the botanical imprecision of contemporary Europeans makes it hard to say exactly what and when. Guinea corn pro-

[86] De Brahm, in Weston, *Documents*, p. 179.

[87] Cf. Mason Crum, *Gullah: Negro Life in the Carolina Sea Islands* (Durham, N.C., 1940), Chapter IV, "The Gullah World of Nature." Crum makes several references (pp. 64, 135) to the ability of Sea Island Negroes to tell time by the stars, and he quotes the spiritual recorded by Thomas W. Higginson, which ran:

> I know moon-rise, I know star-rise,
> Lay dis body down.

Slaves were highly capable of telling direction, as well as time, from the sun, moon, and stars. It is suggestive that Negroes had their own appropriate name ("the Drinking Gourd") for the vital constellation which points to the Pole Star and which Europeans call "the Big Dipper."

[88] Cf. Corry, *Observations upon the Windward Coast*, pp. 65–66:

> Indigo and cotton grow in wild exuberance almost everywhere, without culture, and the women collect such quantities as they consider requisite for their families, which they prepare and spin upon a distaff; the thread is woven, by an apparatus of great simplicity, into fillets, or pieces from six to nine inches broad, which are sewed together to any width, required for use. The indigo, in its indigenous state, and a variety of other plants, colour these cloths, an ell of which will serve as a dress for a Negroe of the lower class.

vides a case in point. Maurice Mathews reported during the initial summer of settlement that besides Indian corn, "Guiney Corne growes very well here, but this being ye first I euer planted ye perfection I will not Aver till ye Winter doth come in."[89] This grain or some subsequent variety clearly took hold, for in the next generation Lawson reported Guinea corn to be thriving; he noted it was used mostly for hogs and poultry, while adding that many black slaves "eat nothing but . . . *Indian* Corn and Salt."[90] The two grains become further commingled—as perhaps they had in fact—in a definition offered by Catesby in 1743: "*Milium Indicum.* Bunched Guinea Corn. But little of this grain is propagated, and that chiefly by negroes, who make bread of it, and boil it in like manner of firmety. Its chief use is for feeding fowls. . . . It was at first introduced from Africa by the negroes."[91] Catesby also recorded "The Leg-worm, or Guinea-worm" among the "insects" he found in Carolina, and Lawson listed among various varieties of muskmelon a "guinea melon" which may have come from Africa. In the course of the eighteenth century the "guinea fowl," a domesticated West African bird, was introduced into North America, as was "guinea grass," a tall African grass used for fodder.[92]

The West African and Carolinian climates were similar enough so that even where flora and fauna were not literally transplanted, a great deal of knowledge proved transferable. African cultures placed a high priority on their extensive pharmacopoeia, and since details were known through oral tradition, they were readily transported to the New World.[93] This applied not merely to such specific arts as abortion

[89] *Coll.*, V, 333.

[90] Lawson, *New Voyage,* p. 81; cf. p. 82.

[91] Mark Catesby, *The Natural History of Carolina, Florida and the Bahama Islands,* 4 vols. (London, 1743), appendix, p. xviii. The relation between Guinea corn and rice is not easy to deduce. John Drayton, *A View of South-Carolina as Respects Her Natural and Civil Concerns* (Charleston, 1802), p. 125, referred to "Guinea rice, bearded rice, a short grained rice." *Henderson's North Carolina Almanack* of 1816 described Guinea corn as a "Substitute for Rice. There is a delicate white farinacious seed, called by some Guinea corn, which is raised, a few stalks in many of our gardens."

[92] Catesby, *Natural History,* appendix, p. xviii; Lawson, *New Voyage,* p. 83; *A Dictionary of American English* (Chicago, 1938–44), II, 193. The dictionary points out that Henry Laurens, the South Carolina merchant, was known to have imported seed for Guinea grass "from remote parts of the globe" (as was George Washington in Virginia). St. Julien R. Childs, a senior historian of the region, states in a letter to the author (June 14, 1973), "When I was a boy, the vegetable now generally called egg plant was known to Charlestonians as Guinea squash."

[93] Jan Vansina, "Once Upon a Time: Oral Traditions as History in Africa," *Daedalus,* C (Spring 1971), 443.

and poisoning, but also to more general familiarity with the uses of wild plants. Negroes regularly gathered berries and wild herbs for their own use and for sale. John Brickell noted of slaves in North Carolina, for example, that "on Sundays, they gather Snake-Root, otherwise it would be excessive dear if the Christians were to gather it."[94] The economic benefits to be derived from workers with such horticultural skills were not lost upon speculative Europeans. In 1726 Richard Ludlam urged the collection and cultivation of cochineal plants, specific plants upon which the cochineal beetle (an insect used to produce red dye) might feed and grow. According to Ludlam:

Two or Three Slaves will gather as many Spontaneous Plants in one day, as will in another Day regularly Plant Ten Acres, by the Same hands and for the Quantity of Plants Growing here on the Banks of Rivers & in the multitudes of Islands on the Sea Coasts, I can Safely Assure you . . . Thousands of Acres might, at a Little Charge, be Stock[d] with them.[95]

A variety of plants and processes were known to both West African and southeastern American cultures, and such knowledge must have been shared and reinforced upon contact. Gourds, for example, served as milk pails along the Gambia River[96] in much the same way calabashes had long provided water buckets beside the Ashley. It is impossible to say whether it was Africans or Indians who showed white planters, around 1700, how to put a gourd on a pole as a birdhouse for martins (that would in turn drive crows from the crops) or who fashioned the first drinking gourd which would become the standard dipper on plantations.[97] The weaving of elaborate baskets, boxes, and mats from various reeds and grasses was familiar to both black and red. "The Mats the Indian Women make," wrote Lawson, "are of Rushes, and about five Foot high, and two Fathom long, and sew'd double, that is, two together." He reported these items to be "very commodious to lay under our Beds, or to sleep on in the Summer Season in the Day-time, and for our Slaves in the Night."[98]

The palmetto, symbol of the novel landscape for arriving Europeans, was well known to Africans and Indians for its useful leaf. They made fans and brooms from these leaves and may well have entered

[94] Brickell, *Natural History*, p. 275.

[95] A copy of this letter (Jan. 10, 1726) is in volume II (labeled volume III) of the typescript marked "Charleston Museum, Miscellaneous Papers, 1726–1730," SCL.

[96] Grant, *Fortunate Slave*, p. 24.

[97] Lawson, *New Voyage*, p. 149.

[98] *Ibid.*, p. 195; cf. p. 196.

into competition with Bermudians who were already exporting baskets and boxes made of woven palmetto.[99] South Carolina's strong basket-weaving tradition, still plainly visible along the roadsides near the coast, undoubtedly represents an early fusion of Negro and Indian skills.[100] The "Palmetto chairs" and "Palmetto-bottom chairs" which appear frequently in early inventories may at first have been a particular product of black hands, as suggested by one surviving mortgage. In 1729 Thomas Holton, a South Carolina chair- and couchmaker, listed as collateral three of his Negro slaves: "by name Sesar, Will, and Jack by trade Chairmakers."[101]

A very different practical activity which derived from similar sources was the poisoning of streams to catch fish. The drugging of fish was well known in West Africa[102] and was also practiced in the West Indies, first by Island Caribs and later by Negro slaves. They dammed up a stream or inlet and added an intoxicating mixture of quicklime and plant juices to the water. They could then gather inebriated but edible fish from the pool almost at will.[103] Inhabitants of

[99] *Ibid.*, p. 14; cf. Corry, *Observations upon the Windward Coast*, p. 66: "They manufacture . . . fine mats, baskets, hats, ornaments, quivers, arrows, &c. which all prove the taste and ingenuity of the natives." Edith M. Dabbs' striking volume of historical photographs from St. Helena's Island, entitled *Face of an Island* (Columbia, 1970), contains a picture taken in 1909 which shows Alfred Graham, an ex-slave who had learned to weave baskets as a boy in Africa, teaching these traditional techniques of basketry to his grandson.

[100] D. E. Huger Smith's recollections of slaves on Smithfield Plantation in the nineteenth century suggest the continuity which persisted. Alice R. Huger Smith, *Carolina Rice Plantation*, p. 71:

> Many of them were expert basket-makers for which on every plantation there was a demand. Some of the men were excellent coopers, and the "piggins" and buckets used on the plantations were mostly made there. The usual drinking vessel for the negroes was a gourd—otherwise called a calabash. This grew on vines which ran along every garden fence. The vine, being an annual, died at the end of the summer, and the calabashes were allowed to dry on the vine. The smaller ones took the place of cups, etc., and the larger ones were used as pails for water or to hold grain and other things. Before use they had to be boiled a long time to extract the bitterness.

[101] WIMR (1729–31), p. 27. Cf. E. Milby Burton, *Charleston Furniture, 1700–1825* (Charleston, 1955), pp. 36–37.

[102] See, for example, the letter of Henry Smeathman, an amateur botanist who lived on the coast of Sierra Leone between 1771 and 1775, quoted in Fyfe, *Sierra Leone Inheritance*, p. 96.

[103] Carroll Quigley, "Aboriginal Fish Poisons and the Diffusion Problem," *American Anthropologist*, LVIII (1956), 508–25; Richard Price, "Caribbean Fishing and Fishermen: A Historical Sketch," *American Anthropologist*, LXVIII (1968), 1363–83. Price gives an excellent discussion of fishing slaves as a privileged subgroup (cf. Chapter

South Carolina in the early eighteenth century exploited a similar tactic, for in 1726 the Assembly charged that "many persons in this Province do often use the pernicious practice of poisoning the creeks in order to catch great quantity of fish." The legislature imposed a public whipping upon any slave convicted of the act, but the misdemeanor seems to have continued.[104] Such an activity implies an awareness of available herbs and their effects, and a knowledge of fish as well.

Fish and fishing, in fact, represent a separate area of expertise. While some Africans had scarcely seen deep water before their forced passage to America, many others had grown up along rivers or beside the ocean and were far more at home in this element than most Europeans, for whom a simple bath was still exceptional. Lawson, describing the awesome shark, related how "some Negro's, and others, that can swim and dive well, go naked into the Water, with a Knife in their Hand, and fight the Shark, and very commonly kill him."[105] Similarly, the alligator, a freshwater reptile which horrified Europeans (since it was unfamiliar and could not be killed with a gun), was readily handled by Negroes used to protecting their stock from African crocodiles.[106] These same slaves were inevitably knowledgeable about the kind of marsh and cypress swamp which their masters found so mysterious. From the start they tended, along with local Indians, to dominate the fishing of the region, for Englishmen, while capable of hauling nets at sea from an ocean-going vessel, were not at home in a dugout canoe.[107]

VII, section IV, below), and he comments (p. 1364) that "in the realm of fishing . . . Amerindians and Africans borrowed mutually and as social equals."

[104] *Statutes,* III, 270; cf. *SCG,* April 6, 1734.

[105] Lawson, *New Voyage,* p. 158. Interestingly, salt-water bathing did not gain fashion among Englishmen until after 1750. A. S. Turberville, *English Men and Manners in the Eighteenth Century,* 2nd edn. (London, 1929), p. 126.

[106] Lawson, *New Voyage,* p. 132; Grant, *Fortunate Slave,* pp. 13, 23. For a vivid description of Negro slaves ("who are very dextrous at this work") killing an alligator near Cape Fear in the eighteenth century, see Janet Schaw, *Journal of a Lady of Quality,* edited by Evangeline W. Andrews and Charles M. Andrews (New Haven, Conn., 1922), pp. 149–51.

[107] The English experience in Carolina must have been comparable to that of the French among the Island Caribs of the Antilles at the same time. R. P. Raymond Breton's *Dictionnaire Caraïbe-Français* of 1665 (rpt. Leipzig, 1892) states (p. 331):

The French learned from the Savages to hollow out trees to make canoes; but they did not learn from them to row them, steer them, or jump overboard to right them when they overturned: the Savages are not afraid of overturning, wetting their clothes, losing anything, or drowning, but most French fear all of these things. . . . Every day one sees disastrous accidents.

These slender boats, however, were the central means of transportation in South Carolina for two generations while roads and bridges were still too poor and infrequent for easy land travel.[108] They were hollowed from a single cypress log by Negroes or Indians, who were then employed, along with an occasional white servant, to pole, row, or paddle them through the labyrinth of lowland waterways. To make the larger canoe, known as a pettiauger, two or three trees were used, giving the boat additional beam for cargo without significantly increasing its draft; fifty to one hundred barrels of tar or rice could be ferried along shallow creeks and across tidal shoals in these vessels. They were frequently equipped with one or even two portable masts for sailing and often ventured onto the open ocean.[109] As early as 1696 an act was passed, patterned on laws already in force in the West Indies, which threatened any slave who "shall take away or let loose any boat or canoe" with thirty-nine lashes for the first offense and loss of an ear for repetition.[110] Such legislation, repeated several times in the eighteenth century, underscores the fact that slaves who were involved in building and manning these boats inevitably found occasions to use them for travel or escape.

VII

No DISCUSSION of pioneer existence is complete without mention of frontier warfare, and this was an element of life in which Negroes

[108] In 1682 Thomas Newe found that horses brought from New England were still scarce and expensive (Salley, *Narratives*, p. 184), "so there is but little use of them yet, all Plantations being seated on the Rivers, they can go to and fro by Canoo or Boat as well and as soon as they can ride." Newe added that "the horses here like the Indians and many of the English do travail without shoes."

[109] Lawson, *New Voyage*, pp. 103, 104, 107; F. W. Clontes, "Travel and Transportation in Colonial North Carolina," *N.C. Hist. Review*, III (1926), 16–35. Clontes notes (p. 18) that in 1711 word of the Tuscarora War was sent from Cape Fear to Charlestown via canoe. Cf. Marshall B. McKusick, "Aboriginal Canoes in the West Indies," in Sidney W. Mintz, comp., *Papers in Caribbean Anthropology* (*Yale University Publications in Anthropology*, no. 57, New Haven, 1960).

[110] *Statutes*, II, 105. "In Antigua, where runaways were common and a small revolt took place in 1687, a law passed during the Restoration required the owners of small boats to lock up all masts, oars and paddles when not in use." Higham, *Leeward Islands*, p. 176.

played a full if rather unheralded role. From the first days of settlement it was apparent that external forces could pose a threat to
anyone within the colony, irrespective of race. All able hands were
therefore kept on the alert.[111] When the French and Spanish attempted
an invasion in August 1706, it was a Negro who brought word to
Charlestown in the predawn hours that the enemy had actually
landed.[112] Whether this man was simply an early riser and fast runner
or a regular lookout with a fixed assignment is uncertain, but slaves
were often employed as military messengers and with increasing frequency as drummers as well. Jeams Ingerson took in an extra pound
per month in 1707 through his Negro's drumming for a militia company, and the muster roll for an expedition against the Yamasees in
May 1728 included "Prince the Drummer."[113] A Frenchman who was
among the Cherokee in 1742 made note of the method which English
traders used for drawing recruits: "After having had their drum beaten
by one of their negroes who was a drummer, and enlisted 70 men, they
distributed among them, from their storehouses, the munitions necessary."[114] But in the earlier proprietary era slaves were by no means
confined to such peripheral roles.

Longstanding Negro involvement in defense was acknowledged
in 1704 with the passage of "An Act for Raising and Enlisting such
Slaves as shall be thought serviceable to this Province in Time of
Alarms," and this statute was revised in 1708.[115] Thomas Nairne stated
that "For Defence of the Colony, our Laws oblige every Male Person
from 16 to 60 Years of Age, to bear Arms," and he added, "There are
likewise enrolled in our Militia, a considerable Number of active, able,
Negro Slaves." He pointed out that any slave "who in the Time of an
Invasion, kills an Enemy" would be granted his freedom and his mas-

---

[111] See Chapter I, notes 28 and 29, above.

[112] BPRO *Trans.*, V, 167; cf. 178.

[113] *SCCHJ, 1707–1708*, p. 53; BPRO Trans., XIII, 196. The readiness with which
Africans took up this task may have diminished the attractiveness of the job among race-
conscious Europeans. At a time of military activity in 1702 the governor remarked to the
Assembly that "Sev^{r}all Companys want drumers, and tho⁻ in ev^{r}y Beat there are men
enough quallified for it yett few or none will doe it." *SCCHJ, 1702*, pp. 64–65.

[114] Newton D. Mereness, ed., *Travels in the American Colonies* (New York,
1916), p. 250. In the nineteenth century, and probably in the eighteenth century as
well, it was a Negro who stood before the guardhouse on Broad Street and stroked
out the evening and early-morning "drum-beat" which signaled the beginning and
end of Charlestown's nightly curfew for slaves. D. E. Huger Smith, "A Plantation Boyhood," in Alice R. Huger Smith, *Carolina Rice Plantation*, p. 94.

[115] *Statutes*, VII, 347–49, 349–51.

ter would be recompensed.[116] Several such manumissions for service were made after the 1706 hostilities.[117] In 1708 the governor submitted the following report:

The whole number of the militia of this province, 950 white men, fit to bear arms, viz 2 regiments of foot, both making up 16 companies, 50 men, one with another, in a company; to which might be added a like number of negro slaves, the captain of each company being obliged by an act of Assembly, to enlist, train up, and bring into the field for each white, one able slave armed with a gun or lance, for each man in his company.[118]

For colonial leaders after the turn of the century, arming the slaves was an increasingly problematic question. The issue was not whether they could be trained to use certain arms, but rather whether they could be contained in the usage of weapons with which many were already expert. This applied equally to the gun and the lance.[119] These and other weapons had been in steady use in the wars over territory and trade which had become a familiar part of life throughout much of West Africa.[120] Prior military experience must have been at least as common among Africans reaching South Carolina as it was among arriving Europeans, and a few slaves may actually have been deported to the New World because of their skill in warfare.[121]

[116] Nairne, *Letter from S.C.*, p. 31. Nairne was assertive in his description of the sharpshooters on the early frontier (pp. 31, 32):

Every one among us is versed in Arms, from the Governour to the meanest Servant, and are all so far from thinking it below them, that most People take Delight in military Affairs. . . . If regular Troops excel in performing the Postures, this Militia is much superiour in making a true Shot. The Habit of Shooting so very well is acquired by the frequent Pursuit of Game in the Forests.

[117] See Duncan, "Slave Emancipation," pp. 64–66.

[118] Rivers, *Sketch*, pp. 232–33.

[119] While I use the words "spear" and "lance" interchangeably here, it is worth considering their traditionally separate English usages. Though virtually synonymous, the first of the two words has had connotations of primitive tribalism, while the latter has implied military chivalry. (President Kennedy's Pentagon code name was "Lancer," not "Spear-carrier.")

[120] C. W. Welman, *The Native States of the Gold Coast: History and Constitution* (London, 1969), part 2, contains vivid examples of the expert use of firearms by warring Africans allied to rival European powers along the Gold Coast in the late seventeenth and early eighteenth centuries (pp. 21–22, 31–35, 44–46). The stakes for being captured in such wars very often involved slavery (p. 41).

[121] Aptheker, *Slave Revolts*, pp. 181–82, cites the case of Samba, a slave long trusted by the director of public plantations in French Louisiana, as described by the director himself. In 1730 Samba was implicated in a conspiracy and condemned with several others to be broken on the wheel. "In the meantime," wrote the director, "I learnt that Samba had in his own country been at the head of the revolt by which the French lost Fort Arguin [to the Dutch in 1711]; and when it was recovered again by

Once present in South Carolina, slaves often hunted for themselves and their masters, and it was not until after the threat of a slave
conspiracy in 1712 that restrictions were imposed. A slave was still free
to hunt on his master's property, but he was not allowed to carry any
firearms beyond the limits of the plantation unless accompanied by
a white or carrying a certificate from his master or overseer. Slaveowners were directed to keep guns "in the most private and least frequented room in the house" and to search the Negro houses every
several weeks not only for fugitive runaways but also for "guns, swords,
clubs and any other mischievous weapons." At the same time, however, masters could be fined in times of alarm for failing to muster out
each slave enlisted on the militia roles, "armed either with a serviceable lance, hatchet or gun, with sufficient ammunition."[122] As in other
young colonies, firearms were at a premium, and it is not surprising to
find that in the emergency efforts to mobilize troops in 1715 at the
outset of the Yamasee War, the legislature adopted a resolution "That
a sufficient number of lances be made immediately, to arm the negroes
who cannot be supplied with guns in the present expedition."[123]

In simple proportional terms, Negroes may never have played
such a major role in any earlier or later American conflict as they did
in the Yamasee War of 1715. The history of this obscure struggle,
which was so vital to the separate interests of red, white, and black in
the Southeast, has never been adequately pieced together and cannot
be fully recounted here. Tensions between the Yamasee Indians and
the overseas settlers were felt as early as 1713[124] and persisted until
after 1720, but the height of the conflict came in 1715 and 1716. The
Rev. Le Jau of Goose Creek, a valuable chronicler of this episode
as of other events, reported on May 10, 1715, that the outlook was

---

M. Perier de Salvert [1724], one of the principal articles of the peace was, that this
negro should be condemned to slavery in America."

[122] *Statutes*, VII, 353–54, 348.

[123] *De Bow's Review*, XXIX (1860), 580. Cf. Wilkinson, *The Adventurers of
Bermuda*, p. 332. During the Dutch-English War (1667–73) the security of Bermuda
was in doubt and the "habilments of war" were typically scarce. Six companies of
foot soldiers were mustered, and, according to Wilkinson, "Male negroes over fourteen
years were instructed to take their places with lances and axes."

[124] An act ratified Dec. 18, 1713, in *SCCHJ*, stated that "Whereas the Yamasee
Indians, and other Indians inhabiting about this Province, having made a most Wicked
and Devilish Conspiracy to cut off and utterly destroy the Inhabitants of this Province,"
the governor is empowered when it proves necessary to declare martial law, to embargo
vessels in port, "and also to press several of the Inhabitants and Several Slaves for the
Service of this Province."

"Dismal in all respects. The Province is in Danger of being Lost & our Lives are Threatened." He added: "The Town is Crouded with people and it is an Unhealthy place[;] we fear pestilential Distempers. . . . I continue at my Parsonage endeavouring to do wt I can to Encourage my Parishioners whom I meet in our Camp 6 Miles of me Noward. The greatest Part of their Women & Children are in Town."[125]

Several days later Le Jau stated that several "good partyes of Men, White, Indians and Negroes," were already in the field against the Yamasees.[126] White manpower in the colony was limited and Indian assistance was highly suspect.[127] The result, which is clear from a variety of sources, was that blacks were drawn into the fray first in dozens, then in scores, and finally by the hundred.[128] Throughout the summer, intensive efforts were made to raise a standing army consisting of "600 whites . . . and 400 Negros."[129] A letter from Charlestown in September 1715 states that these troops were "to protect the Settlements till the Crops are all got in & then march to fight the Enemy where they can find them."[130]

The journal kept by an officer with the unfortunate name of Chicken affords glimpses of the active part Negroes played in the ensuing campaign.[131] Their importance was increased by the absence of significant aid from Virginia. The neighboring colony asked for thirty shillings per man per month "besides a Negro Woman to be sent to Virginia in lieu of each Man Sent to Carolina to Work till their Returne." The white Carolinians were willing to pay out high wages in inflated money, but—and this deserves special note—they found it "impracticable to Send Negro Women in their Roomes by reason of the Discontent such Usage would have given their husbands to have their

[125] *Le Jau*, pp. 152–53. For another minister's description of the outbreak of the war, see *SCHGM*, L (1949), 175–77.

[126] *Le Jau*, p. 155.

[127] For the description of a fatal ambush of an integrated colonial force, directed by an Indian who had received his liberty not long before from Col. Moore, see *ibid.*, p. 159.

[128] Cf. *Le Jau*, pp. 156, 158–61, 165; *Johnston*, p. 176; BPRO Trans., VI, 118.

[129] BPRO Trans., VI, 107. The same document of July 19, 1715, states (p. 105): "The Governor Marched Yesterday from the Ponds [a garrison about twenty miles from Charlestown; see BPRO Trans., VII, 54] for Colᵒ Broughtons with about 100 White Men & 100 Negroes & Indians with a design to pass Zantee River to meet and joyn Colᵒ Moor & then make some Attempt upon the Northern Indians."

[130] BPRO Trans., VI, 127; cf. 132.

[131] Col. George Chicken, "A Journal from Carolina in 1715," *Charleston Yearbook, 1894* (Charleston, 1895), appendix, pp. 338–51.

Wives taken from them wch might have occasioned a Revolt also of the Slaves."[132]

Concern that those Negroes who fought effectively for the English colony might also fight against it was not based on idle speculation. It has been shown that socially marginal individuals, many of them subject to no direct military obligation, "were precisely the men who, if given the chance, were most willing to go to war," but this was hardly a reflection of total loyalty, and among Negro slaves the number of armed fugitives speaks for itself.[133] Blacks readily became a part of any opposition movement, and it is notable that in literally every conflict in eighteenth-century South Carolina there were Negroes engaged on both sides. This applies to the conflicts with the Spanish and the Revolution against England, as well as to slave uprisings and Indian wars. In the brief Tuscarora War of 1711–12, for example, some slaves were captured and tortured along with their masters,[134] while other Negroes who had run away were sheltered by the Tuscaroras in North Carolina and even provided them with invaluable assistance upon occasion.[135] A similar situation, highly disturbing to the whites,

---

[132] BPRO Trans., VI, 262, 263 (cf. 107). This memorial to the Lords of Trade (Dec. 5, 1716) states that the colony finally brought from Virginia, on harsh terms,

> ab^t 130 Men the farr greater part of whom were poor Ragged Fellows. Raw Servants . . . just Landed from England & Ireland whose Masters Considering the Profitt would be greater by this Agreem^t then keeping them to Work at home, . . . who Coming to Carolina unseasoned to America many of them fell Sick and were intirely unserviceable & inexperienced in Armes; nor were they in any Action, and did not Stay above Eight Months before remanded and Sent home.

[133] John W. Shy, "A New Look at Colonial Militia," *WMQ*, 3rd ser., XX (1963), 182. Cf. Chapter IX, notes 60 and 61, below.

[134] In 1711 the Tuscaroras captured Baron Von Graffenried, John Lawson, and Lawson's Negro slave. They tortured all three and eventually killed the latter two. An extraordinary contemporary drawing still exists of the three bound men before a campfire. It is reproduced in Lawson, *New Voyage*, p. xxxiii (over the caption "The Torture of Lawson and Von Graffenried"), cf. p. xxxvi.

[135] Col. John Barnwell of South Carolina (later known as "Tuscarora Jack") led an expedition against King Hancock's Indian stronghold in the spring of 1712 in an effort to secure the release of Negro and white captives. One entry in Barnwell's journal stands out as a small but fascinating illustration of the way in which specific wartime skills carried from Africa could be put into use on the Carolina frontier. After days of marching, Barnwell came within range of King Hancock's fort on March 5. Taking part of his force, he circled through the woods to a point overlooking the backside of the fortification. Barnwell's account continues: "I imeadiately viewed the Fort with a prospective glass and found it strong as well by situation on the river's bank as [by] Workmanship." *Va. Mag. of Hist. and Biography*, VI (1898), 44.

Barnwell reported that besides a large trench, a high earthwork, and two tiers

must have recurred during the war with the Yamasees, which immediately followed.

By 1716 it was clear that the English colony, threatened with extinction by native Americans twelve months before, had survived its most difficult frontier war. The relieved Proprietors in London, who had contributed little to the cause, reported to the Lords of Trade in July that "a Peace is with the greatest Nations of Indians concluded, which we have all imaginable Reason to hope will continue & be lasting." While this was valid enough, they went on to express a belief that the white colonists would be able "upon any great Emergency to arm their Negroes, & by these means . . . to resist a greater Force than the Indian Enemy will in all humane probability be able at any time to bring against them."[136] This assertion illustrates the insensitivity to affairs in South Carolina which was to lead to the overthrow of the proprietorship within several years, for it reflects little awareness of the significant changes under way in the colony. There, Europeans were coming to realize that even as external dangers diminished, internal dangers increased. With the return of peace, the importation of slaves from Africa began in earnest, further augmenting a black population which already seemed to be outstripping the white.[137] As the colony's first half century drew to a close, pioneering life was giving way to plantation life as the dominant mode of existence, and Europeans and Indians were rapidly giving way to Africans as the dominant demographic presence in the coastal lowlands.

---

of portholes, he also found large tree limbs which had been placed to make approach difficult and to hide innumerable "large reeds & canes to run into people's legs." Reliable intelligence sources informed him that "*it was a runaway negro taught them to fortify thus, named Harry, whom Dove Williamson sold into Virginia for roguery & since fled to the Tuscaruros.*" (*Ibid.*, p. 45, emphasis added.) Gaining access after a lengthy siege, Barnwell reported (p. 54) that in late April he "had gone thro' the Fort (which amazed me) . . . , for I never saw such subtill contrivances for Defence."

[136] BRPO Trans., VI, 231.

[137] When the colony's agent, Joseph Boone, was asked near the end of the decade, "Are the Inhabitants increased or decreased of late and for what Reasons," he gave the following reply:

Within these last 5 years the White Inhabitants have annually Decreased by Massacres of Indians and flying off Great Numbers to places of greater safety. . . . Yett the Number of Blacks in that Time have very much increased for the Pitch and Tarr Trade Prodigiously increasing here made the Inhabitants [word faded] in to buying of Blacks to the great endangering [of] the Province.

"Query for Mr Boon," The Wake Letters, mfm, SCDAH. Cf. Chapter V, note 50, below.

☙ V ❧

"More Like
a Negro Country"

I

DURING the first twenty-five years after the founding of South Carolina, roughly one out of every four settlers was a Negro. These first black Carolinians, scarcely more than a thousand in number, came from the West Indies, and most were retained as slaves by a small number of aspiring white immigrants from Barbados. During the quarter century after 1695 this racial balance shifted markedly, so that by the time the colony's Proprietors gave way to a royal government in 1720, Africans had outnumbered Europeans for more than a decade. But South Carolina's population, when free Indians are excluded, still totaled fewer than nineteen thousand people.[1]

In 1722 the settlement's central town, with its low houses and unpaved streets, remained small enough so that a suggestion to change the name from Charles Town to Charles City was easily ignored.[2] Already, however, twenty-five thousand barrels of rice and nearly as many barrels of tar and pitch were crossing local wharves annually.[3] By this time, moreover, the regular importation of slaves directly from Africa rather than from the West Indies had been under way for several years, and as rice production expanded, the number of these shipments would increase. Only in 1741, as a result of the Stono Uprising and other disturbances, was a prohibitive duty imposed upon new slaves in an effort to curtail further growth of the black majority. But

[1] A different version of this chapter, giving further attention to slave imports, appears in Stanley L. Engerman and Eugene D. Genovese, *Race and Slavery in the Western Hemisphere: Quantitative Studies* (Princeton, N.J., 1974).

[2] SCUHJ, June 15, 1722, mfm BMP/D 487, SCDAH.

[3] Sirmans, *Colonial S.C.*, p. 132.

by then the racial demography of the colony had been firmly established. "Carolina," commented a Swiss newcomer named Samuel Dyssli in 1737, "looks more like a negro country than like a country settled
by white people."[4]

Dyssli's remark expressed both a psychological response and a
factual observation; on both counts, the comment could not have been
made about any other mainland colony at the time. If early demographic patterns were determined by the nature of the settlement,
they also helped shape that settlement, and it is difficult to consider any
part of the history of colonial South Carolina without having some
factual knowledge of who was living there, and in what numbers. Certain gross population data are available through government records,
and import statistics yield information on the annual arrival of slaves.
A separate and sometimes more detailed source of information on the
growth of the settlement in the early eighteenth century is the correspondence from Anglican ministers representing the newly created
Society for the Propagation of the Gospel in Foreign Parts. The S.P.G.
provided a missionizing arm for the Church of England, which had
begun to assume increasing precedence in Carolina after the staunchly
tolerationist decades of the early Proprietors.[5] The first S.P.G. missionary reached Charlestown on Christmas Day 1702, and within four
years the Church of England had been proclaimed the "established"
faith of South Carolina and the first formal parishes had been laid out.
From then on, the Anglican parishes provided the main demographic
as well as religious units of the colony, and the handful of ministers
who struggled to preside over them sent back to London an annual
flow of fact and opinion about conditions in the lowlands. Before
exploring the numerical data to which these S.P.G. missionaries contributed on a regular basis, it is worth taking a brief look at their more
general role as commentators and proselytizers.

[4] Samuel Dyssli, Dec. 3, 1737, *SCHGM*, p. 90.
[5] Sirmans, *Colonial S.C.*, p. 18. While a good deal has been written by Frank J.
Klingberg and others concerning the S.P.G. in America, the records have so far been
used more for their religious than for their demographic or anthropological interest. The
most recent addition to the literature is John Calam, *Parsons and Pedagogues: The
S.P.G. Adventure in American Education* (New York, 1971). (Sidney Charles Bolton
has written a doctoral dissertation at the University of Wisconsin on social and cultural
aspects of Anglicanism in early South Carolina.)

II

THE CORRESPONDENCE of the S.P.G. ministers is a rich and under-utilized resource for the history of the early colony, providing a clear if narrow window into the frontier society of the second and third generations. The letters assume particular interest because their authors were concerned not only with fellow Europeans but also with Africans and Indians to a greater degree than were the random preachers who preceded them.[6] In fact, as missionaries, the professional interest of S.P.G. personnel lay in the salvation of those souls with least prior access to the word of the Christian gospels.

Whatever their theoretical commitments, when plunged into the rude, egalitarian "Hotch potch"[7] surrounding Charlestown, the orderly young Anglicans could scarcely determine where to begin. "I have here a multitude of ignorant persons to instruct," wrote Samuel Thomas, the first arrival, after a month; "too many profane to awaken, some few pious to build up, and many Negroes, [and] Indians to begin withall."[8] Ignorant of Indian languages, lacking for resources, and eager to start work, Thomas passed over his assignment to minister among the Yamasees and took up residence instead at the Cooper River plantation of Sir Nathaniel Johnson (governor of the colony for the next six years), where he began instructing the numerous slaves to

[6] This is not to say that the few lay ministers roaming the colony before the Anglicans arrived were at all discriminatory in their gospelizing. Indeed, it was widely recalled that in 1683 "one Atkinson Williamson who was a great Lover of strong Liquor" had inadvertently baptized a bear ("and some Wicked people doubtless they were that made him first fudled and then got him to Christen the Bear")! Thomas Smith to Robert Stevens, Jan. 16, 1708 (cf. letters of Dec. 10, 1707, and Feb. 3, 1708), S.P.G. mfm I, SCDAH. Cf. *Le Jau*, pp. 72–73.

[7] *Johnston*, p. 2. Commissary Johnston exclaimed (Sept. 20, 1708):

The People here, generally speaking, are the Vilest race of Men upon the Earth they have neither honour, nor honesty nor Religion enough to entitle them to any tolerable Character, being a perfect Medley or Hotch potch made up of Bank[r]upts, pirates, decayed Libertines, Sectaries and Enthusiasts of all sorts who have transported themselves hither from Bermudas, Jamaica, Barbados, Montserat, Antego, Nevio, New England, Pensylvania &c; and are the most factious and Seditious people in the whole World. Many of those that pretend to be Churchmen are strangely cripled in their goings between the Church and Presbytery, and as they are of large and loose principles so they live and Act accordingly.

[8] *SCHGM*, IV (1903), 226.

read English.[9] The Rev. Thomas died of a fever in October 1706, but his place was taken that same month by Francis Le Jau. Expressing his broad hopes for "instructing the poor and ignorant from among the white, black & Indians,"[10] Le Jau settled at Goose Creek and soon earned a reputation among his few colleagues for paying particular attention to the Negro slaves.

The odds at work against these ministers were formidable. Their numbers rarely approached and never exceeded a dozen at any one time, so that even in the early decades, when their zeal still ran high and the population remained small, significant contact was hard. Dispersed settlement and difficult travel conditions imposed severe limits: "our houses are so scatter'd and remote," stated Le Jau, "that it is not without great difficulties that we meet so many as we do." He later added, "I wish I had strength to be perpetualy Rideing abt. but I cant., and tho I am better than before as to [the] matter of health, I cannot say that I ever was thoroughly well in this Climat."[11]

When concerned with slaves, the ministers faced several other impediments besides long distances, poor weather, and ill health. The language of the Africans (considered in the next chapter) posed one obstacle; the opinions of their masters posed another. While various Negroes and Indians expressed interest in the activities of the S.P.G., the attitudes of their white owners were problematic at best.[12] The ministers assured slaves and owners alike that baptism contained no implication of earthly freedom, and they went out of their way to accommodate the practical concerns of parishioners short on labor:

I took a particular day of the week [wrote Le Jau] and invited the Children, Servants and Slaves to come to be instructed in the Church, leaving to the discretion of the Parents and Masters to send such of their families as they cou'd spare by Turns, and whom they thought best disposed: I am sorry I can give no satisfactory Account of Success. . . . I am not blamed openly, . . . but it seems by their Whispers & Conduct, they wou'd not have me urge of Contributing to the Salvation, Instruction and human usage of Slaves and ffree Indians.[13]

9 Klingberg, *Appraisal*, pp. 8–9.

10 *Le Jau*, p. 22.

11 *Ibid.*, pp. 69, 105.

12 *Ibid.*, pp. 76, 81, 167. Le Jau stated (pp. 16, 105) that in a land where "Mammon has hitherto got too many Worshippers," white concern often focused upon the money value of black laborers. "I recommend to the Masters that care be taken of their [slaves'] Souls, some submit to my Exhortation (few indeed) and all Generally seem to be more Concerned for loss of their Money."

13 *Ibid.*, p. 50.

Besides hearing the inevitable arguments that slaves might use catechism lessons to avoid work or widen earthly contacts, ministers also listened to "the Old pretext that Baptism makes the Slaves proud and Undutifull."[14] Le Jau took considerable pains to see that any slaves he baptized maintained the most abject and servile humility, but he continued to find, with some exceptions, that masters "will not suffer their Slaves to come to Church to Learn their Prayers, because, say they, knowledge makes them worse, this is now their main Argument."[15] "I cannot to this day," he stated, "prevail upon some to make a difference between Slaves and free Indians, and Beasts." Among such parishioners, many of whom had Caribbean backgrounds, was one who "resolved never to come to the Holy Table while slaves are Rec[eive]d there." Another white person, blissfully confident of her own salvation, was so direct as to ask the minister: "Is it Possible that any of my slaves could go to Heaven, & must I see them there?"[16]

Despite opposition, Le Jau and some of his associates did argue Negro rights and resist racial bigotry upon occasion. "All Men shall speak well of us, if we give them the Liberty to be as badd as they please," wrote the minister in 1710; "but I am sure I never was sent here for that end, and I thank God I've resolution enough to call evil, evil; let it be where it will."[17] Such righteousness, however, carried a social price which the missionaries frequently were unwilling to pay, and their sporadic protests focused upon only the worst excesses of frontier justice. In 1709 Le Jau wrote, "a poor Slavewoman was barbarously burnt alive near my door without any positive proof of the Crime she was accused of, wch was, the burning of her Master's House, and [she] protested her innocence even to my self to the last."[18] Three years later, using biblical citations, he vigorously opposed the clause in the sweeping slave law of 1712 which sanctioned the castration of repeated runaways—punishment that had been accepted locally for several decades.[19]

[14] *Ibid.*, p. 125.

[15] *Ibid.*, p. 133. They informed Le Jau of "the impossibility of bringing the Slaves into a right order" (p. 86), and when he sought actively to bring African social mores into conformity with European patterns, they answered merely (p. 52) that "such a thing cannot be helped."

[16] *Ibid.*, pp. 52, 102.

[17] *Ibid.*, p. 79; cf. p. 90.

[18] *Ibid.*, p. 55; cf. p. 78.

[19] *Ibid.*, pp. 108–9 (Feb. 20, 1712):

I have had of late an opportunity to oppose with all my might the putting of a very unhumane Law and in my Judgmt. very unjust it is in Execution in Relation

During the same year the Rev. Le Jau protested to little avail the increased brutality of individual masters which seemed to follow the fear of rebellion in 1712:

> they are more Cruel Some of them of late Dayes than before. They hamstring main [maim] & unlimb those poor Creatures for small faults, A man within this Month had a very fine Negroe ba[p]tized, Sensible Carefull & good in all Respects who being wearyed with Labour & fallen asleep had the Mischance to loose a parcell of Rice wch by the Oversetting of a Periogua fell into a River. The man tho Intreated . . . to forgive the Negroe, who had Offended only through Neglect without Malice, thought fit to keep him for several Dayes in Chains, & I am told muffled up that he might not Eat & Scourge him twice a Day, and at Night to put him into a hellish Machine contrived by him into the Shape of a Coffin where [he] could not Stirr. The punishmt having continued Several Dayes & Nights and there being no Appearance when it should End, the poor Negroe through Despair Ask't one of his Children for a knife & manacled as he was Stabb'd himself with it; I am told this is the 5th Slave that Same man has destroyed by his Cruelty within 2 or 3 Yeares, but he is onely an hired Overseer the Owner of the Slaves lives out of this Province.[20]

In general, however, pious objections to such behavior proved ineffectual. Outspoken criticism was therefore considered impolitic by ministers who, despite their protestations, were thoroughly worldly when it came to calculations of social standing.

III

For the most part, S.P.G. ministers, attuned to formality and hierarchy, must already have felt uneasy at the indiscreet democratizing of the frontier, without making it their special mission to challenge the emerging inequalities of a slave society. Even Le Jau resorted at

---

to run away Negroes, by a Law Enacted in this Province some years before I came; such an Negroe must be mutilated by amputation of Testicles if it be a man. and of Ears if a Woman. I have openly declared against such punishment grounded upon the Law of God, which setts a slave at liberty if he should loose an Eye or a tooth when he is Corrected. Exod. 21. and some good Planters are of my opinion. . . . when I look upon the ordinary cause that makes those poor Souls run away, and almost dispaire I find it is imoderate labour and want of Victualls and rest. God Alm: inspire the Honourable Society my most Illustrious Patrons to Consider those things so that they may be remedyed for the Encouragemt. of those poor Creatures.

20 *Ibid.*, p. 129; cf. p. 108.

first to simple comparative judgments about the slaves' lot: "they are well used in this place," he wrote soon after arrival, "better than in the Islands."[21] As representatives of a conservative institution engaged in the patronizing work of propagating the gospel, the ministers were acutely aware of a need to be accepted and eventually elevated by the leading white planters, whose self-proclaimed status represented the only rise in the lowland colony's social landscape. Moreover, they themselves regularly became the owners of black slaves and grew dependent in part upon the very labor system they confronted. The perquisites of St. Philip's Parish in Charlestown, for example, included "a Negro man and Woman," and it was understood that the occupant of the parsonage would "let out the Said Slaves to the Best advantage."[22]

Socially insecure and temperamentally cautious, the ministers adopted postures of extreme restraint in conducting their affairs. Samuel Thomas recommended "an humble and obliging carriage" and "a moderate and prudent conduct . . . to remove prejudices . . . agst our Church and Ministers." Gideon Johnston was careful not to preach sermons which might offend prominent listeners, since "it wou'd look too much like pointing, and wou'd disoblige and disgust rather than any thing else."[23] Even the Rev. Le Jau (who once raised a question about "marrying and baptizing slaves without the consent of their masters," which had to be referred to the Archbishop of Canterbury) generally found it practical to remain circumspect. "The Caution I have taken & which the Society is pleased to approve of," he wrote, "to do nothing without the Masters good testimony and consent, is a sufficient answer to them that oppose most the happyness of their Slaves."[24] As this indicates, in order to please the Society and their white parishioners and to allay misgivings about their own abilities to judge the souls of black folk, missionaries often relied upon direct testimony from the *masters* of those they intended to baptize. Indeed, the measure of Christianization applied to the few slaves who actually received baptism remained the degree to which they continued to render financial and psychic rewards to their owners.[25] Obviously

[21] *Ibid.*, p. 26. In 1700 Le Jau had served as a missionary on St. Christopher in the West Indies for a year.

[22] *Johnson*, pp. 22 *n*, 104; Church Commissioner's Book (1717–42), minutes for meeting of October 2, 1717, msv, SCDAH.

[23] *SCHGM*, IV (1903), 280; *Johnston*, p. 38.

[24] *Le Jau*, pp. 55, 76; cf. pp. 58, 104.

[25] *Ibid.*, pp. 48, 57, 60, 76, 86.

there was a severely limiting circularity built into such an approach.

Perhaps nothing indicates the cramped nature and dubious results of these efforts at Christian benevolence better than the missionaries' lofty stand concerning the doctrine of the Sabbath. Proper observance of the Sabbath seemed a more important problem to the ministers than the dismemberment of black recalcitrants.[26] The issue affected their own work directly, and their steady protests provide insight into both the attitudes of the Anglicans and the activities of Afro-Americans. The Rev. Thomas, on a trip to England in 1705, had informed the Society that slaves were being kept at their usual tasks on Sundays, and the matter was even referred to the Bishop of London.[27] Le Jau still protested in 1712 that "they are Sufferd, some forced—to work upon Sundays, having no other means to subsist,"[28] and a communication from all the ministers delivered by Commissary Johnston in the same year gave a more detailed picture:

There are many planters who, to free themselves from the trouble of feeding and clothing their slaves allow them one day in the week to clear ground, and plant for themselves as much as will clothe and subsist them and their families. In order to do this, some Masters give their slaves Saturday, some half that day, and others Sunday only; which they endeavour to justify saying, that if they were not obliged to work that day, they would be employed in that which is worse. 'Tis needless to show the weakness of this excuse, and, therefore, I will only observe, that those who have Saturday given them seldom fail of working more or less on the Lord's Day too . . . , and that it is not just to debar a poor slave from that which is no loss or injury to his master, and upon which his food and raiment and the support of his family . . . does so absolutely depend.[29]

Moreover, signs of *leisure* on the Sabbath were as upsetting to

[26] *Ibid.*, p. 121. Le Jau wrote (Aug. 30, 1712):

There has been a severe Act, to punish our Slaves, lately past in this province. Runaway Slaves are to be Mutilated; and at last put to death if they absent themselves for the fourth time for fourteen days. I have taken the Liberty to say Mutilation and Death too Great punishments in that respect But what I most complaine of is that upon Sundays they are Confin'd at home by the Letter of the Act[.] I urg'd to the Magistrates in this parish these poor souls should have the liberty to come to Church. I was answered that it was so Implyed with their Masters leave, but I fear as the greatest part of the Masters is against their Slaves being Instructed they'll take an Advantage of the Tenour of the Act.

[27] *SCHGM*, V (1904), 26, 43.

[28] *Le Jau*, p. 116.

[29] Klingberg, *Appraisal*, p. 7. References to Sunday work regulations for slaves in other colonies appear in Miles Mark Fisher, *Negro Slave Songs in the United States* (Ithaca, 1953), p. 50 *n.*

zealous ministers as signs of work. Le Jau wrote in 1709 of the Negroes at Goose Creek that it "has been Customary among them to have their ffeasts, dances, and merry Meetings upon the Lord's day." He claimed such activities were "pretty well over in this Parish, but not absolutely,"[30] and the following summer he could boast: "The Lord's day is no more profaned by their dancings at least about me."[31] Le Jau's strictures about keeping the holy days soon went too far, for the Negroes, feigning literal-mindedness, "took that opportunity and wou'd not work which made the Masters angry and none Came to Church, so I am forced to forbear."[32]

But in whatever way the insistence upon the Fourth Commandment was moderated to suit white planters, it still conflicted directly with the Negroes' brief hours for rest and fraternization on the one hand and with their meager chance for self-sufficiency and betterment on the other. Therefore churchmen argued increasingly for removing altogether these vestiges of black autonomy. Early pioneering conditions, with land plentiful, food scarce, and discipline superficial, had made it logical for slaves to have certain open plots and weekend hours for themselves. In the coming decades this degree of freedom would gradually dwindle. Less independence to provide their own food and clothes and to apportion certain hours of their week might make slaves both more profitable to their owners and also more accessible to propagators of the English gospel. It would be some time before these overlapping white economic and religious interests triumphed completely, but as early as 1710 Le Jau saw signs that increasingly "the Slaves shall be fed and provided for by the Masters, and the whole time of the Slaves shall be their Masters." He added that "this is what I have continually urged; knowing how idly and criminally the Slaves spent the time given to them to Work for themselves," and he concluded, "I bless God for having at last rendred the Masters sensible of their own Advantage in that respect."[33]

Anglican treatment of the doctrine of wedlock for Africans is also indicative. The ministers' own accounts reveal that, despite trying

---

[30] *Le Jau*, pp. 60–61. He continued: "I tell them that present themselves to be admitted to Baptism, they must promise they'l spend no more the Lord's day in idleness, and if they do I'l cut them off from Comunion. . . . I see with an incredible joy the fervor of several of those poor Slaves."

[31] *Ibid.*, p. 77. The very existence of these dances, which were no doubt African in origin, is of greater significance than Le Jau's brief curtailment of them.

[32] *Ibid.*, p. 86.

[33] *Ibid.*, p. 76.

conditions, stable alliances were far from unknown to the average slave, who would labor during every free moment in "support of his family and all that is dear to him in this world."[34] The circumstances in the frontier settlement—mortality among white owners, constant indebtedness, absenteeism, and incessant demands for labor—intensified the movement of slaves and reduced the possibility of maintaining family relationships.[35] But where they did exist, whites may not always have accepted or even perceived them, since European and African patterns of family culture inevitably differed somewhat. And when whites did not recognize black ties, they no doubt broke them with greater impunity. It is exceptional to come across a transaction so neatly ordered as the one in 1686 in which a white man in Berkeley County bought "One Negroe man by name Tom . . . One Negroe Woman by name Mareah . . . one Negroe boy by name Jack and One ffeather bed."[36] Masters could easily tear couples apart, and they could also separate children from their parents, as is apparent from the early will of Henry Samways, who gave his wife twenty head of cattle and a slave couple, Peter and Betty, "but in case of death or marriage the negro man & woman *with half their encrease* to befall to my Sonn."[37]

One other fact is striking: despite the preponderance of men in the slave population as a whole, one man is sometimes found grouped with several women and children in the record of a slave sale or division of an estate. Whether this represents pure chance, or monetary

[34] Letter to the S.P.G. from the clergy in South Carolina, 1713, in Klingberg, *Appraisal*, p. 7.

[35] The early career of a Negro boy named Mingo is suggestive. He probably came to Carolina from Jamaica with his owner, Thomas Gunn, a cooper by trade. When Gunn died in 1694, not long after his arrival, Mingo became the property of the cooper's two small sons and their guardians, a surgeon and a draper in London. These distant parties empowered local merchants to administer the estate, and they in turn sold Mingo to a leather tanner in Colleton County. Before reaching manhood, therefore, he had moved from an island to the mainland and from making barrels to tanning hides. RSP (1694–1705), pp. 19–20; also Charleston County Wills (1694–1705), p. 19, mfm, SCDAH.

[36] MR (1682–90), p. 268. In one of the few seventeenth-century documents where slaves are listed roughly by families (e.g., "Great Jack & wife"), confusion apparently arose over their division in the owner's estate. WMR (1687–1710), p. 23.

[37] RSP (1675–95), p. 439. (Italics added.) Masters could not only tear couples apart but also thrust them together, as appears to have been the case when Sarah Waight gave her nephew "one Negroe boy by name Jack and one Negroe woman by name Rose togeather with all their increase." RSP (1675–95), p. 435; cf. *SCHGM*, VIII (1907), 164–65. For sensitivity on this point, see Chapter IV, note 132, above.

considerations of the white owners, or some concession to a West African pattern of polygamy is impossible to say.[38] But the clergy remained mortified by challenges to their strict ideal of monogamous marriage (which owed much to the culture from which they came and little to the Old Testament from which they read). Le Jau soon took to reading a brief warning to each Negro man he baptized: *"The Christian Religion does not allow plurality of Wives, nor any changing of them: You promise truly to keep to the Wife you now have till Death dos part you."*[39] He later noted, "I have proposed to some Masters a thing that seems to me very easy to be done and will prevent horrid Crimes and Confusions amongst Negroes and Indian Slaves for the future." His scheme was to make sure "that none of those that are not yet married presume to do it without his Masters consent, and likewise those that are now Marryed do not part without the like Consent (I know some will transgress) but I hope 'twill do good to many."[40] Increasingly with marriage, as with the Sabbath, the Anglican wish to impose social conformity and to render the Negroes spiritually tractable led to ideas of intervention and control. "Their working upon Sundays for their maintenance," warned Le Jau, "and their having Wives or Husbands at a great Distance from their Masters Plantations, in my humble Judgement dos much harm and hinders much good."[41]

Through their zeal and tenacity these few ministers were inadvertently helping to tighten the hold of the white master over the black slave, but their calculated influence among the thousands of Negroes who surrounded them remained slight indeed. No doubt they took heart, as have their historians, from the belief that there is virtue in saving one soul in a hundred, but their performance by their own admission was hardly that good. Thomas Hasell, after eleven years in St. Thomas' Parish, claimed in 1720 to have baptized eight or nine of

[38] Cf. Wills (1671–1727), pp. 37–38, msv, SCDAH. While it seems likely that during the earliest generations a tentative balance was struck—to be altered in later years—between the desires of Africans for stable personal connections and the demands of Europeans for a supply of unattached and purchasable labor, it is worth remembering that the differences in life-plan between white and black may well have been considerable as African and European culture patterns crossed initially. It will take a great deal more attention by historians and anthropologists to judge such differences accurately. For a suggestive introduction to many aspects of the distinctive world view which Africans brought with them, see John S. Mbiti, *African Religions and Philosophy* (New York, 1969).

[39] *Le Jau*, p. 60. The emphasis is added by Le Jau.

[40] *Ibid.*, p. 77; cf. pp. 93–94.

[41] *Ibid.*, p. 54.

some eight hundred slaves, and when Brian Hunt quit St. John's in 1728 after five years he left behind fifteen hundred Negro slaves, "none of them baptized or instructed in Christianity."[42] "The conversion of slaves," the ministers had informed their society candidly in 1713, "is, considering the present circumstances of things, scarcely possible. 'Tis true, indeed, that an odd slave here and there may be converted when a minister has leisure and opportunity for so doing. . . . But alas!" they added, "success must be little and inconsiderable in comparison of what might be expected because there are so many rules and impediments that lie in the way."[43]

It might conceivably have been otherwise. A Huguenot clergyman who lived in the Santee region, writing to the Secretary of the S.P.G. in 1710, reminded him that Catholic priests elsewhere readily christened any Negro who came before them. The minister suggested that Anglican baptism might be offered on a comparably broad scale and volunteered his services to prepare candidates.[44] If widespread baptism had been undertaken at such an early date, so that English masters, even while keeping black laborers in servile status, were forced to concede their full "humanity" through use of a European ritual, later Afro-American history could have been significantly different. Instead, however, access to this vital foothold in the dominating culture was made extremely difficult in accordance with the tantalizing doctrine of "preparation." As a result, while no one can deny the later importance of Protestant sects among black Americans, it appears that initial efforts to propagate the Christian faith among the Negroes in Carolina had for them a direct impact which was almost negligible and indirect effects which were less than fortunate.

IV

WHATEVER THE WEAKNESS of the established parishes in religious terms, they began to serve an immediate demographic function with regard to all inhabitants, irrespective of race or status (though the actual term "inhabitants" was regularly used by ministers to designate only white residents). Prior to the organization of distinct parishes beginning in

---

[42] Klingberg, *Appraisal*, pp. 32, 52.
[43] *Ibid.*, p. 6.
[44] *Ibid.*, p. 24 *n*.

1704, population statistics had been scarce and a bit confused, though by the end of the previous century it seemed clear that the percentage of blacks in the tiny settlement had begun to increase. A manuscript from shortly before 1700 states: "South Carolina hath nott above 2000 whites & those not ye wealthyest of men in Americah; yett . . . they have procured as many or more Negroes whose labours are Equall to ye English."[45] After the turn of the century, with the arrival of Anglican missionaries and the expansion of the small colonial bureaucracy, census figures gradually became more abundant and precise. It is possible to piece together a significant amount of data concerning the colony's demographic growth in the decades following 1700.

The exact moment at which black inhabitants exceeded white appears to have fallen around the year 1708, for data collected at that time showed the two groups almost even, with just over four thousand in each. This census report, although rough, provides a valuable profile of the colony, for the governor and council broke the survey into distinct categories by age, sex, and race, and indicated the change in each group over the five years since 1703. Their report is summarized in Table I.[46] Due to commerce in war captives, Indian slaves can be seen as the fastest-growing segment of the population between 1703 and 1708.[47] This was a short-term trend that contributed directly to the frontier wars of the ensuing decade, after which the Indian presence would diminish rapidly.[48] Among whites, the number of adults de-

[45] "Some weighty considerations relating to America. . . ." This anonymous and undated manuscript appears as item 64 in the Archdale Papers, mfm, SCDAH.

[46] BPRO *Trans.,* V, 203–4, rpt. in Rivers, *Sketch,* p. 232. Sirmans (*Colonial S.C.,* p. 60) has added these figures wrongly. More significant, however, may be the fact that Verner W. Crane seems to have obtained slightly different totals from the actual BPRO manuscripts, Colonial Office papers, 5:1264, p. 82. Crane, *Southern Frontier,* p. 113.

[47] English colonists had overpowered the Savannah Indians during these years. It is noteworthy that the percentage of Indian women reported was high, the percentage of children low. The free Indians mentioned in the previous chapter do not appear in the report. For an estimate of their numbers, see Rivers, *Sketch,* p. 239.

[48] Le Jau wrote (*Le Jau,* p. 109) at the time of the Tuscarora War (Feb. 20, 1712):

> our Traders have promoted Bloody Warrs this last Year to get slaves and one of them brought lately 100 of those poor Souls. . . . I don't know where the fault lyes but I see 30 Negroes at Church for an Indian slave, and as for our free Indians—they goe their own way and bring [up] their Children like themselves with little Conversation among us, I generaly Pceive something Cloudy in their looks, an Argumt. I fear, of discontent. I am allso Informed yt. our Indien Allyes [the Yamasees] are grown haughty of late.

clined by nearly 6 per cent during the five-year span, despite the arrival of newcomers. By contrast, the number of Negro adults rose more than 20 per cent in the same period, due to natural increase as well as importation. The high proportion of children among the whites (42 per cent) suggests a populace with a high rate of mortality. Among black slaves the proportion of children is lower (29 per cent), but

TABLE I

South Carolina Population as Reported by the Governor and Council, Sept. 17, 1708

	PROJECTED FIGURES FOR 1703	REPORTED CHANGES SINCE 1703	REPORTED FIGURES FOR 1708	
Free men	1,460	−100	1,360	
Free women	940	− 40	900	
Free children	1,200	+500	1,700	
White servant men	110	− 50	60	
White servant women	90	− 30	60	
TOTAL WHITES	3,800	+ 280		4,080
Negro men slaves	1,500	+300	1,800	
Negro women slaves	900	+200	1,100	
Negro children slaves	600	+600	1,200	
TOTAL NEGRO SLAVES	3,000	+1,100		4,100
Indian men slaves	100	+400	500	
Indian women slaves	150	+450	600	
Indian children slaves	100	+200	300	
TOTAL INDIAN SLAVES	350	+1,050		1,400
TOTAL POPULATION	7,150	+2,430		9,580

their total number of children doubled in the course of five years, arguing a high rate of natural population growth among Africans. These different growth rates continued through the ensuing decade.

The contrast between black and white growth rates in the proprietary colony is suggested by the graph in Table IV. Epidemics, Indian wars, and emigration meant that the white population rose by scarcely 2,500 between 1708 and 1721 inclusive, while the Negro population added over 4,000 by natural increase and above 3,600 more through imports during this same period. Using data drawn from Table II, it is possible to demonstrate that the annual rate of black population increase in excess of the number of immigrants was a surprising 5.6 per cent during the thirteen years before 1721.[49] Support for these numerical calculations can be found in a 1714 statute which raised the duty on Negro slaves in hopes of reducing their importation. The legislators observed that "the number of negroes do extremely increase in this Province, and through the afflicting providence of God, the white persons do not proportionably multiply."[50] By the time the Crown assumed control in 1720 it was apparent to all contemporaries that South Carolina, unlike the other mainland English colonies, was dominated demographically by migrants from West Africa. They predominated in terms of total numbers, pace of immigration, and rate of natural increase.

In 1720 the rough population figures accepted in London for the new royal colony were 9,000 whites and 12,000 Negroes, and as is often the case with colonial statistics the figure for Africans was notably more precise than that for Europeans.[51] But it was not until the following March, when census data from each parish were de-

---

[49] The annual rate of population increase in excess of the number of immigrants was computed by: (1) subtracting the total imports during the interval from the net change in population over the period; (2) adding the net increase in excess of the imports to the initial year population; and (3) computing the compounded annual rate of increase between the initial year's population and the final year's estimated population as calculated in (2). To interpret this calculation as referring to the natural increase of the initial year's slave population requires the assumption that births to the imported slaves are equal to the deaths among the imports.

[50] *Statutes*, VII, 367. It is necessary to keep in mind that some part of the increase in slaves during these years was due to masters importing individual Negroes from the West Indies for their own personal use rather than for sale. No duty was paid on these slaves (*Statutes*, III, 56–68), hence they may not appear in a tabulation of imports such as Table III below. See Clowse, *Ec. Beginnings*, p. 204.

[51] This is not to say that slave totals were never misrepresented. For example, in 1720 colonial agents put South Carolina's Negro population at "14 or 15000" when they were trying to dramatize the threat of insurrection. (BPRO Trans., VIII, 253–54.) But it is safe to state that officials usually possessed better demographic information on blacks than on whites. "The White Inhabitants," wrote Gov. Glen in 1749, "may be in number Twenty five Thousand, and the Negroes at least Thirty nine Thousand, of these I can be more positive, as Taxes are paid for them." BPRO Trans., XXIII, 369–70.

livered under oath to the tax commissioners in Charlestown, that a detailed picture was available. The interim governor, James Moore, Jr., promptly forwarded to England "An Exact account of the Number of Inhabitants who pay Tax in the Settlement of South Carolina for the yeare 1720 with the Number of Acres and Number of Slaves in each parish."[52] Moore's account, which provides the basis for Table II, places the slave population at 11,828, or within 1 per cent of the estimated figure of 12,000.[53]

TABLE II

Population Figures for South Carolina by Parish, 1720

FIGURES SUBMITTED BY GOVERNOR MOORE

PARISHES (LISTED FROM SOUTHWEST TO NORTHEAST)	A. TAXABLE ACRES	B. TAXPAYERS	C. SLAVES
St. Helena	51,817	30	42
St. Bartholomew's	30,559	47	144
St. George's	47,457	68	536
St. Paul's	187,976	201	1,634
St. Andrew's	197,168¾	210	2,493
St. James Goose Creek	153,267½	107	2,027
St. Philip's (Charlestown)	64,265	283	1,390
St. John's (Berkeley)	181,375	97	1,439
St. Thomas & St. Dennis	74,580	113	942
Christ Church	57,580	107	637
St. James Santee	117,274	42	584
TOTALS	1,163,319¼ °	1,305	11,828

° Moore actually gives 1,163,239¼ acres as the total for this column, which reflects an error in either the transcription or the addition. For comment on this mistake and for further breakdown of acreage figures, see Clowse, *Ec. Beginnings*, pp. 253–55.

52 BPRO Trans., IX, 22–23; also in *Calendar of State Papers Colonial*, XVIII, 39.
53 This total is higher but apparently more accurate and inclusive than several which followed. After an act of 1721 imposed a tax "upon Negro, Indian, Mustee and Molato Slaves from the age of Seven Years to the Age of Sixty inclusive," a revenue estimate for 1724 put 9,100 persons in this category. (BPRO Trans., XI, 51.) Limitations by age, incomplete returns, or even the incursions of an epidemic could all help explain the similarly smaller figure of 9,570 slaves submitted to the S.P.G. in 1722. S.P.G. "Facsimiles," p. 61, Library of Congress.

ADDITIONAL CALCULATIONS

	D. ESTIMATED FREE POP. (B × 5)	E. ESTIMATED TOTAL POP. (C + D)	F. ESTIMATED % SLAVES (E/C)	G. TAXABLE ACRES PER PERSON (A/E)
St. Helena	150	192	22	270
St. Bartholomew's	235	379	38	80
St. George's	340	876	61	54
St. Paul's	1,005	2,639	62	71
St. Andrew's	1,050	3,543	70	56
St. James Goose Creek	535	2,562	79	60
St. Philip's (Charlestown)	1,415	2,805	50	23
St. John's (Berkeley)	485	1,924	75	94
St. Thomas & St. Dennis	565	1,507	63	50
Christ Church	535	1,172	54	49
St. James Santee	210	794	74	148
TOTALS	6,525	18,393	65	63

Moore's totals for taxable land (over 1,100,000 acres) and for South Carolina taxpayers (1,305) as given in columns A and B can be confirmed from other sources.[54] Moreover, since the number of taxpaying heads of households in each parish is known, it is possible to estimate the full number of white inhabitants through the accepted formula of multiplying by five.[55] The resulting total of 6,525 whites (column D) checks remarkably well with the total of 6,400 obtained a year earlier by Col. Johnson, using the other traditional formula of multiplying militia rolls by four.[56] The estimate of 6,525 white colo-

[54] A revenue estimate of 1724 lists 1,116,000 acres of taxable land, and an earlier representation to the king puts the number of taxable inhabitants near 1,300. BPRO Trans., XI, 51; *ibid.*, 19.

[55] James H. Cassedy, *Demography in Early America, Beginnings of the Statistical Mind, 1600–1800* (Cambridge, Mass., 1969), p. 73.

[56] *Ibid.* Johnson, then governor, had informed the Lords of Trade, Jan. 12, 1720 (BPRO Trans., VII, 233–34):

Tis computed by the Muster Roles & other observations that at present we may have about 1600 Fighting Men, from 16 to 60 Years of Age every body in the

nists in 1720 represents a more informed if less optimistic calculation than the guess of 9,000 accepted in London.[57] Using this sum of 6,525 Europeans, a figure can be reached for the total population of each parish (column E) and for the percentage of residents who were slaves (column F).

A final column (G), based on the ratio of occupied acreage to total population, indicates how sparsely settled the coastal colony remained in 1720.[58] The parishes are ordered geographically in Table II, and it is clear from the accompanying map that the southernmost precincts of St. Bartholomew's and St. Helena, lying beyond the Edisto River in the region which had recently been devastated by the Yamasee War, contained few whites and by far the lowest proportion of blacks.[59] Slaves were far more numerous among the small French settlements in the parish of St. James Santee on the northern boundary, and for the colony as a whole, slaves already outnumbered free whites

---

Province within that Age being inlisted, and obliged to bear Arms and by the Comon Computacon of 4 Persons in each Family, the whole of the Whits are 6,400, tis bleived that since the Indian Warr which broke out in Aprill 1715 We are Increased about 100 Inhabitants, wee haveing lost about 400 in the Warr and have had the Accession of about 500 from England, Ireland and other places.

[57] Sirmans, *Colonial S.C.*, p. 132, arrived at a total of 7,800 whites from Moore's figures. This plausible figure was accepted by Hawkins, who recently reviewed general population data in his "Legislation Governing the Institution of Slavery," Chapter II. Various estimates for the colonial period appear in Evarts B. Greene and Virginia D. Harrington, *American Population before the Federal Census of 1790* (New York, 1932), pp. 172–79.

[58] Slightly earlier, Thomas Nairne had observed, "This Province is capable of containing about 60 times the Number of its present Inhabitants." *Letter from S.C.*, p. 8.

[59] Francis Yonge, "A Narrative of the Proceedings of the People of South-Carolina in the Year 1719," in Force, *Tracts*, II, 7: "In this War near 400 of the Inhabitants were destroy'd with many Houses and Slaves, and great numbers of Cattle, especially to the Southward near Port-Royal, from whence the Inhabitants were entirely drove, and forced into Settlements near Charles Town." Cf. BPRO Trans., XVII, 88–144; BPRO Trans., XIX, 131. Several years later in "A View of the Trade of South Carolina" (BPRO Trans., X, 2), Yonge, who was one of the colony's agents, told the Lords of Trade and Plantations:

The trade for Beef and pork which was to Barbado's and the several Leeward Caribee Islands ye Bahamas Jamaica &c has been very much interupted by the late Indian Warr which not only destroyed the Stocks of Cattle but drove most of the Inhabitants to the southward where the great stocks of Cattle were, from their plantations who yet dare not return for fear of the Yamazee Indians who frequently disturb the settlements near Port Royall murder the planters and carry the slaves to St Augustine.

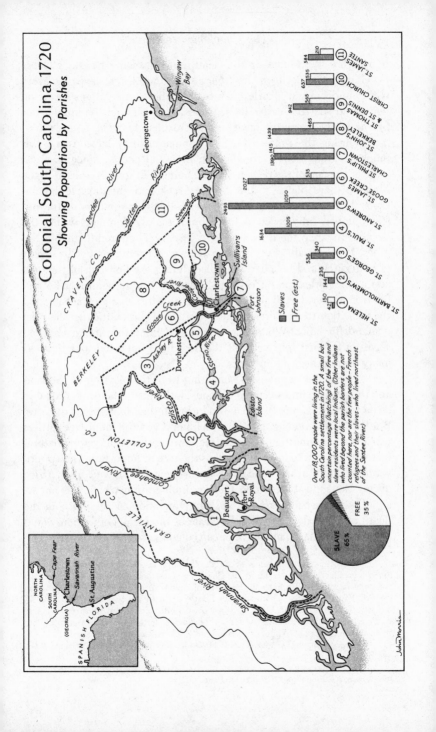

Colonial South Carolina, 1720
Showing Population by Parishes

Slaves
Free (est)

1 ST HELENA — 150 / 42
2 ST BARTHOLOMEW'S — 235 / 144
3 ST GEORGE'S — 536 / 340
4 ST PAUL'S — 1634 / 1005
5 ST ANDREW'S — 2493 / 1050
6 ST JAMES GOOSE CREEK — 2027 / 535
7 ST PHILIP'S CHARLESTOWN — 1390 / 1415
8 ST JOHN'S BERKELEY — 1439 / 485
9 ST THOMAS & ST DENNIS — 942 / 565
10 CHRIST CHURCH — 637 / 535
11 ST JAMES SANTE — 584 / 210

Over 18,000 people were living in the
South Carolina settlement in 1720. A small but
uncertain number were free or slave Indians (hence high)
of the free and slave residents here (hatching). (Other Indians
who lived beyond the parish borders are not
counted here, nor are the few people — French
refugees and their slaves — who lived northeast
of the Santee River.)

SLAVE 65%
FREE 35%

NORTH CAROLINA
Cape Fear
SOUTH CAROLINA
Charlestown
Savannah River
(GEORGIA)
St. Augustine
SPANISH FLORIDA

CRAVEN CO.
BERKELEY CO.
COLLETON CO.
GRANVILLE CO.

Peedee River
Santee River
Sewee R.
Winyaw Bay
Georgetown
Goose Creek
Cooper River
Ashley R.
Dorchester
Stono River
Edisto River
Edisto Island
Combahee River
Savannah River
Charlestown
Fort Johnson
Sullivan's Island
Beaufort
Port Royal

John Morris

by roughly two to one. In the wealthy rice-growing parish of Goose Creek near Charlestown there were more than three slaves for every white, and only in Charlestown itself (where calculations based on household size are least reliable) does it appear that the numbers of free and unfree may still have been approximately even.

During the 1720s the white population may have risen by as much as 50 per cent to roughly ten thousand people, since one estimate at the end of the decade put the number fit to bear arms at "2500 Men or thereabouts,"[60] and another reckoned the taxable inhabitants "to be two thousand Whitemen." But the numbers of the unfree climbed fully twice as fast, approximately doubling within the decade. By 1729 there were "above Twenty Thousand Tythable Negroes,"[61] presumably between the ages of seven and sixty. The export of both pitch and tar nearly doubled during the first half of the decade, and confident producers bought slaves on credit before the bottom fell from under the naval stores market in 1727.[62] The drop accelerated the transition to rice already under way, and this shift intensified the demand for labor. Where the colony had imported fifteen hundred slaves in the first four years of the decade, it imported four times as many during the last four years.

The white population, benefiting from the clearing of the land and the gradual improvement of food, clothing, and housing, probably owed more of its increase to natural growth than in previous decades. But the same economic growth which improved the lot of free settlers worsened the condition of the unfree. Among slaves the rate of natural increase appears to have declined as the rate of importation swept upward. All told, nearly nine thousand newcomers arrived from Africa during the 1720s (see Table III), an immigration which was almost equal to the net increase in the slave population. A slight rise in the death rate and decline in the birthrate of the black population would not be surprising. In many European colonies of the South Atlantic the

[60] James Sutherland came to South Carolina in Nov. 1722 and served as the commander of Johnson's Fort on Charlestown Harbor. Sometime between 1729 and 1732 he submitted a letter to the Lords of Trade, an undated copy of which is in the Coe Papers, SCHS: "Charleston, my Lord, . . . hath ab^t 300 brick Houses in it, the rest Timber, & is inhabited by about 600 white Men from 16 to 60 years of Age. . . . I believe there are 2500 Men or thereabouts, fit to carry Arms, from 16 to 60: But as to the number of Whites & Negroes in this Colony, I cannot be certain."
[61] George Burrington to the Lords of Trade, July 23, 1730, BPRO Trans., XIII, 373–74.
[62] For a discussion of major economic and demographic trends in this decade, see Clowse, *Ec. Beginnings,* Chapters VII and VIII.

TABLE III

Record of Annual Slave Imports, 1706–1739
as It Appears in Gentleman's Magazine of 1755 (XXV, 344)

YEARS	NEGR.	VESSELS	YEARS	NEGR.	VESSELS
1706	24	68		4,504	1,919
a 1707	22	66	1724	604	122
1708	53	81	1725	439	134
b 1709	107	70	e 1726	1,728	146
1710	131	92	1727	1,794	126
1711	170	81	1728	1,201	141
1712	76	82	1729	1,499	157
1713	159	99	1730	941	165
1714	419	121	1731	1,514	184
c 1715	81	133	1732	1,199	182
c 1716	67	162	1733	2,792	222
d 1717	573	127	1734	1,651	209
1718	529	114	1735	2,907	248
1719	541	137	1736	3,097	229
1720	601	129	1737	2,246	239
1721	165	121	1738	2,415	195
1722	323	120	1739	1,702	225
1723	463°	116			
	4,504	1,919		32,233	4,843

ᵃ The trade of this province to 1708 was only in exporting provisions to the sugar islands, from whence they had their supply of *European* goods, &c. and there were not above 200 negroes in the province, although now there is above 50,000.

About this time they began to make tar, pitch, and turpentine.

ᵇ At this time they began to make and export rice.

ᶜ Time of the great *Indian* war, when many inhabitants left the prov.

ᵈ Before this time the trade was chiefly carried on in small coasting vessels, who made three or four voyages *per ann.* but after this in large ships to *Europe*, and smaller vessels to *America*.

ᵉ About this time two new ports of entry, &c. for shipping was allowed, *viz.* Port Royal, to the southward, and *George Town*, to the northward, each about 60 miles from *Charles Town*, and the number of negroes or vessels in those parts are not in this account.

° Donnan (*Documents*, IV, 255) reprints the annual totals, 1706–24, which were given in the *Report of the Committee of the Commons House of Assembly of the Province of South Carolina on the State of the Paper Currency of the said Province* (London, 1737) and were repeated in McCrady, *Proprietary Government*, p. 723. They are identical to those in Table III, except for the difference—apparently an ancient copying error—for 1723, where 436 is given. There is no way to know which figure is correct. (Obviously, the total of "200 negroes" given by the English author of note a above falls short by a factor of 20.)

TABLE IV

*Population Trends
in Colonial South Carolina, 1700–1740*

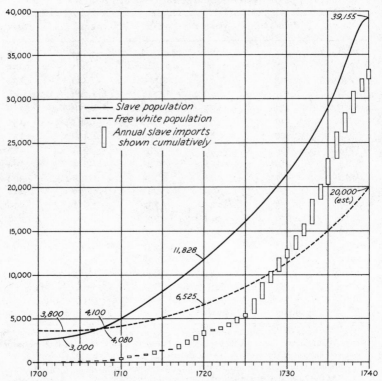

drive to secure profits or remove debts by increasing the production of a plantation economy created a willingness to buy Negroes on credit, a callousness toward the conditions of resident slaves, and a general sense of the expendability of black labor. All these tendencies worsened the prospects for natural population growth among slaves and simultaneously heightened the demand for slave imports. A vicious circle was thereby established in which it appeared advantageous to stress the importation of "salt-water" slaves rather than the survival of those at hand. On some Caribbean sugar islands the natural rate of increase fell below zero for generations with the advent of intensive staple agriculture.[63]

[63] Curtin, *Atlantic Slave Trade*, p. 32 n and Chapter III.

Somewhat the same phenomenon seems to have occurred in South Carolina during the decades after 1720, as rice rose from the status of a competing export to become the colony's central preoccupation. White colonists who responded to the opportunity for profit by investing in labor and expanding the production of staples soon faced declining prices which in turn intensified the urge to broaden production further.[64] Pressures to expand cultivation, increase crop yield, raise efficiency, and reduce overhead all worked directly to depress the lot of the slave.[65] Intensification of the plantation system may have reduced life expectancy and impaired the comparative family stability usually associated with a high birthrate,[66] for the Negro population scarcely sustained itself for several decades. Only because of expanded importation did the total number of blacks rise more rapidly than ever. Guesses made in 1734 as to the number of slaves range from 22,000 to 30,000, with the proper total probably falling almost halfway between.[67] Assuming the correct figure to be around 26,000, it is notable that even though roughly 15,000 new slaves were imported from Africa over the next six years, the colony's black population was tabulated at only 39,155 in 1740.[68]

[64] Gov. Nicholson had written to the Lords of Trade, April 21, 1723 (BPRO Trans., X, 77): "We have already had more ships and vessels in respect of Tonnage than was ever known in the Country and it is supposed there is loading enough for them and for those that are expected but the people are afraid that their Comoditys of Rice pitch and Tarr there being so much of it will come to a Low market."

[65] The squeeze produced by this downward spiral was suggested in Gov. Johnson's report of 1731. The governor pointed out that during the previous decade South Carolina had "more than doubled the produce in Rice, which imploys more than double the Negroes." But he went on to lament that the price of this commodity had declined so rapidly that fifty thousand barrels of rice exported in 1731 returned hardly £4,000 more than had been brought by fewer than half that many barrels in 1721, "altho it is the Labour of Double the Number of Negroes, near three times the quantity of Land Planted, and the same proportion of Labour to make it marketable." "Governor Johnson's Answers to Queries," Dec. 16, 1731, Parish Trans., box marked "Md. and other colonies," folder for S.C. (1720–52), p. 18.

[66] Cf. Patterson, *The Sociology of Slavery*, pp. 108–10.

[67] Document of April 9, 1734, BPRO Trans., XVI, 398–99; "Extract of the Reverend Mr. Bolzius's Journal" in Force, *Tracts*, IV, part 5, 18. An estimate of "twenty four Thousand Negroes" was probably a bit low. Document of March 8, 1734, Parish Trans., p. 15a of folder cited in note 65 above.

[68] A committee report to the colonial legislature, March 2, 1742, listed 2,447 town slaves and 36,708 slaves in surrounding counties, on the basis of assessments made the previous spring for the year 1740. *SCCHJ*, 1741–1742, p. 460.

Using the precise counts of the black population made in 1720 and 1740, along with available import data, it is possible to calculate the annual rate of black population increase for the two decades in excess of the number of immigrants (leaving aside

The arrival of great numbers of new slaves in increasingly large shipments, directly from Africa, inevitably affected the black demography of every parish. Fewer than 15 per cent of the newcomers at this time were ten years of age or younger, and an equally small proportion were elderly. One South Carolina inventory, drawn up for the estate of John Cawood in 1726, is especially valuable in showing this distribution, since it lists age as well as value for each of thirty-nine slaves.[69] Youth predominates, for almost half (nineteen of thirty-nine) are eighteen or under, while only six are over forty. For the younger slaves exact ages are given, and most were probably born on Cawood's estate. But among the sixteen who were born before 1700 ages are rounded off, and it is interesting to speculate about their origins. Most, like Angola Phillis, whose age was estimated at thirty, were undoubtedly born in Africa and imported after the turn of the century, although Indian Jane (also thirty) was clearly an American by birth. The two most elderly slaves, Old Cate born in 1662 and Old Betty born in 1666, probably began life in the West Indies, since their exact ages were known to the appraisers.

If the slave trade helped shape age distribution, it also played a part in determining the sex ratio among slaves. Rising imports reflected a consistent preference for men over women, which perpetuated the imbalance of earlier years and limited the prospects for a high birthrate which could restore a more even ratio between the sexes. A Charlestown merchant wrote to the owner of a schooner in Barbados that ideal slave cargoes for Carolina would include "especially Boys & Girls of abo^t 15 or 16 y^{rs} of Age . . . 2/3 Boys & 1/3 Girls."[70] An

---

the departures via escape or exportation). A population which had been increasing at a rate of 5.6 per cent per annum before 1720 appears to have been decreasing at a rate of 1.1 per cent per annum over the next twenty years. (See note 49 above for the basis of the calculation.) If substantial exportations to North Carolina are taken into account, the shift becomes less drastic, but it does not disappear.

[69] "Inventory of John Cawood, Esq.," Jan. 4, 1726, MR "B" (1726–27), pp. 542–52. Cawood was a well-to-do citizen whose diverse enterprises illustrate the state of the young economy. In Charlestown, where Cawood's older and more valuable slaves were located, he maintained a town house, a "skin store," and a smith shop, but he also owned a plantation at Ashepoe employing twenty-eight slaves. His brother-in-law, William Gibbon, was a Charlestown merchant. *SCHGM*, XIX (1918), 69. But Cawood himself appears to have been—like many others of his generation—part merchant, part Indian trader, part artisan, and part planter.

[70] Robert Pringle to Edward Pare, owner of the *Charming Sarah*, Pringle Letterbook, May 5, 1744. This is not dissimilar to the advice which Henry Laurens conveyed

analysis of the twenty-three inventories filed in the eighteen months after January 1, 1730, for estates with more than ten slaves yields a sample of 714 slave names.[71] Of the 663 persons who can be identified by sex, 64.2 per cent (426) are men and only 35.8 per cent (237) are women. In the future, even broader statistical samples taken from import and inventory records over a longer time span may yield a more precise and continuous demographic picture.

V

FOR THE PRESENT, the single most valuable source of data on the increasing Negro population remains correspondence of the S.P.G. ministers. The accuracy and detail of the figures, and the nature and usefulness of the accompanying insights varied, depending upon each minister's interests and the location of his parish. Thomas Hasell, for example, from the northern parish of St. Thomas east of the Cooper River, was in a position to provide clear evidence of the continuing relative and absolute decline in the number of Indian slaves after 1720.[72] In that year Hasell noted the nonwhites in his parish as more than 800 Negroes and 90 Indian slaves. Four years later he recorded 950 blacks but only 62 enslaved Indians, and in 1728 he estimated, "There are in this parish about 1,000 negro and 50 Indian slaves."[73] In the survey of 1730 inventories mentioned above, only 18 of 714 lowland slaves were identified explicitly as Indians or mustees. This represents only 2.5 per cent of the slave population. Eight of them resided

---

to his slave-trading agents, Smith & Clifton, in the following decade: "Purchase that number of very likely healthy People, Two thi[r]ds at least Men from 18 to 25 Years old, the other young Women from 14 to 18." *Laurens*, I, 295.

[71] I have drawn these documents from WIMR (1729–31), vol. 62-B.

[72] This significant shift had begun well before the Yamasee War and was accompanied by a decline in the cash value of Indian slaves. In 1722 (when Negro slaves were worth several hundred pounds in Carolina currency), the government offered Col. Theophilus Hastings £50 for each remaining Yamasee he could take, dead or alive. It was added that "in Case he Engages the Creeks or any other Indians utterly to destroy the Said nation of Yamasees the Said Hastings for such Extraordinary Service Shall be paid out of the Publick Treasury of the Province the Sum of One Thousand pounds." SCUHJ, June 14, 1722, mfm, BMP/D 487, SCDAH. (Hastings returned with five scalps and three captive Indians, two of whom were set aside by Gov. Nicholson as gifts for the Prince and Princess of Wales. *SCCHJ, 1724*, pp. 15, 50.)

[73] Klingberg, *Appraisal*, pp. 32, 34.

on the two largest plantations, and the majority were women and children.

Letters from St. Bartholomew's, between the Edisto and Combahee rivers, suggest the evolution of a frontier parish into a predominantly Negro rice district within a generation. In 1715 the Rev. Nathaniel Osborne estimated there were "near an Hundred and Twenty Familys" in this region, but most were forced out by the Indian war and five years later there were less than half as many whites and only a minority of blacks. No missionary settled there again until the 1730s, but by 1736 Thomas Thompson reported to the S.P.G. Secretary that, "In the parish of St. Bartholomew there are one hundred and twenty families of white people, and twelve hundred negroes."[74] In the next seven years, with the expansion of rice production, the free population rose from roughly 600 to more than 900,[75] while the number of slaves fully tripled to "between three and four thousand."[76] When William Langhorne submitted "An Account of the Spiritual State of St. Bartholomew's Parish" in 1752, he numbered the Europeans at 1,280 and the "Heathens and Infidels" at 5,200.[77] Dramatic population shifts such as this in the rice-growing parishes south of Charlestown must have proven significant factors in the unrest which filled the colony in the late 1730s and early 1740s.

The most precise population data acquired by the S.P.G. derive from St. George's Parish, offering a localized perspective for some of the patterns already mentioned. This thin strip of prosperous lowland stretched toward the northwest from just below Dorchester, touching the Ashley River on one side and the Edisto on the other. It had been split off from the older parish of St. Andrew's during the expansion which followed the Yamasee War, and by 1720 it already had nearly seventy taxpayers and more than five hundred slaves.[78] Rapid growth

[74] *SCHGM*, L (1949), 175 (cf. Table II above), 178.

[75] This estimate is based upon Thompson's statement, April 23, 1743, that "There are not above 240 White men in this parish." *SCHGM*, L (1949), 180.

[76] *SCHGM*, L (1949), 182–83. Thompson wrote of his white parishioners (Aug. 16, 1743):

> They pretend that their parish is poor and cannot well defray the charges of a Church and parsonage; but tis well known that for some years past there is no parish in the Province That has produced a greater, and few (if any) so great a quantity of rice; that there are between three and four thousand slaves in it, and several considerable Stores, which besides the land, make it richer than some parishes in England itself.

[77] *SCHGM*, L (1949), 200.

[78] Table II above.

over the next few years meant that there were more than one hundred households with a total of thirteen hundred slaves in St. George's when the Rev. Francis Varnod filed his unique census of the parish in January 1726. This minister's account, long published, has been subjected to almost no analysis, yet it provides an invaluable close-up of one segment of the colony at the end of the first quarter of the eighteenth century.[79]

Varnod listed by name 108 heads of households, probably in some geographical order, and placed a "D" after those fifty-two who were religious dissenters. After each name he recorded six figures: the numbers of white people ("Men," "Women," and "Children") and the numbers of slaves ("Men," "Women," and "Children") within that household. Two of the land holdings—totally dissimilar in nature—clearly belonged to absentees: "Sam Wraggs Plant[ation]" was the property of the leading Charlestown slave merchant and contained fifty-seven slaves and a white overseer; "Nath Wickams Pl:" was worked by four slave men, one woman, and a child entirely on their own. Eleven of the households are listed in the names of women, in some cases even when white men were present.

Below the list of householders Varnod records the presence of twenty-four people under the separate category of "Free negroes and Indians." Guy (a Negro), Nero (an Indian), and a woman named Sarah all lived alone, while an Indian named Sam Pickins and a Negro named Robin Johnson each lived with a wife and four children. The latter had nine slaves in his household: three men, three women, and three children. The presence of these two dozen people is significant, for it illustrates the fact that free nonwhites could still find ways to subsist, at least marginally, within the confines of this frontier society. As slavery based on race became increasingly central to the colony's social and economic system, the incongruous status of such people grew more and more untenable. Already in 1726 the most striking fact about this group was its small size. Whatever the social importance of these anomalous residents, statistically they represent less than 2 per cent of the parish's non-Europeans. It is logical to leave them aside while examining the bulk of both the free and slave population more closely, and therefore they have been excluded from the calculations which follow.

The parish's white minority in 1726 totaled 537. Just over 50 per

[79] Varnod's census is printed in Klingberg, *Appraisal,* pp. 58–60. Sirmans, *Colonial S.C.,* p. 145, makes brief use of it, but the number of slaves has been added incorrectly.

cent (271) were regarded as adults, and 56 per cent of these were men. There were eight households with no white men and seven others with more women than men, but almost half the holdings contained one man and one woman listed as white. Assuming most of these couples to be conjugal units, the sizes of the families they were raising can be summarized as follows:

TABLE V

Children in 53 White Households
with One Man and One Woman

Children per household	0	1	2	3	4	5	6	7	Totals
Number of households	3	13	14	7	10	3	2	1	53
Number of children	0	13	28	21	40	15	12	7	136

Nearly 40 per cent of these homes (21) contain two or three children; 16 have one child or none, and 16 others have four offspring or more. The child/parent ratio in these 53 households averages to 2.57 children for every mother. This ratio is somewhat higher (2.82/1) when calculated from the 73 households with one white woman present (but not necessarily one white man), and it is slightly lower (2.24/1) when the total number of white children is divided by the total number of white women in the parish.

The number of white men varied little from household to household. Apart from the large farm of Benjamin Perriman with eight men (plus two women, nine children, and a slave man and child) and that of Roger Sumner with five men (plus two women, three children, and three adult slaves), all the other households in the parish contained fewer than four free men. There was a single white man on 70 of the holdings and two or three on 28 others, not a surprising distribution in a recently settled parish where fresh land was readily available for new arrivals and for children as they came of age. (Numerous family connections can be seen among the names of property owners on Varnod's list.) The size of white households as a whole is worth noting. If one discounts the two plantations with absentee owners, the 1726 census shows 106 households with 536 white members, or 5.06 per household. This figure varies little in accordance with the size of the plantation, and it lends specific confirmation to the process of multiplying the number of heads of households by five to estimate the white population.[80]

VI

THE SLAVES in St. George's Parish by 1726 were almost entirely Negroes, and there were scarcely half a dozen Negroes present who were not slaves, so it is possible to view the black population and the unfree population as roughly co-equal. Varnod's list enumerates exactly 1,300 slaves, more than 70 per cent of the parish's total inhabitants. By this time, therefore, slaves numbered 12 per household (as opposed to 8 in 1720), and since 21 residences in the parish included no slaves at all, there were an average of 15 Negroes on each of the remaining 87 tracts. However, they were by no means evenly distributed, as Tables VI and VII show, and a slave born in St. George's Parish or brought there to work was far more likely to dwell on a large plantation than on a small one. There were 40 tracts with from 1 to 5 slaves and a total of 90 holdings which contained fewer than 20 slaves, but only one third of the unfree population worked on these lands. Two thirds of the slaves resided on only 18 plantations in groups ranging in size from 25 to 94, and more than 20 per cent were located on the largest three of these.

The contrasting distribution of Africans and Europeans is seen more clearly in Table VII which sorts out households according to their combined total of free and unfree persons. There were fewer than 10 people in half the units (column A) and here whites outnumbered slaves by five to two. But in the other half (columns B through F), which contained five sixths of the total population, slaves outnumbered whites by nearly four to one. On the seven plantations listed by Varnod as having over 50 residents (two of which were run by women), there were more than 13 slaves for every white person.

As Table VIII indicates, the ratio between the sexes among the adult slaves (129 men to 100 women) was almost exactly the same as the ratio among their white owners (128 to 100). But this similarity is deceptive in considering family patterns, for slave distribution was extremely arbitrary and was dictated by white economic considera-

---

[80] See Table II and note 55 above.

TABLE VI   Distribution of Slaves per Household

Number of slaves per household	0	1	2	3	4	5	6	7	8	9	10	
Number of households	21	13	4	12	8	3	4	1	3	2	3	
Number of slaves	0	13	8	36	32	15	24	7	24	18	30	
% of total slave pop.				8.0					7.9			

Number of slaves per household	0–24
Number of households	90
Number of slaves	435
% of total slave pop.	33.4

tions. Although in half of the white homes adults were balanced by sex, less than one sixth of the adjacent slave quarters had an equal number of men and women. Fifteen slave men and 6 women belonged to Lilia Hague; 18 men and 8 women lived on the Warring plantation; 6 men and 13 women were bound to John Baker's estate. Negro women outnumbered men on 31 per cent of the slaveholding estates while females predominated in only 13 per cent of the white households, but more often Negro men were in a majority. Not surprisingly, this was especially true on the largest plantations. Two hundred men labored on the seven biggest tracts, where the ratio was 155 men to 100 women. As plantation agriculture expanded and intensified, masters increasingly sought and obtained shipments of slaves which were nearly two thirds men. As a result, while the sex ratio for Europeans grew more balanced, that for Africans was becoming more disproportionate. The sample of slaves taken from inventories in 1730 and 1731 shows that by that time the ratio of slave men to women on sizable plantations throughout the colony was 180 to 100.[81]

[81] See note 71 above.

eorge's Parish, South Carolina, 1726

11	12	13	14	15	16	17	18	19	20	21	22	23	24
2	2	2	6	0	1	0	1	2	0	0	0	0	0
22	24	26	84	0	16	0	18	38	0	0	0	0	0
		12							5.5				

25–49	50–74	75–99	Totals
11	4	3	108
371	232	262	1,300
28.5	17.9	20.2	100

Although the slave population was undoubtedly young as a whole, the St. George's census shows a low percentage of Negro children. While only half of the white inhabitants were listed as fully grown, nearly two thirds of all slaves (66.2 per cent) were numbered as adults. Few explanations seem sufficient.[82] Undoubtedly slave imports, which concentrated upon young adults, raised the percentage of

[82] The difference might in some measure arise from (1) the economic double standard whereby full duty was paid on any African over ten, with young slaves assuming adult work loads before their white contemporaries, but it seems doubtful that Negro children were classed as adults much earlier than their white counterparts. (2) Since high rates of mortality and large numbers of children often fit together in demographic data, another source of the discrepancy between slave and white age distribution could be a continuation of the higher death rate among Europeans which had characterized the colony in the previous generation. (3) Conceivably the sale of slave children could have decreased their percentage somewhat, but since labor was clearly in demand in the parish it is unlikely that Negro children would have been sent elsewhere. (4) A few mulatto children born to slave mothers might have passed into the household of a white father (a dissenter named Bacon had no white women and one slave woman, no slave children and five free children, on his plantation), but miscegenation would have increased the numbers born into servitude.

TABLE VII　*Distribution of Slaves and Whites in Relatic*

	A	B
Number of slaves and whites in household	1–9	10–19
Number of households	54	31
% of total households	50	29
Number of people	305	449
% of total population	16.6	24.4
Number of slaves	86	277
% of all slaves	6.6	21.3
Number of whites	219	172
% of all whites	40.7	32
Ratio of slaves per one white	0.4/1	1.6/1
Ratio of slaves per five whites (average size of white household)	2/5	8/5

Details of the Seven Largest Househo

	WHITE PEOPLE	
	Men	*Women*
Walter Izard	2	1
John Williams	1	1
Alex Skeene, Esq.	3	2
Sus: Baker D[issenter]	3	3
Eliz. Diston D[issenter]	2	1
Sam Wragg Plant[ation]	1	–
Jos: Blake	1	1
	13	9

grown-ups somewhat, but by the same token they introduced numerous women of childbearing age. It would therefore seem that the birthrate itself among potential Negro mothers was lower in 1726 than it had been earlier, for there was an average of only 1.17 children for each slave woman in the parish, scarcely half the average (2.24) of the free population.

al Household Size, St. George's Parish, South Carolina, 1726

C 20–29	D 30–39	E 40–49	F 50–99	G Totals
6	5	5	7	108
6	4.5	4.5	6	100
146	185	220	532	1,837
8.0	10	12	29	100
100	147	196	494	1,300
7.7	11.3	15.1	38	100
46	38	24	38	537
8.6	7.1	4.5	7.1	100
2.2/1	4/1	8.2/1	13.4/1	2.4/1
11/5	20/5	41/5	67/5	12/5

olumn F above) as Listed in Varnod's Census

Children		SLAVES	
	Men	Women	Children
4	29	23	39
1	48	24	22
1	27	18	32
5	26	17	18
2	19	18	24
–	35	12	10
3	16	17	20
16	200	129	165

No single argument explains the high proportion of adults and the associated low birthrate. They are best understood in terms of the general worsening of black living conditions associated with the intensification of staple agriculture. This process would never result in quite the degree of malnutrition, overwork, abortion, and infant mortality which prevented slave populations in the Caribbean from sus-

TABLE VIII *Distribution of Slaves and White*

	MEN	WOMEN	CHILDREN	TOTAL
Slaves	484	376	440	1,300
Whites	152	119	266	537
Combined	636	495	706	1,837

taining themselves. But already in the 1720s and 1730s the arbitrary grouping of slaves to create and maintain plantations in the wilderness had adverse effects upon Negro family life. Men and women were thrown together in increasingly random proportions on increasingly large holdings as the period progressed. And far from giving license to any innate promiscuity imagined by white masters, such conditions apparently served more to frustrate desires for enduring intimacy and reduce the likelihood of procreation.

This reduced rate of natural growth is easily overlooked in view of the considerable net increases in the black population. The slaves listed by Varnod generated enough profits for their owners so that hundreds of new Negroes were brought into the parish every year. When Varnod's successor, the Rev. Stephen Roe, filed a parochial report in 1741, the number of slaves owned in St. George's had risen to roughly 3,300, an increase of more than 250 percent in fifteen years.[83] According to Roe's report, there were by this time "Few or no wandering Indians," and what was more striking, the white population had actually diminished to 468 persons in 139 households. Errors on the minister's part or sickness among his parishioners could account for this decline in slight measure, but emigration was undoubtedly the

[83] Klingberg, *Appraisal*, p. 87. Roe stated that the 468 white inhabitants owned 3,347 slaves, but he listed the number of heathens and infidels as 3,287. Two things contribute to this discrepancy. One is the fact that certain Negroes were counted as Christians (roughly 85 professed to be of the Church of England and 15 were communicants); the other is the fact that some slaves were "settled at Remote Plant[ati]ons out of ye Parish."

x and Age, St. George's Parish, South Carolina, 1726

% OF TOTAL POP.	CHILDREN PER WOMAN	MEN PER 100 WOMEN	% OF ADULTS
70.8	1.17/1	129/100	66.2
29.2	2.24/1	128/100	50.5
100	1.43/1	128/100	61.6

primary factor.[84] As a result of these shifts in the population, the average number of slaves per household in St. George's Parish in 1741 was three times higher (24) than it had been twenty years before. Moreover, in the two decades after 1720 this parish near the geographic center of the colony had altered from a situation where scarcely 60 per cent of its inhabitants were unfree to a point where nearly 90 per cent were enslaved.

These demographic changes were being repeated in varying degrees in each of the other lowland parishes. Everywhere during the period between the beginning of royal government in 1720 and the imposition of the slave embargo in 1741 plantation agriculture expanded and intensified. For the Negroes, directly involved in the grueling process of rice production, the birthrate declined and the mortality rate (and runaway rate) may have increased. As natural population growth slackened, the importation of new slaves intensified greatly, with the net result that the number of Africans rose more rapidly than the number of Europeans.

"If a great number of negroes could have made South Carolina secure," wrote Benjamin Martyn in 1741, the English colony would have had little to fear, "for she is computed to have at least forty thousand blacks." But the presence of so many African slaves offered little in the way of security to Europeans whose adult males numbered "not above five thousand; and these . . . at too great a distance from one

[84] As lowland holdings were enlarged during the 1740s there is evidence that the number of households in St. George's decreased. After 1750 a further number of white residents would take their slaves and move to Georgia.

another for the public safety." On the contrary, said Martyn, repeating a generalization which was common among whites at this time,

The greater number of blacks, which a frontier has, and the greater the disproportion is between them and her white people, the more danger she is liable to; for those are all secret enemies, and ready to join with her open ones on the first occasion. So far from putting any confidence in them, her first step must be to secure herself against them.[85]

It is not surprising, therefore, since the early eighteenth century in South Carolina was characterized demographically by the emergence of a clear-cut black majority, that the third generation of the colony's settlement witnessed increasing social anxieties and mounting racial tensions.

[85] [Benjamin Martyn], *An Impartial Inquiry into the State and Utility of the Colony of Georgia* (London, 1741), rpt. in Ga. Hist. Soc., *Collections*, I (1840), 167.

Gullah Speech:
The Roots of Black English

I

DEMOGRAPHIC surveys, such as those by ministers and officials cited in Chapter V, serve to underscore the full numerical presence of people whom white colonial society consistently slighted. (The portion of the Constitution proclaiming an enslaved person equal to three fifths of a free person represented more than a legislative compromise; it rested on generations of ambiguous reasoning among English colonists, in South Carolina and elsewhere, about the presence of a non-European labor force.) Through demography African men and women assume equal weight with the merchants who imported them and the planters who purchased them. Demographic analysis, however, cannot in itself convey the actual life experience of these enslaved immigrants, for it remains outside, rather than inside, the heads that are being counted. In fact to speak of involuntary servants as "immigrants" (which implies a vivid life experience) has itself become plausible only recently, even though Negroes constitute one of the earliest and most distinctive ethnic groups to enter North America.[1] There are numerous contrasts between the experience of an

[1] One ironic explanation for this lies in the fact that the Afro-American had, as C. Vann Woodward points out, "completed his immigration before the word 'immigrant' came into use." But Woodward goes on to point out a deeper reason for the omission of the Negro: "He has never been accorded the status of immigrant either by official census or by the historiography of American immigration. To have done so would have been to acknowledge him as a candidate for graduation from that status—to make him potentially assimilable, and that he has been denied." C. Vann Woodward, *American Counterpoint: Slavery and Racism in the North-South Dialogue* (New York, 1971), p. 5. Negro immigrants in the national period have been given some consideration, as in Ira DeA. Reid, *The Negro Immigrant: His Background, Characteristics and Social Adjustment, 1899–1937* (New York, 1939). But it is interesting that even so

African reaching Charlestown in the eighteenth century and that of a European entering New York or an Asian entering San Francisco in later times, but there are also unexamined similarities.[2] Among the experiences shared by most immigrants to America (whatever their legal status, date of arrival, genetic makeup, or continent of origin), none was more universally significant than the acquisition of a common language. This chapter, therefore, explores the distinctive manner in which the first three generations of slaves entering the Carolina lowlands responded to the challenge of mastering the foreign language of English.

Inevitably, personal accounts of first-generation Africans in South Carolina are rare compared to testimony concerning Europeans arriving at Ellis Island more recently. But suggestive glimpses can still be found in the recorded reminiscences of aged ex-slaves. Two such interviews, which were transcribed in the 1930s, give special attention to the factor of language. A resident of Union, South Carolina, named Richard Jones, when well over one hundred years old, recalled the stories of his African grandmother, who had herself lived more than a century and must have endured the middle passage in the late eighteenth century:

Uncle Tom come along with Granny Judith. Two womenfolks come with dem, Aunt Chany and Daphne. Aunt Chany and Aunt Daphne was bought by de Frees dat had a plantation near Jonesville. Uncle Tom and Granny was bought by Marse Jim Gist, but deir marsters always allowed dem to visit on July Fourth and Christmas. When dey talk, nobody didn't know what dey was talking about. My granny never could speak good like I can. She talk half African, and all African when she got bothered. I can't talk no African.[3]

---

impressive a volume as Oscar Handlin's *The Uprooted* (Boston, 1951), although subtitled "The Epic Story of the Great Migrations That Made the American People," dismissed newcomers from Africa in a single line (p. 5).

[2] For a statement on the importance of comparing Negro migrations (to and within this country) with the migration experiences of other Americans, see Stephan Thernstrom, "Up From Slavery," *Perspectives,* I (1967), 434–39.

[3] Norman R. Yetman, *Life Under the "Peculiar Institution": Selections from the Slave Narrative Collection* (New York, 1970), p. 192. Parrish, *Slave Songs,* p. 45, prints the reminiscence of a slave born in Liberty County, Ga., who recalled the African songs of Dublin Scribben, a Negro on the neighboring plantation: "Ole man Dublin he belong' to de Andersons o' Sunbury an' every day or two Miss Bertha would sen' me ober fo' him—to talk de ole African talk. I heered him, but I was too small to remember what he said, but I remember de songs, 'cause I always p'int it on my mind about de t'ing." (Recollection of African words and phrases spoken by elders on the porch of his boyhood home would prompt the writer, Alex Haley, to undertake the unique genealogical odyssey described in his forthcoming volume, *Roots.*)

A few black Carolinians living in the 1930s, like Charley Barber of Winnsboro, were themselves first-generation Americans, the children of slaves imported illegally during the nineteenth century. Barber recalled of his parents, "They both come from Africa where they was born. They was 'ticed on a ship, fetch 'cross de ocean to Virginny, fetch to Winnsboro by a slave drover, and sold to my marster's father. Dat what they tell me." With a mixture of pride and embarrassment typical for a first-generation American son, he related that "They never did talk lak de other slaves, could just say a few words, use deir hands, and make signs. They want deir collards, turnips, and deir 'tators, raw. They lak sweet milk so much they steal it."[4]

Add to these accounts the testimony of Olaudah Equiano, an Ibo from the region of Benin who was brought to the New World aboard a British slaver in 1756 and survived to obtain his freedom and write a dramatic and picaresque autobiography. Equiano recalled the relief he had felt when, stopping in Barbados on the passage to America, "there came to us Africans of all languages." But within weeks he found himself isolated from all his shipmates on a mainland plantation, weeding grass and gathering stones with older slaves. "I was now exceedingly miserable, and thought myself worse off than any of the rest of my companions, for they could talk to each other, but I had no person to speak to that I could understand. In this state," he continued, "I was constantly grieving and pining, and wishing for death rather than anything else."[5]

Charlestown (a port with which Equiano himself became familiar) was rivaling the older cities of New York and Boston as North America's Babel even during the proprietary era, and in the decades after 1720 it became more linguistically diversified than any other spot in the mainland colonies. The sources of the seaport's population stretched from Scotland to Mozambique, and the newcomers entering the colony there were as varied in speech as in appearance. To the related languages of western Europe were added a larger number of

[4] *Slave Narratives: A Folk History of Slavery in the United States from Interviews with Former Slaves,* 17 vols. of typewritten records prepared by the Federal Writer's Project, 1936, 1938, assembled by Library of Congress (Washington, 1941), XIV, part 1, 30. See also *ibid.,* II, part 7, 20; XVI, part 1, 14; XVI, part 4, 78. These items are cited by Bobby Frank Jones, "A Cultural Middle Passage: Slave Marriage and Family in the Ante-Bellum South," unpublished Ph.D. dissertation (University of North Carolina, 1965), p. 134.

[5] "Life of Equiano," pp. 32, 34; cf. p. 35.

distinctive tongues and dialects from the language families of West Africa. Negroes who had grown up in Barbados, like Caucasians raised in Ireland, spoke comprehensible English (with distinctive accents) upon arrival, but with people coming directly from Africa, as with settlers from continental Europe, there was little knowledge of the colony's official tongue. They must therefore have experienced all the confusion and loneliness shared by legions of non-English-speaking immigrants in the national period. They strained to hear familiar words or accents; they struggled to repeat the meaningless phrases shouted at them; they lapsed often into disconsolate silence.

The trauma of verbal isolation may well have outweighed, or at least intensified, the shocks of legal enslavement at first, and the struggle to renew and broaden communication began immediately. In large measure this involved an effort to learn English, and in South Carolina, as in all the other provinces, individuals could be found at every stage of this task.[6] On the other hand, demographic conditions encouraged a somewhat easier retention of African elements of speech than was possible in any other mainland colony, for nowhere else did Afro-Americans constitute so large a proportion of the population in so limited a space. From these opposite tendencies—the acquisition of English and the retention of African tongues—there developed a dialect which evolved gradually into the distinctive form of English known as Gullah.

Negro speech in the Sea Island area has long been a source of fascination and speculation among whites. Generations ago writers of fiction began imitating local speech patterns in the region. "The Gold Bug," by Edgar Allan Poe, for example, is set on Sullivan's Island and includes a believable Gullah speaker named Jupiter. Before 1900 folk-lorists, and later anthropologists, had begun to transcribe and analyze this speech, so that over the years an unusual and copious body of literature has evolved around the Gullah language of coastal South Carolina (along with the roughly synonymous "Geechee" dialect of the Georgia Sea Islands). As a result of considerable study and controversy, much has gradually been learned about the structure of Gullah and about its relation to other creole dialects of "Atlantic English" on

---

[6] This is the basic observation which Allen W. Read drew from a brief survey of ads for runaways, "The Speech of Negroes in Colonial America," *JNH*, XXIV (1939), 247–58.

the one hand and to the broader North American phenomenon of "black English" on the other.[7]

Yet the exact historical origins of this English dialect, which was once very nearly a separate language, have still not been adequately explored. Anthropologists and linguists dealing chiefly in present-day "survivals," dependent upon live informants and wary of archival sources, have been in a poor position to reach back across several centuries of time, and partly for this reason a series of ahistorical notions has prevailed for decades.[8] In listening to twentieth-century Gullah speech, scholars have heard only a faint echo of a previously stronger dialect, as they themselves concede.[9] There is room, therefore, for historical evidence to be marshaled briefly in the hope of adding to a fuller picture of Gullah's historical roots. At the same time, such a consideration should also contribute to a clearer awareness of the concrete immigration experience of slaves in colonial South Carolina.

[7] I have omitted a lengthy summary of what is now understood about Gullah on the assumption that detailed analysis will be clearer and more authoritative if taken directly from the linguistic sources. The most important monograph is still Lorenzo D. Turner, *Africanisms in the Gullah Dialect* (Chicago, 1949), but general introductions to these matters are becoming more numerous. See, for example, Ivan Vansertima, "African Linguistic and Mythological Structures in the New World," in Rhoda Goldstein, ed., *Black Life and Culture in the United States* (New York, 1971), pp. 12–35. The most important recent addition is J. L. Dillard, *Black English* (New York, 1972), which contains a useful bibliography.

[8] Some of these notions are described in Wood, "Black Majority," Appendix D. The situation has begun to change, as can be seen from the articles of William A. Stewart, such as "Sociolinguistic Factors in the History of American Negro Dialects," in V. P. Clark, P. A. Eschholtz, A. F. Rosa, eds., *Language: Introductory Readings* (New York, 1972). Dillard's *Black English* is a significant departure in this regard. Regrettably, however, in the process of emphasizing the broad distribution of a Negro dialect from early times, he mistakenly goes out of his way to diminish the linguistic importance of the Sea Island region, where black English had its most formative development among the most highly concentrated group of Afro-Americans during the colonial era.

[9] Cf. Robert A. Hall, Jr., *Pidgin and Creole Languages* (Ithaca, N.Y., 1965), p. 15:

In the southeastern part of the United States, the original English of the Negro slaves seems to have been a creolized variety, going back to a pidgin of which we have no record. This American Negro Creole English began quite early to take over more and more features of standard speech—and hence to disappear through assimilation. . . . By now, most American Negro speech has lost virtually all of these characteristics, which have come to be regarded as badges of inferiority; but markedly aberrant Negro creoles are still spoken in the coastal region around Charleston and Savannah.

II

THE INITIAL ENCOUNTER with English by Negroes reaching Carolina, the intermixture of various European and African languages, and the continuous stimulation for linguistic change through intensive importation of blacks were all steady features of colonial life which disappeared after 1800. Lydia Parrish, an expert on black folk music in the Sea Islands, surmised that most secular songs had evolved to their standard forms by roughly 1760, and were no doubt more conspicuous then than after such music had been largely silenced or transformed by Baptist and Methodist missionaries in the 1800s.[10] "If we knew the period in which certain groups of slaves came to America, and the section of Africa from which they were obtained," wrote Parrish, "we might learn more about their musical background."[11] With respect to speech, as with respect to music, further awareness of the origins of this stream of black immigrants and of their separate cultural contributions still lies ahead.[12] But it is already possible to offer a brief his-

[10] Parrish, *Slave Songs*, pp. 5, 238. In Fisher, *Negro Slave Songs*, p. 13, it is noted that "The great majority of the original texts of slave songs are not available, for the earliest language which Negroes used was the African, and only a few African songs have been preserved."

[11] Parrish, *Slave Songs*, p. 164 n. Parrish noted a similarity between the intonations and rhythms used in the ring-shouts of the Sea Islands (Negro circle dances unknown elsewhere on the continent) and those used in dances recorded in the Congo area, which led her to speculate that "the slaves of South Carolina and Georgia might have come from that region." This observation is particularly interesting in light of the apparent preponderance of slaves brought from the Congo–Angola region during some of the formative years before 1740. See Appendix C.

[12] Cassidy, *Jamaica Talk*, p. 17, remarks on a relationship between the types of Africanisms most prevalent in Jamaican Creole and the dominant slave nationalities present "at the time when the basis of Jamaican folk speech was laid." In his article, "Some New Light on Old Jamaicanisms," *American Speech*, XLII (1967), 191–92, Cassidy has pointed out, among other examples, that the Doulla-Bakweri language of the Cameroon River area provided the Jamaican creole word for the crayfish or river prawn. ("This part of Africa, indeed, took its name from the plentiful shrimps or prawns in the river: Cameroon is from Portuguese *camarão* 'shrimp.'")

Similar sorts of analysis are less advanced in South Carolina. The etymology of the term "Gullah" itself remains in some doubt. It could represent an abbreviated form of Angola, which would fit with the import data cited in the previous note. But it could also derive from the Gola tribe of the Windward Coast, which would relate to expressed preferences for slaves from that rice-growing region. The most likely answer is that both sources contributed to the word, and that it has a multiple etymology of the sort cited in note 51 below.

torical interpretation of how Africans confronted and "pidginized" the English language in South Carolina within the first century of settlement.

"Pidgin" is a term applied to any speech evolved from several languages and used by speakers for whom it is not the primary tongue. "In connection with the slave-trade in the late seventeenth and eighteenth centuries," points out Robert A. Hall, there grew up a "kind of pidginized English on both sides of the Central Atlantic—in West Africa on the east, and in the Caribbean area and what is now the south-eastern part of the United States." This Central Atlantic Pidgin English has continued as a pidgin (or secondary) speech in parts of West Africa and still survives in creolized forms (that is, as a primary language) in the Caribbean regions.[13]

The pidginizing process began around the slave baracoons of the West African coast. There, captured blacks from separate regions were forced to blend their distinctive languages as best they could while awaiting deportation to the New World.[14] There too, at the ports frequented by British traders, slaves first heard a pidgin English being used by the Africans who were selling them, as well as by the sailors who would carry them away. A knowledge of this tongue was at a premium around coastal factories. William Chancellor, aboard a slaving vessel off the Gold Coast in 1750, recorded in his journal that "As soon as you arrive at Annamaboo, you will have negroes come off to you to desire you to take their Sons on board, to learn them English, which they generally do, & keep them in the cabbin to wait on you." He added that "neither is there any thing, the negroes so much esteem as a negro who talks English." The following week Chancellor noted that in selling slaves local trading men, "that is those that talk English," were regularly able to withhold considerable profits from the provincial slave catchers "that live in the bush or Country, and are ignorant not only of trade, but English."[15] In certain regions other European languages left traces in this trading language. An interesting example, probably drawn from Portuguese Angola, is the survival in

[13] Hall, *Pidgin and Creole Languages*, p. 9; cf. p. 25. See also Dell Hymes, ed., *Pidginization and Creolization of Languages* (Cambridge, England, 1971).

[14] Dillard, *Black English*, pp. 6, 74, 76, 140. Cf. Samuel G. Stoney and Gertrude M. Shelby, *Black Genesis* (New York, 1930), p. xi; Basil Davidson, *Black Mother: The Years of the African Slave Trade* (Boston, 1961), p. 218.

[15] Darold D. Wax, "A Philadelphia Surgeon on a Slaving Voyage to Africa, 1749–1751," *Pa. Mag. of Hist. and Biography*, XCII (1968), 476, 478.

Gullah (as in Jamaican Creole) of the term "crawl" for pen, deriving from the Dutch and Portuguese word *kraal*.[16] (Our word "corral" may derive as much from this source as from the regularly cited Spanish root, *corro*, meaning "ring.") Another term derived from the language of Iberian slave traders was "pickaninny," after the Portuguese or similar Spanish phrase, *piqueño-nino*, meaning "very little one."[17]

For Africans being forced into enslavement, further linguistic interaction took place in the course of the middle passage itself. It has recently been suggested that Wolof speakers from Senegambia, being located closer to Europe and North America than other blacks, "were frequently employed as interpreters or mariners during early European voyages along the African coast," and in this way they transferred Wolof names for African foodstuffs such as *yams* and *bananas* into European vocabularies.[18] As the slave trade grew, black linguists became common fixtures aboard English vessels, where they translated orders and conveyed information. A mate aboard the snow *Rainbow*, which carried slaves from Benin to St. Thomas in 1758, testified before the Vice Admiralty Court at Charlestown that "Captn Harrison at Benin, hired One Dick, a free Negro Man as a Linguist between him and the Slaves to proceed on the said Voyage." It was acknowledged under oath "that his being onboard the Said Snow was of great Consequence to the Interest of the Voyage."[19]

Every British West Indian island provided conditions in which a form of Central Atlantic Pidgin English could prosper. In the late seventeenth and early eighteenth century slaves transferred from the

[16] Memoirs of D. E. Huger Smith, in Alice R. Huger Smith, *Carolina Rice Plantation*, p. 68:

> The cow-minder resided at the "hog crawl." . . . The name seems to have come from "Kraal," a Dutch-Portuguese-African word for a cattle-pen. It has no affinity to the English word meaning "to creep," even though it has borrowed that spelling. The word was in very general use in the first days of Carolina, almost interchanging with "cattle-pen," which meant a range for cattle, the raising of which was an early occupation of the colony.

[17] Although the *Dictionary of American English* does not record usage of this term in the U.S. before 1800, the word appears in an S.C. inventory as early as 1682. See Appendix B. Cf. Dillard, *Black English*, pp. 19–20, 77, 135, 154–55. The word was in use in Barbados by 1653.

[18] David Dalby, "Americanisms that may once have been Africanisms," London *Times*, July 19, 1969.

[19] Deposition of John Dawson, June 22, 1758, The King v. Joseph Harrison, Admiralty Court Records, mfm, reel 3, pp. 45–52, SCDAH. The court case arose from the fact that when English sailors told Dick he would be sold as a slave, the linguist raged and sulked so bitterly that the captain decided to let him take physical revenge on several crewmen.

Caribbean to the new colony of South Carolina must have brought along an English dialect with considerable African ingredients. Mainland settlers would occasionally comment upon a slave who "was either born or lived in the West-Indies by which he has acquired their peculiar Way of speaking."[20]

Ironically, the first generation of slaves in South Carolina may have spoken a more standard English than those who followed them. They constituted a minority of the colony's small population, and almost none had come directly from Africa as yet. Moreover, they lived and worked on intimate terms with their English-speaking masters in the early years. Consequently, unlike their more numerous and isolated contemporaries in Jamaica, slaves in pre-plantation South Carolina acquired a considerable amount of common English which would underlie the black dialect of later generations.[21] The first Anglican missionary in the colony estimated in 1706 that roughly four out of five slaves could "speak English tollerably well."[22] By 1722, however, the minister of Christ Church was notably more cautious, reporting that his parish contained "about 700 slaves, some of which understand the English tongue."[23]

III

ACCORDING TO the Rev. Thomas Hasell in St. Thomas Parish, "the Negroes born and brought up in South Carolina, were civilized and spoke English as well as himself, whereas those newly brought from

---

[20] *Virginia Gazette*, Aug. 14, 1752. (This particular notice concerned a slave named Jasper who ran away after being taken to Virginia from New York and who was thought to have committed suicide.)

[21] Cassidy, *Jamaica Talk*, p. 19. The lot of the small number of slaves who reached the mainland colonies in the seventeenth century had an important bearing on the nature of Afro-American culture in this country. Whatever their theoretical status, in practice it was difficult to separate African slaves from English servants on the early settlements, and this *de facto* integration reduced the base upon which African survivals could rest, not simply in speech, but other elements of culture. Richard M. Dorson points out in *American Folklore* (Chicago, 1959), p. 185, that the African folk tales of Anansi, the spider, which are frequent in the West Indies, are rare in the South.

[22] The Rev. Samuel Thomas, *SCHGM*, V (1904), 42. "Tollerably well" may be synonymous with "at all," for in his own parish of Goose Creek Thomas conceded (p. 32) that of two hundred slaves only twenty "come constantly to church, and these and several others of them well understand the English tongue and can read."

[23] The Rev. Benjamin Pownall, quoted in Crum, *Gullah*, p. 175.

their own country seldom attained good command of English."[24] Such an observation, although made in 1713, was to gain in significance as slave imports grew to more than one thousand per year before the end of the next decade. Blacks increased in proportion to whites; foreign-born Negroes increased in proportion to native-born; slaves arriving directly from Africa increased in proportion to those who had spent time in the West Indies. It is not surprising, therefore, that the Charlestown newspaper (which began in the 1730s) carried ads for numerous runaways who spoke "little," "bad," or "broken" English, or sometimes none at all.[25]

For blacks as for whites, fluency in English would always remain too complex a variable to correlate directly with time spent in America. The age, temperament, and immediate surroundings of each immigrant were important factors.[26] Some slaves, such as a sawyer named Topsham who left his job in 1734, spoke "very good English" after only several years in the province,[27] while others never learned. Rev. Le Jau withheld baptism from an exemplary slave near Goose Creek because "after having been above 20 Years in this Province . . . he can hardly Speak, even Comon things, so as to be understood & Consequently cannot make such a formal Confession of faith as is Comonly requisite."[28]

To complicate matters, English was not always the first Euro-

24 The Rev. Thomas Hasell, March 12, 1713, quoted in Klingberg, *Appraisal*, p. 31. Almost twenty years later Hasell tried to require all the Negro adults in the parish who could understand English to attend religious service. *Ibid.*, p. 32.

25 For examples, see *SCG*, Nov. 4, 1732; Feb. 15, 1735; Jan. 22, 1737; Nov. 5, 1737; Feb. 2, 1740; Oct. 3, 1743. (Whites as well as blacks fell into these categories; Alexander Vander Dussen advertised in the *SCG*, June 4, 1741, for two runaways: "one an Irish Man, . . . had a great Brogue in his Speech: The other is a Palatine, spoke little or no English, . . . had on a long Negro Cloth Gown.")

26 John W. Blassingame, *The Slave Community, Plantation Life in the Antebellum South* (New York, 1972), pp. 22–23. Arna Bontemps, *Great Slave Narratives* (Boston, 1969), p. xii, gives the following account of the well-known slave Phillis Wheatley, who was kidnaped in Senegal and transported to Boston in 1761 at the age of seven:

Within sixteen months after her arrival, according to her owner, Phillis "attained the English Language," as he said, "to such a degree as to read the most difficult parts of the sacred Writings, to the great astonishment of all who heard her." Books were placed at her disposal in the home of the Wheatleys, and within six years after her kidnaping, when she was no more than fourteen, she wrote an attractive poem addressed "To the University of Cambridge, in New England."

27 *SCG*, June 22, 1734. (An ad in the next column concerned an Irish indentured servant who spoke three languages with a brogue.)

28 *Le Jau*, March 12, 1715, p. 150.

pean language which Africans encountered. South Carolina documents written in French attest that numerous slaves were purchased
by Huguenots in the early eighteenth century, and it is safe to assume
that most acquired a working knowledge of their masters' language.[29]
(Among the men on Philip Gendron's estate in 1724 were *Latronche,*
a cooper, *Esperance,* a shoemaker, *Pierot* and *Francois.*[30]) In the Huguenot settlement along the Santee on the northern edge of the province, French must have remained the means of communication on
some plantations for several generations. Just prior to the Revolution
the jailer in King and Queen County, Virginia, noted the presence of
a mulatto runaway from South Carolina named Louis Patterson, who
had been living there twelve years, and who spoke French but only
broken English.[31]

Other South Carolina slaves had experienced Portuguese or
Spanish as their first European language. The Anglican minister at
Goose Creek reported in 1710, "I have in this parish a few Negroe
Slaves . . . born and baptised among the Portuguese."[32] And an account drawn up in 1739 declared: "Amongst the Negroe Slaves there
are a people brought from the Kingdom of Angola in Africa, many of
these speak Portugueze."[33] During this same period "Spanish Negroes"
were mentioned among the runaways in the *Gazette,* and if they did
not head for Spanish Florida they were sometimes suspected of seeking out plantations where other Spanish-speaking slaves were most
numerous.[34]

With such diverse exposure, a few slaves became considerable
linguists in European tongues. In 1740 the printer Elizabeth Timothy
offered a reward for her own slave ("a Negro Fellow named Pierro,
but commonly stiles himself PETER") who she claimed "speaks
good English, French and Dutch." Several runaways who disappeared
from Purrysburg fifteen years later "spoke English, French, Spanish,

[29] RSP (1675–95), p. 282; *ibid.* (1712–13), p. 47; *ibid.* (1719–21), p. 24.

[30] WIMR (1722–26), pp. 443–45.

[31] *Virginia Gazette,* Sept. 1, 1774, "Supplement." Twenty years later a mulatto
runaway in the same region named Joe Cully was known "to pass a Frenchman and
alter his tongue to a broken language," a device which made him "very perceivable to
any one that would converse with him." *Virginia Herald and Fredericksburg Advertiser,*
Sept. 18, 1794.

[32] *Le Jau,* p. 69; cf. p. 102.

[33] "An account of the Negroe Insurrection in South Carolina," CRSG, XXII, part
2, 233.

[34] See SCG, Sept. 17, 1737.

and German."[35] Usually, however, slaves who learned French or German from their master had little hope of conversing with black neighbors who were acquiring English, and while this must have been a stimulus to learn English as a common tongue it would also have been an inducement to return to African forms of speech wherever possible.

IV

OF THE AFRICAN LANGUAGES which slaves brought with them, Arabic was undoubtedly the most international. The Rev. Le Jau, anxious to begin proselytizing Indians in 1706, reported word of a "transcendent Language of America, spoke every where thro' the Continent as Latin was formerly in Europe and Arabick is still in Affrica." An Englishman living among the Fula in Gambia slightly later reported, "they are much like the Arabs, whose language is taught in their schools." He added that "they are generally more skilled in Arabic than the Europeans in the Latin; for most of them speak it, though they have a vulgar tongue of their own, called Fuli."[36] As with Latin in medieval Europe, however, a knowledge of Arabic in West Africa was most common among the best educated, wealthiest, or most devout segments of the population. When such people found themselves enslaved, they were likely to establish the clearest contact with other Africans through more local tongues. The celebrated Job Ben Solomon, who engineered his return from Maryland to Gambia in 1731 through his knowledge of written Arabic, first explained himself to a slave in the Chesapeake colony by speaking Wolof.[37]

Instances of slaves familiar with Arabic must have occurred in the Carolina region from the beginning and can be documented for a somewhat later period. Omar ibn Seid, a Fula born in Africa before 1775 and trained in Arabic, was transported to Charlestown after the American Revolution. He was an elderly slave living in North Carolina at the time of Nat Turner's Rebellion.[38] A similar individual alive in

[35] *SCG*, June 14, 1740; June 26, 1755.

[36] *Le Jau*, p. 19, letter of Dec. 2, 1706; Francis Moore, c. 1730, quoted in Parrish, *Slave Songs*, p. 28.

[37] Grant, *Fortunate Slave*, p. 84.

[38] "Autobiography of Omar ibn Seid, Slave in North Carolina, 1831," *AHR*, XXX (1925), 791–95. (While examining a collection in the SCL of an eighteenth-century Carolina tavern keeper, I uncovered a remarkable scrap of paper from Africa concerning the return of a woman slave, *signed in Arabic*.)

the nineteenth century was Bilali, an African slave on a plantation near Savannah. He had been born near Timboo in the Kingdom of Bambara and educated in Arabic writing and the Muslim faith. He always wore a cap resembling a Turkish fez, prayed to Allah three times each day and was buried with his Koran and praying sheepskin. A slave on a neighboring plantation was also from Bambara, having been born in Kianah on the Niger River between Jenne and Timbuctoo. When he and Bilali conversed they used the Fula language. Bilali's children spoke French, English, and Fula and continued to practice the Mohammedan faith.[39]

Familiarity with Arabic could never have been common enough among newcomers in the region to assist communication, and yet the comparative ease with which slaves in South Carolina could locate other speakers of their own or similar African languages is worth emphasizing. Throughout most of the eighteenth century, the colony had a higher density of blacks and a lower percentage of whites than any other part of the North American mainland. Most of the populace was confined to the coastal lowlands, and the arrival of new slaves from stated African ports was well publicized. Some newcomers wore their hair or clothing in traditional styles; others bore the distinguishing scarification of a particular nationality. Most white colonists would have marveled at the ignorance of their descendants, who asserted blindly that all Africans looked the same.[40] The slaves themselves were

[39] Parrish, *Slave Songs*, pp. 26–28. See also Joseph H. Greenberg, "The Decipherment of the 'Ben-Ali Diary,' A Preliminary Statement," *JNH* (1940), 372–75.

[40] Slaveowners advertising in the *SCG* for their runaways often mentioned place of origin (along with such things as age, stature, scarification, clothes, and language ability) so that the Negroes might be easily recognized. There are examples of uncertainties on this point: "Basey is a short well set Fellow of a tawny Complexion, speaks broken English, and is either an Eboe or Calebar Negro." (*SCG*, Feb. 2, 1740.) But masters were generally familiar with these terms, and occasionally used them in sale and rental ads as well, to inform purchasers about the nature of the slave.

Distinctions made by purchasers of Africans in the eighteenth century bear a striking resemblance to attitudes characteristic of the employers of cheap European and Asian labor within the last hundred years. The stereotypes applied to Gambians, Ibos, Coromantees, and Angolans were not different in kind from those later applied to Irish, Chinese, Jews, Slavs, and Italians. Racial, cultural, and religious distinctions were mixed; shrewd analysis and sensible lore became intermingled with shifting social and personal prejudices. Word of a shipboard rebellion in Benin or of several Ibo suicides in Carolina could do a great deal to shape labor demands. The influential slave merchant Henry Laurens once wrote to his agent to send "fine, healthy, young Negro lads & Men, if such [are available] of any Country except Ebo." *SCHGM*, XXVII (1926), 211. At another time he stated his desire for slaves from "Gambia & Windward coast [rice regions] . . . or the Angola Men such as are large." *Laurens*, I, 258.

more aware of regional distinctions, and newcomers must sometimes
have been able to seek out by appearance Negroes who understood
their native tongue. Even where appearances did not suggest an immediate bond, spoken words sometimes proved surprisingly familiar.
In his autobiography, Equiano, describing his passage to the New
World, relates how he stood wide-eyed near the dock in Bridgetown,
Barbados, absorbing his first view of men on horseback. "While I was
in this astonishment, one of my fellow prisoners spoke to a country-
man of his, about the horses, who said they were the same kind they
had in their country. I understood them, though they were from a
distant part of Africa."[41]

Under such conditions, trial and error in communication often
revealed common elements of grammar or vocabulary. Thus almost
from their first arrival here, slaves were distinctly aware of interrela-
tions between African languages, yet whites remained oblivious to
these links. In fact, most planters put great stock in the assertion that
African language differences, occasionally reinforced by national an-
tipathies, served to divide the slaves among themselves.[42] It was an
article of faith among the English in late-seventeenth-century Barbados (from whom South Carolina's first generation of slaveholders
was largely derived) that "the whites have no greater security than
the diversity of the negroes' languages."[43] Few masters acknowledged
the fact that the accepted policy of mixing slaves from different backgrounds was itself an inducement to the evolution of a common pidgin.

[41] "Life of Equiano," p. 32. The thirty-six prisoners from the Windward Coast
region involved in the *Amistad* affair in the nineteenth century (Chapter II, note 94,
above) were perhaps the only slaves ever interviewed systematically upon reaching
America. The findings reflect the diversity of language background but also the inter-
connections: "Although a Bandi, he appears to have been able to talk in Mendi."
"Besides Mendi, he speaks Vai, Kon-no and Gissi." "He can count in Mendi, Timmani,
and Bullom." Barber, *Amistad Captives*, pp. 9–15.

[42] Cassidy, *Jamaica Talk*, p. 17, quotes Charles Leslie (1739), who had some
knowledge of the regional origins of Africans in Jamaica: "The Slaves are brought
from several places in Guiney, which are different from one another in Language, and
consequently they can't converse freely; or, if they could, they hate one another so
mortally, that some of them would rather die by the Hands of the *English* than
join. . . ."

[43] Gentleman Planters of London, Journal of the Lords of Trade, Oct. 8, 1680,
Calendar of State Papers Colonial, 1677–1680, no. 1535. The Planters pointed out as
an argument against Protestant missionizing that this diversity "would be destroyed by
conversion, in that it would be necessary to teach them English."

V

THE WAYS IN WHICH Africans held to their linguistic heritage while integrating it with English speech are illustrated vividly through the names which they retained. In contrast to later times, when African names were used less frequently, less publicly, and with less sense of their original meaning, steady immigration lent support to a wide variety of non-English names during the eighteenth century. One South Carolina master who died before the Revolution listed the following among his slaves: *Allahay, Assey, Benyky, Bungey, Colley, Cumbo, Cush, Dusue, Esher, Into, Jehu, Jeminah, Matillah, Meynell, Minto, Quamino, Quash, Quashey, Rinah, Sambo, Satirah, Sibbey, Tehu, Temboy, Tiffey, Yeabow,* and *Yeackney.*[44]

For many Africans their name had considerable social significance or reflected unique personal circumstances.[45] One common practice involved naming children after the day of the week on which they were born, and the seven African day-names, in their masculine and feminine forms, can all be found in the records of early South Carolina. (Actually these names only approximate the European weekdays, since Africans recognized lunar rather than numerical months.[46]) Enslaved persons entering the colonial labor force from a different culture struggled consistently to retain their names,[47] but as with countless

[44] Estate of William Walter, Inventory Book Y (1769–71), pp. 183–85, SCDAH. Observations in this section dovetail with Dillard's comments (*Black English,* pp. 123–35) concerning "West African Naming Practices Outside Gullah Territory."

[45] Turner, *Africanisms,* pp. 31–43; H. A. Wieschhoff, "The Social Significance of Names Among the Ibo of Nigeria," *American Anthropologist,* XLIII (1941), 212–22; Richard and Sally Price, "Saramaka Onomastics: An Afro-American Naming System," *Ethnology,* XI (1972), 341–67.

[46] Mbiti, *African Religions and Philosophy,* Chapter III, "The Concept of Time."

[47] The African who eventually accepted the name of Gustavus Vassa (after a famous sixteenth-century king of Sweden) describes vividly in his autobiography the series of European names forced upon him before and after he reached Virginia. "Life of Equiano," pp. 35–36.

In this place I was called Jacob; but on board the *African Snow,* I was called Michael. I had been some time in this miserable, forlorn, and much dejected state, without having anyone to talk to, which made my life a burden, when . . . the captain of a merchant ship, called the *Industrious Bee,* came on some business to my master's house . . . and liked me so well that he made a purchase of me. . . . While I was on board this ship, my captain and master named me *Gustavus Vassa.* I at that time began to understand him a little, and refused

other Americans down to the present day, the pressures for accommodation to the dominant English were often overwhelming.[48] One regular compromise was to accept a direct English translation; Negroes
were called *Monday* or *Friday*, as well as other temporal names such
as *March* and *August*, *Christmas* and *Midday*.

A more significant and common compromise was that whereby
slave and master settled upon the English name which bore the closest
relation in sound, rather than in meaning, to the African day-name.
For example, a man named *Cudjo* (Monday) frequently became
known as *Joe* to his master. When I drew up from inventories a sample
of more than four hundred black men on South Carolina plantations
in 1730, there were ten *Quashies* (Sunday) and nine *Cuffies* (Monday). Both names were pronounceable for Englishmen and neither
one suggested obvious alternate names (although the variants *Coffee*
and *Squash* both appeared). On the other hand, only six slaves retained the African name *Cudjo*, while five others were known by the
English alternative, *Joe*. Most strikingly, while a mere four men were
named *Quaco* (Wednesday), fully twenty others were called by some
form of *Jack*. Among these forms were such variations as *Jacco* and
Jacky, which clearly suggest an etymology from the African to the
English name.[49]

The same process can be seen with female day-names. J. L. Dillard points out that *Cuba* (Wednesday) was among the most common,

---

to be called so, and told him as well as I could that I would be called Jacob;
but he said I should not, and still called me Gustavus: and when I refused to
answer to my new name, which I at first did, it gained me many a cuff; so at
length I submitted, and by which I have been known ever since.

[48] Professional literature, both historical and psychological, is surprisingly thin
with regard to the impact of changing one's name under duress, a circumstance which
the majority of American families have faced or continue to face. John Womack, Jr.,
"The Chicanos," *New York Review of Books*, XIX (Aug. 31, 1972), 13, pointed
out that in recent times Chicanos in the Southwest have seen "their children smacked
for speaking Spanish at school and given new Christian names by the teachers (Jesús
mutated into Jesse, Magdalena into Maggie)."

[49] During the 1930s Martin Jackson, born a slave in Victoria County, Texas, in
1847, recollected how Negroes had registered their surnames after Emancipation. Most
working with him assumed the name of their former owner, "more because it was the
logical thing to do and the easiest way to be identified than it was through affection
for the master." But while others were taking the name Fitzpatrick, "I made up my
mind I'd find me a different one," he recalled. "One of my Grandfathers in Africa was
called Jeaceo, and so I decided to be Jackson." George P. Rawick, ed., *The American
Slave: A Composite Autobiography*, vol. IV, *Texas Narratives* (Westport, Conn., 1972),
part 2, 187–92.

"possibly because the owners thought it represented the island." *Phiba* or *Phibbi*, the name often given a female child born on Friday, was easily heard and perpetuated as *Phoebe* by Europeans. "Given the obvious condition that both southern Negroes and southern whites early learned to accommodate to the different phonological systems of the other," Dillard writes, "the slave girl was probably quite unaware that her master thought her name referred to a classical name for the moon—or on the part of the owner that the slave herself considered her name to be Friday." He goes on to point out that the name *Benah*, from *Cubena* (Tuesday), "was frequently misanalyzed" as *Venus*, and *Abba* (Thursday) often evolved into *Abby*. "In some cases," he adds, "the slaves themselves may have misunderstood the relationship. More frequently, perhaps, they simply chose to keep their own practices to themselves. West African naming practices have long given considerable latitude for giving the same person different names under different circumstances."[50]

The same kind of compromise must have occurred over other names, and it seems probable that close analysis of the most frequent biblical and classical names accepted among slaves will reveal that they often resemble African words (as with *Venus* above). The noun *keta*, quite similar to *Cato*, occurs in Bambara, Yoruba, and Hausa.[51] *Hagar*, besides being an appropriate Old Testament name for a servant, corresponds with *Haga*, the feminine name meaning "lazy" in Mende. Occasionally meaning as well as sound coincided. One reason that the name *Hercules*—often pronounced and spelled *Hekles*—was applied to strong slaves may well be the fact that *heke* in Sierra Leone, was the Mende noun meaning "a large wild animal."[52] With slave names, therefore, those which survived most readily from Africa were the ones which were particularly commonplace, or significant, or familiar in a variety of regions, and day-names suited all these categories.

Other names survived in exact or altered forms for a variety of different reasons, making their way into the general vernacular of the region. Some, as has been suggested, corresponded closely to an English word, and there is no telling how many of the thoroughly English

---

[50] Dillard, *Black English*, pp. 129–30.

[51] Turner, *Africanisms*, p. 109. For a description of the principle of multiple etymologies which explains such overlapping, see Frederic G. Cassidy, "Multiple Etymologies in Jamaican Creole," *American Speech*, XLI (1966), 211–15.

[52] Turner, *Africanisms*, p. 92.

slave names in eighteenth-century inventories had a similar-sounding African name in their origin. Survival was particularly likely on those rare occasions when an African and a European word approached each other in both sound and meaning. In the Mende language *sasi* constituted a noun meaning "boaster" or "pride" and a verb meaning "to treat contemptuously" or "to ridicule." Since this coincided so closely with the English word "saucy," it is not surprising that the term *sasi* meant "proud one" or "to ridicule" in Gullah and that it probably reinforced the use of "sassy" and "to sass" in American English.[53] From an early date, African names were fastened to certain lowland places and wildlife species with which slaves had special familiarity. Lorenzo Turner included the following names for coastal rivers and islands among those which derive totally or partly from Africa:[54]

Okatee	*okati* (Umbundu, Angola)	"middle, interior"
Peedee	*mpidi* (Kongo, Angola)	"a species of viper"
Tybee	*tai bi* (Hausa, N. Nigeria)	"fertile, low-lying farmland"
Wahoo	*wahu* (Yoruba, S. Nigeria)	"to trill the voice"
Wassaw	*wasaw* (Twi, Gold Coast)	name of a district, tribe, and dialect

Lydia Parrish, gathering oral data in the Sea Islands somewhat earlier and less professionally than Turner, observed:

Years ago I heard the great blue heron in the marshes called "Poor Joe," and judged his lean body had given him his name. Not at all. *Podzo* is the name of a similar heron in Africa. We call a certain type of southern tortoise a "cooter." In the neighborhood of Timbuctoo its near relative is called a *kuta*. When I first visited the Georgia coast I heard the name "tackies" applied to the small wild horses found on the salt marshes of the sea islands of South Carolina and Georgia. Now I find that *taki* is the West African name of a horse.[55]

Alongside the linguistic and cultural circumstances which allowed certain African names to survive, it is worth noting the long-

---

[53] *Ibid.*, pp. 201, 208.
[54] *Ibid.*, p. 307.
[55] Parrish, *Slave Songs*, p. 41. She continued:

The same with the "tabby" houses built for [by] the slaves out of old oyster shells, sand, and cement (made from burning live oyster shells in pine cribs built for the purpose). In Africa the name for a house of similar construction is *tabax*. When a Southerner hears the word "tote" he knows that it means to carry; a very similar word, *tota*, from the Congo, means to pick up. Southern children know the "joggle board," or seesaw, but they do not know that the name comes from the West African word, *dzogal*, meaning to rise.

term social pressures which caused many personal names to disappear, at least from public use. Repeatedly in America, when non-English-speaking groups have imported names which had laudatory or at least neutral implications at first, these have gradually been made common nouns and given a negative connotation by the culturally dominant class. African day-names illustrate this New World phenomenon. By the late nineteenth century in Jamaica all fourteen of the traditional day-names had taken on specific pejorative meanings, which caused Negroes to limit their further use.[56] The name *Sambo* provides a similar example for North America: among the Hausa it was a name given to the second son of a family, and other African groups used the same word in different ways (interestingly enough, to signify "disgrace" in Mende and Vai). But in America *Sambo* gradually assumed insulting implications which could only be avoided by adopting the English biblical alternative of *Samuel,* or *Sam.*[57]

Roughly the same principles which governed the survival and alteration of proper names must have determined more general accommodations and adjustments in the syntax and morphology of slave English. The Negroes in South Carolina developed a language in which sounds and constructions comprehensible to the widest number survived, while those understood by the smallest numbers or subjected to the greatest degree of white derision were lost or suppressed. This idea of linguistic reinforcement and compromise is highly significant, since it explains the comparative simplicity of early Gullah without reverting to old arguments of European condescension or African mental,

[56] David DeCamp, "African Day-Names in Jamaica," *Language,* XLIII (1967), 139–49; esp. 146–47. DeCamp points out dozens of meanings, usually derogatory, which became associated with each day-name, masculine and feminine. For example:

Sunday	*Quashee*	a stupid or gullible man; an irresponsible ne'er-do-well
Monday	*Cudjo*	a drunkard or dunce; a troublesome schoolboy
Tuesday	*Cubena*	a fool; a liar; a trickster or con-man
Wednesday	*Quaco*	an insane, illiterate or feeble man; a spendthrift
Thursday	*Quao*	a freak; a lunatic; an ignorant rustic
Friday	*Cuffee*	a simpleton; a bully; a left-handed man
Saturday	*Quame*	a fat man; a greedy man; a glutton
Sunday	*Quasheba*	a foolish, ne'er-do-well woman; a prostitute
Monday	*Juba*	a sexually promiscuous girl; a type of fish
Tuesday	*Beneba*	a flirt; a tease; a pretty but highly vain girl
Wednesday	*Cuba*	a fussy old woman; a domestic servant; a homosexual
Thursday	*Abba*	a shiftless, no-account woman; a girl who stammers
Friday	*Phiba*	a foolish woman; a hard-working drudge
Saturday	*Mimba*	a headstrong girl; a menial servant; a laundress

[57] Dillard, *Black English,* pp. 130–32.

moral, or physiological weakness.[58] It is now accepted as being characteristic in the formation of a pidgin language for complexities of vocabulary, pronunciation, and grammar to diminish at first. "In general," explains Hall, "this reduction is in the direction of whatever features are common to the languages of all those using the pidgin, for mutual ease in use and comprehensibility, thus arriving at a kind of greatest common denominator."[59]

VI

ACCORDING TO the common denominator theory, the increasing predominance of slaves and the steady influx of new Africans are enough to explain why Negro dialect in the colony diverged considerably from white English. But several related factors also contributed to the early evolution of a distinct pidgin tongue. In the first place, Englishmen were openly ambiguous about imparting their language to blacks. When a planter limited his speech in addressing slaves, it may have been prompted as much by a fear that they *would* master English as by a condescending belief that they *could not*. Every master whose Negroes knew no English was courting inefficiency and misfortune.[60]

[58] Cf. Cassidy, *Jamaica Talk*, pp. 49–50:

The structure of the West African languages, as we know today, was quite as complex as that of the European, though of course in many ways very different. As might be expected, when English and Niger-Congo languages had some feature in common, that item had a good chance of surviving in the new compromise speech. Features that differed markedly in English and African would be harder for the learner to acquire or to preserve. Thus, not only was a lot of English grammar ungained, but a lot of African grammar was unkept: such were the inevitable terms of the compromise.

[59] Hall, *Pidgin and Creole Languages*, p. 25. Cf. Dillard, *Black English*, p. 75:

The term "pidgin" is not well understood, and many people feel—without cause —insulted when told their ancestors depended upon such a language. From the point of view of the linguist, such a feeling is irrational. A pidgin language has rules (regular principles of sentence construction) like any other language. Syntactic rules of a high order of regularity can be written for any pidgin. . . . In short, pidgins are not formed by distortions of the syntactic patterns of the "standard" language, even if the prejudice of Europeans has usually led them to conclude that this is true.

[60] Occasionally Negroes were shot dead if they failed to respond to the order or query of a white watchman. Some of these victims may well have been unable to understand or answer the vital summons adequately. *SCCHJ, 1725–1726*, pp. 20, 22, 23; *SCG*, Feb. 3, 1733.

But slaves who developed the greatest facility in English were also the most forward leaders in other ways, and whites were quick to emphasize this dangerous relationship. "The Negroes are generally very bad men," the Rev. Le Jau was informed, "chiefly those that are Scholars."[61] Such observations among whites meant that after the first generation, contrary to accepted dogma, most new Negroes learned the local language not from Englishmen but from other slaves, a factor which reinforced the distinctiveness of the dialect.[62]

Quite apart from any white reluctances, the slaves had serious reservations of their own about the acquisition of English. Proficiency could be a means of advancement, but standard English could not, and never would, provide so simple a key to upward mobility for blacks as it did for white newcomers.[63] And if knowledge of "good" English could occasionally be used to advantage, as in eavesdropping or newspaper reading, "bad" English was discovered to be an equally effective weapon.[64] To cultivate a dialect few whites could understand and to

[61] April 15, 1707, *Le Jau*, p. 24. A subsequent incident convinced Le Jau that it was "most convenient not to urge too far that Indians and Negroes shou'd be indifferently admitted to learn to read" (Feb. 1, 1710, *ibid.*, p. 70), and other ministers accepted the same view. The Rev. Richard Ludlam, who followed Le Jau at Goose Creek, told of "secret poisonings and bloody insurrection" attributed to slaves who had received Christian instruction. Klingberg, *Appraisal*, p. 46.

[62] Dillard, *Black English*, p. 97. Cf. Cassidy, *Jamaica Talk*, p. 19: "the chief models after the seventeenth century must have been the native Negroes rather than the whites."

[63] Since "passing" would always represent a complex psychological challenge for Negroes, the anxieties of borderline status for certain slaves may if anything have brought forth speech impediments. This interesting suggestion is put forth by Gerald W. Mullin, Jr., in his Ph.D. dissertation, "Patterns of Slave Behavior in Eighteenth Century Virginia" (U. of Cal., Berkeley, 1968), pp. 188–89, 224–35. The necessity of speaking more than one language, or of speaking English in more than one way, could have introduced further dislocations into the already slightly schizophrenic world of an enslaved immigrant from Africa. Renewed interest in American ethnicity is now leading psycho-historians and others to consider more fully the psychological and social complexities of selecting, adopting, or rejecting a "mother tongue."

[64] Cf. the following passage from Frederick Douglass, *The Life and Times of Frederick Douglass* (Boston, 1881):

> Slaveholders ever underrate the intelligence with which they have to grapple. I really understood the old man's mutterings, attitudes and gestures, about as well as he did himself. But slave-holders never encourage that kind of communication, with the slaves, by which they might learn to measure the depths of his knowledge. Ignorance is a high virtue in a human chattel; and as the master studies to keep the slave ignorant, the slave is cunning enough to make the master think he succeeds. The slave fully appreciates the saying, "where ignorance is bliss 'tis folly to be wise."

be able to adopt a stance of incomprehension toward their masters' speech proved effectual elements of resistance. Such things considered, colonial slaves could not have felt the same eagerness to acquire the dominant language that seized voluntary immigrants in later times. After all, total acceptance of the master's tongue might be felt or perceived psychologically as one more emblem of capitulation. Nevertheless, non-English-speaking workers entering Charlestown harbor in the eighteenth century were still much like those entering New York harbor in the nineteenth century, in that linguistically they had ahead of them a long period of personal and generational travail, laboring to retain old and familiar modes of communication against the erosion of time, struggling to develop new modes through which they might better understand their fate.

One further hurdle for these slaves must have been the transition from an oral to a written language. All Africans (including those few who wrote Arabic) were heirs to oral traditions, the scope and importance of which are difficult to appreciate. The urge to retain the significant spoken forms of the old country—a recurrent theme in American immigrant history—must have been strong among newcomers who carried so much of their cultural heritage in their minds. "I asked once a pretty ancient and very fine slave whether he cou'd read," recorded the Rev. Le Jau; "his answer was he wou'd rather choose hereafter to practice the good he could remember."[65]

Some Africans, motivated in part no doubt by prohibitions on teaching slaves to read English, expressed an eagerness to "talk to books," as many whites could do.[66] But it is logical, given all the reservations mentioned above, that many Negroes mocked the minority who took most quickly to the Christian faith and to the language in which it was offered. Thus ridicule from both whites and blacks must have been a final source of inhibition for Africans contacting written and spoken English. Le Jau noted that a few baptized Negroes bravely

[65] June 13, 1710, *Le Jau*, p. 77. See David P. Henige, "Oral Tradition and Chronology," *Journal of African History*, XII (1971), 371–89; David Dalby, ed., *Language and History in Africa* (London, 1970), *passim;* Vansina, "Once Upon a Time," p. 442. All would agree with Ben Sidran, *Black Talk* (New York, 1971), p. 1: "Literate society often turns a deaf ear to the implications of an oral culture."

[66] "Life of Equiano," p. 39:

I had often seen my master and Dick employed in reading; and I had a great curiosity to talk to the books as I thought they did, and so to learn how all things had a beginning. For that purpose I have often taken up a book, and have talked to it, and then put my ears to it, when alone, in hopes it would answer me; and I have been very much concerned when I found it remained silent.

"prayd and read some párt of their Bibles in the field and in their Quarters in the hearing of those who could not read, and took no notice of some Profanne men who laught at their Devotions."[67] Another minister pointed out that one of the primary drawbacks to preparing slaves for baptism was the fact that "all other slaves do laugh at them."[68]

The conjunction of all these forces led to the emergence during the early eighteenth century of a simple and distinctive pidgin dialect in frontier South Carolina. No sooner had this basic amalgam emerged, however, than transition toward a more elaborate and nativized creole language began. After 1740 the percentage of African newcomers in the expanding slave population dropped off gradually, even though the annual total of imported workers increased during subsequent decades. The number of American-born children learning Gullah as their primary language increased, and the language itself began to take on a greater complexity through intensive use. As is common in the rapid development of a creole language out of a pidgin, the changes were "in the direction of re-expansion of both structure and vocabulary."[69]

[67] March 19, 1716, *Le Jau*, p. 174. A typical incident of white derision for Africans struggling with a new language is provided by a Harvard graduate named Hugh Hall whose Letterbook is in Harvard's Houghton Library. Having recently returned to Boston from Barbados, he wrote to a friend in London (May 15, 1718) concerning the:

> Comical Surprise of a Young New Negro Boy brought with us here, who in a Raw Cold Morning on this Coast was sadly Complaining of the Cold, & in his Gibberish Dialect vehemently Express'd it was no Boon Country;—but Seing [seeing] his own Breath (which You know we all do in Cold Weather) was struck with a strange Consternation; & Running to his Master Acquainted him there was a Fire in his Mouth, for he saw the Smoke; which Occurrence I'le Assure You gave us a great deal of Diversion, for which End I have now Informed You of it.

[68] James Gignillat to John Chamberlayne, Santee, S.C., May 28, 1710, Klingberg, *Appraisal*, p. 24 n.

[69] Hall, *Pidgin and Creole Languages*, p. 25. Cf. pp. 122–23:

> All evidence available so far indicates that the type of linguistic change and the mechanisms involved—sound-change, analogy, borrowing of various kinds—are the same for pidgins and creoles as they are for all other languages. The only difference lies in the rate of change—far faster for a pidgin (because of the drastic reduction in structure and lexicon) than for most languages. When a pidgin has become nativized, the history of the resultant creole is, in essence, similar to that of any other language. . . . We consider that . . . languages such as . . . Gullah . . . have had this type of origin because the extent of restructuring they have undergone, in contrast to the languages from which they are clearly derived, is of a kind that normally takes thousands of years, whereas we know from historical sources that they arose in a century or two; and because we know that pidgins or pidgin-producing conditions existed in the regions where these languages are now spoken.

For the increasing population of native-born slaves in the colony, this distinctive variety of black English became not only more elaborate and self-contained, but also more widely shared and more easily conveyed. Its African elements were undoubtedly far greater than those which have survived into the twentieth century, for they were constantly being reinforced and revitalized by "salt-water" slaves from the other side of the Atlantic. These newcomers in turn gained their knowledge of English from Gullah-speaking Negroes, which served to put added distance between black and white speech in the colony. In 1734 an advertisement described "Four young Negroe Men slaves and a Girl, who . . . speak very good (Black-) English."[70] Increasingly slaveholders came to define "good" English among slaves simply as English which whites could comprehend. Even before 1750 whites were distinguishing between "new Negroes" and "sensible Negroes," the latter being any who understood their commands.[71]

There is evidence, according to J. L. Dillard, "of complicated variation in the English of the Afro-American population as of about 1750,"[72] and after 1800 the curtailing of slave imports and the tightening of plantation controls gradually gave rise to a further degree of local variation in slave language. By the middle of the nineteenth century in the Sea Islands "each plantation had its own particular songs for beating rice, just as its rowing songs were unlike those of other plantations."[73] Separation from whites increased as well: when the Union Army occupied the South Carolina coast they reported that some Sea Island Negroes did not understand the English words for "left" and "right."[74] The incomprehension was of course mutual, and

[70] *SCG*, March 30, 1734. This is the earliest known American record of the specific term "black English."

[71] *SCCHJ, 1744–1745*, p. 354. The committee looking into improper trade with St. Augustine reported the testimony of a pilot who had seen a vessel unloading "five new Negro Men . . . and a sensible Negro Man." William A. Stewart, "Continuity and Change in American Negro Dialects," *The Florida FL Reporter* (Spring, 1968), n.p., note 2, suggests "the possibility that in the parlance of slave owners a term like 'good English' might have meant something very different when applied to Negroes than it would have if applied to whites." Cf. Dillard, *Black English*, p. 85.

[72] Dillard, *Black English*, p. 86.

[73] Parrish, *Slave Songs*, p. 235. According to John Bennett, "Gullah: A Negro Patois," *The South Atlantic Quarterly*, VII (1908), 336 n, "Singular peculiarities upon one plantation may be—or once were—totally lacking upon the next holding though but a few miles distant."

[74] Fisher, *Negro Slave Songs*, pp. 150–51.

the standard Sea Island reaction to such strangers was said to be: "Dey use dem mout' so funny."[75]

During the century after the Civil War Gullah speech eroded gradually as word meanings were lost and constructions were dropped, until now there are only limited remains from what was once the primary language of the region's majority. But from another perspective, it is extraordinary how tenaciously this mode of speech has persisted and how directly it relates to the broader patterns of black English which remain prevalent throughout the United States. Gullah might be described as an early, localized, and intensified form of an accommodation process between separate speech traditions that has not yet run its course in this country. The exact historical relationship between the concentrated regional tradition and the more diffuse national pattern has not yet been adequately analyzed. But whatever the linguistic implications of Gullah for later times, it would be hard to overestimate the importance of this common dialect to South Carolina slaves in the eighteenth century. Gullah became their central mode of communication and expression, linking together people of widely disparate backgrounds. It provided a mutually intelligible mode of discourse for the thousands of laborers at work in the rice fields of Babel. It was an outgrowth of their ingenuity, not of their ignorance, and it served its function well.

[75] Bennett, "Gullah," p. 340.

❧ PART THREE ❧

Rising Tensions

ᥫ VII ᥬ

Growing Initiative
Among Blacks

I

BY the time South Carolina became a royal colony, the growing number of Africans provided a nucleus around which distinctive social patterns could cohere and develop. Unlike the slaves in Virginia, these Negroes were not dispersed among a far larger group of Europeans, nor were they spread as yet over so wide an area. On an increasing number of separate plantations, and perhaps in the coastal settlement as a whole, there existed the "critical mass" necessary for preserving and synthesizing traditions of behavior, speech, and myth. There was a tendency toward social, and occasionally economic, self-sufficiency among blacks as their numbers expanded. A voluntary separation from the white community went along with denser population, wider contacts, and increasingly independent living quarters.

Indications of even the most limited black autonomy, however, proved increasingly threatening to the white minority; signs of independence and assertion were countered with measures for regulation and control. As a result Negroes, despite rising numbers, felt themselves increasingly hemmed in and suppressed, losing ground in absolute as well as comparative terms. In a variety of ways they were being pushed from the dubious position of unfree laborers to the degrading status of racial slaves. White Americans would later argue that the transition evolved naturally and was accepted as inevitable by all concerned, but such naturalness is belied by the wealth of anxieties which the English minority expressed. The thorough social imbalance between the races which later generations came to accept as God-given was created out of severe tensions in the eighteenth century, and if white supremacy could one day be taken as a foregone conclusion through the benefit of biased hindsight, contemporaries found themselves drawn into a conflict in which everyone's situation was precarious and no one's survival was assured.

After the Yamasee War, as the settlement evolved from a frontier outpost to a staple-producing colony, distinct social changes emerged by slow degrees. The diminishing white fraction of the populace, which controlled the colony's government and economy ever more securely with time, bound the Africans increasingly tightly to their servile status. As the eighteenth century progressed, Negroes found themselves pushed out in a variety of ways from the positions of forced intimacy and tenuous equality with Europeans which frontier conditions had tended to create. Increasingly the social separation of black from white became less horizontal and voluntary, more vertical and involuntary. But so significant and lasting a realignment of social forces could not take place overnight. The adjustment to a new equilibrium occurred only after a generation of increasing turbulence.

At first the indications of conflict and suppression were comparatively slight. Undeniably, a rapidly growing absolute number of Negroes and an increasing percentage of the slave population were being confined to the laborious production of staple crops. Hundreds of newcomers were being subjected annually to the arduous and monotonous routine of rice cultivation which their descendants in the lowlands would follow with little variation for over a century to come. At the same time, however, the period after 1720 was marked by continuing diversity in the activities of the Negro population as a whole, for as the colony grew, the demand for more varied and specialized labor increased. Slaves from abroad as well as native-born Negroes whose parents had worked in close proximity with earlier European settlers, took up their share of these tasks. Far from being prohibited at first, such diversification was often encouraged, and, as this chapter illustrates, many of the traditional and acquired skills of black workers continued to be exercised to the full. For the time being, therefore, the black labor force retained a variegated character similar in many ways to that of the smaller white population.

II

As THE COLONY GREW, the demand for experienced craftsmen of all sorts was intense enough so that such questions as whether workers were free, indentured, or slave, or whether they were red, white, or black, often mattered less than their availability and aptitude. Specific skills which a worker did not already possess could be developed under service to a master. In 1727 a Charlestown clockmaker owed £20 to "an Indjon for Cutting Clock Wheels."[1] An ad in the *Gazette* somewhat later read: "Any white Man or Negro having a mind to learn the Coopers Trade, to correct spoiled Wine and to distill, may apply to PETER BIROT, who will teach them under reasonable conditions."[2] After mid-century the *Gazette*'s owner, Peter Timothy, having just fired a "villainous Apprentice," wrote to his fellow printer Benjamin Franklin, "I am, (and have been these 4 Months) the sole Inhabitant of my Printing office, (excepting a Negro boy, whom I'm teaching to serve me at the Press)."[3]

Under such conditions, signs of useful initiative on the part of black slaves did not go totally ignored. Two Negro men from a group sold at public auction in 1743 were advertised as follows: "one understands the Dairy, and the other has an extraordinary Inclination to learn the Carpenter's Trade." Several years later Robert Pringle felt enough confidence in a slave girl named Peggy to pay £20 to board her for a year with a woman who would teach her sewing.[4] The slave Equiano relates that the following conversation occurred after he was purchased in Montserrat by a Quaker merchant named Robert King, and similar discussions between slave and master must occasionally have taken place in colonial Charlestown:

Mr. King soon asked me what I could do; and at the same time said he did not mean to treat me as a common slave. I told him I knew something of seamanship, and could shave and dress hair pretty well; and I could refine wines, which I had learned on shipboard, where I had often done it; and that I could write, and understand arithmetic tolerably well, as far as the Rule of Three. He then asked me if I knew anything of gauging; and on my answering that I did not, he said one of his clerks should teach me to gauge.[5]

---

[1] Inventory of James Batterson, Aug. 1, 1727, MR (1726–27), p. 648. (Indian excellence at this kind of precision handwork was noted early by Europeans, and it is interesting that certain watch companies make use of reservation labor to the present day.)

[2] *SCG*, Oct. 5, 1734. Such a notice implies knowledge among slaves of the contents of the *Gazette*, as do the occasional published offers of rewards to Negroes for the apprehension of runaways or the return of stolen goods.

[3] Peter Timothy, June 14, 1754, *SCHGM*, XXXV (1934), 125.

[4] *SCG*, Feb. 7, 1743; "Journal of Robert Pringle, 1746–1747," *SCHGM*, XXVI (1925), 97, 101.

[5] "Life of Equiano," p. 70.

More often than not, slaves belonging to white artisans worked at the trade of their own master. When the estate of a South Carolina gunsmith was sold in 1739 (days before the Stono Rebellion renewed debate over slave access to firearms), it included "a Negro Man and boy both [of] which can work at the Gunsmith's Trade, and two extraordinary House wenches with their Children." A white butcher who died the following spring left a household near Charlestown which contained "Five Negro Butchers by Trade, One Plantation Negro Man, One good House Wench," and the inventory of silversmith Andrew Dupuy's estate made in 1743 included a Negro silversmith named Limus appraised at the exceptional value of £300.[6] In many situations a young slave must have learned a craft from an older slave in the same household, as in the case of the twenty-year-old Negro who was sold in 1734 as "a Cook, having serv'd three Years under a regular bred Cook."[7]

Often slaves mastered their trade so thoroughly that their owners sold them, along with their tools, as accomplished artisans. In December 1742 Elizabeth Bampfield offered to sell "A Fine young Negro Man, born in this Country, . . . brought up to the Ship Carpenter's Trade, and can Caulk very well,"[8] and two weeks later another white woman named Anne Lorey advertised "A likely Negro Fellow to be Sold, . . . a Ship Carpenter and Wheelwright by Trade." The following February the owner of a choice waterfront lot in Beaufort put up for sale—separately or together—his dwelling house, the adjoining smith's shop and tools, and the Negro smithy who worked there. In Charlestown during the same month three young Negroes, employed as tallow chandlers and soap boilers, were sold along with the utensils they used when their owner decided to leave the province.[9] Over the ensuing years it became a common practice for urban tradesmen to train up slave apprentices with specific skills who could then be sold to planters for a high price. This pattern of exporting black artisans to the country helped further the self-sufficiency of plantations to such a degree that by the time of the Revolution it posed a real dilemma to

[6] *SCG*, Sept. 1, 1739; July 5, 1740; E. Milby Burton, *South Carolina Silversmiths, 1690–1860* (Richmond, Va., 1942), p. 209.

[7] *SCG*, April 6, 1734.

[8] *SCG*, Dec. 2, 1742. Nine years before, the same woman had sold "a young Negro Fellow . . . bred a Butcher, and a Negro Woman that is a very good Cook, Washer, and understanding any Sort of Household Work." *SCG*, May 12, 1733.

[9] *SCG*, Dec. 16, 1742; Feb. 7, 1743; Feb. 28, 1743.

the white artisans themselves, who had inadvertently undercut their long-term profits by the short-term maneuver of selling talented slaves.[10]

While some trades were learned in Charlestown and carried to the hinterland, it is apparent from primary sources that there was still a continuous overlap between the activities of town slaves and their more numerous counterparts in the country. Sewing and blacksmithing, cooperage and carpentry were as essential to life in the outlying parishes as in Charlestown itself.[11] In many instances the variety of tasks essential to plantation life must have fostered particular diversity, as suggested by an ad in the *Gazette* of February 1, 1739, for the sale of "3 choice young Plantation Negroes, 2 Men and one Wench." The men were said to be at home "in Boats and Perriauguas and understand very well how to manage Cattle," while the woman was "fit either for the Field or House, being used to both." She was able to "milk very well, wash and iron, dress Victuals, and do anything that is necessary to be done in the House." They were all well clothed, and their various plantation tools were to be sold with them. The same issue contained an ad from Goose Creek for a runaway named Sampson, born and raised on a plantation, who was "a good Ploughman and works a little at the Cooper's Trade." A slave on the nearby estate of William Smith was considered "a very good Plough-Man and Mower."[12]

The active involvement of Negroes in the full range of plantation activities is demonstrated by the fact that slaves not only undertook all the routine tasks but were also thoroughly involved wherever experiments were made with new products. When French settlers along the Santee River sought to develop silk culture, a key consideration was the fact that "it requires a great Number of small Negroes to pick

---

[10] Richard Walsh, *Charleston's Sons of Liberty: A Study of the Artisans, 1763–1789* (Columbia, 1959), p. 25.

[11] Consider the following message which Eliza Lucas Pinckney sent to town via her slave June in Oct. 1745:

> June comes for thread, for the negroes are in want of their Cloaths. Please send a Cooper's broad ax for Sogo. It must be turned for the left hand, Smith Dick knows how to do it, and a Cross Iron. . . . Pompey has been very bad Twise with the Pleurisy & I could not get the new barn finished being obleeged to take Sogo to make barrells.

Harriott Herry Ravenel, *Eliza Pinckney* (New York, 1896), p. 127. Cf. Chapter IV, note 52, above.

[12] *SCG*, Feb. 27, 1742.

the Mulberry leaves & keep the Worms clean."[13] When John Lewis Poyas proposed a government-backed silk plantation in 1737, he intended to instruct a group of Negroes in the entire management process. Although he obtained half a dozen slaves "to gather Leaves and feed Worms," little came of the project, and Poyas was dismissed and the slaves resold in 1741.[14] Hemp was the experimental crop on Joseph Crell's Santee River plantation when he put it up for sale in September 1739. His property included a new house and outbuildings, livestock, and vegetables, "as also Wheat and Hemp already gather'd, the latter being water'd and put up for working; moreover about 8 Bushels of Hemp Seed . . . , [so] there may be raised the next Summer a large Crop of Hemp." And along with these holdings Crell was offering "three choice healthy Slaves that have had the Small Pox and [are] acquainted to manage the Hemp and to dress Deer Skins."[15]

It is worth quoting one further advertisement to illustrate the degree to which differing levels of responsibility and degrees of expertise were acknowledged among slaves on the larger plantations toward the middle of the century. The choice estate of the Lake family from Barbados, which covered several hundred acres between Ashley River and Wappoo Creek, was being used in the 1750s to raise corn and indigo. Holdings included, "upward of FIFTY likely strong NEGROES, among which is a very good driver who understands the management of a plantation, and planting perfectly well." There were two coopers: "one that makes tight casks," and a second that "has served Three years to the trade." Two other men were skilled in the kitchen: "one of which is a professed cook and fit for any person in the province, and the other a very good one." In addition there were "seamstresses that were also good housewenches; washer women, house-wenches, and waiting-men; plantation slaves, and handy boys and girls."[16]

III

THE PARTICULAR SKILLS of slaves familiar with the water had been readily acknowledged during the first half century of colonial settle-

[13] Undated letter of James Sutherland in the Coe Papers (Docs. of the Lords Commissioners, 1719–42), SCHS. On Negro involvement in a projected experiment with cochineal dye, see Chapter IV, note 95, above.

[14] *SCCHJ, 1736–1739*, pp. 395–96. Also see *ibid.*, pp. 344, 634, and *SCCHJ, 1739–1741*, pp. 273, 500.

[15] *SCG*, Sept. 1, 1739.

[16] *SCG*, Jan. 5, 1759; cf. *SCHGM*, XX (1919), 76–77.

ment, as was suggested in Chapter IV. If anything, these talents were utilized more extensively in the generation after 1720. Slavers returning from Africa could attest to the long tradition of coastal fishing in dugout canoes which prevailed in many places and which helped the slaving vessels meet their need for provisions. A doctor named William Chancellor aboard the *Wolf*, a New York sloop trading along the Gold Coast in 1750, reported that the extensive fishing there with both hooks and nets was carefully regulated, and that near Cape Coast Castle he had seen a fleet of more than one hundred canoes set out to catch herring.[17] Many of the slaves exported to America came from the coastal regions, and it is not surprising that in both the West Indian and mainland colonies Africans quickly proved able to supply both themselves and their European owners with fish.

In Charlestown, an entire class of "fishing Negroes" had emerged early in the eighteenth century, replacing local Indians as masters of the plentiful waters.[18] "There is . . . good fishing all along this Coast, especially from October till Christmas," wrote an official during the 1730s. He added, apparently with only limited exaggeration, "I've known two Negroes take between 14 & 1500 Trouts above 3 feet long, wch make an excellent dry fish."[19] A French Catholic, whose ship anchored near the confluence of the Ashley and Cooper rivers early in the next century, found himself "in the midst of twenty-five dug-outs, each containing four Negroes who were having excellent fishing, such as one might well desire on the eve of Good Friday."[20]

Many Negro fishermen also made use of a variety of nets, and the art of net casting, which became an established tradition in the tidal shallows of Carolina, may have derived directly from West Africa. The surgeon visiting the Gold Coast at mid-century recorded in his journal: "It is impossible to imagine how very dextrous the negroes are in catching fish with a net."[21] The know-how of Afro-Americans skilled in fishing provided steady profits for colonial slaveowners. A Carolina

[17] Wax, "Slaving Voyage," pp. 475–76.

[18] See note 22 below and also notes 102 to 110 in Chapter IV.

[19] Letter of James Sutherland cited in note 13 above. Sutherland came to the colony in 1722, was commissioned the commander of Johnson's Fort overlooking Charlestown Harbor in 1730, and died in 1740.

[20] Baron de Montlzun, "A Frenchman Visits Charleston, 1817," *SCHGM*, XLIX (1948), 136. The Baron continued: "Ten minutes doesn't go by without there being hauled into the dugout fish.weighing from Twelve to fifteen pounds. After they are taken on the line, they are pulled up to the level of the sea where one of the black fishermen sticks them with a harpoon."

[21] Wax, "Slaving Voyage," p. 474. Dr. Chancellor added, "this morning I watch'd one man throw one [net] of 3 yards deep, and hale it in himself with innumerable fish."

planter from Wando Neck, deprived of these profits when one of the Negroes disappeared in 1737, offered a reward for the runaway named Moses: "he is well known in Charlestown, having been a Fisherman there for some time, & hath been often employed in knitting of Nets."[22] Not surprisingly, even now, generations after the end of slavery, professional Negro fishermen continue to be prevalent along the southeastern coast.

Numerous men who did not fish regularly spent considerable time in boats. As the traditional historian of the crown colony explained admiringly:

The oldest plantations were all upon the rivers; indeed a water front and landing was an essential to such an establishment, for it must have the perriauguer for plantation purposes, and the trim sloop and large cypress canoe for the master's use. So, besides the master of the horse, the coachman, there was a naval officer too, to each planter's household, and he was called the patroon—a name no doubt brought from the West Indies. The patroon had charge of the boats, and the sounding of his horn upon the river told the family of his master's coming from town. He, too, trained the boat hands to the oar and taught them the plaintive, humorous, happy catches which they sang as they bent to the stroke.[23]

The earliest rowing songs were probably African remnants recalled by the patroon, and the boats themselves may have represented a blend of diverse coastal traditions from West Africa, where cypress wood was used to fashion both round- and flat-bottomed craft.[24] Plantation boats varied considerably in size and were frequently brightly painted, as ads in the *Gazette* indicate: "a Cypres Canoe, 15 Feet 8 Inches long, and 2 Feet 8 Inches over, the Inside painted red," "a canow 25 feet long and 4 feet wide, with a white bottom, yellow sides, black gunnels,

[22] *SCG*, Nov. 5, 1737.

[23] Edward McCrady, *The History of South Carolina Under the Royal Government, 1719–1776* (New York, 1899), p. 516. (McCrady first offered this description in an address to the Society of the Colonial Dames of South Carolina in 1897 on "The Social Development of the Colony During the First Hundred Years of Its Existence.")

[24] Consider the following entries in the journal of William Chancellor (Wax, "Slaving Voyage," pp. 474, 478), aboard ship off the Gold Coast, 1750:

Cape Coast Castle, June 5: There is nothing in which the negroes so much differ in Africa as the make of their Canoes & paddles, here they are flat bottom'd every where else on the Coast thr. bottoms are round.

Annamaboo, July 11: Early this morning the King of the Fantees . . . sent his Canoe wth. 12 negroes for me, . . . [and] from the Ship to the Shore I was attended with the Singing of them.

and the storm sheets painted with Prussian blue."[25] Larger boats like the latter were equipped with sails and also with oarlocks, and in the nineteenth century uniformed black crews from different plantations sometimes rowed against one another in races.

Young men were often advertised in terms of their abilities on the water: "a very good Sailor, and used for 5 years to row in Boats, . . . a Lad chiefly used to row in Boats," "a fine strong Negro Man, that has been used to the Sea, which he is very fit for, or to go in a Pettiaugua," "all fine Fellows in Boats or Pettiau's." Such dexterity often represented a direct carryover from Africa, as can be seen from an ad for a runaway in the Virginia colony: the notice concerned "a new Negro Fellow of small Stature" from Bonny, on the coast of Nigeria; it stated that "he calls himself Bonna, and says he came from a Place of that name in the Ibo Country, in Africa, where he served in the Capacity of a Canoe Man." The tradition of black familiarity with boating was clearly recognized among whites by the time Henry Bedon (in 1741) advertised a pair of Negro men "that is capable to go in a Pettiauger, and has practis'd going by the Water above 10 Years, and understands their Business as well as most of their Colour."[26]

Men like these literally provided the backbone of the lowland transportation system during most of the colonial era, moving plantation goods to market and ferrying and guiding whites from one landing to another with such regularity that notice is taken of their arduous and sometimes dangerous work only when a mishap occurs. "Tuesday Night last," related the *Gazette* in 1732, "a Pettyawger laden with a considerable Quantity of Rice, was unfortunately lost in her Passage from the Country to this Town, wherein two very valuable Negroes were drown'd." A subsequent story related a "very melancholy Accident" which befell the son of Capt. Bellinger of Ashley Ferry and the Negro who was carrying him back to boarding school at Charlestown in a canoe: "they both were missed, and great Search being made after them, they were found dead on Tuesday last sticking in the Mud in the said River, their Arms clasping one another." This same white family also affords an illustration of the increasing supervision which was imposed upon black ferrymen; in 1741 Capt. Bellinger's widow was granted the lucrative ferry franchise across Ashley

[25] *SCG*, March 14, 1743; Nov. 6, 1752; cf. Feb. 7, 1743.
[26] *SCG*, April 6, 1734; April 11, 1739; Jan. 31, 1743; *Virginia Gazette*, Dec. 24, 1772; *SCG*, Feb. 18, 1741.

River with the understanding she would "find and provide two able and sufficient persons to Row in the Boat with one white man who shall constantly attend the Said Ferry as well by night as by day."[27]

The rigors of servitude on land made service on the water seem all the more attractive. The steady demand for ships' hands in the coastal colony therefore offered a degree of mobility to many slaves and clear profits to their masters. After one of several Negro crewmen aboard David Godin's coastal schooner drowned in a canoe accident along with the patroon and several other men, a local merchant commented, "he was a Young fellow this Country born & brought up in ye Boat from his Infancy wch business he understood very well & upon that Acc^t was ye more Valluable."[28] When a vessel loaded with flour ran aground south of Charlestown in 1743 Robert Pringle, another merchant, responded by hiring a local pilot and "Four Stout Negro Men to assist" in the salvage. Pringle wrote to the stranded captain that these slaves were "used to be upon the Water, & understand to Work on Shipboard, & [I] Desire you may Lett the Said Negroes have Provisions & Drin^k while on board, as I have agreed with them."[29] In 1747 Pringle sent two of his own slaves to sea for profit. Tom worked six weeks on a local vessel at ten shillings per day, and London, whom Pringle outfitted with two frocks, two pairs of trousers, and a new hat, embarked aboard the privateer *Isabella*. The terms for such ventures seem to have been standard, for when Henry Laurens later sent two Negro seamen aboard the schooner *Brother's Endeavor*, he instructed the captain, "The negroes are entitled to no wages being my property as slaves, except clothing & provisions from me & good usage from you."[30]

The Negroes whose seamanship came closest to being a liability for whites were those who served aboard Charlestown pilot boats or

[27] *SCG*, Feb. 9, 1732; Jan. 22, 1737; "An Act for vesting the Ferry over Ashley River in Elizabeth Bellinger Widow . . . ," March 26, 1741, Parish Trans., S.C., Box I, folder 5, p. 24.

[28] Guerard Letterbook, March 4, 1753. Compare "the Petition of John Daniel Carpenter setting forth that a valuable Negro of his had been shot in the Knee Pan by one of the Men enlisted in the Service of the Publick, on board the Schooner Ranger by which Means he was rendered incapable of working for his said Master." *SCCHJ, 1736–1739*, p. 497.

[29] Pringle Letterbook, Jan. 24, 1743.

[30] "Journal of Robert Pringle, 1746–1747," pp. 95–98, 104; Henry Laurens to Capt. Magnus Watson, Feb. 15, 1770, cited in Leila Sellers, *Charleston Business on the Eve of the Revolution* (Chapel Hill, N.C., 1934), p. 67.

were otherwise knowledgeable in local navigation. For such strategic skills to become available to an international rival, as when the Negroes from Thomas Poole's pilot boat were carried to St. Augustine by a Spanish privateer in 1741, was always a cause for alarm among English settlers.[31] They were well aware that for several decades Bermuda had suffered serious depredations from Spanish vessels piloted by Bermuda Negroes who had defected.[32] In 1745 a slave named Arrah was seized from Hugh Cartwright's schooner and "great encouragement was offered to be given him by the enemy if he would join with them against the English, and assist them as a pilot for . . . Carolina." When he stoutly refused and succeeded in making his way back to Charlestown after several years, the grateful Assembly granted him his freedom by a special act.[33]

IV

ALL THESE VARIED ACTIVITIES of the Negro majority, whether based on skills transmitted from Africa or acquired in Carolina, were controlled to serve the white economy. Slaves were obliged by law to submit to the fact that their labor could be directed arbitrarily to suit the designs of their owners or the needs of the white colony at large. Often, therefore, masters hired out their slaves to provide themselves with an additional source of revenue. At mid-century Gov. Glen went so far as to propose a tax of six pence per pound "upon the Gettings of Negroes

[31] *SCCHJ, 1741–1742*, p. 272. *Virginia Gazette*, Dec. 2, 1773, carried an advertisement for a runaway Negro pilot.

[32] Wilkinson, *Bermuda in the Old Empire*, p. 112. Several unusual documents found in the Bermuda Archives are worth mentioning here. In 1762 three slaves named Charles Cuff, Tom, and Peter were among those convicted of involvement in an intended rebellion and "Sentenced to be banished off these Islands to some Remote part of Maryland never to return here again under pain of Death." But it was pointed out to the governor that these men were "well skilled in the Channels in and about the East End of Our s^d Islands and that should [one of them] . . . happen to fall into the hand of Our Enemies it may be attended with more Dangerous Consequences to Our . . . Islands and Our People . . . than if the said Slave . . . should be permitted to remain within Our said Islands under certain Restrictions." Gov. Popple was prompted to revoke their banishment, ordering that they should "never henceforth Pilot or Conduct any Deckt Vessel coming into or going out from Our . . . Islands," and confining them to dry land in order that none might "fall into the hands of any Enemy by means of his . . . service on the sea." Bonds, Bills, and Grants (1739–66), VIII, 107–9, Bermuda Archives.

[33] *Statutes*, VII, 419–20.

who are good Tradesmen, and bring considerable Gains to their Masters."[34]

Occasionally public and private interests overlapped for these slaveowners. As public works were undertaken on an increasingly large scale, Negro hands were regularly placed in service. An excerpt from the colonial accounts for 1722 illustrates the steady presence of Negro labor in the public sector:[35]

To Noah Serce for Negroe Hire at Winyaw   2–5–0
To Mr Thomas Lloyd for Negroe Work, & Several things done to
    the ffortifications in Charles City   43–13–9
To Jacob Bond for Boards & the hyre of a Negroe Carpenter for
    fort King George   99 – –
To Messrs Wm Gibbon & Andrew Allan for Negroe Hyre for
    carrying Bricks for ffort King George   9–0–5

Military dangers created occasional demands for workers; over 240 Negroes were among those mobilized for several weeks in the summer of 1742 during the threat of a Spanish invasion. The majority were set to work on the fortifications in Charlestown, but more than seventy were enlisted aboard the vessels sailing to the relief of Georgia. Their masters, very few of whom sent more than one slave, received seven shillings, six pence for each day of public service.[36]

Most hiring, however, remained in the private sector, where white owners moved slaves about profitably in response to continuing demands for labor. Even hands to do regular household chores were often in short supply, and it was not strange for a Charlestown homeowner to seek notice of "Any Person that wants to let out by the Year, or dispose of, a Negro Wench that can wash and smooth Linnen."[37] An ad in the *Gazette* early in 1743 offered an accomplished mustee house boy "to be hired by the Year," and another six months later mentioned "Two very good House Wenches to be hired out by the Month."[38] Negro sawyers were generally owned and rented in pairs; a Charlestown hatter claimed to have four men who could "whet, set

[34] James Glen, "Description of South Carolina," March 1751, a typed copy of the manuscript in the Clements Library is in the folder marked "S. C. History COLONIAL Misc." at the SCHS.

[35] SCUHJ, Feb. 23, 1723, mfm BMP/D 487, SCDAH.

[36] *SCCHJ, 1742–44*, pp. 81, 325–32, 338, 339, 435, 440, 441, 491, 518, 519, 550; *SCCHJ, 1744–45*, pp. 8, 50, 263, 332, 370.

[37] *SCG*, Sept. 23, 1732.

[38] *SCG*, Jan. 3, 1743; July 25, 1743.

and lay Timbers."[39] Patrick Brown, a storekeeper, must have planned to hire out the three skilled slaves which he bought in 1744 for more than £280 each: "Two Angola's and [one] Iboe known by the names of Carolina, Anthony and Prince one of the three being a Cooper and the other two Sawyers."[40] Numerous Negro bricklayers were also in demand, and on at least one occasion the labor of several was actually bequeathed. It was the last wish of Mary Mullins that future proceeds from the work of her "two Negroe Bricklayers . . . employed about the Rebuilding of the Presbiterian Meeting House" be divided between the minister and the church.[41] And yet not all the proceeds from such exertions entered the pockets of free whites, for South Carolina slaves showed remarkable enterprise in their efforts to salvage for themselves some small individual profit in a system designed to preclude it. Indeed, the two bricklayers (Tony and Primus by name) who appear in the will of Mary Mullins provide a case in point. Not long after they were assigned to the Presbyterian Church, it was discovered that both craftsmen were selling their services secretly for their own profit.[42]

Of course certain remunerations remained legal, if practically unattainable. Where slaves had once collected a bounty for killing beasts of prey, they could still earn two shillings, six pence for every fox or raccoon skin they brought to the Charlestown hatters. In 1735 the price offered to freemen or slaves taking Tuscarora Indians was £50 if dead, £60 if alive, but heavy restrictions on travel and firearms prevented slaves from seeking these bounties on either animals or humans. As early as 1722 the Assembly complained that certain town slaves had struck bargains with their owners whereby they were allowed on certain days to seek money by fair means or foul, returning a prearranged sum to the master in the evening and pocketing whatever extra they acquired.[43]

When a black artisan's skill was uncommon his reputation could

[39] *SCG*, Feb. 1, 1735. The expression used here was apparently common to describe overall excellence in the trade. William Scott sold "Two Negro Men, choice Sawyers (who can whet and set and lay-out their Work) with their Wives and Children." *SCG*, Feb. 13, 1742.

[40] Deed of Sale, July 24, 1744, Charleston County MR, 1736–1740, WPA Typescript, vol. 106, n.p., SCDAH.

[41] WIMR, 1729–1731, vol. 62-A, p. 490, SCDAH.

[42] *SCG*, June 17, 1732; Oct. 5, 1734.

[43] *SCG*, Oct. 26, 1734 (cf. Chapter IV, note 9, above); June 21, 1735; *Statutes*, VII, 380.

be widespread: Sampson, a West Indian–born slave who was finally executed for his repeated efforts to escape, was "well known in Town & Country for his painting and glazing." But on the other hand, there was a whole class of nearly anonymous black porters and carters in Charlestown who did heavy jobs at cheap rates and returned a set weekly payment to their masters. Typical of this group was Aaron, a tall Negro man from Guinea-Bissau on the coast of Sierra Leone. He belonged to Daniel Bourget on Old Church Street, a white brewer who also kept a stable, and before he ran away in 1732 Aaron "used to go about the Town with a Cart & Mule" earning odd fares.[44]

Frequently, slaves with marketable talents took occasional jobs, and wages, without their owner's required approval, as numerous newspaper notices illustrate.[45] Jack, "by Trade a Ship-Carpenter," pretended to be free and received wages for work done aboard vessels in Charlestown Harbor after the death of his master in 1737. Several years later, Limas, a Negro carpenter who was sold after his owner died, slipped away from his new master and "for some Time wrought clandestinely about Town, and thereby defrauded his Master of several Sums of Money."[46]

Repeated public notice often was not enough to prevent an ambitious slave from finding employment. The following ads, printed almost a year apart, make this plain in the case of one individual:[47]

Whereas a Negro-Man named Lancaster, commonly known about the Town for a White washer, and Fisherman, has of late imposed upon his Employers, and defrauded me of his Wages; I do therefore advertise all Persons not to employ the said Lancaster, without first agreeing with me, or his

[44] *SCG*, Nov. 17, 1739; Jan. 10, 1743; Oct. 7, 1732.

[45] The following notices from the *SCG* (Jan. 20, 1733; March 10, 1733; July 31, 1736) are samples:

This is to forewarn all Manner of Persons whatsoever, not to employ two Negro Carpenters, . . . Mingo and Norwich, belonging to Lawrence Dennis of Charles town, without first agreeing with the said Dennis, or his Spouse for the same.

THIS is to give Notice to all Persons, that they do not hire or employ these following Negroes . . . Cuffee and Beavour, two Caulkers, and Anselm a Bricklayer, without first agreeing with . . . Nicholas Trott, or Sarah his Wife.

John Vaughan and Ralph Rodda Bricklayer[s] having two Negro Boys brought up to their Trade, which are employed by Persons without their Master's Leave or Licence, they hereby forewarn all and every Person from doing so in the future.

[46] *SCG*, Sept. 3, 1737; Aug. 15, 1741.
[47] *SCG*, Dec. 25, 1740; Oct. 17, 1741.

producing a proper Ticket, unless they are willing to pay the Fine pre-scribed by Law; and all Negroes who shall carry the said Lancaster a Fish-ing, shall be rigorously prosecuted by Elizabeth Smith.

WHEREAS I have formerly advertis'd all Persons not to employ my Negro-Man Lancaster in white washing or any other kind of Work whatever, but to little Purpose; since he constantly earns Money (which he losses either by Gaming or spends among the little Punch-Houses.) altho' he has been run away for this Month past: I do therefore once more peremptorily forbid all Persons from employing the said Lancaster in any Manner whatever, unless they first agree with, and have a Ticket from Dr. Dale, and pay unto him whatever Money the said Lancaster shall earn, otherwise they will assur-edly be prosecuted according to Law.

Elizabeth Smith

Lancaster's case suggests the degree to which labor needs often overcame legal scruples among white employers. His situation also underscores the fact that diligence in earning and diligence in saving were two very separate matters, and social forces were organized even more strongly against the latter than the former. Though a small quan-tity of cash could be obtained through extra exertion, there was every chance it would be snatched away arbitrarily and almost no prospect of conserving or investing it profitably. Pressures were all toward spending such money quickly or else running the risk of never spend-ing it at all. Thus slaves who were hired out by the week to accumu-late a fixed amount for their masters and who succeeded in earning an additional margin of cash through their personal initiative or ingenu-ity were still likely to part with this pocket money immediately in what can only be considered a sound principle of investment under the circumstances.[48]

[48] Free colonists took regular advantage of economic initiative among slaves, paying them small sums for special services while seeking to assure that such money would recirculate into white hands as rapidly as possible. The ale houses and gaming shops, which provided the readiest means for recirculation, were then cited by Europeans as evidence of the Negro's slothful nature. Complaint was made before the Grand Jury, March 10, 1734: "that it is a common Practice by Several Persons in Charles Town, to suffer their Negroes to work out by the Week, and Oblige them to bring in a certain Hire which is not only Contrary to a Law now subsisting, but a Great Inlet to Idleness, Drunkenness and other Enormities." *SCG*, March 30, 1734; rpt. in *SCHGM*, XXV (1924), 193.

Dr. James P. Comer, *Beyond Black and White* (New York, 1972), p. 24, describes black steel workers in a northern city two hundred years later who, even when almost broke, would insist on buying a round of drinks. "Trying to feel adequate in a society that demands and then limits one's opportunity to be adequate takes unusual forms. Buying the drinks is one of them."

Yet even in spite of the thoroughly negative incentives for thrift among black workers, whites were chagrined to find that some Negroes were cleverly working their meager earnings into investments which could yield an interest. There is clear evidence of slaves entering upon organized efforts to slice out a small wedge of profit from their masters' economic pie. By 1720 goods as well as services were being sold regularly to willing European colonists through a network of informal contacts, and Gov. Nicholson's message to the Assembly the following year concerning the government of Charlestown suggested that "a sufficient provision be made against trading with Negroes, or other Servants, & Slaves, and receiving anything from them."[49] But this commerce continued to increase, and in 1734 Charlestown Negroes were accused of shrewdly buying up a large enough proportion of the country produce brought in by plantation slaves in order to force an increase in the rates being paid for provisions by white town dwellers. "We present as a very great Grievance and an intollerable hardship," Chief Justice Wright was told, "that Negroes are suffered to buy and sell, and be Hucksters of Corn, Pease, Fowls &[ca] whereby they watch Night and Day on the Several Wharfs, and buy up many Articles necessary for the Support of the Inhabitants and make them pay an exorbitant price."[50]

Such industriousness had unsettling effects upon the white minority. Labor rates appeared unstable and food prices seemed high. The concern of Europeans over the growing preponderance of blacks and their continuingly diverse activities was reflected in the changing statutes of the colony. Examined together, the successive slave laws of the South Carolina colony reveal a gradual movement toward forced dependence, with slaves being allowed to manage fewer things for their own use or profit and masters being required to provide more. Rations of clothing material and food were to be made available by the owner as a means of curtailing black initiative, and time itself was a commodity of which the slaves were allowed only a limited amount for themselves. Restricted in what they could produce on their own and sell, plantation residents increasingly took to selling goods which were legally the landlord's. Among the bills ratified in 1738, therefore,

[49] SCUHJ, Aug. 28, 1721, mfm, BMP/D 487, SCDAH.

[50] BPRO Trans., XVII, 304; cf. *SCHGM, XXV* (1924), 193 *ff*. Seven years later the Clerk of the Market protested against this forestalling and "Negro-huckstering" by the food venders, whose tuneful street cries would become one of the city's particular legacies. *SCCHJ, 1741–1742,* p. 16.

was "an Act for licencing Hawkers, Pedlers and petty Chapmen, and to prevent their trading with indented Servants, Overseers, Negroes and other Slaves."[51]

Early in the same year the Assembly proposed a statute to prevent Charlestown slaves from buying goods during market hours and to prohibit them from buying fish, fruit, or vegetables at any time. The intent of this measure was to stop white residents from sending Negro slaves to do their marketing, but the members of the council, representing the wealthy families among whom this practice was most common, opposed the idea.[52] The two houses disputed the issue for some time, and in 1741 the Clerk of the Market blamed a good deal of confusion and fraud on the fact that "Negroes went so much to Market for the Families." By this time it was illegal for slaves to sell any goods in the markets without a ticket, although the clerk admitted he was unable to keep track of "such as shaggle up and down."[53]

Not only were white merchants hurt by the enterprise of slaves around the marketplace, but commercial activities in the countryside could undermine the entire Charlestown market. An act of 1751 made it unlawful for slaves outside the town limits to sell rice or Indian corn to any person except their master, and any person purchasing such commodities illegally was to be fined forty shillings.[54] No penalty against the Negro sellers or their white buyers was fully effective, but the increasing strictures did serve to drive this considerable portion of the colony's commerce underground into what can only be described —in both senses—as a black market.

V

THE FACT THAT SLAVES struggled to maintain a covert place in the colony's regular economy through the profitable exchange of goods and services was less disquieting to white residents than the fact that many frequently chose, or were obliged, to subvert the standard economy altogether. Active bartering could be seen as a dubious extension of the free enterprise system, through which much was accomplished and little harm was done. But for blacks to "appropriate" items of per-

[51] BPRO Trans., XX, 266.
[52] *SCCHJ, 1737–1738*, pp. 429, 512–15.
[53] *SCCHJ, 1741–1742*, pp. 22–23, 16–17.
[54] *Statutes*, VII, 423.

sonal property from whites without permission or payment constituted a form of direct resistance, and this pattern grew more pervasive with time. As the slaves' relative status deteriorated and their opportunities became more circumscribed, they resorted increasingly to the dangerous practice of simply taking what they needed, or were denied, and then using or trading it as suited their purposes.

As early as 1714 a statute, no doubt imperfectly enforced, had ordered a twenty-pound fine for masters who continued to "suffer or allow any . . . slaves to plant for themselves any corn, peas or rice or to keep for themselves any stock of hogs cattle or horses."[55] The Negro Act of 1722 conceded there was considerable "stealing of fowles" and "robbing of hen-roosts," and it acknowledged that "negroes and other slaves, under pretence of hunger, do frequently break open corn-houses and rice-houses, and steal from thence corn and rice."[56] Certainly hunger and other basic needs were not generally mere pretense. An English traveler who had seen slaves from Charlestown to the Chesapeake in the 1740s observed: "They are, no Doubt, very great Thieves, but this may flow from their unhappy, indigent Circumstances, and not from a natural Bent."[57]

The appropriation process is most clearly illustrated in the case of horses and cattle, since these animals were among the most available and valuable targets in such an agricultural settlement. From the beginning of the colony Negroes occasionally helped themselves to the livestock which they attended, and the methods of branding introduced before the turn of the century did little to deter this practice. Slaves altered brands with such dexterity that it was soon felt necessary to prohibit them from owning livestock altogether. The act of 1722 which denied slaves the right to keep horses, cows, and hogs (as well as boats or canoes) explained that "great inconveniences do arise

[55] *Statutes,* VII, 368.

[56] *Statutes,* VII, 374. Compare Henry C. Wilkinson's description of mid-eighteenth-century Bermuda, where "nocturnal marauders . . . stripped every edible object so completely and over such a radius that agriculture fell into more notorious neglect than would have seemed possible. In truth, those who improved their land really suffered for their industry, with the result that Bermuda, in its internal economy, lagged far in arrears of most colonies in the western hemisphere. Bermudians did not have to await Adam Smith's *Wealth of Nations* to learn the economic disadvantage of slavery." *Bermuda in the Old Empire,* p. 245 and note.

[57] "Itinerant Observations in America," Ga. Hist. Soc., *Collections,* IV (1878), 38. The author added, "and when they have robb'd, you may lash them Hours before they will confess the Fact." Any underlying differences between West African and western European ideas of "property" have not been fully explored, but see William R. Bascom, "Acculturation," pp. 43–50.

from negroes and other slaves keeping and breeding of horses, whereby they convey intelligences from one part of the country to another, and carry on their secret plots and contrivances for insurrections and rebellions."[58]

Harsh deterrents did not stop slaves from appropriating forbidden livestock, and the columns of the *Gazette* contain occasional ads for horses "strayed or stolen." An item from 1733 reads: "On Saturday last, a Negro Fellow belonging to Mr. Isaac Mazyck, sen. pull'd a young Ladd off his Horse, on the Board Path, and rode away with the Horse, and Bags thereon, in which were Cloathes of Value: He was taken on Sunday, on Monday brought to Town, tried and condemned; and the next Day, about Noon, he was hanged."[59] As on most frontiers, animals not used by those who took them could be sold at a profit, and at times there was apparently a brisk intercolonial traffic in stolen horses. Negro participation in livestock rustling was great enough so that when the Assembly drew up "An Act to prevent Stealing of Horses and Neat Cattle" in 1743 it went so far as to declare, "That it shall not be lawfull hereafter for any Slave whatsoever to brand or mark any horses or neat Cattle but in the Presence of some white Person under the penalty of being severely whip[p]ed."[60]

Stealing, or at least stealth, was already familiar in 1690, for a law of that year exempted from action any white who killed "a slave stealing in his house or plantation by night, the said slave refusing to submit." The incidence of larceny by slaves increased with time, and white suspicions escalated even faster, until they reached a point where nearly anything lost by a European or possessed by an African was assumed to be stolen. When the sum of £143 "bound up in a letter" was lost in the vicinity of Dorchester by James Postell in 1733, he immediately advertised a £10 reward and added: "*N.B.* All Persons are desired, that if any Negro shall offer to pay any large Bills, to give Notice to the . . . above-named."[61]

---

[58] *Statutes*, VII, 382.

[59] *SCG*, Jan. 27, 1733. A promotional tract from this time stated that "Horses, the best Kind in the World, are so plentiful, that you seldom see any body travel on foot, except *Negroes*, and they oftner on horseback." Purry, "A Description of the Province of South Carolina, . . . 1731," rpt. in Force, *Tracts*, II, 9. And in 1735 it was estimated that eight hundred horses were used annually in South Carolina's Indian trade. BPRO Trans., XVII, 413.

[60] *Statutes*, III, 604; cf. similar clause in act of 1768, *Statutes*, IV, 285. Both acts provide for repeal of a law passed Feb. 17, 1704, entitled "An Act to prevent stealing of horses and neat cattle."

[61] *Statutes*, VII, 347; *SCG*, March 10, 1733.

The following spring an advertiser sought information concerning the person, "(supposed to be a Negro)," who had stolen a bag full of clothes, sheets, and books from the edge of Richard Wright's pasture, and several months later when Thomas Bolton lost a silver snuff box from his home on the bay, he announced that "it is supposed to be stolen by a Negro." Such suspicions were not dismissed idly, and white colonists assumed the right to demand any article in a Negro's possession. In a typical incident, a slave of Mr. Stanyarne was made to relinquish "a Piece of blue Taffety, suspected to be stolen" to Richard Powers, who then placed a notice in the *Gazette*.[62]

Members of the watch, the patrols, and the local constabulary had special responsibility for control in this area, as is clear from the activities of Lewis Lormier, one of four Charlestown constables in the early 1740s. According to an ad printed on New Year's Day, 1741, he had paid two shillings "to a Negro for finding: two Silver Casters, one large Spoon, two Tea Spoons, and a small Box with some Jewels therein." A year later Lormier announced having found "In the Possession of a Negro Boy . . . a Gold Ring which I suppose to have been stolen or lost," and the following January he advertised that some good leather, suspected of being stolen, "was taken from two Negroes (who immediately made off)" and would be sold for the use of the poor if not claimed within a month.[63]

Despite efforts at surveillance, slaves became adroit at acquiring valuable or useful articles. Certain Negroes made a practice of taking up goods in their owners' names;[64] others may well have pretended carelessness in making goods disappear.[65] Still others resorted to bolder methods of petty larceny, especially those slaves who were allowed to work where they wished so long as they returned a prearranged fee to their master at the end of the day or week. The Negro Act of 1722 charged that this arrangement prompted "slaves to spend their time in looking for opportunities to steal, in order to raise money to pay their

[62] *SCG*, April 6, 1734; Aug. 10, 1734; Jan. 31, 1743.

[63] *SCG*, Jan. 1, 1741; Jan. 9, 1742; Jan. 3, 1743.

[64] For example, the following ad appeared in the *SCG* for Dec. 27, 1742, and Jan. 10, 1743: "WHEREAS my Negro Fellow nam'd Hercules, hath taken up Things at divers Places in my Name, without my Knowledge; this is therefore to forewarn all Persons from trusting him hitherto on my Accounts. ELIZABETH SMITH."

[65] E.g., *SCG*, Aug. 23, 1735: "Dropt by my Negro Girl between Mrs. Harris's and Mr. Gooding's House, a Suit of Flanders laced Head clothes, 2 laced Mobs, 2 laced Handkerchiefs Whoever has taken them up and will bring them to Elizabeth Lions, at Mrs. Harris's, shall have 20 l. paid at the delivery, and no Questions ask'd."

masters, as well as to maintain themselves, and other slaves, their companions. . . ." It imposed a five-shilling fine on offending masters which was raised to £ 10 per offense in the Negro Act of 1735.[66]

In outlying areas runaway slaves were common participants in these activities during the colonial period, and it is not surprising to find that at least one spot along Charlestown Neck was "commonly . . . known by the Name of Pick Pocket," for the pathway leading out of town was a notorious place for vandalism, most of which was attributed to absentee slaves.[67] The *Gazette* related how several Catawba Indians departed from Charlestown in the summer of 1736,

and going up the broad Path, the Head Man of them lying down to sleep on this Side the Quarterhouse, he was robb'd of his Gun, Powder and Shot Pouch, an Otter-Skin bag, Shoes, Hat, and all what he had about him, which is supposed to be committed by some Run-away Negroes, who lurk about the Town, having no fear of being disturb'd by the Patrol, that Law being expired.[68]

Within the town limits it appears as though groups of Negroes were occasionally involved in what must at least be called semiorganized crime. In New York City in the mid-1730s a band of slaves who had shared in certain larcenies and punishments became known as "the Geneva Club" after appropriating some Geneva gin,[69] and similar loose associations may well have been at work in Charlestown. The *Gazette* for June 21, 1735, reported that three Negroes, apparently armed, had broken into Capt. Windham's brewhouse the previous Tuesday night, and although driven off by the brewer, they had ventured to return later in the week. The scale which some of these undertakings could assume is revealed by another item in the same column:

In Thursday a Discovery was made of a Theft, committed by some Negroes belonging to Mr. James Crockatt of Charlestown Merchant, they had stolen out of their Master's Store a considerable Quantity of Goods to the value of above 2000 Pounds, hid and buried several of them under Ground in his own Yard, carried others to such houses and persons as they knew would receive and conceal the same, and gave some to other Negroes of their Acquaintance. It is supposed a great many Negros are concern'd in this

[66] *Statutes,* VII, 380; *Statutes,* VII, 393.
[67] *SCG,* Oct. 13, 1739.
[68] *SCG,* July 10, 1736.
[69] Thomas J. Davis, *The New York Conspiracy* (Boston, 1971), p. xiii.

robbery, and no doubt but some white Persons that are concealers of such Goods will be detected at the Tryal of these Negroes, and brought to condign punishment.[70]

Two years later a carpenter's apprentice, aided by three other young Negroes, entered a Charlestown residence at night "and carried away a Trunk with Paper Currency, Notes of Hand, gold Buttons, and silver Buckles to the value of 600 *l.*"[71] All were caught by their "liberal spending," yet while the accomplices were whipped through the town and the leader was threatened with branding and deportation, the valuables were not readily found.

The most interesting aspect of the appropriation process, however, is not how the goods were obtained but what ultimately became of them. Some items could be returned with profit as having been "found" when the owner offered a reward. Other things could be pawned to whites, who gained handsomely from such bargains and therefore encouraged the process. (There was never strict enforcement of the 1714 statute which made receivers of stolen goods subject to prosecution, or of the later act which threatened peddlers dealing in such articles with fines and loss of license.[72]) But a surprising amount of usable items entered the black market mentioned earlier. A substantial underground economy seems to have developed, involving a steady flow of a wide variety of goods.

Naturally the traffic in appropriated goods was heaviest around Charlestown, where the concentration of slaves was largest and the opportunities for mingling legal and illicit trade were greatest. No materials left unguarded on the docks were considered safe.[73] And waterfront Negroes were said to watch constantly at the wharves for black patroons from the country with whom they might do business.[74] The Grand Jury which met in October 1737 stated as a grievance, "the Practice of Negroes buying and selling Wares in the Streets of Charles-

[70] *SCG*, June 21, 1735.

[71] *SCG*, June 25, 1737. For other incidents of slaves arrested for breaking and entering, see SCUHJ, March 19, 1734, SCDAH, and *SCG*, "postscript," Jan. 9, 1742.

[72] *Statutes*, VII, 367; *Statutes*, III, 489.

[73] Pringle Letterbook. Robert Pringle wrote to John Erving (Sept. 9, 1740) concerning shipments of bricks: "there is always a very great Breakage of them & as they Lye expos'd on our Common Wharfs after Landing are Lyable to be Stolen and Embezell'd by all Comers which renders them the worst Commodity a Ship Can bring here."

[74] See note 50 above.

Town, wherby stolen Goods may be concealed and afterwards vended undiscovered."[75]

But city streets were not the only place for illicit traffic. The same Grand Jury presentment of 1737 protested against "Negroes going in Boats and Canoes up the Country trading with Negroes in a clandestine manner." Two months later the Assembly urged that slaves no longer "be suffered to go atrading in the Country."[76] Despite official opposition, however, the commercial interaction between town dwellers and plantation residents continued, for in October 1744 the Grand Jury presentments included as a grievance: "Negroes being allowed to go from Town in[to] the Country under the Pretence to pick Myrtle Berrys &c[a] and who at the same time carry Rum & Liquors to trade with Negroes in the Country." The jury complained that plantation slaves were thereby "debauched & Encouraged to steal & robb their Masters of their Corn & Poultry & other Provisions."[77] And yet the more the Negro community was explicitly prohibited from earning, purchasing, and possessing goods, the more respectable, justifiable, and necessary such clandestine activity would become as an economic way of life.

[75] *SCG,* Nov. 5, 1737.
[76] *Ibid.; SCCHJ, 1737–38,* p. 364.
[77] BPRO Trans., XXII, 82.

VIII

Mounting Anxiety
Among Whites

I

FOR Europeans, fears and fantasies based on skin color had pre-dated the entire process of overseas colonization.[1] The formation of a settlement such as that in South Carolina in no way automatically intensified these fears. Far from being augmented and elaborated in the new colony, certain European anxieties may have dissipated be-fore the realistic demands of life on a thoroughly interracial frontier. But in the face of a distinct majority of blacks, the apprehensions felt by white colonists gradually deepened. Concern stemmed first from a simple awareness of numbers, but it spread out to encompass a variety of ambiguities concerning the identity of the colony and the tenu-ous position of the Europeans who were ostensibly its masters.

Not even straightforward population awareness came easily, for numbers, after all, are a highly subjective matter. Even after the sys-tematic enumeration of slaves had begun, it was hard for Europeans to come to terms directly with the demographic situation which was so thoroughly apparent around them. The way local population figures were analyzed and altered suggests the dimensions of this uneasiness. The number of blacks, first of all, was simply exaggerated. And not only newcomers struck by the contrast with Europe but also residents of long standing misrepresented conditions. Samuel Wragg, the owner of land in St. George's Parish and elsewhere and a magnate in South Carolina commerce for nearly two decades, testified before the Com-missioners for Trade and Plantations in 1726 that "that country for-merly had but very few negroes, but now they employ near 40,000,"

[1] Jordan, *White Over Black*, Chapter I.

fully twice the number actually enslaved. Though 1726 was the first year in which black arrivals approached 1,000, Wragg minimized his own role in Carolina's African trade by claiming that "they now *usually* import 1,000 per annum."[2] Several years later John Peter Purry wrongly estimated "above 40,000 Negroes."[3] And in 1734, as annual slave imports were passing 2,000 for the first time, Capt. Von Reck could claim "there are imported generally 3,000 fresh Negroes every Year."[4]

A further confusion arose from the tendency to measure white male adults against the entire black population. This statistic took on increasing importance for European colonists as they felt themselves physically threatened by the number of Africans, and numerous population estimates after 1720, contrasting men on the muster rolls with all adults and children in the slave quarters, reflect the emerging concept of white manhood opposing a preponderant race. This explains why Von Reck stated in 1734 that "There are five Negroes to one White."[5] It also helps make understandable (although not correct) the assertion of a European in 1737 that "In Charleston and that neighborhood there are calculated to be always 20 blacks . . . to one white man,"[6] as well as the claim of another visitor five years later that "the heathen slaves are so numerous here that it is estimated that there are fifteen for every white man."[7]

Even after framing the disproportion in its starkest form, white colonists faced the added realization that the slave population was being augmented annually while their own numbers scarcely rose. Indeed, an Anglican minister noted in 1725, "we have some reason to believe that we rather decrease than increase in the small number of Christian white inhabitants." He went on to explain candidly, "As matters stand with us we make use of a wile for our present security to

---

[2] Hearing before the Board of Trade, May 4, 1726, in *Journal of the Commissioners for Trade and Plantations* (London, 1928), pp. 251–54, italics added. Cf. Wood, "Black Majority," p. 369 n. For a useful cautionary statement on these matters, see Curtin, *Atlantic Slave Trade*, Chapter I.

[3] Purry, "A Description of the Province of South Carolina, . . . 1731," rpt. in Force, *Tracts*, II, 6.

[4] "Extracts of Mr. Von Reck's Journal," in Force, *Tracts*, IV, 9.

[5] *Ibid.*

[6] Samuel Dyssli to friends in Switzerland, Dec. 3, 1737, *SCHGM*, XXII (1922), 90.

[7] *Muhlenberg*, I, 58. On a later visit to Charlestown, Sept. 8, 1774, this prominent minister recorded (II, 567) "At first it strikes one as strange to see so many Negro slaves, for here, it is said, there are twenty blacks for every white man."

make the Indians and negros a check upon each other lest by their vastly superior numbers we should be crushed by one or the other."[8] Slaves, who had generally been taken as an asset in the thinly settled proprietary colony, were now viewed in part by whites as a liability. First of all, the presence of an enslaved majority anxious for liberation increased the chances of invasions by foreign powers and reduced the colony's ability to resist such attacks. And moreover, quite apart from the inducement which the slaves provided to foreign enemies, they constituted a rebellious threat in their own right.

Two weeks after South Carolina became a crown colony in 1720, a document drawn at Whitehall described the settlement as being in "great disorder," pointing out that "the Inhabitants are exposed to incursions of the Barbarous Indians" and "the Encroachments of their European Neighbours," and adding that "ye whole Province was lately in danger of being massacred by their Own Slaves, who are too numerous in proportion to ye White Men there."[9] The white colonists, observed Sir Alexander Cuming in 1730 after six months in the province, "are in danger of the Blacks Riseing up against them, who are Six times the Number of the Whites [that is, white adult males]." Cuming blamed this state of affairs upon "the Mutinous Disposition of their Masters," almost all of whom conceded the colony "to be in a miserable Condition but being divided in their Measures and particular Interests No two of them can agree in any common Measure for their Relief."[10] Four years later, Von Reck's report contained this ominous appraisal:

There are computed to be 30,000 Negroes in this Province, all of them Slaves, and their Posterity for ever: They work six Days in the Week for their Masters without pay, and are allowed to work on Sundays for themselves. . . . Being thus used, lays amongst them a Foundation of Discontent; and they are generally thought to watch an Opportunity of revolting

----

[8] Richard Ludlam to David Humphreys, Goose Creek, March 22, 1725, quoted in Klingberg, *Appraisal*, p. 47. Ludlam continued: "This I imagine one cause that intimidates the planters from being willing that their sensible slaves should be converted to Christianity lest as they allege they should make such an ill use of meeting to do their duty to God as to take the opportunity at such times of seizing and destroying their owners."

[9] Lords Commissioners for Trade and Plantations to their Excellencies the Lords Justices, Aug. 30, 1720, BPRO Trans., VIII, 99–100. Compare the statement by Benjamin Martyn, Chapter V, note 85, above.

[10] "The humble Memorial of Sir Alexander Cuming Bart to his Grace the Duke of Newcastle," received July 11, 1730, BPRO Trans., XIV, 225.

against their Masters, as they have lately done in the Island of St. John and of St. Thomas, belonging to the Danes and Sweeds; and it is the Apprehension of these and other Inconveniences, that has induced the Honourable Trustees of Georgia, to prohibit the Importation and Use of Negroes within their Colony.[11]

II

As Capt. Von Reck's report makes clear, scraps of news from abroad regarding perils inherent within the slave system were closely watched by Europeans in Carolina. Incidents from the slave trade itself offered repeated evidence of the desperate ends to which captive people might be driven, and white Carolinians took a wary interest in the frequent stories of reversals on the Guinea Coast. The fate of the *Clare*, as reported in London and Boston, must have been a subject of common gossip along Charlestown piers in 1729:

We have an account from Guinea by Way of Antigua, that the *Clare* Galley, Capt. Murrell, having compleated her Number of Negroes had taken her Departure from the Coast of Guinea for South Carolina; but was not got 10 Leagues on her Way, before the Negroes rose and making themselves Masters of the Gunpowder and Fire Arms, the Captain and Ships Crew took to their Long Boat, and got shore near Cape Coast Castle. The Negroes ran the Ship on Shore within a few Leagues of the said Castle, and made their escape.[12]

When South Carolina got its own newspaper in 1732, the second issue carried an account of an uprising aboard the *Dolphin,* a brigantine taking on slaves at "Taboe, near Cape Palmas, on the windward Coast." In November the *Gazette* printed news from Africa that "Capt. John Major, in a scooner from New-Hampshire, was treacherously murdered, and his Vessel and Cargo seized by Negroes." And in December came word of another uprising in which the commander, sev-

---

[11] "Extracts of Mr. Von Reck's Journal," in Force, *Tracts,* IV, 9.

[12] *Boston News-Letter,* Sept. 25, 1729. This item is in Donnan, *Documents,* IV, 274, with the comment by the editor that "There is nothing unusual about this disaster to the *Clare* save the wide publicity which it seems to have received." Note that the incident reflects a prior knowledge of guns and gunpowder among the slaves, as does an item from the *SCG,* July 14, 1733: "The Robert, Capt. Hamilton, was lately blown up by the Negroes on the Coast of Guinea." For a general discussion of such insurgency, see Darold D. Wax, "Negro Resistance to the Early American Slave Trade," *JNH,* LI (1966), 1–15.

eral crewmen, and some Negroes were killed; despite aid from shore, no slaves were able to get away. "About the same time," continued the *Gazette's* report, "the Slaves on board a Guinea-man belonging to Bristol, rose and destroyed the whole Crew, cutting off the Captain's Head, Legs and Arms."[13] During this same period the paper featured reports of extended warfare between the Spanish and the Moors around Oran and Ceuta, a conflict which must have assumed racial significance in pitting Europeans against Africans.[14]

The items which struck closest to home, however, were those from the nearby Caribbean. The revolts in the Virgin Islands in 1734, as Von Reck had noted, were carefully followed by white Carolinians. In early March the *Gazette* relayed the news that the slaves on St. John's "had intirely massacred all the white People on that Island, consisting of about 200 Families, and were very inhuman in the Execution of their Murders." The next issue carried a story that white landing parties from St. Kitts and St. Thomas had attacked the rebels "with such vigour, that in less than one hour they cut them all to pieces, some were taken Prisoners, and afterwards hang'd and quarter'd as they deserved, and not one of 'em escaped." But in fact the suppression was by no means so thorough, and not until nine months later did the *Gazette* report that French and Indians trained in slave hunting had finally been imported from Martinique to track down the resisters. Dozens of the Negroes committed suicide to escape torture, and it was recounted that "one of the Rebels was so hardy, that he would not go in with the rest, but was resolved to kill some body before he was taken, upon which a Company went out and shot him, so an End was put to the melancholly Scene." Meanwhile, the word came of an attempted rising in St. Kitts, "by setting Six Houses on Fire," and a similar effort must have occurred several years later, for Robert Pringle wrote to a friend on St. Kitts in 1739 that he was "much Concern'd to hear . . . of your being alarm'd for fear of an Insurrection of the Negroes but hope their wicked Designs will prove abortive & turn to their own Confusion."[15]

---

[13] *SCG,* Jan. 15, 1732; Nov. 18, 1732; Dec. 9, 1732. Cf. Donnan, *Documents,* II, 461: "The *Boston Weekly News Letter* . . . published a gruesome account by one of the two survivors of the *Mary,* lost on a voyage from Cachao to Lisbon with slaves. *News Letter,* Sept. 8, 1737."

[14] See *SCG* for Sept. 1732, also Feb. 10 and June 9, 1733. One issue (Nov. 11, 1732) relates an incident in the conflict between the Spaniards and "Musketo Men" in the Caribbean.

[15] *SCG,* March 2, 1734; March 9, 1734; Dec. 21, 1734; May 11, 1734; Robert Pringle to Francis Guichard, Feb. 5, 1739, Pringle Letterbook.

The most dramatic stories of Caribbean upheaval during the 1730s, however, proceeded from Jamaica, and the *Gazette* chronicled the violence there as fully as possible. Word came via Rhode Island in 1732 that a Jamaican militia company had seized "a large Negro Town, . . . had killed and taken above 40 Negroes, and expected Recruits every Day to secure the Town for the English Inhabitants."[16] In May 1734 the *Gazette* quoted the letter of a white Jamaican saying that "Our rebellious Negroes are so numerous that they attack us everywhere, and are not afraid of our greatest Force. About ten Days ago," the source continued, "they attacked near 100 Men most Soldiers. carried away their Arms, Provisions, and what plunder they pleased; most of our people fled; we can get no body to stand before them."[17]

The following January, Carolina readers were informed that in the fall a British man-of-war had been dispatched from Gibraltar "to quell the Rebellious Negroes in Jamaica" where martial law was in effect. The *South Carolina Gazette,* which printed only several columns of news per week, continued to feature intermittent dispatches. In September it reported that a force of more than seventeen hundred was pursuing the rebels and roads were being cut through the island to speed their suppression, but the following month word came from Jamaica "that it is as bad there with the rebellious Negroes as ever, being there runs every Day over to them 3 for every one that is taken."[18] With fascination and horror, slaveholders in the southern colonies followed these dispatches on the Maroon War through to the final treaty in 1738.

For Carolina, with its rapidly increasing African trade, there were dire implications, and even in Virginia, where the free populace would never become a minority, the repercussions of high slave im-

[16] *SCG*, Nov. 1, 1732. For details of race relations in Jamaica between 1729 and 1739, including the war between the Maroons and the English, see George Metcalf, *Royal Government and Political Conflict in Jamaica, 1729–1783* (London, 1965), Chapter II.

[17] *SCG*, May 18, 1734. The issue of Sept. 7, 1734, carried other letters from Kingston written about the same time. One correspondent related:

We are at present more apprehensive of a Civil than a Foreign War, the rebellious Negroes that are settled in the Mountains having been very troublesome of late, and are now become more numerous by . . . those that are daily running away from several of the Adjacent Settlements to join them; they have lately made Incursions into some of the Neighbouring Plantations, and done considerable Damage; and it is feared, if some effectual Means are not taken to reduce them they may in a Little Time render themselves stronger than the Force that can be sent against them.

[18] *SCG*, Jan. 18, 1735; July 12, 1735; Sept. 20, 1735; Oct. 11, 1735.

ports were becoming the subject of growing concern. In 1736 Virginia's William Byrd wrote the Earl of Egmont congratulating him on the prohibition of slavery in Georgia and urging an end to the slave trade. Byrd described at length the ambivalence which made mainland planters feel increasingly foolish and furious, and numerous South Carolina slaveowners, scanning reports from the Caribbean at this time, must have shared his anxious thoughts.

They import so many Negroes hither, that I fear this Colony will some time or other be confirmed by the Name of New Guinea. I am sensible of many bad consequences of multiplying these Ethiopians amongst us. They blow up the pride, and ruin the Industry of our White People, who seing a Rank of poor Creatures below them, detest work for fear it should make them look like Slaves. . . .

Another unhappy Effect of Many Negros is the necessity of being severe. Numbers make them insolent, and their foul Means must do what fair will not. We have however nothing like the Inhumanity here that is practiced in the Islands, and God forbid we ever shoud. But these base Tempers require to be rid with a tort Rein, or they will be apt to throw their Rider. Yet even this is terrible to a good naturd Man, who must submit to be either a Fool or a Fury. And this will be more our unhappy case, the more Negros are increast amongst us.

But these private mischiefs are nothing if compard to the publick danger. We have already at least 10,000 Men of these descendants of Ham fit to bear Arms, and their Numbers increase every day as well by birth as Importation. And in case there shoud arise a Man of desperate courage amongst us, exasperated by a desperate fortune, he might with more advantage than Cataline kindle a Servile War. Such a man might be dreadfully mischeivous before any opposition could be formed against him, and tinge our Rivers as wide as they are with blood.[19]

III

THE DILEMMA posed by events in the West Indies had particular acuteness for whites in South Carolina. Their province, after all, was something of an anomaly to both the mainland and Caribbean colonial worlds, as is suggested by the fact that wills and travel accounts still

[19] Col. William Byrd to Earl of Egmont, July 12, 1736, printed in Donnan, *Documents,* IV, 131–32.

referred to "Carolina in the West Indies" upon occasion.[20] While these Carolinians admired the numerical strength and economic diversity of Europeans farther north, they shunned the well-known commercial subservience of the provision colonies; and although they envied the luxurious life-style of associates in the sugar islands, they were newly fearful of the risks it entailed. By the early 1730s they could feel both horns of the dilemma sharply, for no sooner had rice been removed from the empire's list of enumerated commodities in 1730 and the way cleared for South Carolina's triumph as a staple colony than word from the Caribbean raised fresh concern about the dangers of plantation life: should white Carolinians view the trouble in the West Indies as a windfall to speed their ascendancy, or as an omen to warn against destruction?

Nothing illustrates their awareness of the two contrasting worlds to the north and south of them more clearly than a pair of letters which received equal attention in a single issue of the *Gazette* in 1732. One was a representation to the king from New York's legislature ("most loyal and dutiful Subjects of these Bread Colonies") opposing the mercantile policies which forced their goods toward the English West Indies. They beseeched the king, in terms Carolinians could understand, not "to cut us off from being of any other Use to our Mother Country, than to be the Bondsmen and Slaves of her Sugar Colonies, by confining us to them for the Vent of the Produce of our Industry." The adjacent letter expressed West Indian grievances. The author in Jamaica complained to London that white inhabitants were "going off daily," taking their slaves and leaving wide areas still uncultivated, on account of

the declining Condition of their Estates, the Increase of our Rebel Negroes, and the Loss of our Trade.

These unhappy Circumstances have struck such a Damp on the Inhabitants of this Island, that nothing is heard but Preparations for the Northern Colonies; and Carolina begins to encourage great Numbers to adventure there, forasmuch as by the great Goodness of his Majesty, and the Wisdom of the Parliament, the Enumeration of Rice is taken off.[21]

For more than a decade the white minority in South Carolina would wrestle with ways to obtain the best of both worlds, keeping

[20] *SCHGM*, IV (1903), 235; cf. Chapter I, note 63, above, and note 27, below.
[21] *SCG*, July 1, 1732.

the price of rice up and the percentage of slaves down. One of the most ingenious plans for combining the advantages of a staple colony with those of a provision colony was that offered to readers of the *Gazette* by "Agricola" the following winter. He dispensed with the recurrent idea of crop diversification by remarking "how improbable 'tis that a Planter, who has engaged his Crop for Negroes, (which is, perhaps, the Case of too many of us) should venture on new, and uncertain Projects." He also dismissed well-intentioned efforts to mechanize rice production with mills and dams on the simple grounds that there were too few artificers to maintain them. Instead, "Agricola" urged intensification designed to reduce the quantity and improve the quality of rice. According to his argument:

if in lieu of five Acres to a Hand, our Planter were obliged to plant no more than two; it is reasonable to presume, that in a short Time, the Produce of the two Acres, would yield as much at Market, as the Produce of the five. And I would fain know, whether a Man could not find what to do with the rest of his Negroe's Time? Yes certainly. He would apply it to the Improvement of his Cattle, and preparing Beef, and Pork for the Islands; and our old Rice Fields would then be of singular Use for Pasturage: The Situation of our Country would enable us to be the earliest of all the Northern Colonies at Market, & of course, to engross all that valuable Trade: The surplus Time also would, without inconveniency, enable us to endeavour to cultivate all other useful Manufactures.[22]

Rice planters already realized, as did tobacco growers in Virginia, that to decrease acreage per slave was almost impossible in an economy where land was cheap and labor scarce. But there seemed another means by which the colony might have its cake and eat it too: if forced migration from Africa could be offset by voluntary immigration from Europe, then white colonists could reap the benefits of plantation agriculture without being dangerously outnumbered or limited to a single crop. A memorial filed in 1720, apparently by English merchants trading with South Carolina, had contained suggestions as to "What may be done to retrieve the desolation of Carolina, to strengthen that frontier of our colonies on the continent & to encrease its inhabitants & trade." One recommendation was the enactment and enforcement of a law by which the number of slaves was limited to ten per white man and their distribution was carefully recorded, "whereby ye negros may be prevented from rising."[23]

[22] *SCG*, Feb. 3, 1733.
[23] BPRO Trans., VIII, 228.

In line with this argument, the colonial Assembly made repeated efforts to impose a limit upon the ratio of slaves to whites, and in 1727 it passed "An Act for the better Securing this Province from Negro Insurrections, & for Encouraging of Poor People by Employing them in Plantations." Gov. Johnson noted in several of his letters to England at the end of the decade, "Nothing is so much wanted in Carolina as White Inhabitants," and in 1735 the legislature determined to put the income from the duty on Africans directly into subsidies for importing poor Protestants,[24] but slaveowning assemblymen were still less than total in their commitment to offsetting black labor with white. In 1738, during debate over a Negro bill, a clause giving planters three months to comply with the requirement for the presence of one white man to every ten slaves was voted down, as was a proposal that the regulation "should be read in the Churches throughout the several Parishes."[25]

IV

EVEN THOUGH official encouragement was sporadic, there did exist a steady flow of poor white immigrants. Their numbers were by no means adequate to offset the heavy importation of Negroes, but shiploads of servants arriving from Europe were occasionally advertised in the *Gazette,* and surviving vestry books show a marked increase in concern over indigent Europeans.[26] According to one description of their lot from 1738: "Only in and around the towns are houses to be found, but in the country only shacks or shanties made of boards and covered with brush, in which the people stay." Most newcomers were said to subsist on cakes made from Indian corn and baked over a fire (a diet more familiar to Africans and Indians than Europeans), and

[24] BPRO Trans., XII, 231; BPRO Trans., XIII, 425 (cf. BPRO Trans., XIV, 237); *Statutes,* III, 409.

[25] *SCCHJ, 1737–1738,* p. 429. It was finally agreed that the measure should be read before every militia company twice each year. Several days later word came from Jamaica that an act had been passed there "For Obliging every owner to keep a White for every 30 Negroes &c or pay £3-5-0 a Quarter Deficiency." BPRO Trans., XIX, 37.

[26] *SCG,* Sept. 30, 1732. Several early vestry books have been published; others are available in typescript in the SCL. Benjamin Joseph Klebaner, "Public Poor Relief in Charleston, 1800–1860," *SCHGM,* LV (1954), 210, points out that in 1734 the St. Philip's Parish Vestry rented a house for the purpose of giving paupers "proper attendance," and two years later the parish obtained authorization for erecting a substantial workhouse which would absorb paupers, vagrants, and common beggars. Cf. BPRO Trans., XIV, 86–87; *SCHGM,* XXI (1924), 193–94.

the very poor, claimed the account, "get nothing all the year round for their sustenance but potatoes, which they dig out of the ground themselves. With these alone they have to keep themselves alive, and they see neither bread, meat, or anything else."[27]

Conditions facing this immigrant class were comparable to those faced by the first white settlers, but unlike their predecessors they found themselves at the bottom of an existing social order—or almost. Officials shared William Byrd's misgivings that the presence of bondsmen below the whites in this hierarchy would lead to laziness, but there was also concern that even the most industrious newcomers would not be able to compete with slaves for jobs. The unfree workers, who were involved in almost every colonial activity, earned low wages—lower when employed illegally—and were not directly responsible (it was argued) for maintaining themselves or their families.[28] White slaveowners therefore found themselves confronted with trying to curb a variety of Negro economic activities (from which they themselves usually gained), or else risking a rise in the parish poor rolls and a decline in the arrival of European immigrants.

Tension between black and white workers, a recurrent theme in America's later history, increased with the number of whites, and the hard-earned predominance of the Negro majority in parts of the colony's varied labor force was called into question. When debate began on a new Negro bill in 1737 it was proposed that no Charlestown slaves "be permitted to buy or sell or to be employed for Hire as Porters, Carters or Fishermen." This was amended to allow that "the Negroes be at Liberty to fish and ply as Porters and Carters under Lycense from the Commissioners of the Work House."[29] The owners of slaves sent out as carters and porters paid a weekly sum for the privilege, and every Negro fisherman was charged £5 per annum for a license. Each received a numbered badge for identification, and the fees were used in support of the town watch.[30]

At the same time pressure mounted against the participation of

---

[27] Trachsler, "Brief Description of a Journey," p. 103.

[28] The Clerk of the Market protested in 1741 that his daily fee of seven shillings "was not Negroes' Hire; and sure then not a living for any white Man of the lowest rank in Life." *SCCHJ, 1741–1742*, p. 21.

[29] *SCCHJ, 1737–1738*, p. 364.

[30] *Ibid.*, pp. 365, 428. For mention of the brass badges traditionally worn by Negroes allowed to work out, see the memoirs of D. E. Huger Smith in Alice R. Huger Smith, *Carolina Rice Plantation*, pp. 94–95.

slaves in a variety of skilled crafts. The Negro Act of 1735 imposed a fine of £50 upon any master who allowed slaves to maintain any "houses of entertainment or trade," whether in their own names or under his protection, and two years later a protest was issued against the "too common Practice" of barbers, many of whom were Negroes, shaving customers on Sundays.[31] During the reappraisals which followed in the wake of the Stono Uprising, a "Committee appointed to consider the most effectual Measures to bring into this Province white Persons to increase our Strength and Security" reported to the Assembly "that a great Number of Negroes are brought up to and daily employed in mechanic Trades both in Town and Country." The committee recommended a statute "prohibiting the bringing up [of] Negroes and other Slaves to mechanic Trades in which white Persons usually are employed,"[32] but a formal prohibition was not enacted until 1755 and appears never to have been totally enforced.[33] As suggested in the previous chapter, pressures exerted against Negroes in the trades were paralleled by efforts to curb Negro involvement in the commerce of the province.

V

ONE SPECIFIC RESULT of these economic pressures is worth noting separately. Where blacks and whites had previously shared most activities, distinguished only by the fact that the latter gave the commands and took the proceeds, workers were now occasionally set apart by race. At the same time that Negroes were being forced away from certain skilled trades, they were receiving more exclusive custody of the society's most menial tasks. Jobs which were in various ways taxing or offensive became, as Byrd had feared, "unfit" for white labor. As slaves assumed the entirety of the onerous business of rice production, they were also made to take on other oppressive chores as well.

[31] *Statutes*, VII, 396; *SCG*, Nov. 5, 1737.

[32] *SCCHJ, 1742–1743*, pp. 345–46.

[33] *SCG*, Supplement, May 8, 1755. An industrial census of Charlestown in 1848 shows that Negroes outnumbered whites in more than one third of the forty-nine occupations listed. Blacks were a majority in the following categories: "Carpenters and joiners, Masons and stone cutters, Painters and plasterers, Wharf builders, Tailors and cap makers, Barbers and hairdressers, Bakers, Coopers, Ship carpenters and joiners, Other mechanics and journeymen, Coachmen, Draymen, Wherfingers, stevedores and porters, Apprentices, Domestic servants, Laborers, Fishermen." Phillips, "The Slave Labor Problem," p. 435.

The collection and disposal of refuse, to cite one example, was increasingly delegated to slaves. An early request of the first royal governor in 1721 was that "all necessary Houses, draines, and Sinks . . . be kept clean and [free] from noisome smells." And in 1734 "the Want of a Scavenger, and proper Regulations for keeping clear the Streets of Charles-Town" was presented as a grievance to the Grand Jury, with particular note being taken of the fact that the sewer ditch which ran across Church Street and through Mrs. Bettison's garden was generally stopped up, "whereby the way to and from the Church is often almost unpassable." Subsequently, a government committee issued a report suggesting the division of the city into four districts, in each of which an elected official could assess every household for at least one slave above the age of nine. Every three months, or whenever a white citizen filed a legal complaint about offensive dung hills in the streets, the official would send out word via the corporal of militia or the parish constable that on a set day these men and women were "to meet at the Court House by Beat of Drum at six oClock in the Morning." Each Negro was to bring "a Box, Basket, Spade or Shovel," and it was hoped that their unpleasant labors would keep the town healthy, clean, and "beautified."[34]

As in any society, many of the lowest jobs were also the most laborious. Besides the actual production of rice and naval stores (and later indigo), all of the hauling and loading of these commodities was done by Negroes, as was the building of roads and the cutting of canal passages. Black porters, carters, and stevedores on land were matched by hundreds of black oarsmen on the water. Even the boats which taxied persons to and from ships in the harbor were manned by slaves.[35] While all of these tasks were essential, others exploited Negro strength in far more dubious ways. When sailors were being pressed into service against pirates in 1718, it was four slaves who executed the pressmaster's orders for a month.[36] In later years Negroes were encouraged to take part in the apprehension of white sailors who deserted their ships, and owners were promised compensation from the Public Treasury "if any Slave shall be killed or maimed in apprehending such fugi-

---

[34] SCUHJ, 1721, mfm BMP/D 487, SCDAH; *SCHGM*, XXV (1924), 194; "Report on Ways and Means to cleanse and keep clean the several Streets in Charles Town . . . ," March 5, 1737, *SCCHJ, 1736–1737*, p. 288.

[35] "Life of Equiano," p. 96.

[36] *SCCHJ, 1725*, p. 59.

tive Seamen."[37] Slaves themselves were often put to work on local privateers, and occasionally while at sea, captains allowed or even forced slaves to beat European crewmen.[38]

The use of Negroes as roughnecks was even more common on land. A statute of 1712, reiterated in 1714 and 1722, made it a crime for slaves to strike a white except in defense of their masters, "Provided always, that such striking, conflict or maiming, be not by command of . . . their master, mistress, or owner of their families, or of their goods."[39] This proviso was made necessary by the fact that it was common practice for insolvent slaveholders to urge their Negroes to resist seizure in payment of debts. This was generally a place where the interests of owner and slaves coincided, and the job of the provost marshal was made almost untenable as a result. After 1713 the provost marshal was empowered to summon indebted planters to Charlestown, but in 1726, at a time when few slaveowners were solvent, the Assembly forced a return to the older system of *capias*, whereby this official had to go and personally lay hold of slaves or other property belonging to the debtor. Thomas Lowndes, who had been granted the post the previous year, reported that an officer hazarded his life in making seizures outside Charlestown and often had slaves "rescued" from him while returning. He claimed that frequently "the Negroes are let loose upon him, and he . . . whipped or drawn through a ditch," and all this without legal recourse since it can never be proven "that it was by their Masters order tho' every one knows it could not be done without it."[40]

The allegiance of the Assembly at this time can be seen by the fact that when one provost marshal sought to use a group of Negroes in his own right to force a debtor to prison, he was promptly removed from office.[41] And yet at the same time whites who were private citizens seem to have been condoned in using slave muscle not only to

[37] *SCCHJ, 1742–1743*, pp. 228, 230, 284.

[38] SCUHJ, June 22, 1722, mfm BMP/D 487, SCDAH; *SCG*, Nov. 6, 1740; Admiralty Court Records on mfm in SCDAH. See "Harvey & others vs. Ebsworthy," Aug. 1738 (reel 2, pp. 176–78), in which the captain of the *Sea Flower* was charged by his crewmen with having encouraged the slaves on board to beat a white shipmate; also "The King vs. Joseph Harrison," June 1758 (reel 3, pp. 45–52), in which a black linguist aboard the snow *Rainbow* was allowed revenge upon white crewmen.

[39] *Statutes*, VII, 359; cf. 366, 377.

[40] BPRO Trans., XV, 72–73, 309.

[41] *SCCHJ, 1726–1727*, p. 24.

keep the government at bay but also to settle private scores as well.[42] To a few slaves such brutal activities may have afforded an outlet for aggressions and perhaps a certain notoriety. But nothing could offset the broader degradation which came with the forced acceptance of the society's most tedious, harsh, and squalid tasks.

Numerous laws reflected indirectly, and also furthered, this process of economic and social subjugation. The prohibition of the use of firearms by slaves, for example, and severe constraints upon their movements curtailed innocuous as well as subversive ambitions. Even clothes became a matter of legislation: the Negro Act of 1735 took special note of the many Negroes who wore "clothes much above the condition of slaves, for the procuring whereof they use sinister and evil methods." The easiest way to remove the incentive for earning or taking money with which to purchase good clothes was to prohibit such apparel altogether. The law, therefore, prescribed the materials suitable for slave clothing, allowing only the cheapest fabrics: "negro cloth, duffelds, course kearsies, osnabrigs, blue linnen, checked lin- nen," and also "course garlix or callicoes, checked cottons or scotch plaids," if these last were not valued at more than ten shillings per yard. Any slave wearing a garment of some finer, different, or more valuable material could have it stripped away. This dress code was intended (as were those enacted earlier among Englishmen in the northern colonies) to impose and emphasize social stratification, to enforce the maintenance of social distance through the emblem of apparel. One sure indication that the law had deeper significance for whites than simply preventing slaves from stealing expensive clothes is the fact that when the question was put in debate as to whether Negroes should be allowed to wear the cast-off clothes of their masters and mistresses, it carried in the negative.[43]

An even more serious measure of involuntary separation and forced inferiority concerns the rationing of food. Inevitably, as wealth built up among the whites, their general fare became more expensive

[42] *SCG*, July 24, 1736:

We are inform'd that a certain Gentleman in the Country having some business in Town left one of his reputed Friends at his House to take care of his Spouse and to manage his Affairs in his absence. The Gentleman at his return hearing by one of his Negroes that his Friend had used a little too much Familiarity with his Wife, immediately took a loaden Pistol and went to meet his Friend in the Fields, who avoiding the blow, fell to wrestling with him, but the Gentleman calling his Negroes to assistance, cut off his Friends Ears, and for fear of loosing the Use of his Wind pipe is gone to Cape Fear.

[43] *Statutes*, VII, 396; *SCCHJ, 1734-1735,* p. 145.

and diversified, while the diet of slaves remained cheaper and less varied. Moreover, this widening distinction, like that in clothing, was given official sanction during the 1730s and 1740s. In public accounts, food for Negroes was budgeted separately at half to three quarters the rate allowed for whites, and it was becoming accepted doctrine among freemen that slaves needed—and got—smaller quantities of cheaper foodstuffs with minimal allotments of meat. On a six-month military venture against the Spanish in 1740 it was projected that one thousand white foot soldiers would each consume seven pounds of beef, fourteen quarts of rice, and an equal amount of corn each week, while the weekly food allotment for eight hundred "Pioneers" was put at half a piece of beef and twelve quarts of corn per man.[44]

Legal authorities were even worse than military authorities with respect to rations. In 1741 the official at a trial submitted to the Assembly two bills, "one for 10 Days' Diet of 50 white Persons, the other for as many Days Diet of the same Number of Negroes," and the Committee on Accounts appraised them at £100 and £20, respectively.[45] The annual budget submitted by the provost marshal for 1743 suggested a rate of one shilling, three pence for each white person's daily ration ("allowing one Pound of Bread and one Pound of Flesh all wholesome Provisions") and only nine pence for the rations of Negroes in his custody. This latter figure was the only one which the Assembly questioned among hundreds of diverse fees, and after several hours of debate they reduced the daily allotment of food for Negroes to a value of six pence.[46] As yet, little is known about the exact implications of pervasive and long-term differences in the nutrition available to the African and European populations in America.

VI

INCREASED DISCRIMINATION regarding food and clothing was matched by deepening white anxiety over the even more basic issue of physical intimacy. As the ratio of white men to women became more balanced

[44] *SCCHJ, 1739–1740,* p. 175. In the previous century in Barbados, slaves enrolled in the militia who performed commendably under fire earned the right to receive a white servant's allowance of food from their masters. Harlow, *Barbados,* pp. 209–11.

[45] *SCCHJ, 1739–1741,* p. 493 (see also pp. 184–85, 284). The committee responded to another bill, submitted by the same official two years later, "that eighteen Pence per Day for Negroes and five Shillings per Day for white Men will be a sufficient Allowance," *SCCHJ, 1742–1744,* p. 377 (see also pp. 138, 367, 370).

[46] *SCCHJ, 1742–1744,* pp. 148, 196. Cf. *SCCHJ, 1736–1739,* p. 511.

with time, one motive for sexual relations between freemen and slaves diminished,[47] and as the size of the Negro population grew, the impetus among Europeans for white offspring increased.[48] From the minority's point of view, every baby born to European parents "improved" the dangerous racial imbalance, while each child with a white father and a black mother increased the ranks of the slaves and served as a reminder of the Europeans' precarious social and genetic position. Mulattoes, editorialized the *Gazette*, "are seldom well belov'd either by the Whites or the Blacks."[49] But their presence, however limited, could hardly be denied. "The whites mix with the blacks and the blacks with the whites," commented a European in 1737, "and if a white man has a child by a black woman, nothing is done to him. . . . It also occurs that the English marry . . . black women, often also Indian women."[50] Six years later the presentments of the Grand Jury in Charlestown included the following grievance: "We present THE TOO COMMON PRACTICE OF CRIMINAL CONVERSATION with NEGRO and other SLAVE WENCHES IN THIS PROVINCE, as an Enormity and Evil of general Ill-Consequence."[51]

Twice during the 1730s full-scale debates erupted in the public press concerning this sensitive issue. The use of poetry and the attempts at cleverness cannot disguise the underlying anxieties in either case. Early in 1732 the *Gazette* ran a brief poem entitled "The Cameleon Lover" which suggested half-whimsically that whites with a

[47] See Jordan, *White Over Black*, p. 175.

[48] The *SCG* made pointed allusions to notable instances of European longevity or fertility and encouraged large families with such notes as the following, from the third issue (Jan. 22, 1732): "We are told, there are several Weddings upon the Anvil, we therefore take the Freedom to advise the young Sparks that are concern'd, to strike, whilst the Iron's hot, and we doubt not, but in time, we shall be a numerous, and flourishing People."

[49] *SCG*, March 22, 1735. The full passage is reprinted in Jordan, *White Over Black*, p. 170.

[50] Samuel Dyssli to friends in Switzerland, Dec. 3, 1737, *SCHGM*, XXIII (1922), 90. During the same year an Anglican missionary in Prince Frederick's Parish northwest of Georgetown baptized "one *Negroe* Woman, and six of her Children *Mulattoes;* she herself and her three elder Children could read well, and repeat the Church-Catachism; and two of the remaining three could repeat the Creed and the Lord's-Prayer." Quoted in Klingberg, *Appraisal*, p. 85.

[51] *SCG*, March 28, 1743. A slave woman advertised several months earlier as being capable of "almost any Work required either in publick or private House" was given the halfhearted endorsement of being "neither a Theif, Whore, or Drunkard." *SCG*, Dec. 27, 1742. It can be guessed that prostitution was among those onerous tasks mentioned above to which an increasing number of Negroes found themselves consigned.

taste for black lovers, being "Stain'd with the Tincture of the Sooty Sin," might well "imbibe the Blackness of their Charmer's Skin."[52] This harmless threat prompted a much longer and more serious prose piece from "Albus" (a double-edged pseudonym invoking the Latin words for "white" and "English"), who described miscegenation as an "*Epidemical Disease*" less natural and more odious than the smallpox distemper then infecting the colony.[53] The gist of his arguments and the degree of his indignation presaged a long history of tirades on this matter, but for the moment the last word was given to "Sable," who promptly provided a sympathetic verse entitled "Cameleon's Defence."[54]

In 1736 male settlers in Georgetown tried to induce white women from elsewhere in the colony to join them, but the death of several upon arrival discouraged others, and the bachelors turned to a motley shipment of sixty women from Bermuda.[55] These newcomers were said to be healthier, but apparently few in Georgetown could afford to pay the cost of their transport, upon which the women's importer placed a bitter notice in the *Gazette*. He suggested to single men, "that if they are in a Strait for Women, to wait for the next Shipping from the Coast of Guinny. Those African Ladies," the author continued caustically, "are of a strong robust Constitution; not easily jaded out, able to serve them by Night as well as Day. When they are Sick, they are not costly, when dead, their funeral charges are but *viz* an old Matt, one Bottle Rum, and a lb. Sugar."[56]

The following week a correspondent was prompted to argue defensively that "our Country-Women are full as capable for Service either night or day as any African Ladies whatsoever, unless their native Constitution is much alter'd," and an anonymous warning accompanied the letter:

Certain young Men of this Town are desired to frequent less with their black Lovers the open Lots and the Chandler's House on the Green between old Church-street and King's Street, there being something intended to coole their Courage and to expose them; but they have no need to be idle, since of their own Colour are lately arrived so many buxom Ladies,

[52] *SCG*, March 11, 1732.
[53] *SCG*, March 18, 1732.
[54] *Ibid.*
[55] *SCG*, July 10, 1736.
[56] *SCG*, July 17, 1736.

who are tender-hearted and no doubt will comply easily with their request on small rewards, to cure their Itch and Courage. *N.B.* Be careful of Fire.[57]

This veiled threat was quickly parried in the next issue by a bit of doggerel which asked, *"Kiss black or white, why need it trouble you?"*[58] And there the exchange ended for the time being.

The white anxieties which underlay such interchanges found their most profound and succinct psychological expression in the fantasy of rape. Negroes were threatening to compete too successfully economically; they were shouldering an awesome proportion of the colony's physical labor; they were gradually asserting their power through sheer force of numbers. It is no surprise that the weekly paper of the Europeans, seeing nothing newsworthy in the ravishments of Negro women by whites, which could not have been an unknown occurrence, seized upon stories of rapes committed by slaves in distant provinces. During its first year the *Gazette* published an italicized item about the scheduled execution of a Negro man convicted of raping a white woman on the Massachusetts frontier. In October 1734 a similar offense, also in Massachusetts, was reported in considerable detail, and two months later readers were informed that the suspect had subsequently "set the Prison on fire, and . . . made his Escape, but was taken again."[59] The following year an issue which contained news of the rebellion in Jamaica and of the efforts of several slaves to poison a white family in New England also carried a story from Philadelphia about a Negro who was "whip'd round the Town at the Cart's Tail, 63 Lashes, for attempting to ravish a white Child about 12 Years of Age."[60]

Such mounting preoccupation with ravishment reflected not only the personal fears of white readers, but also the collective anxieties of the white minority as well. Individual rape if committed by a black man was suggestive of social overthrow, just as broad upheaval had implications of personal rape. And occasionally these two elements were brought into close conjunction in local lore, much as they

---

[57] *SCG,* July 24, 1736.

[58] *SCG,* July 31, 1736.

[59] *SCG,* Nov. 11, 1732; Oct. 26, 1734; Dec. 21, 1734.

[60] *SCG,* Sept. 20, 1735. It was not surprising for a Baptist minister from South Carolina, traveling to Virginia several decades later, to take special note of such incidents in his diary; as in his entry of Dec. 1, 1769, or of Jan. 16, 1770: "This Town is called New London and is about 120 Miles from Richmond . . . —a negroe lately executed here for ravishing a white young woman." Journal of Oliver Hart, SCL.

were in the tale of the Sabine women, which had inspired ancient
Romans and which horrified the English colonists. One story which
found its way into the *London Magazine* in 1757 described how each
leader of a South Carolina slave plot in 1730 had confessed, before
execution, "whose wife, daughter, or sister he had fixed on for his
future bedfellow."[61] There was an actual conspiracy in August 1730
for which only limited evidence has been found. It is clear, however,
that the incident made a lasting impression, for almost the same account was given to a Hessian officer who served in Charlestown during
the Revolutionary War. Although the listener got the year wrong
(1736), he eagerly recorded the more lurid details. The black conspirators, according to these white recollections of the incident, had intended to massacre the entire European population, sparing only those
women who could be enslaved or used to gratify their lusts.[62]

The increasing white obsession with physical violation, therefore, must be taken as an integral part of the white minority's wider
struggle for social control. The degree of shared interest and unavoidable intimacy which had held the two races in uneasy coexistence during the proprietary period was breaking down. Slaves were becoming
a more numerous and distinctive group, and their very real efforts
toward social and economic self-assertion prompted the anxious white
minority to fantasies of ravishment and to concrete measures of containment. The general guardedness among whites increased percep-

[61] *London Magazine*, XXVI (1757), 330–31. A contemporary account of this
plot said nothing about such confessions. *Boston News-Letter*, Oct. 22, 1730. See
Aptheker, *Slave Revolts*, pp. 180–81.

[62] "The Diary of Captain Johann Hinrichs," in Bernard A. Uhlendorf, trans. and
ed., *The Siege of Charleston* (*University of Michigan Publications, History and Political
Science*, vol. XII, Ann Arbor, 1938), p. 323. This vision was by no means confined
to South Carolina, and upon occasion rumors from other colonies no doubt became
entwined with local stories. The Stephen Bordley Letterbook, 1738–40, Md. Hist. Soc.,
Baltimore, contains a letter written in Annapolis, Jan. 30, 1739 or 1740. (Historians
are not clear on the date: see Aptheker, *Slave Revolts*, p. 192 n; Land, *Bases of the
Plantation Society*, p. 228.) Bordley claimed that a plot which had been brewing
among slaves there for eight months involved destroying "their several families Negro
women and all except the young white women only whom they intended to keep for
their wives."

It is said, before the Appointment of any day for the execution of the design a
negroe woman lying abed in a quarter overheard several of the negroe fellows
talking in their country language, concerning this very affair, and she accordingly
told her mistress of it the next morning, but could not gain relief; foolish woman!
that sooner than give herself the trouble of looking into the affair would run the
hazard of having her throat cutt; but perhaps she had a mind for a black
husband.

tibly, and it is not surprising that as they grew more concerned about Negro intimacy and forwardness on the one hand, they also became more watchful regarding slave absences and disappearances on the other. Such concern was justified by—and helped add to—the increasing number of slaves who elected to run away. The experience of these numerous runaways presages the larger pattern of overt controls and desperate resistance described in the concluding chapters.

IX

Runaways:
Slaves Who Stole Themselves

I

NO single act of self-assertion was more significant among slaves or more disconcerting among whites than that of running away. This common practice, which has often been oversimplified by historians and novelists, offers insights into the tensions that were building up within the South Carolina colony after 1720. While the number and percentage of blacks in the colony were growing, individual Negroes were finding it increasingly difficult to exercise even the rudimentary aspects of independence and autonomy which had been possible during earlier decades. Personal and social initiatives among slaves were gradually being checked by the evolving economic patterns and legal codes imposed by the European settlers. Changing circumstances prompted an increasing number of runaways. In a society where slaves were defined as property and where blacks were becoming artful in appropriating things they were denied, these were the people who, in a real sense, elected to "steal themselves."

Runaways, of course, had existed in the colony from the start. As early as 1688 the governor had sent an envoy to St. Augustine to negotiate the return of Negroes "that roned away from Carolina."[1] At first, notices of slaves lost or taken up were posted at the guard house in Charlestown, but as the settlement spread and the number of absentees increased, such notification proved inadequate. By 1714 it had already become standard for the provost marshal to give notice in writing of any runaways brought to Charlestown "by sending up the names, ages, and sexes, to the several parish churches, and the most

[1] *SCHGM*, XXXIV (1933), 4–5.

notorious marks belonging to . . . slaves . . . in his custody."[2] In
the spring of 1734 the marshal placed a notice in the *South Carolina
Gazette* "of what Negroes or Slaves are brought to the Common Goal,"
and the Assembly ordered that he continue this list every week.[3] Moreover, from the founding of the newspaper in 1732, subscribers began
to advertise some of their own slave losses, and these advertisements
for runaways, taken in conjunction with other sources, provide an important category of historical evidence. An initial survey of all such
ads from the *Gazette,* simply through the mid-1740s, offers detailed
and revealing information.

The runaways found in this survey number well over three hundred, yet this group must represent little more than the top of an ill-
defined iceberg. In the first place, the time lag which often existed
between date of disappearance and date of advertisement suggests that
newspaper notices were only a last resort. Many slaves must have been
caught before any ad was necessary, and others, as will be suggested,
returned from short absences on their own initiative. Some slaves may
have escaped so completely that advertising seemed futile. Nor could
all masters afford to advertise in the *Gazette,* and one would expect a
bias within the notices toward owners who were wealthy town-
dwellers and toward slaves who were highly valued. Nevertheless, an
examination of this newspaper evidence can suggest a great deal not
only about those who ran away but about the tensions faced by all
slaves, whether or not they ever chose to take flight.

Historians have only recently recognized the need and the opportunity for quantifying such data,[4] yet already the analysis of runaway ads by date and region is beginning to reflect the variation of
the American slave experience at different times in different places.
For example, in colonial Virginia, young men, frequently mulattoes
who knew a trade, figured disproportionately in the runaway ads, but
in South Carolina the absentees of the 1730s and 1740s appear to have
approached a cross section of the colony's slave population.[5] Only 6

[2] *Statutes,* VII, 366. The Negro Act of 1722 required the marshals to give
written accounts of slaves in their custody to every session of the court. *Statutes,* VII,
379.

[3] *SCG,* May 25, 1734; June 1, 1734.

[4] Jordan, *White Over Black,* p. 392. In discussing forms of slave resistance in the
eighteenth century, Jordan states: "The present need, of course, is for quantitative
studies of these occurrences; we simply do not know how much this sort of thing went
on, though even the most cursory reading in the newspapers suggests persuasively that
there was enough of it to give contemporaries genuine cause for alarm."

[5] Mullin, "Patterns of Slave Behavior in Eighteenth Century Virginia," pp. 464–65.

per cent of the runaways cited in the *South Carolina Gazette* during the 1730s were identified as artisans, and an equally small percentage were described as house servants or personal slaves. Not surprisingly, there is evidence that skilled craftsmen who had been born in America and possessed a thorough command of English stood the best chance of obtaining permanent freedom and were the most determined in seeking it, but the vast majority of the Carolina slaves who disappeared for any length of time seem to have been a representative sampling of field hands with no single distinguishing attribute.[6]

Seventy-seven per cent of the runaways advertised during the 1730s were males, and the ratio of more than three men for every woman persisted in later decades. The overall sex ratio among Carolina slaves was not unbalanced to the same extent, so it is safe to say that men ran away somewhat more frequently than women. On the other hand, statistics show that women runaways were more likely than men to visit other slaves and then return of their own accord in a pattern less likely to prompt public advertising, so the imbalance by sex among all runaways may not have been great.[7] The distribution by age also seems to have been roughly representative. Babes in arms were among those listed as missing, and adolescents sometimes ran away on their own. A boy named London was "about 12 or 14 Years of Age" when he left his master, and an Angolan girl who spoke "pretty good English" was "about 14" when she deserted her mistress.[8] Young adults predominated among the runaways as they did among the black populace as a whole. For slaves who survived past their forties, increased age by no means precluded the urge to run away. A number of slaves described as "old" and "aged" were still considered worth advertising for when they disappeared.[9]

Much of this study, which makes extensive use of runaway materials in early Virginia, has been published as a book, *Flight and Rebellion: Slave Resistance in Eighteenth-Century Virginia* (New York, 1972). I am indebted to Russell L. Blake (note 6 below) for sharing with me the results of his initial quantification study concerning ads for runaways in colonial South Carolina.

[6] Russell L. Blake, "Slave Runaways in Colonial South Carolina," unpublished paper prepared for Dr. Kenneth Lockridge (University of Michigan, 1972), pp. 8, 22.

[7] *Ibid.*, pp. 1, 20.

[8] *SCG*, March 4, 1732; Dec. 21, 1738. In 1735 the governor himself reported the disappearance of "a young Negro Wench about 14 or 15 Years of Age." *SCG*, Feb. 1, 1735.

[9] The *SCG* contained such ads frequently. (Cf. note 27 below.) In 1733 "an old Negro Woman nam'd Juba" ran away from her new master, and "an old Negro Man named Jack," who commanded very little English, was taken up near Ashley River (April 21, June 23). In 1735 a runaway named Charles, "about 50 or 60 Years of

II

SO DIVERSE AN ASSORTMENT of runaways could only be prompted by a variety of motives. Quite often the immediate act hinged upon the slave's relation to a single European: a stranger, a fellow renegade, or a master. Some slaves actually departed against their will, for incidents were common in which Negroes were stolen away by whites. As early as 1673 two white men ran away from Charlestown with a Negro belonging to Nathaniel Sayle. They were overtaken and condemned to death but obtained reprieves because of their "extraordinary penitency" and the need for labor; the fate of the slave is unknown.[10] The Negro Act of 1722 imposed a £25 fine on any "evil and ill-disposed" white person who "attempted to steal away negroes or other slaves, by specious pretences of promising them their freedom in another country." Any person caught and convicted of attempting to "actually convey away" slaves from the province was to "suffer death as a felon."[11] Blacks who had already set out on their own could still be subject to exploitation by white strangers. In 1741, for example, two young Negro men named Bob and Isaac, who had been absent from a Winyaw plantation for some time, "were taken up by white Men near Bond's Ferry," according to the report of a fellow deserter, but their whereabouts was not made known to officials.[12]

---

age," who spoke English "indifferently," was apprehended in a stolen canoe (June 21). Later a Dorchester man lost "an old well set Negro wench named Doll, formerly a Milk-woman," and a Ponpon planter advertised for "an aged Negro Fellow nam'd Job" (Sept. 4, 1736; Aug. 8, 1743).

[10] *Coll.*, V, 420–21; *Journal of the Grand Council, 1671–1680*, pp. 54–55, 58.

[11] *Statutes*, VII, 376. Slave-stealing continued, as implied by a notice from 1734 concerning the loss of a Negro boy named Jacob ("he is this Country born, & speaks no other tongue but English"). Since this ten-year-old had been purchased recently, homesickness may have prompted his departure (see note 39 below), but the owner vouched that Jacob had never disappeared before and "had no manner of Provocation to run away." "I am apt to believe he is stolen," wrote the master, "being he was put to look after a Corn-field just by a pretty public Road, where two white Men were seen that Day, enquiring the way to Dorchester." *SCG*, June 22, 1734. Cf. *SCG*, Dec. 5, 1741.

[12] *SCG*, June 18, 1741. A vivid firsthand account of local kidnaping techniques appears in "Life of Equiano," pp. 122–23:

one day while I was a little way out of the town of Savannah, I was beset by two white men, who meant to play their usual tricks with me in the way of kidnapping. As soon as these men accosted me, one of them said to the other, "This is the very fellow we are looking for, that you lost," and the other swore I

No servant could avoid altogether the thought of absconding, and it is important to keep in mind that white runaways were commonplace.[13] For this reason black and white fugitives, with distinct but overlapping interests, were occasionally thrown together as fellow renegades to assist and exploit one another briefly in relationships reminiscent of Huck Finn and Jim. In such instances it is difficult to say where kidnaping ends and willing complicity on the part of blacks begins. When an Irish soldier deserted the garrison at Port Royal in 1734, it was believed that he had "taken with him two Negroes belonging to Ensign Farrington,"[14] and the next year the following ad appeared in the *Gazette:*

Run away from Mr. Bryan Reily and Mr. John CarMichael, two Irishmen Servants, both talking broad Scotch. . . . They stole from the said Masters a new yellow stocked trading Gun. . . . Run away likewise from the said Masters two Negro Men (which we suspect they have taken with them) one this Country born, named George, he speaks good English, a short thick well set sensible fellow, the other named Derry, a tall likely young Ibo Negro branded on the breast I.C.[15]

Two months later Lt. Gov. Thomas Broughton "received Information that several White persons and Blacks, have Committed many Outrages and Robbery, and lye in the Swamp at the Head of Wando River, where they bid defiance to the Chief Justices Warrant."[16] Broughton ordered that the nearest militia company be sent to "apprehend those disturbers of the Peace by taking them alive, . . . or in case of resistance from them to Exercise Military discipline, either by shooting them or otherwise." Later that same summer, when

---

was the identical person. On this they made up to me, and were about to handle me; but I told them to be still and keep off, for I has seen these kind of tricks played upon other free blacks, and they must not think to serve me so. At this they paused a little, and one said to the other—it will not do; and the other answered that I talked too good English. I replied I believed I did; and I had also with me a revengeful stick equal to the occasion; and my mind was likewise good. Happily, however, it was not used; and after we had talked together a little in this manner the rogues left me.

[13] One issue of the *SCG* (Jan. 24, 1743) carried adjacent notices for a Negro who had run away from his master in Winyaw, a West Country indentured servant who had slipped off from James Island, and a freckle-faced white servant boy of about fifteen who had left a plantation at Goose Creek.

[14] *SCG*, March 16, 1734.

[15] *SCG*, March 22, 1735.

[16] "Order for apprehending some Whites and Blacks," May 29, 1735, Parish Trans., S.C., Minutes of the Council in Assembly and House of Burgesses (1734–40), p. 2.

a sandy-haired young felon escaped from the constable in George-town and stole a horse, he "enticed with him a short lusty well set Negro Wench, she speaks plain English, is very well Cloathed and about 30 Years old, supposed to be in Man's Cloaths." Similarly, the following year a white servant boy who had worked in a tavern and was renowned as a thief ran away from Edisto Island and artfully obtained a pass from the local justice. The *Gazette* reported that "he has enticed an Angola Negro to go along with him, named Dick, speaks good English, a middling Stature, has on a homespun Jacket and breeches."[17]

The association between black and white deserters was too dangerous to be frequent, however, and most often if any white person figured in a slave's disappearance it was his own master. A decision on the owner's part to change a Negro's location or line of work could provide the final impetus for running away. For example, three Negro sawyers named Primus, Venture, and Syphax were employed making cypress shingles for Mrs. Catherine Bettison. In the spring of 1733, when Col. Bull led a group from Charlestown to assist Oglethorpe's newly arrived Georgian contingent, the three men were hired out "for the service of Georgia," but before Bull's party could transport them they gathered up their clothes and blankets and disappeared in the night.[18]

Perhaps more important than any specific assignment was the general quality of the master's treatment. Already by this period slave-owners had begun to debate the degree to which kindness and leniency were inducements to resistance rather than deterrents against it. There is no way to judge whether the many runaways whose masters considered them well used disappeared because of benevolent treat-ment, such as it was, or in spite of it. Tokens of generosity within an overwhelmingly hostile system may well have engendered further bitterness, although it seems more likely that few acts of kindness were significant enough to be determinative. Acts of particular cruelty, on the other hand, may well have tipped the balance for individual slaves, and it is interesting to notice, even in the terse columns of the *Gazette,* how the names of certain owners stand out. Several seem to

---

[17] *SCG,* Aug. 30, 1735; May 29, 1736.
[18] *SCG,* April 14, 1733. When Bull himself arrived in Georgia he "brought with him 4 of his Negroes, who were Sawyers, to assist the Colony, and also brought Pro-vision for them." *SCG,* March 31, 1733.

advertise for runaways with peculiar frequency and in vindictive tones
which may suggest their deeper feelings.

A Goose Creek planter named Alexander Vander Dussen, for
example, appears repeatedly in these pages. In 1733 he offered a £10
reward for "a Negro Man named Thomas Butler, the famous Pushing
and Dancing Master . . . [said to be] lurking at Ashley River Ferry."
In June 1735 he put a similar price on Guan, a "Spanish Negro Man
. . . supposed to lurk about Town,"[19] and six months later he was
advertising the disappearance of two Negro men: "the one a tall elderly Fellow named Guan, a Taylor by Trade, has on a blew livery
Coat trimm'd with red, the other a short thick Fellow, named Steven,
had on a white Negro Cloath jacket & breeches."[20] That same year a
single issue of the *Gazette* carried an ad for a new Negro who had run
away from Vander Dussen after being branded and an ad for a rented
slave who had been missing from Vander Dussen's plantation for three
months. In 1738, after advertising fruitlessly for a runaway Angolan
field hand, he went so far as to insert an italicized paragraph in the
newspaper stating, *"I am inform'd that there are certain Persons, who
entertain Run aways, and in Time send them out of the Settlements."*
He offered a reward of £50 to *"any Person that can inform me . . .
in order that such Persons may be prosecuted according to Law."*[21]

But no slaves could have felt a greater urge to escape from a vindictive master than those belonging to Francis Le Brasseur. Not long
after this man opened a general store on Elliott Street, he announced
in the *Gazette* that his Negro named Parris had "absented himself . . .
to avoid punishment," adding: "The Boy is about 16 Years of Age,
well-set, qualified for any plantation Work, provided it be far off from
Charlestown. The Owner is willing to Hire, or sell him."[22] By the following week the slave had reappeared, but a year later Le Brasseur
gave sharp notice that

whosoever at any time finds a young lusty Negro, named *Parris*, without a
Ticket from myself (which he never shall have,) . . . [is] desired to take
him up as a Runaway. . . .

[19] *SCG*, May 26, 1733; June 21, 1735. Earlier he had posted a £20 reward for
a slave who was probably the same man: "RUN away from Goose-Creek Point, a tall
elderly spanish Negro Man named John. . . ." *SCG*, Jan. 20, 1733.

[20] *SCG*, Dec. 13, 1735. Steven was identified as the patroon of Vander Dussen's
pettiauger.

[21] *SCG*, Nov. 29, 1735; Feb. 2, 1738.

[22] *SCG*, Feb. 10, 1733.

N.B. If he do refuse to surrender, knock him down, or shoot him with small shot about his Breech to make him stand.

> Mr. *B-------s* Advertisement continued.
> *Against my Negro man nam'd Parris*
> *From this day forth denounced War is:*
> *For now the Dog is grown so wicked*
> *He's run away without a Ticket.*
> *Which he shall never have, I tell ye,*
> *Nor maigre soup to fill his belly.*
> *If he don't halt at your command,*
> *Pray knock him down to make him stand,*
> *Or pepper him well about the A--e*
> *Be gar, dis make one pretty farce.*[23]

There was nothing farcical in the situation for Parris, who managed to return in the middle of the night at one point and depart again before day despite "a Chaine and 3 Spurrs on each of his legs."[24] His endurance finally prompted an anonymous outburst of frustration and hatred in the *Gazette* which could only have come from Le Brasseur:

Whereas a stately *Baboon* hath lately slipp'd his Collar and run away: He is big-bon'd, full in Flesh, and has learn'd to walk very erect on his two Hind-Legs, he grins and chatters much, but will not bite, he plays Tricks impudently well, and is mightily given to clambering, whereby he often shews his A---. If any one finds him, or will send any news of him to ----- Office, in ----- street, shall be rewarded proportionally to the Merit of the Creature.[25]

In the spring of 1735 Le Brasseur advertised vigorously for a Negro woman named Filledy, and he successfully prosecuted a slave named Peter River for having harbored her. The next year he gave notice that a man, a woman, and three boys had been gone from his Habshaw plantation on Wando River for three months.[26] Le Brasseur died not long after this, but in 1737 his widow saw fit to run her own threaten-

[23] *SCG*, March 2, 1734.

[24] *SCG*, March 30, 1734.

[25] *SCG*, May 4, 1734. Jordan quotes this passage in *White Over Black* (p. 238) and discusses the "extraordinarily pervasive and enduring character" of the notion which underlay this man's crude joke (pp. 228–39). John Appel has pointed out that nineteenth-century cartoonists often showed Irishmen with similar characteristics, while zookeepers sometimes named their gorillas Mike and Pat.

[26] *SCG*, May 3, 1735 (cf. issues from April 5 through May 17, 1735); Sept. 4, 1736.

ing notice in the *Gazette* concerning "an old Negro Woman" who had run away.[27]

In many cases, therefore, immediate provocation from the master in terms of punishment or abuse must have prompted a slave's disappearance. Olaudah Equiano recalls in his autobiography how, as a young slave in Africa at about this time, he once hid from his master through fear of being punished,[28] and the same response was common among slaves in Carolina. Such a reaction to immediate circumstance cannot in the least be seen as a reflection of unreasoned and spontaneous behavior in a childlike people; instead it is an appropriate if desperate response to a vicious circle of fear and reprisal. Fettered runaways testify to the degree to which harsh punishments could prompt fresh resistance: Hercules "had on when he went away 2 Irons on his Feet"; Tom had "one Leg galded by wearing a Spurr"; Billy "has a Chain & Pad lock on his Neck."[29]

Several notices concerning a slave belonging to Lewis Timothy, the printer of the *Gazette*, illustrate the early stages of this brutal spiral. A youth named London, purchased by Timothy from a local vintner, had his head shaved by his new master as a means of punishment or humiliation. That must have been one reason for his running away in the fall of 1735, with a red silk handkerchief over his head.[30] He was apparently apprehended, but the following spring Timothy gave notice in his paper that London had disappeared again, this time "with an iron head-piece on his Head." John Brickell observed that in North Carolina at this time servants and slaves who persisted in running away despite increasingly harsh laws were often made to wear cumbersome neck-yokes as a punishment and deterrent.[31]

[27] *SCG*, July 2, 1737. Cf. *SCG*, June 21, 1742: "Mrs. *Anne Le Brasseur*, a Widow Gentlewoman of considerable Fortune; a prime Disciple of Mr. *Whitefield's*, . . . shot herself with a Pistol, . . . professing her full Assurance of her Salvation, and that she longed to be in the blessed Mansions which she knew were prepared for her."

[28] "Life of Equiano," pp. 21–22.

[29] *SCG*, July 2, 1737; May 11, 1738; Aug. 1, 1740. In 1741 a slave of Joseph Wragg's brought in a runaway who "had on when taken up, a large Iron Chain, Shackle and Pad-lock on his right Leg, but will confess neither his own nor Master's Name." *SCG*, May 14, 1741.

[30] *SCG*, Oct. 25, 1735. Mullin, cited in note 5 above, shows that such penalties were familiar elsewhere. Hannah, an eighteen-year-old slave girl in Prince George County, Virginia ("the Daughter of Sykes's Doctor . . . the well known Fiddler"), ran away six times in half a year and therefore had her hair cut "in a very irregular Manner, as a Punishment for offences." *Virginia Gazette*, Oct. 17, 1777.

[31] *SCG*, April 3, 1736; Brickell, *Natural History*, p. 270.

III

But DWELLING AT LENGTH upon aspects of white involvement seriously distorts the actual experience of black runaways. It lends misleading support to the traditional assumption of white interpreters that slaves, stripped of initiative in so many ways, were incapable of independent thought and action. Even in the act of running away, when they quite literally and obviously took their lives in their own hands, these individuals have been misrepresented as passive objects, "forced," "urged," "allowed," or "provoked" to escape by various whites. This bias began among the early slaveowners themselves, who refused to acknowledge among runaways signs of rationality, emotion, and independence, which they hoped to both ignore and suppress. The furthest they could go in recognizing any Negro initiative in these matters was to accept a perverse obstinacy as motivating numerous slaves. In 1783, for example, the legislature on the island of Antigua complained about "the late frequent running away of their Slaves who generally without any other Reason, than the Dictates of their own Vicious Inclinations, absent themselves from their Duty, and till they are apprehended and Compelled will not return thereto."[32] Such begrudging statements, if the following evidence from South Carolina sources earlier in the eighteenth century offers any indication, do little justice to the complex and personal motives of the Negro runaway. Within the varied web of reasons which could prompt a slave to run away, at least three patterns emerge which are worth examining more closely. One grouping involves slaves with obvious family ties; another contains newly arrived Africans; a third includes Negroes who have recently changed masters.

The drive to sustain family connections was a significant motivation of which white owners were only occasionally aware. Olaudah Equiano relates from personal experience how this concern could take hold with captivity in Africa and persist in the face of overwhelming odds. Equiano's regard for his sister seems paralleled by the case of Ben, a pockmarked young Negro who disappeared from Edward

[32] Minutes of the Antigua Council, July 31, 1783, quoted in Elsa V. Goveia, *Slave Society in the British Leeward Islands at the End of the Eighteenth Century* (New Haven, Conn., and London, 1965), p. 257.

Thomas' lowland plantation in 1735. According to the *Gazette*, this slave had been "waiting man to Mr. John Wright deceased, when he was in England," so it was suspected that he might be near the Wrights' plantation at James Island, but the advertisement also mentioned as a hint to Ben's whereabouts that "he has a Sister at Dorchester at Mr. Tidmarsh's." A slave named Jack, who had gone to a new master and then disappeared for six months, was "suppos'd to be lurking about Mr. Maybank's Plantation, with his Wife." A similar notice appeared for a young Negro carpenter named Primus, who had also changed owners recently: "He pass'd over Combahee Ferry about 6 Weeks ago, and is suspected to be at Port-Royal Island, having a Wife at or near Mr. Hazard's Plantation."[33] But the most extreme example of the way in which a black family bond could be severed by a white owner comes from the letterbook of Robert Pringle. In the fall of 1740 this Charlestown merchant placed a Negro girl named Esther aboard the snow *Dorsett*, bound for Lisbon, Portugal. "She is a Very Likely Young Wench," he wrote to his contacts there, "& can doe any House Work, such as Makeing Beds, Cleaning Rooms, Washing, Attending at Table &c. & talks good English being this Province Born, & is not given to any Vice." Pringle stated he had "always found her honest" and added: "—The only Reason of my sending her off the Province, is that she had a practice of goeing frequently to her Father and Mother, who Live at a Plantation I am Concern'd in, about Twenty Miles from Town." Since "there was no Refraining her from Running away there, & Staying every now & then," Pringle had decided to ship her away and hoped his colleagues in Lisbon might "sell her to good Advantage."[34]

For every province-born slave deported during these years, hundreds of newcomers were arriving from Africa. Though it is sometimes stated that acculturated slaves were most likely to run away, a striking number of "salt-water" slaves managed to disappear. Some of these slaves were from the Caribbean—"Francisco a Spanish Negro"; "Tony, Barbadian born, about 30 years of age"; "John, West-India born, aged about 40"[35]—but most of them were from Africa. More than a quarter of all runaways advertised during the 1730s were cited as having been

---

[33] "Life of Equiano," pp. 20, 23–24; *SCG*, April 26, 1735; April 3, 1742; Oct. 3, 1743.

[34] Pringle to Edward and John Mayne and Co., Sept. 19, 1740, Pringle Letterbook.

[35] *SCG*, March 6, 1736; Nov. 16, 1734; Oct. 30, 1736.

born in Africa, and nearly half of these were indicated as recent imports. Where specific origins were given during the colonial period, the proportion of runaways from Gambia, Guinea, and Angola correlated fairly directly with the proportion of the slave population arriving from each region. The only marked exception was among Ibo tribesmen from the Bight of Biafra, who represented only several per cent of the incoming slaves but who constituted more than one tenth of the colonial runaways whose African origins are known, a fact which may explain in part why Carolina merchants avoided dealing in Ibo slaves.[36]

The ads for newcomers who ran away provide insight into the initial shock of debarkation and sale which all imported Negroes shared. A sense of bewilderment was inevitable for every immigrant. At times it must have grown overwhelming, and some new arrivals, like the old man brought to the workhouse from Ashley Ferry in 1742, sound more lost than escaped: "speaks very bad English, says his name is Bendar and that his Country is Mundingo, but cannot tell his Master's Name."[37] An ad placed in the *Gazette* by Henry Laurens suggests the real or pretended innocence of another Mandingan newcomer:

STROLLED away from my house, about midnight . . . , a tall well-made new negro man (of the Mindinga country) of a yellowish complexion, can speak no English, had on a new osnaburg shirt, and long trowsers, and a new romall handkerchief about his head. The hair of his forehead, about two or three inches up toward the crown of his head, was lately cut with scissars, and will appear as a mark for some time to come. His name is John, but he will more readily answer to the name of FOOTBEA, which he went by in his own country. He is supposed to have been decoyed away by some other negro. . . .[38]

But some slaves did a great deal more than "stroll away." There were instances reported in Virginia of Africans striking out overland, "being persuaded that they could find the Way back to their Country."[39] Smug Europeans may have overlooked the fact that the exertions of newcomers were less likely to be simplistic attempts to return to Africa than herculean efforts to retain contact with families and

[36] Blake, "Slave Runaways," pp. 5–7.
[37] *SCG*, May 22, 1742.
[38] *SCG*, Sept. 3, 1753.
[39] Quoted in Mullin, "Patterns of Slave Behavior in Eighteenth Century Virginia," p. 140.

countrymen, despite the weakness which followed their ocean crossing. Juno, a girl of scarcely fifteen who was "slender and strait Limb'd, and of the blackest Colour," arrived at Charlestown aboard the ship *Speaker* in June 1733 and was sold in Joseph Wragg's auction yard to an owner from Dorchester. But in two weeks she disappeared, still carrying "a large Scar on her right Knee" which may have been a mark of her voyage.[40] An Ibo boy of similar age was taken up in Charlestown in June 1735 by a local hatter scarcely a month after he arrived in port aboard the galley *Rainbow* from Africa. During the same spring a man with "one sore eye," who arrived among 318 slaves from Angola aboard the *Morning Star*, took his blanket and departed at the end of his first week of work on a rice plantation.[41] Such fugitives did not even have recognized names when they disappeared, as was also the case with four slaves taken up in Charlestown early in 1737. They had been among 350 slaves imported from Angola aboard the *Shepherd* the previous fall and sold at auction by Joseph Wragg. They spoke no English and did not know their master's name, but they had managed to make their way back to Wragg's slave pen in a vain search for relatives and shipmates.[42]

The odds for such strangers remaining at large were slim, but some managed to avoid starvation and capture for months at a time.[43] In 1734 a planter took up two Negroes swimming across the Combahee River; they had been branded and wore long white frocks after the African fashion. He reported that "they can't speak English (or will not) but I understand by one of my Negroes, who is of their Country, they have been out four Months."[44] While many of these runaways must have depended upon seasoned slaves for clandestine assistance, some newcomers appear to have helped and encouraged each other. Three of the slaves imported from the River Gambia aboard the *Princess Carolina* and auctioned in August 1736 disappeared from their new home in St. John's Parish within ten days, and

[40] *SCG*, July 21, 1733. A slave named Fellow, one of three new Angola men who ran away from James Bulloch after being branded, had "Bumps on the Joints of his two Knees and Elbows" which probably came from confinement below decks. *SCG*, Dec. 7, 1738.

[41] *SCG*, June 14, 1735; May 10, 1735.

[42] *SCG*, Jan. 22, 1737.

[43] One of many unforeseen dangers is illustrated by the Angolan woman taken up at Ponpon one December with feet so badly frostbitten that she could not be sent to town. *SCG*, Feb. 1, 1739.

[44] *SCG*, June 22, 1734.

from another ad a month later it appears as though two of their shipmates soon left the same plantation to join them.[45] It is natural that
recent arrivals sought out shipmates from the same passage, with whom
they shared not only the experience of the voyage but perhaps a common origin, a common language, or even blood ties as well. Yet it is
also worth noting that slaves from separate parts of Africa occasionally
joined in running away (usually after mastering a common pidgin
language), for such associations suggest the failure of the owners' conscious strategy to put Africans from different regions together so as to
minimize their chances to conspire.[46]

If the odds were heavily against such newcomers, the desperation driving them was often great. This is seen both in the distances
they traveled[47] and in the obstacles they overcame. One new Angola
man, being led to his master's Willtown plantation with his arms pin-
ioned, managed to escape and avoid discovery for at least six months.[48]
"A big belly'd run away Negro Woman," apparently well along in
pregnancy, was taken up beyond Ashley Ferry by another slave and
brought to the workhouse; she spoke no English and bore African
markings on her cheeks and breast.[49] But the best index of the frenzy
to escape which could consume a new arrival can be found in the instances where Africans were no sooner captured and punished than
they broke away again. In 1734 planters took into custody at Santee

---

[45] *SCG*, Sept. 11, 1736; Oct. 30, 1736. Cf. *SCG*, June 16, 1733: "Run away
from Dr. Samuel Stevens's Plantation at Westoe Savannah above Dorchester, a Negro
Man named Pompey of Callabar, who has been in the Country about 7 Months . . . ;
two new Ebo Negroes are run away from a neighbouring Plantation, and supposed to
be with him."

[46] In 1738 a planter named Richard Wright lost four slaves, "one named Cyrus,
born in Carolina, formerly belonging to Mrs. Trott, one called Cain a Bambra Negro,
Two Angola Negro Men, one named Ben the other Symon." The same year an
Angolan and an Ibo, assigned to handle William Martin's pettiauger, ran away to-
gether, and in 1743 Edward Fisher offered a reward for "two Negro Fellows, named
Cyrus and Caesar, the former is an Ebo, and the other an Angola Fellow." See *SCG*,
June 29, 1738; Jan. 19, 1738; April 4, 1743.

[47] The following announcements appeared in *SCG*, Oct. 26, 1734:

Brought to Goal in Charlestown

The 22d Instant a likely young Ibo Negro man, taken up near Capt. Charles
Russells 100 miles from Town near the Congeres, speaks no more English than
to say his name is Jack.

The 24th a likely young Angola Negro man, speaks no English, named Dick,
taken up at Stono Bridge.

[48] *SCG*, Jan. 18, 1739.

[49] *SCG*, June 11, 1741.

"a Negro Man, about 30 Years of Age, a very large strong Fellow, speaks no English at all." They reported that the slave had been "sent several times to Charles Town, in order to put him in Goal, but always has made his Escape, and return'd back." The next year a new Negro named Flanders escaped from Edisto Island in February 1735 and was taken up on a neighboring island a month later "but made off again" immediately.[50] Harry, an Ibo man, was picked up near Cooper River and confined to the jail in November 1740; in less than four weeks he was at large again, only to be apprehended on Charlestown Neck and reconfined.[51]

If newcomers were prompted to escape by a sense of bewilderment and desperation, another group of runaways defected for a different set of motives. Slaves who ran away upon confronting the prospect of a new owner were moved by a more calculated awareness of their present and future. The fact that so many absent slaves are described as "formerly the property of" someone else is in part simply a reflection of the fact that few Negroes belonged to one master for an entire lifetime. But the personal dislocations caused by a change of ownership in which the slave had no say could be catastrophic enough in their own right to spur escape. Often such changes came without warning in accordance with the shifting economic status of the master, for his financial losses, as well as his financial gains, generally occurred at the expense of his slaves. As the economy expanded, an ever-increasing number of Negroes were exchanged as payment on mortgages and other debts.[52]

When death came to a master, it made a change in ownership automatic, and a planter's will often had greater import for residents of the slave quarters than for anyone else. Sometimes an owner bequeathed slaves by name; other times their distribution was left to executors. In either case, for those Negroes who had been waiting their chance, the interregnum which followed the passing of a master

[50] *SCG*, May 25, 1734; April 19, 1735.

[51] *SCG*, Nov. 6, 1740. Cf. the later case of "a Calabar negro man, named Ben" who escaped from the Georgetown constable. (Naturally the owner blamed the white official, "who let him make his escape by neglect or design.") *SCG*, Feb. 22, 1756.

[52] E.g., "a Negro Wench named Kate" ran away from her new owner in 1733 not long after she had been "taken in Execution [of a debt] and publickly sold." *SCG*, March 10, 1733. The printer of the *Gazette* sold standard forms for mortgages for Negroes (*SCG*, Nov. 4, 1732). When property owners wished to sell land promptly, they would offer to "take Negroes, Liquors, or dry Goods in Payment" (*SCG*, Oct. 12, 1734).

could provide the breakdown of authority necessary for escape. A document from the turn of the century illustrates this point: Richard Baker died early in 1698 while his slaves were planting a crop, and his widow drew up an agreement with her sons for the year, "the better to manage and Govern the s^d Slaves and . . . for the Management of ye s^d Cropp and to Prevent any Disorder and Disobedience that may happen to Arrise by the Unrulyiness of the s^d Slaves." The inventory of an estate from 1737 is not unique in listing among the slaves of the deceased several "in the woods" and one "disputed in ye Estate."[53]

The uncertainty and fear connected with such transitions are obvious enough to explain any increase in disappearances, but one other factor may have had an important bearing upon these early generations of American Negroes: the West African tradition of slavery frequently frowned upon the sale of members of an estate. Francis Moore, who was living in Senegambia at this time, reported:

Several of the Natives have many Slaves born in their Families. . . . And tho' in some Parts of Africa they sell their Slaves born in the Family, yet in the River Gambia they think it a very wicked thing; and I never heard of but one that ever sold a Family-Slave, except for such Crimes as would have made them to be sold had they been free. If there are many Family-Slaves, and one of them commits a Crime, the Master cannot sell him without the joint Consent of the rest; for if he does, they will all run away, and be protected by the next kingdom, to which they fly.[54]

IV

WHAT THE RUNAWAYS took with them gives some indication of their various situations and intents. A few slaves brought into the Charlestown jail scarcely had clothes to cover themselves: several were wrapped in Negro blankets when apprehended; one man had on "only an Arse-cloth"; still another was entirely naked.[55] Pierro, or Peter, the twenty-five-year-old man who delivered *Gazettes* for the printer and who had been wearing his black leather printer's breeches, along with a white shirt and woolen cap, when he ran away in 1740, was located late one Friday night in a home outside Charlestown. According to

    [53] RRP (1696–1703), pp. 74–75; Inventories (1736–39), vol. II, p. 197, msv, SCDAH.

    [54] Francis Moore, *Travels into the Inland Parts of Africa* (London, 1738), p. 43.
    [55] SCG, May 8, 1736; June 7, 1740; June 12, 1736; Jan. 31, 1736.

the paper, "In making his Escape he left his Breeches and Hat in the House, so that 'tis uncertain whether he has any on, he having been since seen without them in the Swamp there." In contrast, some runaways wore their best clothes and many took extra garments with them so as to belie their newspaper description. Sue, a dark-haired mustee woman who disappeared in 1734, "carried all her cloaths with her, but being this Country born, and having many Relations, it is supposed she has changed them to prevent being discovered."[56]

Often the extra clothes were worn, as in the case of Peter and Bristoll, two Charlestown slaves who set out toward Santee one night wearing "new blue Plains Jackets and Breeches, and their old white cotton cloaths over them."[57] In 1742, Hampshire, a highly valued mustee slave, ignored a severely swollen foot and ankle to run away from the man in Morton Town who had purchased him off the estate of his deceased master. The new owner reported that the man had probably returned to Charlestown or James Island, "and had on when he went away white Negro Cloth Jacket and Trowsers, an Oznaburgh Shirt, and a Gown of white Plains."[58] Clothes could also provide a full-fledged disguise: an Indian slave named Sarah who disappeared from John's Island wearing "a strip'd flannel Gown" was thought ten months later to have "gone over to Hobkoy in Men's Apparel."[59]

Some runaways gathered up money or valuables: an eighteen-year-old named Phyllis "broke open her Master's Box and took from thence £110 and some other Money" before departing. Other slaves took along weapons or were able to acquire them later. It was claimed in an act of 1751 that "slaves which run away and lie out for a considerable space of time, at length become desperate, and stand upon their defence with knives, weapons or arms." When two Angolan brothers left a plantation on Wando Neck in 1734 in a stolen canoe, they "carried with them their Axes and Howes." Another Angolan named Tim possessed a gun when taken up at Stono in 1742.[60] The following year word reached Boston from South Carolina that "30 of their sensible

[56] *SCG*, June 14, 1740; July 13, 1734.

[57] *SCG*, Jan. 4, 1735. A black cooper named Bristol ran away the previous winter, "having on Two Jackets, one Green and one Blew, a red Cap and Hat with a pair of Indian Boots." *SCG*, Feb. 9, 1734.

[58] *SCG*, Jan. 3, 1743.

[59] *SCG*, June 17, 1732; March 10, 1733. Cf. note 17 above.

[60] *SCG*, May 20, 1732; *Statutes*, VII, 424; *SCG*, Feb. 9, 1734; Sept. 13, 1742. Cf. note 15 above.

Negroes, 15 of whom had Fire Arms," had run away in a group and
were heading for St. Augustine.[61] In the 1750s the *South Carolina
Gazette* illustrated its ads for runaways with a woodcut of a Negro
(branded with an R on the chest and wearing a skirt-like garment)
who was carrying a lance.

As for transportation, some slaves who were good riders and
hoped to cover a broad distance dared take horses, even though this
inevitably raised the owner's wrath and also increased the possibilities
of being spotted. In 1732 a slave named Owen took the bay horse of
his new master, tied some clothes and a white blanket behind the sad-
dle, and rode away under the pretense of going to see his wife on a
nearby plantation.[62] About the time of the Stono Uprising an "old
Negro Man named England, And a young slim Mustee Fellow, named
Prosper (his Son) about 19 Years of Age" disappeared suddenly from
Joseph Wragg's Goose Creek plantation. The notice in the *Gazette*
reported that several weeks later there departed

another young Mustee Fellow, named Prince, about 22 Years of Age (also
Son of England) with an Iron round one Leg, he took with him out of the
Stable, a large Bay natural pacing Stallion. . . .

It is supposed they are together near Dorchester, or about the Plantation of
Bethal Dewes to whom they did belong, the old Fellow England is well
known, having worked at the Bricklayer's Trade at several Plantations in
this Province and his Sons with him.[63]

Taking a boat was more commonplace than taking a horse, especially when several slaves departed together. Shortly after William
Webb moved his slaves from James Island to Maggot's Island in 1732,
three men and two women, "being very clever Negroes," disappeared
in his twenty-five-foot poplar canoe. Two women, one nursing a baby,

---

[61] *Boston Weekly-Magazine* (no. 2, p. 16), March 9, 1743.

[62] *SCG*, April 1, 1732. "He is about 30 Years of Age, tall, and somewhat lean:
He had on when he went away a brown Coat, a blue under Coat with Breeches of the
same, and blue Negro Boots."

[63] *SCG*, Oct. 13, 1739. The frequency with which family members escaped
together is suggestive. Earlier in 1739 John Cattell had advertised for "a Negro Man,
named Pompey, a short well set Fellow, and Barbary his Wife a Yellow Wench, big
with Child," and a year later he advertised for "a Negro Fellow named Will, lame in
one of his Legs, . . . and Hannah his Wife." That same year an Angolan couple
named Pompey and Menda absconded from North Edisto with their two small children,
and a mulatto woman named Judy disappeared from a James Island plantation with
her young ones, ages ten and six. Each of these slaves except Judy had recently changed
owners. (See *SCG*, Jan. 11, 1739; Jan. 19, 1740; Feb. 19, 1741; Feb. 16, 1740.)

stole a cypress canoe and escaped from their master several months later.[64] Such incidents continued to be as frequent as they had been in the earliest years when overland trails had been minimal, but as the colony spread out, an increasing majority of those who disappeared seem to have made off on foot.

V

BY NO MEANS all runaways were bent upon quitting the colony altogether, but for those who had such extreme ambitions, whether they left via water or over land depended upon their intended destination. These destinations varied widely, and the old stereotype, not even thoroughly valid for the nineteenth century, of the slave who follows the Drinking Gourd toward freedom in the North has little applicability in colonial Carolina. When runaways did navigate by the stars, and many were capable of doing so, they only occasionally headed due north, for in this period each point of the compass offered a different prospect of escape. The paths of some slaves were naturally determined by misinformation or ignorance about local geography, but a far greater number had a clear sense about where they were heading and why, having weighed at least to some degree the comparative dangers and prospects associated with each direction.

To the east the open ocean was an inevitable lure, and Charlestown harbor became a common locale for runaways. In 1725 well over one hundred local merchants and freeholders signed a petition which commended the captain of Johnson's Fort on the south side of the bay, for "the many good Services done . . . in Apprehending run away Servants & Negroes" and assured him sufficient men and boats to continue.[65] If a few newcomers entertained fancies of recrossing the Atlantic to Africa, most of those who hoped to depart illegally by sea had gained a clearer sense of their actual prospects through observation or experience. For example, a young Charlestown runaway named Harry, who was suspected of putting to sea in 1732, had no doubt seen

[64] *SCG*, May 6, 1732; June 17, 1732.
[65] BPRO Trans., XIV, 124–25. It was not unknown for ships in the West Indies to encounter runaways on the high seas (sometimes in canoes) and to smuggle them into Charlestown in hopes of selling them at a profit. See the case of "Dom Rex vs. Three Negro Slaves," July 28, 1737, Admiralty Court Records, mfm, reel 2 (1736–38), SCDAH.

and heard a great deal during the years he was the attendant in the "Physick and Surgery" shop of Daniel Gibson and Thomas Stitsmith beside the bay. When he vanished from Stitsmith's house on Broad Street, readers of the *Gazette* were warned: "Be it at the Peril of any Captain to take him off."[66] A similar warning was issued for Sampson, a well-known painter and glazier in Charlestown, who disappeared in the uneasy fall of 1739. Since he had been raised in the West Indies, his owner advertised that "He is likely to be hid on Board of Vessels, therefore I desire all Commanders to make enquiry on board their respective Vessels."[67]

Some of these runaways had prior experience at sea which they hoped would assist their efforts to escape. In 1743 Toney, a slave who had once belonged to Capt. Ebenezar Simmons of Charlestown, ran away from a purchaser who had taken him north to a rice plantation along the Peedee; he was described as "a lusty tall Gambia Fellow, . . . about 35 Years of Age, speaks pretty good English, . . . and affects to dress like a Sailor." Less knowledgeable runaways who frequented the docksides may have been trying to assess the sea as a possible avenue of escape. In 1737, for example, the *Gazette* reported that "a young Negro Fellow named Peter," who had already had four owners including an Indian trader, "has been lately seen with the fishing Negroes, at the Markett Place."[68] Slaves escaping to the north or south could also travel by water, and Lt. Gov. Bull reminded the Assembly in 1741 that the maintenance of scout boats at Hilton Head and Dawfuskee Islands was crucial to "prevent the Desertion of our Negroes, who might (perhaps) make frequent Attempts if those Places were left unguarded."[69]

As official vigilance and commercial traffic grew, the numerous coastal passages became more difficult avenues for escape, and runaways were obliged to test more thoroughly the colony's inland borders. North Carolina, thinly populated and rarely on good terms with its southern neighbor, had served as a refuge since the seventeenth century, and in 1722 South Carolina's agents in London were instructed to argue for the annexation of that region "by Shewing how

---

[66] *SCG*, Dec. 16, 1732; Jan. 7, 1733. Pierro of the *Gazette* office would have been similarly knowledgeable (see note 56 above), and his owner warned "All Persons as well Captains of Vessels as others" against harboring or employing him.

[67] *SCG*, Nov. 17, 1739.

[68] *SCG*, Jan. 17, 1743; Nov. 5, 1737.

[69] *SCCHJ*, 1741–1742, p. 56.

much this Province Suffers by the Inhabitants and Slaves running away there where they are Succour'd."[70] Some of the runaways who headed north were undoubtedly slaves brought from that direction who desired to return. When Toney, "a Virginian middle sized yellow-ish Negro Fellow," ran away from a plantation in Christ Church Parish he may well have hoped to reach Virginia again, although in fact he was brought to the workhouse in Charlestown within ten days.[71] Other slaves traveling in the lowland region claimed with varying degrees of honesty and success that they were "born free in Virginia."[72]

Exodus toward the south retained an even greater attraction for

[70] Instructions sent from S.C. to Francis Young and John Lloyd in London, received May 9, 1722. Parish Trans., Box marked "Maryland and other colonies," folder 168 (S.C., 1720–52), p. 2.

[71] *SCG*, May 29, 1742; June 5, 1742.

[72] *SCG*, Dec. 26, 1741. It was understood among whites that captured runaways were never to be fully trusted in giving their owner's name, much less in their other statements. (For such references as "perhaps maliciously will say he belongs to . . . ," see *SCG*, May 25, 1734; April 19, 1735; Feb. 7, 1743.) Some absentees sought to preserve their autonomy by literally playing "dumb," feigning ignorance, inarticulateness, or deafness. It was reported that Caesar, a man "well stricken in Years" taken up at Port Royal, "can't or wont tell his Master's Name." (*SCG*, May 9, 1743.) The considerable language barrier was also something behind which numerous black immigrants must have hidden occasionally during the eighteenth century, just as their white counterparts would do in the nineteenth and twentieth centuries.

But other slaves dissembled in the opposite manner by assuming a "smart" aspect, bluffing glibly and assertively. Roger Saunders (*SCG*, Aug. 4, 1733) offered a reward of £20 each for two such dissemblers:

> Run away near two Years, two Negro Men (being Sawyers) . . . , by Names Quamino and Quacco short, but very well Set, they both speak English very well, and are so crafty, that they would almost deceive any Body, and if taken, will frame a very Plausible Story that they are not runaways: The said Quacco is mark'd in the Forehead with Gunpowder thus RS.

Ten years later (*SCG*, Aug. 29, 1743) Richard Wright offered a £10 reward for a mustee slave named Nedd:

> about 20 Years old, he is a short well set Lad, full faced, short curl'd Hair, but not woolly, thick lip'd, small Eyes, speaks very plain, and is very artful in making a Story to get off, upon any examination. The last Account I had of him was, that he was about the head of *Strawberry River*, making his way for *Cape-Fear*.

In this same category were a considerable number of runaways who pretended to be free, such as the young mustee woman who left Stono seeking to pass as an Indian and who was occasionally "taken to be a Free Wench"; her owner reported that she "speaks good English, . . . has her Tongue at Pleasure, and her Back will shew the Marks of her former Misdeeds." (*SCG*, June 2, 1733.) The use of such assertiveness as a disguise may help explain why numerous slaves ran away in new and conspicuous clothes. It also heightened the confusion between free and enslaved Negroes, increasing the chances that those who *were* legally free might be taken up as dissemblers. Cf. *SCG*, June 4, 1737; Sept. 6, 1742.

South Carolina slaves because of the continuing Spanish presence in
Florida. Just as Negroes from the Virgin Islands would later defect to
Puerto Rico and work on Spanish fortifications there in exchange for a
plot of land,[73] so Carolina slaves of this period were drawn toward St.
Augustine by the thought of protection and freedom among enemies
of the English. The establishment of Georgia as a nonslave settlement
created new difficulties for black deserters, for as Capt. Massey told
that colony's trustees in 1740: "Georgia is a fine Barrier for the Northern Provinces, and especially for Carolina; And is also a great Security
against the running away of Negroes from Carolina to Augustine, because Every Negroe at his first Appearance in Georgia must be immediately known to be a Run away, since there are no Negroes in
Georgia."[74] But after slavery was allowed (or imposed) there in 1750,
the situation changed, and some of those Negroes heading south in
the following years had actually started in Georgia. In 1758, for example, Austin and Laurens offered a £20 reward for "a slim sprightly
sensible yellow Negro Boy, named Harry, lately sent from Georgia to
be sold, and imagined to be returned to that Province."[75]

As for those slaves who escaped toward the west into Indian
country, the prospect of total absorption into a compatible culture had
to be balanced against the risk of betrayal, captivity, or death. Decades of considerable contact must have made these contrasting possibilities broadly known, but the tensions of wilderness diplomacy kept
red–white–black relations in a state of considerable doubt. Occasionally, the familiar issue of runaways taking refuge with the Indians
gained prominence among whites, as in 1735 when the Assembly announced "that Several Slaves have made their Escape from this Province and very probably are sheltered & protected by the Tuskerora
Indians."[76] The assemblymen charged that tribe with killing cattle and
abducting slaves and undertook "to expel those Tuskeroras out of this
Government" by offering a bounty to freemen or slaves who killed or
captured any Tuscaroras, warning that as "the next step on the like
Provocation we shall endeavour to extirpate them."[77]

For Negroes disappearing westward, Indians consistently
played a major role, stealing some slaves away and helping others

[73] Goveia, *Slave Society*, p. 255.
[74] *Journal of the Trustees*, Jan. 16, 1740, in *CRSG*, I, 363.
[75] *SCG*, Dec. 15, 1758.
[76] *SCCHJ, 1734–1735*, p. 235.
[77] *Ibid.*, p. 233; also p. 217.

escape, but relations were always ambiguous. Upon occasion redmen killed blacks with no clear provocation, as in 1721 when a member of the Cussoe Nation named Toby shot a valuable Negro sawyer named Bram as he was working on his master's plantation.[78] Months later a Negro runaway "was Shott by a Slave Indian by nobody's Order."[79] White colonists encouraged such animosity. Sensing that the interests of these two groups often overlapped, they did all that they could to insure separation and promote hostility between black and red.[80] An early move of the first royal governor in 1721 was to negotiate a pact of "Friendship and Commerce" with the Upper and Lower Creeks, whose head men promised "to apprehend and secure any Negro or other Slave which shall run away from any English Settlements to our Nation," in return for four blankets or two guns if taken up beyond the Oconoy River, one gun if returned a shorter distance. "And in Case we or our People should kill any such Slaves for their Resistance, or running away from us in apprehending them," continued the article, "then we are to be paid one Blanket for his Head by any Trader we shall carry such Slave's Head unto."[81]

The Creeks may have been one of the tribes to steal and redeem slaves simultaneously, for in February 1728 an English agent charged that for several years they had been "Robbing and Plundering us of our Slaves and Goods and laying the blame on the Yamasees."[82] Later that same month a committee appointed to consider ways to make the neighboring tribes "more Serviceable" to the interests of the colony suggested the appointment of Indian Commissioners whose duties would include distributing rewards to Indians who killed or captured runaways. At the same time it was recommended that such officials should be empowered to punish any Negroes who tried to intimidate local Indians from carrying out white orders. It was also hoped that they would "Discourage any Trade or Traffick being carryed on between the Indians and Negroes and likewise prevent any Negroe from

[78] SCUHJ, Jan. 25, 1722, mfm BMP/D 487, SCDAH; *SCGHJ, 1725*, pp. 109–11.

[79] SCUHJ, June 22, 1722 (cf. Jan. 29 and June 23), mfm, BMP/D 487, SCDAH.

[80] For a full discussion of this triangular relationship, see Willis, "Divide and Rule," pp. 157–76.

[81] *SCCHJ, 1736–1739*, p. 110. The scalp of a black runaway may have been harder to take, more difficult to recognize, or less horrifying to show other slaves than the whole head. At any rate, decapitation was used frequently by both Indian and European captors.

[82] BPRO Trans., XIII, 109.

takeing a Wife among the Free Indians, or Free Indians from takeing a Slave a Wife."[83]

By this time reports of "an outlying Negro being shot" by Indians had become a regular occurrence, and their frequency increased as slave numbers and Indian desperation grew.[84] In 1730 seven Cherokee chiefs traveled to London for an audience with the English king. There they signed an agreement similar to that struck with the Creeks nine years before, promising among other things to return Negro runaways for the somewhat reduced payment of a musket and a match coat per slave, alive or dead.[85]

Experience gradually taught the English that runaways who reached the hinterlands were not easily returned to the low country alive, even when spared by the Indians. In 1723 a band of warriors brought two half-starved runaways to a trading post on the Ochese River and settled down to await payment. Though uncertain the slaves could survive the trip or that their ransom would be paid, the trader felt obliged to ship them to Charlestown in a pettiauger and pay off their captors. In 1726 the Assembly granted a trader £50 in restitution for "a wound he received of a Negro bringing him down prison[r]: from the Indians." During the following winter an English captain returning from the Creek tribes ran up a bill of £25 "for men employ'd to pursue a Negro that was taken & made his escape."[86]

[83] SCCH, Feb. 29, 1728, Parish Trans., S.C., Box I, folder 4, p. 19. A week before, it had been recommended that in revising the Patrol Act, "any Indian pursuing a runaway Negro be given a reward if the slave is killed resisting apprehension, and a greater reward if taken alive." *Ibid.*, Feb. 23.

[84] This quotation concerns a slave of Ralph Izard (president of the council) killed by a Eutaw Indian in the spring of 1728. Parish Trans., S.C., Box I, folder 4, p. 17. See pp. 28–29 in this source for an incident brought before the Assembly, Feb. 25, 1731. For other runaways killed by Indians, see *SCCHJ, 1725*, pp. 34, 45, 49; *SCCHJ, 1734–1735*, p. 32.

[85] BPRO Trans., XIV, 21–22. The speech delivered Sept. 9, 1730 (p. 24), by Scalileskin Retagusta, speaking on behalf of all the Cherokee chiefs, provides a stark glimpse of the imbalance of power between the two nations and of their contrasting ideas of slavery:

We came hither naked and poor as the Worm out of the earth, but you have everything and we that have nothing must love you and can never break the Chain of Friendship that is between us.

Here stands the Governor of Carolina whom we know. This small Rope we shew you is all we have to bind our slaves with and may be broken but you have Iron Chains for yours. We shall bind them as well as we can and deliver them to our Friends again and have no pay for it.

[86] John Woort to John Bee in "Charles City," July 30, 1723, BPRO Trans., X, 129–30; *SCCHJ, 1725–1726*, pp. 102–3; *SCCHJ, 1726–1727*, p. 147.

In 1728 another English agent, sent among the Cowetaws, reported that "They have now a Negro belonging to a Man at Pon Pon who has run away from his Master and has been catch'd several times and still gets away. I desire your Order about him," the agent told officials; "I believe it as much as he is worth to bring him down. I believe it would be better to set his head up for an example."[87] An item from the *Gazette* in 1737 told how seven Upper Creeks had come upon an outlaw band composed of a Spaniard, an Indian, a Negro and a mulatto, known to have made forays against whites and Indians alike. The Creeks promptly killed the brigands and sold their stolen Spanish horses to the English.[88] Among the Cherokee, and perhaps among other nations as well, patrolling for runaways became such an accepted occupation that by the middle of the eighteenth century the term "slave catcher" was applied to a certain class of braves.

VI

WHETHER SLAVES DEPARTED singly or together, by sea or land, armed or unarmed, toward north or south, their chances of successful escape became increasingly slight. This did not preclude desperate slaves from undertaking such escapes, as the events surrounding the Stono Uprising will make clear. But it meant that Negroes who actually took flight from South Carolina in various directions were only a minority of the entire runaway population. Many more slaves seem to have succeeded in going "underground," intermittently or for good, without leaving the colony. It is hard to estimate how many people simply disappeared temporarily and endured a set punishment upon return. For practical purposes they were "absent without leave," and one

[87] Charlesworth Glover, March 17, 1728, BPRO Trans., XIII, 116–17, 140–41 (punctuation added).

[88] *SCG*, March 5, 1737. John Brickell wrote of Indians in the Southeast at this time (*Natural History*, p. 357):

> They are very expeditious in finding out the Negroes that frequently run away from their Masters into the Woods, where they commit many outrages against the Christians, as it happened in Virginia not long since, where above three Hundred joined together, and did a great deal of Mischief in that Province before they were suppressed. . . .

> I saw four and twenty of these Negroes hanged in Virginia, for conspiring against their Masters who had taken Sanctuary in the Woods for some time before they were discovered, or hunted out by the Indians, who are very serviceable to the Christians in those Parts, and many other Provinces in the hands of the English.

would not expect such individuals to show up proportionally in the printed ads. Even so, where specific motives can be discerned from notices in the colony's newspaper, South Carolina Negroes were more likely to disappear in order to visit and to maintain contact with other slaves than for any other single reason.[89] Such short-term absences became acknowledged as an effective "coping" process within the system, and both blacks and whites realized that these brief departures could represent a means of relieving tension and avoiding more dangerous confrontations or desertions.

Even the shortest disappearance was by no means a carefree gesture and demanded constant ingenuity and vigilance toward other Negroes, as well as toward Englishmen and Indians. Harboring escaped slaves could draw severe penalties, and although many blacks ran the risk gladly, there were others who would reveal the whereabouts of a runaway to settle a grudge, curry favor with their owner, or lay claim to a small reward. In 1737 the disappearance of a Negro man named Tom prompted his new owner, Thomas Gadsden, to give notice in the *Gazette* that "If any one will bring him to me, I will pay 5 *l.* reward, and I shall be oblig'd to those that will acquaint their Negroes of this, he being known by many." When a sixteen-year-old named Lucy ("formerly belonging to Jonathan Fitch, by whom she is supposed to be harboured") ran away in 1742, her current master advertised: "Ten Pounds reward will be given to any white Person, giving such Intelligence of the abovesaid Girl that she may be had again, and to any Negro Five Pounds for the like Intelligence."[90]

There were always slaves to respond to such inducements, as shown by the weekly lists of runaways brought to Charlestown jail. In late April 1735 a slave boy from Ponpon was "taken up at Wappow at Mr. Harvey's Plantation by one of his Negro Men named Dubb." The next day a new African was turned in by a slave named Tony, and several weeks later a man named Bristol took up another newcomer on his owner's plantation.[91] If the fugitives were very young or old, if

[89] Blake, "Slave Runaways," pp. 11–16.

[90] *SCG*, July 2, 1737; Nov. 22, 1742. When "a new Angola Negro Man, named Clawss" disappeared from Isaac Porcher's Wassamsaw Plantation, the owner offered a £2 reward (*SCG*, Aug. 13, 1737) and added: "*N.B.* As there is abundance of Negroes in this Province of that Nation, he may chance to be harbour'd among some of them, therefore all Masters are desire[d] to give notice to their Slaves who shall receive the same reward, if they take up the said Run-away."

[91] *SCG*, May 3, 1735; June 7, 1735. Neither slave gave his own name or that of

they could not make themselves understood, or if they had been mutilated for previous offenses, they fell easy victims to "loyal" slaves.[92]
But to threaten the freedom of strong men entailed considerable risk.
On the night of March 22, 1743, a runaway named Hannibal appeared
near the slave quarters on John Paggett's plantation. Two resident
Negroes tried to apprehend him, "but he being armed with a Knife
stabbed one . . . (named Harry) in the Heart of which he instantly
died, and maiming the other very much made his Escape."[93] Paggett
was reimbursed liberally for the loss of Harry, in accordance with the
Negro Act, but Hannibal remained at large. Even strong men fully
armed, however, often could not avoid eventual betrayal, and more
than one found himself being shot at by a fellow slave.[94]

Fugitives were not even safe among other absentees. In 1742
several ordinary runaways, encountering a surviving ringleader of the
Stono Uprising, captured him in Cocaw Swamp and collected a reward for turning him over to the hangman. In encouraging slaves for
capturing slaves, white colonists went so far as to accept the logic that
a Negro who "recovered" himself could be eligible for a reward. In
1721 the government voted £5 to Harry, "a Negroe Man belonging to
the Widdow Perry, . . . for his faithfulnes in returning from St Augustine to this Government." Seven years later "a Negroe Man named
Cuffee belonging to Mr. Jones who had been serviceable, in makeing

---

an owner, and they appear to have been at least the third and fourth slaves brought to
jail that spring who spoke little or no English. (See *SCG* for March 29 and April 12.)

[92] *SCG*, Aug. 23, 1740. On Aug. 16 a slave named Booba was brought to
the workhouse in Charlestown: "says he belongs to Mr. Ball at Wando, two Toes upon
each Foot seem as if they were cut off, had on a White Negro Cloth, Jacket and
Breeches, taken by one of Mr. Izard's Negroes at Goose-Creek."

[93] *SCCHJ, 1742–1744*, pp. 387, 388.

[94] The capture of Quash (*SCG*, March 16, 1734) provides a case in point:

On Tuesday last in the afternoon a Negro Man named *Quash*, belonging to
Roger Moore Esq; was apprehended at the Plantation of *Charles Hart* Esq;
He had been run away between six and seven Years: When he was surrounded
he went up stairs over the Kitchin, a white Man and one of His Excellency's
Negroes followed him each with a Musket loaded with Swan-shot, and he jump-
ing down out of the Window received the Fire in the small of the Back, notwithstanding which he ran a Quarter of a Mile, but growing faint, he fell down,
was taken, and brought to Prison in a Cart, where he now lies, in order to be
tried in a few Days.

Aptheker, *Slave Revolts*, p. 183, notes from the Council Journals that "In March,
1734, a reward was urged for the white servant and slaves who had caught and killed
a well-known leader of a destructive band of slave outlaws." (This could not have
been Quash, for his execution is described in Chapter X below.)

his Escape from the Spaniards and giveing Information to this Province" was granted £10 by the Assembly.[95] However, these incidents
in which a reappearing slave was paid for returning stolen property—
himself—were highly exceptional. Whatever the psychological benefits of disappearing for a time and then surrendering, no Negro could
engineer a financial profit through running away.

If anything, the incentives for departed slaves to remain "underground" increased as their absence lengthened. Negroes who continued to stay away, because with the passage of time they had become
increasingly fond of their autonomous status or fearful of added reprisals, were designated by authorities as "notorious fugitive slaves"
after a year at large.[96] Such persons who were prompted in their absence by family ties undoubtedly gained refuge from a relative within
the colony.[97] Other runaways sought out friends from whom they had
been separated. An ad in the *Gazette*, August 8, 1743, suggests that
this practice was acknowledged by both black and white:

RUN away about January last, from John Fenwicke's Plantation at Ashepoo,
a short well set Mustee Fellow, named Cadjoe, formerly belonging to Mrs.
Beamer on Charles Town Neck; He is a sensible Fellow, about 28 Years old,
born in the Province; and not being heard of, about Ashepoo or elsewhere,
for above these three Months, it's supposed, that he is harboured by some
Negroes of his old Acquaintance, especially those formerly belonging to
said Beamer.

Sometimes the whereabouts of an absent slave could only be
guessed by a master, but often the knowledge of a runaway's location
seems strikingly specific. The *Gazette* contains numerous references to
absentees who continued to elude authorities, even after they had
been seen at a distance or located by a reliable source. In 1738 Roger
Saunders noted that an Indian slave named Peter, who had worked
for Thomas Elliott as a carpenter and wheelwright,

[95] *SCG*, Dec. 27, 1742; *SCCHJ*, 1742–1744, p. 263; SCUHJ, Aug. 15, 1721,
mfm BMP/D 487, SCDAH; SCCHJ, Feb. 17, 1728, Parish Trans., S.C., Box I, folder
4, p. 18. Cf. Chapter VII, note 33.

[96] *Statutes*, VII, 421 (1751). The Negro Act of 1722 ordered any master to pay
the patrol fifty shillings for any one of his slaves "they shall take alive, having been
run away above six months." *Statutes*, VII, 380.

[97] A young woman named Sabina, for example, ran away from a Goose Creek
plantation soon after her owner died; a notice published the following month stated
that she was the "Daughter to a Negro Woman, named Tulah, living with Mr. Robert
Pringle Merchant, and is supposed to be lurking or concealed in or near Charlestown."
SCG, July 3, 1736; cf. note 34 above.

has eloped from me several Times, and generally has been taken up on the Town Neck. Also run away about two Years since, a Negro Man, named Abram, who is a good Sawyer, middle sized and middle aged, and speaks broken English, he formerly belonged to Major Tobias Fitch, I have a good deal of Reason to think that he is harboured sometimes about Four hole Swamp, sometimes about Mr. Baccots at Goose Creek, and sometimes on the Town Neck, he having been frequently seen about them Places, and not long since on the latter.[98]

Phillis, "a pretty tall young Negro Wench . . . well known in Charlestown," had been absent less than a week when her master placed a notice in the *Gazette,* but she had already "been seen often about Town at Work, and Friday Evening last was seen going up the Road with Capt. Gadsden's Negroes."[99]

Although hiding in Charlestown was the opposite of hiding in the woods, the crowded anonymity of the city attracted numerous runaways, especially those who had been there before. Franke, "a young Molatto House-Wench . . . known by most People in Charlestown," was sold to a John's Island planter by the executors of an estate in 1734. She soon absconded and was seen in town by several people, "without doubt harbour'd by some free Negroes or Slaves."[100] Fear of being recognized apparently did not deter these runaways, who knew the safety of Charlestown's numbers and had learned to rely on their own shrewdness. The ad for one Negro who deserted his new master reads: "well known about Charles Town but not for his goodness." A slave named Minos who ran off from Mr. Wragg's plantation in 1734 was also "well known in Charles Town, having liv'd there several Years." His master supposed him "to be lurking in or about the Town" and warned readers of the *Gazette:* "He is a very crafty subtil Fellow, and if taken, without great Care, will get away again."[101]

Slaves seeking refuge in Charlestown must occasionally have crossed paths with Negroes running away from the city. In the fall of 1734, for example, the *Gazette* not only carried ads for "a Negro Wench named Flora," who had disappeared from James Island and been seen in town, but also for Hanna, the absent slave of a Charlestown bricklayer. When this woman first left the city in June she was "seen at Capt. Gadsden's and Mad. Guyle's Plantations"; in October

[98] *SCG,* April 27, 1738.
[99] *SCG,* May 7, 1741; cf. Cyrus in *SCG,* Feb. 19, 1737.
[100] *SCG,* May 18, 1734; cf. Bella in *SCG,* July 13, 1734.
[101] *SCG,* Sept. 6, 1735; July 13, 1734.

she was still at large and said to keep "between Mr. Edward's and Capt. Gadsden's Plantations." Some Negroes who disappeared into the countryside must have sought out enslaved relatives or friends while others went into solitary hiding. A Negro who escaped from James Kerr lived for a considerable time on Otter Island before being hunted down. A few found safety on the remote fringes of the colony. London, for example, an Angolan who had been brought to Carolina in 1730 and had lived in St. John's Parish for ten years, ran away from his new master near Pine Tree Creek. Two years later, an ad in the *Gazette* stated that he was "supposed to be harbour'd in some of the Out Settlements."[102]

Therefore, from the center of the port city to the edge of settlement and beyond, the presence—or nonpresence—of absentee Negroes was a fact of colonial existence. As agricultural production intensified during the first half of the eighteenth century, the pressure on Negroes to run away increased, but at the same time the machinery for their containment multiplied: tickets were required, patrols were strengthened, punishments were enforced. Perhaps hardest of all, rewards were offered to buy the loyalty of slaves. Individually and collectively, therefore, Negroes felt their situation becoming more desperate. As the incentives grew higher on the one hand to rebel or escape, the inducements mounted on the other hand to submit and even to inform. For slaves caught in such a vicious circle, running away represented a personal and partial kind of resistance which at one moment seemed too bold and at another moment did not seem bold enough. If the majority of slaves never actually broke out of the circle and ran away, even for a short time, it was due not to any ignorance of the variables involved but to an acute awareness of them. And these specific considerations weighed by every potential runaway were in many ways emblematic of the larger ongoing dilemma which enslavement posed for all black people.

But their masters too were confronting a circular dilemma. Although no single runaway posed a threat to the slave system, scores of absentees constituted not simply a minor nuisance and ominous reminder but a potential nucleus for more concerted acts of rebellion. And the harder the hammer fell, the more likely it was to create further sparks. A subtle spiral of fear and repression had begun to generate around the inner anxieties of the white community.

[102] *SCG*, Nov. 16, 1734; June 15, 1734; Oct. 26, 1734; *SCCHJ, 1734–1735*, pp. 84, 94, 96; *SCG*, March 27, 1742.

PART FOUR

A Colony
in Conflict

X

Patterns of White Control

I

AS the South Carolina colony grew numerically, it spread out geographically along the coastline and began to edge farther inland along the network of creeks and rivers. Life within this expanding settlement became increasingly complex, and the tensions which separated slaves and freemen grew increasingly strong. Confronted with different and more acute anxieties about race relations than their forebears or their counterparts in mainland colonies farther north, white Carolinians addressed with increasing directness the question of the Negro's "place." The fact that this question had not yet become a tradition, the fact that the answer had not yet been entirely foreordained, made the issue all the more vexing and the need for direct answers all the more intense. The net result was a pattern of controls intended to define with increasing clarity and bluntness the social, economic, and even physical "place" of the black Carolinian.

In a culture where running away had become a common emblem of the tensions between blacks and whites, the most elementary form of control was little more than a concerted effort by masters to establish the continuous whereabouts of their slaves. Official worry over what tasks slaves performed was therefore complemented by growing concern over how they spent their free time, particularly in the vicinity of Charlestown. For while certain deceptions were feasible during working hours, these were limited compared to the activities possible on holidays or under cover of darkness. The printer of the *Gazette* reported in 1732 that "On Sunday Evening last, there were nigh 200 Negroes met together on the Green" in Charlestown, and he pointed out that the injury of one "valuable Negro" in a fracas there directly reduced the owner's wealth. Early in 1734 several slaveowners placed an ad charging that Messrs. Blondel, Wyss, and Morphew "in Broad street and others keep and entertain Negroes and Servants, at their Masters great damage," and notice was given that laborers belonging to the advertisers were not to be served "in any publick or private House by day or night, without . . . their Masters Leave." In 1740 the colony's licensed retailers of rum and wine, who already numbered close to one hundred, were all forbidden by law from serving any spirits to slaves without the permission of the owner.[1]

As early as 1712 legislation had been directed against the numerous Negroes who entered Charlestown on Sundays and holidays in order—according to whites—"to drink, quarrel, fight, curse and swear, and profane the Sabbath, . . . resorting in great companies together, which may give them an opportunity of executing any wicked designs."[2] Slaves coming to town on these days were required to carry a ticket from their masters stating their specific mission, and ten years later this ticket system was elaborated to include all slaves away from their home plantation at any time.[3] But efforts to prohibit Negro socializing had limited success as the repetitive presentments to the Grand Jury make clear. In 1734 white citizens presented "as a very great grievance the Negroes Meeting in such Numbers in the Streets of Charles Town on the Lords Day both in and after the Time of Divine Service," for not only was their noise and profanity considered a "Great Scandal . . . [to] all sober and well disposed persons," but also there was always the "hazard of their running into greater Extravagance and endangering the safety of the Inhabitants by such great Licince." In 1737 it was protested that "the Laws for the religious Observation of the Sabbath Day are notoriously violated in Charlestown, by Negroes publickly cabaling in the Streets," and a similar complaint was lodged in 1744 concerning "the great Insolence of the Negroes in Charlestown by gaming in the Streets and Cabballing in numbers thro' most parts of the Town especially on the Sabbath day."[4]

Charlestown was not the only location of suspicious gatherings

---

[1] *SCG*, Oct. 28, 1732; March 9, 1734; *Statutes*, VII, 408. More than fifty individuals paid the £ 12 fee for a license to sell rum or wine in 1725, and more than seventy paid in 1728. Treasury Records, Ledger Book A (1725–30), pp. 55–56, 198–9, SCDAH.

[2] *Statutes*, VII, 354.

[3] *Ibid.*, p. 371.

[4] *SCG*, March 30, 1734; Nov. 5, 1737; BPRO Trans., XXII, 82.

—after the Stono Uprising a fine of £10 was imposed on planters who countenanced "any public meeting or feastings of strange negroes or slaves in their plantations"[5]—but the port had the largest concentration of enslaved people and the greatest prospect of disorder. Town officials therefore organized a formal watch which grew more elaborate with time. An act for "maintaining a Watch and keeping Good Orders in Charles Town," passed in 1721, empowered watchmen to stop any Negro on sight, and slaves appearing in public after nine at night without a satisfactory cause were to be "Confined in the Cage of Charles Town till the next morning."[6] Watchmen went armed, practiced shooting every month, and were instructed to fire on any Negro who refused to stop when ordered.[7] Gov. Nicholson informed the Lords of Trade several years later that without such an act, "We in this Place must be in the Utmost Confusion as in the Primative State of Nature every one doing what is right in his Own Eyes and Dayly and Nightly Suffering Mischiefs and Insults."[8]

The total force consisted of "Twenty one able Watchmen of the age of Twenty one years and one Drummer" (perhaps black) capable of awakening the white populace. There was a commander and two subordinate officers, one of whom was in command each night and all of whom were charged with "the Quelling and Defeating of any Disorders Insurrections or Tumultuous Design's formed and carried on by any Negroes or other Slaves."[9] An additional act was passed in 1737 and published in the *Gazette* on the day that it took effect. Any slaves abroad after 8 P.M. in the winter and 9 P.M. in the summer were required to carry a lantern containing a lighted candle or a ticket signed by their master and stating their precise business. Violators could be taken up by a watchman or any white person and confined to the watch house until morning. At that time the officer in command of the watch would "order every such Negro to be whipped at the publick whipping-post," and collect a fee of five shillings from the victim's master.[10]

5 *Statutes*, VII, 410.
6 Parish Trans., S.C., Box I, folder 1, p. 25.
7 *Ibid.*
8 BPRO Trans., XI, 110.
9 Parish Trans., S.C., Box I, folder 1, p. 26.
10 *SCG*, March 26, 1737.

II

WHAT THE WATCH DID for Charlestown, the patrol system did for the rest of the colony. It was traditional that patrol duty, performed on horseback in every parish and providing an exemption from militia service, fell to those well-to-do whites with the largest personal investments in the slave system. When an act was passed in 1721 which merged the separate patrols with the colonial militia, one purpose was to insure that the "choicest and best" planters in the province could no longer "screen themselves from doing such services in alarms as are required and ought to be done by men of their ability."[11] On the other hand, the merger also served to make the entire militia system available for the surveillance of slaves, and in this respect it marks an important step in the shift of white priorities away from problems of external danger to questions of internal security.

From 1721 until the time of the Civil War the local control of slaves in South Carolina rested with military authorities,[12] and from this date as well there began a transformation of the militia "from a vital defensive agency to one whose principal duty was the police supervision of slaves."[13] Acts passed during the 1720s requiring planters to supply armed whites in proportion to their holdings in land or slaves were designed to strengthen the militia numerically in relation to the potential black enemies.[14] Captains of Patrol were appointed, and efforts were made to clarify their duties and strengthen their hand. In 1728 the Committee to Revise the Patrol Act recommended to the Assembly that each captain be given a statement of his responsibilities and be allowed to collect from the masters in his district a full list of

[11] *Statutes*, IX, 639. There is some question as to whether patrol members had been exempted from, or had simply shirked, their militia duties. SCCHJ, 1701, p. 21, SCDAH; David William Cole, "The Organization and Administration of the South Carolina Militia System, 1670–1783," unpublished Ph.D. dissertation (University of South Carolina, 1953), p. 42 *n*. Since patrol members were also called "alarm" men (because the prospect of internal rebellion increased when the colony was threatened externally), there was clearly disagreement as to who should be where at times of mobilization.

[12] H. M. Henry, *The Police Control of the Slave in South Carolina* (Emory, Va., 1914), p. 32. This work is now rather dated, and it devotes little attention to the formative colonial years.

[13] Cole, "South Carolina Militia System," p. 59. Cf. Shy, "A New Look at Colonial Militia," p. 181: "increasingly the South Carolina militia became an agency to control slaves, and less an effective means of defense."

[14] *Statutes*, III, 183, 255–57, 272.

the slaves on every plantation so that the patrol might check for absentees.[15] Several years later, however, the governor complained publicly that "Our Negroes are . . . become very insolent and ungovernable, for want of proper Amendments to the Law for their Governance, and for settling Patroles."[16]

In an effort to tighten security a new act was passed in 1734 which established a regular patrol along lines which would be followed for the duration of slavery. Under this statute three commissioners were appointed to supervise the patrol in each militia district. The patrol itself consisted of a captain and four men, excused permanently from militia duty, who were to make the rounds of plantations within their district at least once a month. They could question or search any traveling Negro and they could administer up to twenty lashes to any slave stopped outside his plantation without a ticket. They were empowered to search the homes of Negroes arbitrarily and to confiscate firearms or other weapons and any goods suspected of being stolen. They had authority to kill or maim supposed runaways who resisted arrest.[17] For these services each man received £25 annually, with a double stipend for the captain; and while most goods thought to be stolen were to be turned over to the commissioners, fowls and other provisions were left to the patrolmen, who seized them as an incentive for their work.[18]

Not all of these arrangements proved satisfactory, and when the law expired in 1737 a new patrol bill was passed. Certain powers were reassigned in an effort to strike a more efficient balance between mili-

[15] SCCH, Feb. 23, 1728, Parish Trans., S.C., Box I, folder 4, p. 19.

[16] *SCG*, Dec. 16, 1732, Gov. Robert Johnson's address to the Commons House, Dec. 7, 1732.

[17] Whether military or civilian, slave hunters traveled armed, and there was a high mortality rate among Negroes whom they located. Fleeing and resisting were both provocations for which a suspect would be killed, as shown by several petitions for reimbursement from the 1720s. A widow requested "an Allowance for a Negroe shott in persuite," and another white was granted £100 for his slave, "It appearing he was killed in making resistance." (SCUHJ, Aug. 29, 1721, mfm BMP/D 487, SCDAH; *SCCHJ*, *1725–1726*, pp. 38, 75.)

During the month of February 1735 the Assembly was asked to reimburse white citizens for more than half a dozen runaways who had recently met death. Stephen Bull, whose petition concerning "three run away negroes . . . killd by the Indians" was denied because he could not prove ownership, had himself recently shot a Negro man belonging to William Elliott, Sr. (*SCCHJ*, *1734–1735*, see entries for Feb. 12, 13, 14, 24, 26, 27, 28, 1735.) It may not be coincidence that on the final day of that month, mention was first made (p. 76) of a new "Act for the better ordering and governing of Negroes." (See also March 4, 19; April 8, 1735.)

[18] *Statutes*, III, 395–98.

tia authorities and local planters. Moreover, the experiment with paid recruits was dropped in favor of voluntary service by men who owned fifty acres or paid forty shillings in taxes. They were exempted from militia duty during the year in which they rode patrol and were allowed to choose their own captain. More significantly, the size of each patrol was raised from five to fifteen men, and they were required to make regular weekly rounds.[19] Further adjustments were made in 1740 when, in the wake of the Stono Uprising, patrol service became part of the required duty of *every* militiaman, for internal security was now the concern of all whites. Militia districts in the lowlands were divided into "beats"—no single circuit exceeding fifteen miles—which groups of seven whites patrolled for two-month stretches. Every woman who owned ten slaves was expected to provide a horseman, and any whites who defaulted from their duty were charged the full cost of hiring a substitute.[20]

By giving the patrol law renewed consideration every three years, the planters gradually evolved a method for policing Negroes which suited their desired ends. But the system never served its architects perfectly. Patrolmen who took their duties too lightly paid a price for their neglect. Others who construed their mandate too broadly ran the risk of provoking slaves to resistance as often as they forced them into submission. "Many irregularities have been committed by former patrols," noted the act of 1740, "arising chiefly from their drinking too much liquor before or during the time of their riding on duty."[21] Officials grew increasingly aware that, on the one hand, in times of alarm the militia would have more than it could do to maintain discipline over the black majority,[22] yet on the other hand, in more tranquil times it remained difficult to force even partial observance of the Negro code. In 1766 and again in 1772 the Grand Jury in Charlestown listed as one of the major grievances among whites the fact that enforcement of the Patrol Act had grown deplorably slack.[23]

[19] *Statutes*, III, 456.
[20] *Statutes*, III, 473.
[21] *Ibid.*
[22] See Charles Pinckney to Board of Trade, 1756, BPRO Trans., XXVII, 192–93; Report of Gov. Campbell, 1775, BPRO Trans., XXXV, 135.
[23] *SCG*, June 2, 1766; Dec. 10, 1772. Gov. Bull filed the following report on the state of the militia in 1770 (BPRO Trans., XXXII, 283–85):

> The Defense of the province as far as our power can avail, is provided for by our militia against foreign and Patrols against domestic enemies: . . . our

The efforts of individual planters and local patrols, especially in apprehending runaways, were often supplemented by special posses, and the council and Assembly were occasionally willing to grant £25 fees to cover expenses in pursuing Negro absentees.[24] Moreover, one final line of control lay beyond the districts of regular patrol. The scout boats posted along the coast had their counterparts inland in the several garrisons which dotted the perimeter of settlement. Planters clearly viewed these outposts more as a means for controlling runaways than for preventing invasion or protecting trade. Nothing underscores this frame of reference more vividly than a sardonic report from the commander at remote Fort King George:

The Fort (if a place incapable of defence may be called by that name) is situated 150 miles beyond any settlement and in the most desert part of the province for the security of which or any part of its Trade it might as usefully have been placed in Japan. . . .

The accomodations in the Fort both for Officers and Soldiers are fit for none but negroes. . . . I find I am not to expect Redress or Assistance from the Country who I firmly believe (some few persons excepted) would sacrifice not only this unfortunate Company but all His Maj[tys] Forces if in their power could they either save or gain half a score of paltry Negro's by it.[25]

III

FROM THE VIEWPOINT of the plantation slave the local patrols, standing at the head of a long tradition of sanctioned night-riding, represented a considerable reservoir of arbitrary power and constituted the Negroes' only regular contact with the harsh and one-sided system of surveillance known as the law. Beyond the intimidating

---

militia is now encreased to about Ten Thousand men, divided into Ten Regiments unequal in numbers, but equal in want of discipline. . . .

In the country almost every militia man marches on Horseback, of great use for expedition and to avoid fatigue. . . . The interior quiet of the Province is provided for by small Patrols, drawn every two months from each company, who do duty by riding along the roads and among the Negro Houses in small districts in every Parish once a week, or as occasion requires. Though human prudence has provided these Salutary Laws, yet, through human frailty, they are neglected in these times of general tranquillity.

[24] SCUHJ, Jan. 23, 1723, mfm BMP/D 487, SCDAH; *SCCHJ, 1726–1727*, p. 147; *SCCHJ, 1734–1735*, pp. 53, 58, 59.
[25] Report of Edward Massey, April 26, 1727, BPRO Trans., XII, 247–49.

force of the patrols, however, and apart from the crude justice meted out by individual overseers and masters, there remained a further legal mechanism, established by the Negro code, for controlling slaves through punishments and rewards. Justices of the peace were empowered to judge minor offenses and impose corporal punishment, and major felonies were taken before a panel of two justices and three freemen. In either case, swiftness and severity were considered the guiding principles in passing sentence. Whether punishments imposed upon slaves during the eighteenth century became more or less brutal with time has remained a matter of some question. Maiming of convicted Negroes through castration, nose-slitting, or chopping off such extremities as ears, hands, or toes seems to have become less common, or at least less public, during the 1700s. Branding for punishment, like branding for identification, may have declined,[26] as did the practice of burning slaves at the stake, although as late as 1791 the Charlestown paper reported that two Negroes were sentenced to be burned alive on the site where they were accused of having murdered a white overseer.[27]

But even if punishments became less hideous in absolute terms, it seems equally clear that in comparison to penalties imposed upon white offenders the treatment of blacks grew worse and worse, mirroring the relative decline of their condition being felt in many other ways. White lawmakers, increasingly anxious to recruit white settlers, knew that strict punishment of Europeans could damage the colony's reputation, while harsh treatment of blacks could in no way affect the flow of laborers from Africa. Moreover, since slaves were unable to possess property or assume debts, it was impossible to fine them for minor offenses. Therefore corporal punishment remained the rule for blacks, with whipping as the most frequent means, while physical penalties became less common and less brutal for whites, even in an era when all servants were traditionally subject to abuse.[28]

[26] Edson L. Whitney, "Constitutional, Economic, and Social History of the Colony of South Carolina," unpublished Ph.D. dissertation (Harvard University, 1890), pp. 669–80, points out that while branding was not formally abolished until 1833, mention of the practice disappears from the statutes after 1740. But its acceptance among planters must have continued; see note 43 below.

[27] *City Gazette of Charlestown*, Feb. 9, 1791, reprinted in *SCHGM*, LII (April, 1951), 110–11. *SCG*, July 30, 1772, reported of "that notorious Felon" Robert Prine: "He was shot by one of his own Slaves, who has since been convicted and burnt alive." For this and several other burnings, see *SCHGM*, II (1901), 299–300.

[28] Whitney's thesis (note 26 above) contains the fullest summary of all the punishments laid down in the *Statutes.*

Charles Wesley, who accompanied his elder brother John Wesley to America in the mid-1730s as secretary to Georgia's Gov. Oglethorpe, recorded in his journal:

Colonel Lynch cut off the legs of a poor negro, and he kills several of them every year by his barbarities. Mr. Hill, a dancing-master in Charleston, whipped a female slave so long that she fell down at his feet, in appearance dead; but when, by the help of a physician, she was so far recovered as to show some signs of life, he repeated the whipping with equal rigour, and concluded the punishment by dropping scalding wax upon her flesh: her only crime was overfilling a tea-cup! These horrid cruelties are the less to be wondered at, because the law itself, in effect, countenances and allows them to kill their slaves by the ridiculous penalty appointed for it. The penalty is about seven pounds, one-half of which is usually remitted if the criminal inform against himself.[29]

One traveler in the 1740s observed concerning the whipping of slaves: "The common Method is to tie them up by the Hands to the Branch of a Tree, so that their Toes can hardly touch the ground." After touring the southern and Caribbean colonies he concluded there was "hardly a Negro but bears the marks of Punishment in large Scars on his Back and Sides."[30]

Capital punishment, although much more rare, was still surprisingly common, given the fact that each slave represented a considerable investment to the whites. From the passage of the first slave code in 1690, death was prescribed for certain offenses, and to strengthen the enforcement of such laws the act of 1712 established a system of public compensation for the owners of slaves sentenced to death. Otherwise, the Assembly pointed out, the cost of executing slaves "would prove too heavy for the owners of them to bear" and would result in masters concealing crimes to prevent losing their Negroes.[31] But labor was still too scarce and the government too poor for this scheme to succeed, as shown by a change enacted two years later. "Whereas," stated the Negro Act of 1714,

[29] Quoted in James Silk Buckingham, *The Slave States of America*, 2 vols. (London, 1842), I, 105–6.

[30] Campbell, "Itinerant Observations in America," *London Magazine* (July 1746), rpt. in Ga. Hist. Soc., *Collections*, IV (1878), 39. Brickell, *Natural History*, pp. 272–75, related: "I have frequently seen them whipt to that degree, that large pieces of their skin have been hanging down their backs; yet I never observed one of them shed a tear." With a logic common to Europeans Brickell concludes that this "plainly shows them to be a people of very harsh and stubborn dispositions."

[31] *Statutes*, VII, 358.

it has been found by experience, that the executing of several negroes for felonies of a small nature, by which they have been condemned to die, have been of great charge and expense to the public, and will continue (if some remedy be not found,) to be very chargeable and burthensome to this Province; *Be it therefore enacted* . . . That all negroes or other slaves who shall be convicted and found guilty of any capital crime, (murder excepted,) for which they used to receive sentence of death, as the law directs, shall be transported from this province.[32]

This design for ridding the colony of convicted Negroes while still salvaging a profit proved thoroughly unworkable. It was repealed in 1717 after it became clear that the scheme had prompted slaves "to commit great numbers of robberies, burglaries and other felonies, well knowing they were to suffer no other punishment for their crimes, but transportation, which to them was rather an encouragement to pursue their villanies."[33] Executions were renewed, this time at the expense of all slaveowners in the parish. In 1722 cost was spread over the wider county unit, and a maximum value of £80 current money was established for any slave.[34] To meet depreciation in the currency this ceiling was raised to £200 in 1735 and then to £40 proclamation money in the next decade.[35]

In 1740, after the Stono Rebellion, the colonial government officially resumed responsibility for compensating the masters of executed Negroes,[36] but even during the 1720s it seems to have been making payments for slaves sentenced to death. More than 2 per cent (or £500) of the colony's budget for the year ending in September 1724 was allotted "to Arrears due for Negroes killed."[37] Often the payment, such as that to Roger Sanders in 1725, was "for a Negro man killed in takeing who was run away . . . & had robbd several People."[38] In

[32] *Statutes*, VII, 366.

[33] *Statutes*, VII, 370.

[34] *Statutes*, VII, 377. A majority of the Upper House persisted in "thinking it very unreasonable that the Publick Should pay for Negroes Executed." SCUHJ, Feb. 6, 1723, mfm BMP/D 487, SCDAH. This issue was still being debated in 1724. *SCCHJ, 1724*, p. 14.

[35] *Statutes*, VII, 389 (1735); III, 648 (1745); VII, 424 (1751). To prevent masters from secretly seeking higher compensation for offending slaves, the act of 1735 provided that any person exporting a slave who had killed a white, "that such slave may escape execution, . . . shall forfeit the sum of five hundred pounds, half . . . to his Majesty, . . . and the other moiety to the informer."

[36] *Statutes*, VII, 403. Compensation was not paid upon slaves guilty of murder or "taken in actual rebellion."

[37] BPRO Trans., XI, 49; see also 52, 192, 350.

[38] *SCCHJ, 1725*, p. 76.

cases involving formal execution the procedure was longer, but the outcome for the felon was the same. The only scholar to examine the payments made for sanctioned executions of slaves during the colonial period ventured the rough estimate that the "number of slaves executed annually probably varied from four to twenty, averaging probably about eight."[39]

For the white community, most of the cost of these punishments could be measured in monetary terms. The Negro Act of 1722 required masters to pay the marshal or constable two shillings six pence in proclamation money for whipping, branding, or cutting off the ear of any slave.[40] In 1735 the rate was raised slightly to twenty shillings current money, and a charge of £5 (to be taken from the public treasury) was established for executions.[41] Five years later, in the general tightening of controls which followed the Stono Uprising, the government assumed all expenses for the corporal punishment of criminal slaves, and also any "other charges for keeping and maintaining such slaves, as are allowed to the warden of the work house in Charlestown."[42] Thus in 1742, for example, warden William Garns submitted a bill to the Assembly "amounting to the Sum of twenty Pounds and five Shillings, for Fees due on keeping Negro Criminals."[43]

Some of these white officials may have overcharged for their services at times: in 1743 one constable asked £43 for the trial costs and execution of two Negroes; another claimed £8 for detaining, whipping, and branding a slave the following year.[44] Others took on private business in an effort to make ends meet: the warden of the workhouse began offering punishments at a set rate of fifteen shillings per quarter to any Charlestown residents who had "a mind to have their Servants or Slaves corrected."[45] At least some of the constables proved to be slaveowners in their own right. John Roberts of Dorchester, for example, found himself in the bizarre position of earning £12 for executing one slave and whipping and branding several others belonging to John Skene on the same day that another official was

[39] Whitney, "South Carolina," pp. 679–80. He cites the budgets which appear in *Statutes*, III, 155, 213, 264, 361, 362; IV, 70, 141, 204, 252, 282.

[40] *Statutes*, VII, 384.

[41] *Statutes*, VII, 395.

[42] *Statutes*, VII, 404.

[43] *SCCHJ*, 1741–1742, pp. 416–17.

[44] *SCCHJ*, 1742–1744, pp. 367, 370, 525.

[45] *SCG*, Oct. 25, 1742.

receiving £5 for putting to death one of Roberts' own slaves who had injured a white man.[46]

IV

ASSESSING SLAVE PUNISHMENTS in monetary terms allowed whites to distance themselves from the process. However, no similar distancing device was available to the blacks themselves. No slave could be assured protection from this arbitrary system, and as many as possible were made to feel the burden of any individual slave's suffering in a variety of ways. For example, it was not uncommon for one Negro slave to be placed in the position of punishing another. This applied not only to the evolving class of plantation drivers, who (like ethnic foremen in nineteenth-century factories) were allowed a certain private discretion in exerting control over the work force, but also to persons requisitioned to carry out public executions. If convictions ran too far ahead of punishments or there were other grounds for haste, slaves were pressed into service to execute slaves, as had long been the practice in some of the island colonies.[47] In 1740 South Carolina gave official sanction to this practice by empowering constables to force Negroes into inflicting corporal punishment on other slaves, so that "no delay may happen in causing execution to be done."[48]

Promptness was by no means the only consideration at work. In part, use of slaves as executioners reflects the tendency already described for thrusting Negroes into the most loathsome and demeaning tasks. Furthermore, it presented a means by which pain and anguish could sometimes be inflicted upon the individual punisher as well as the person being punished. Whites also saw in this practice a means for humiliating and dividing the rest of the slaves in ways which would make later subjugation easier. John Brickell observed a pattern of punishing slaves in North Carolina which may have been only slightly less regular in the adjacent colony:

[46] *SCCHJ, 1741–1742*, pp. 320, 343, 364, 376, 377, 379, 395, 416.

[47] Wilkinson, *The Adventurers of Bermuda*, p. 304, states that in seventeenth-century Bermuda, executions were often performed by a pardoned felon. "On one occasion a coloured woman had to be reprieved to do execution upon a man who was a greater offender than herself, and, from her time, the duty was usually delegated to a negro; it always was if the victim were coloured."

[48] *Statutes*, VII, 404. Refusal could bring twenty lashes, and compliance brought a five-shilling reward.

There are several laws made against them in this province to keep them in subjection, and particularly one, *viz*, that if a Negroe cut or wound his master or a christian with any unlawful weapon, such as a sword, scymiter, or even a knife, and there is blood-shed, if it is known amongst the planters, they immediately meet and order him to be hanged, which is always performed by another Negroe, and generally the planters bring most of their Negroes with them to behold their fellow Negro suffer, to deter them from like vile practice.[49]

White emphasis upon the importance of public punishment as a necessary form of deterrent grew as slave numbers increased and the potential for resistance among slaves multiplied.[50] Masters were fined for failing to whip unruly slaves, and the heads or bodies of notorious offenders were often left on public display as a grim warning to other Negroes. In 1732 Charles Jones reported having killed a Negro runaway who had robbed him and then offered resistance upon being overtaken. Jones told a justice of the peace he had felled the slave in self-defense with a blow of his musket butt, and the justice, accepting this version, ordered him to cut off the victim's head, "fix it on a Pole, and set it up in a Cross-Road" near Ashley Ferry.[51] Several years later, a slave named Abram, being charged with felonious assault on the high road, was arrested and sentenced to hang. His execution was delayed for a month in the hopes that his accomplice might be caught, and the *Gazette* editorialized: "it is hoped that an Example of Justice in this Case will deter other Negroes from committing such Insolencies and Crimes for the future."[52]

The spectacle of a public hanging was supposed in itself to provide a deterrent. Few onlookers could have been unmoved by the execution of Quash, a runaway who had been at large for seven years before finally being cornered in 1734. Once taken, this unusual renegade who had managed to preserve his African name and his personal independence for so long a time, was tried for various felonies in the morning and executed the same afternoon in a ceremony described fully by the local paper:

[49] Brickell, *Natural History*, pp. 272–75.

[50] Land, *Bases of the Plantation Society*, p. 223.

[51] *SCG*, Jan. 29, 1732. This practice was not unique. The heads of Negroes executed for alleged participation in a poisoning plot near Alexandria, Virginia, in 1767 were fixed on the chimneys of the local courthouse. Aptheker, *Slave Revolts*, pp. 198–99.

[52] *SCG*, Oct. 16, 1736; cf. Nov. 27, 1736.

When he came to the Gallows, he kneel'd down at the foot of the Ladder and prayed very devoutly; after he had ascended the Ladder, he likewise prayed again for some short time, when he turn'd himself gently off the Ladder, with a fervent Petition to' the Almighty, to have Mercy upon his poor Soul. After he was dead his Head was sever'd from his Body, and fixed upon the Gallows.[53]

Given Quash's serene departure, it is difficult to surmise the conflicting thoughts which passed through the minds of the numerous slaves who assembled to see him die or who later walked beneath his impaled head. Some victims, through eloquent silence or strong words, must have offered the opposite of a lesson in submission, and their final moments were left unreported, but the deaths of those who demonstrated contrition were publicized in detail. Few slaves provided white authorities with a more suitable display than Caesar, a slave convicted of trying to lead a band of runaways out of the province early in 1739. According to the *Gazette*'s account:

on Saturday last the said Caesar was executed at the usual Place, and afterwards hung in Chains at Hang-Man's Point opposite to this Town, in sight of all Negroes passing and repassing by Water: Before he was turned off he made a very sensible Speech to those of his own Colour, exhorting them to be just, honest and virtuous, and to take warning by his unhappy Example; after which he begged the Prayers of all Christian People, himself repeating the Lord's Prayer and several others in a fervent and devout Manner.[54]

It was hoped by white colonists that dramatic public punishments had a repressive impact, forcing slaves into patterns of docility. And in large measure the effect could hardly have been otherwise. Such regular displays, and the network of arbitrary controls they reinforced, inevitably drew forth from most blacks a submissiveness which, however unnatural, could be outwardly affected if it represented the price of survival. But external conformity often masked inner conflict, and the existing records make clear that a strengthened system of controls could not deter, and may even have provoked, patterns of resistance.

[53] *SCG*, April 6, 1734. For the account of his capture, see Chapter IX, note 94, above.

[54] *SCG*, April 12, 1739.

XI

Patterns of Black Resistance

I

IT is by no means paradoxical that increasingly overt white controls met with increasingly forceful black resistance. The stakes for Negroes were simply rising higher and the choices becoming more hopelessly difficult. As the individual and collective tensions felt by black slaves mounted, they continued to confront the immediate daily questions of whether to accept or deny, submit or resist, remain or flee. Given their diversity of background and experience, it is not surprising that slaves responded to these pressures in a wide variety of ways. To separate their reactions into docility on the one hand and rebellion on the other, as has occasionally been done, is to underestimate the complex nature of the contradictions each Negro felt in the face of new provocations and new penalties. It is more realistic to think in terms of a spectrum of response, ranging from complete submission to total resistance, along which any given individual could be located at a given time.

As in any situation overladen with contradictory pulls, there were those few persons who could not be located on such a spectrum at all; that is, their personalities "dis-integrated" in the face of conflicting pressures—internal and external—and their responses became unpredictable even to themselves. The Negro Act of 1751 made provision for local parishes to relieve poorer masters of the cost of confining and maintaining "slaves that may become lunatic."[1] This category of individuals is not easy to define, for mental illness, like physical illness, became an element in the incessant game of deception

[1] *Statutes*, VII, 424.

developing between masters and slaves; Negroes pretended outright insanity upon occasion, and owners readily called such bluffs, perhaps more frequently than they occurred.[2] Deception aside, it is no easy matter to define rational behavior within an arbitrary social system. Certain acts of resistance already discussed, such as appropriating goods and running away, usually involved prior calculation by their very nature, as did poisoning, arson, and conspiracy, which will be examined in this chapter. Many other actions represented impromptu responses to trying situations, but even reactions which seemed most irrational in terms of straightforward appearances and consequences rested upon a rational appraisal of the slave environment.[3]

At one end of the spectrum of individual resistance were the extreme incidents of physical violence. There are examples of slaves who, out of desperation, fury, or premeditation, lashed out against a white despite the consequences. Jemmy, a slave of Capt. Elias Ball, was sentenced to death in 1724 "for striking and wounding one Andrew Songster."[4] The master salvaged the slave's life and his own investment by promising to deport Jemmy forever within two months. For others who vented individual aggression there was no such reprieve. In August 1733 the *Gazette* reported tersely: "a Negro Man belonging to Thomas Fleming of Charlestown, took an Opportunity, and kill'd the Overseer with an Axe. He was hang'd for the same yesterday." An issue during 1742 noted: "Thursday last a Negro Fellow belonging to Mr. Cheesman, was brought to Town, tried, condemn'd and hang'd, for attempting to murder a white lad."[5]

Such explosions of rage were almost always suicidal, and the mass of the Negro population cultivated strict internal constraints as a means of preservation against external white controls. (The fact that whites accepted so thoroughly the image of a carefree and heedless black personality is in part a testimony to the degree to which black slaves learned the necessity of holding other emotional responses in outward check.) This essential lesson of control, passed on from one

[2] Inventories from the colonial period note an occasional slave who "pretends to be mad." Cf. "Charles Cotesworth Pinckney's Plantation Diary, April 6–Dec. 15, 1818," *SCHGM*, XLI (1940), 139. Among those "not working" at his Crescent Plantation, Pinckney cites "Old Sambo (pretends to be crazy)."

[3] See Jordan, *White Over Black*, p. 393.

[4] Parish Trans., S.C., Box I, folder 4, pp. 3a–4 (copied from SCCHJ, Jan. 24, 1724).

[5] *SCG*, Aug. 25, 1733; June 28, 1742.

generation to the next, was learned by early immigrants through a painful process of trial and error. Those newcomers whose resistance was most overt were perceived to be the least likely to survive, so there ensued a process of conscious or unconscious experimentation (called "seasoning" or "breaking" by the whites) in which Africans calculated the forms and degrees of resistance which were most possible.[6]

Under constant testing, patterns of slave resistance evolved rapidly, and many of the most effective means were found to fall at the low (or invisible) end of the spectrum. For example, for those who spoke English, in whatever dialect, verbal insolence became a consistent means of resistance. Cleverly handled, it allowed slaves a way to assert themselves and downgrade their masters without committing a crime. All parties were aware of the subversive potential of words (along with styles of dress and bearing), as the thrust of the traditional term "uppity" implies, and it may be that both the black use of this approach and the white perception of it increased as tensions grew. In 1737 the Assembly debated whether the patrols should have the right "to kill any resisting or saucy Slave,"[7] and in 1741 the Clerk of the Market proposed that "if any Slave should in Time of Market behave him or herself in any insolent abusive Manner, he or she should be sent to the Work-house, and there suffer corporal Punishment."[8]

At the same time traits of slowness, carelessness, and literal-

---

[6] An Englishman, after observing the relations of masters to slaves along the American coast, commented:

> as to their general Usage of them, 'tis monstrous, and shocking. To be sure, a *new Negro,* if he must be broke, either from Obstinacy, or, which I am more apt to suppose, from Greatness of Soul, will require more hard Discipline than a young Spaniel: You would really be surpiz'd at their Perseverance; let an hundred Men shew him how to hoe, or drive a Wheelbarrow, he'll still take the one by the Bottom, and the other by the Wheel; and they often die before they can be conquer'd.

"Itinerant Observations in America" (Anonymous), printed in the *London Magazine* (1745–46) and reprinted in Ga. Hist. Soc., *Collections,* IV (1878), 38.

[7] *SCCHJ, 1736–1739,* p. 221.

[8] Memorial of William MacKay, May 21, 1741, *SCCHJ, 1741–1742,* pp. 16–17. MacKay explained that his proposal arose

> from the disorderly Behaviour of several of the Butchers and their Attendants, which indeed was a Reproach to any Christian well governed Country, and which they had been then so long used to that they were become quite ungovernable, and abusive to the Town's People who went to buy, and to the Country People that came to Sell Provisions at Market.

mindedness were artfully cultivated, helping to disguise countless acts of willful subterfuge as inadvertent mistakes.[9] To the benefit of the slave and the frustration of the historian, such subversion was always difficult to assess, yet considerable thought has now been given to these subtle forms of opposition.[10] Three other patterns of resistance—poisoning, arson, and conspiracy—were less subtle and more damaging, and each tactic aroused white fears which sometimes far exceeded the actual threat. All three are recognized as having been methods of protest familiar in other slave colonies as well, and each is sufficiently apparent in the South Carolina sources to justify separate consideration.

[9] Consider the following passage by a Virginia tobacco planter:

There is nothing so absurd as the generality of negroes are. If in the beginning of cutting tob⁰, without watching they will cut all before them, and now when there is danger of losing tob⁰ by the frost should it happen, they will not cut pl[an]ts really ripe because they may be the thicker, just as if there was time to let it stand longer.

"Extracts from the Diary of Col. Landon Carter," *WMQ*, XIII (1905), 223.

[10] Historians have only recently begun to appreciate again the degree to which work slowdowns, the destruction of tools, and general malingering evolved into semiconscious tactics of agricultural sabotage. William W. Freehling, *Prelude to Civil War* (New York, 1965), p. 66, alludes to the stock image which grew up among South Carolina planters of "the seemingly innocent but cunning laborer who could misunderstand adroitly, loiter diligently, or destroy guilefully." "Culpable carelessness" was the vivid phrase coined by one nineteenth-century editor and cited in Herbert Aptheker's brief review of the subject: "Slave Resistance in the United States," in Huggins, Kilson, Fox, eds., *Key Issues in the Afro-American Experience*, I, 163–73. (Historians of American labor have made less progress in documenting and explaining the similar covert and pervasive tactics used by European immigrant workers to contain managerial drives for industrial efficiency in more recent times.)

Among the most interesting discussions of this entire topic is George M. Frederickson and Christopher Lasch, "Resistance to Slavery," *Civil War History*, XIII (1967), 315–29. However, while their article lends considerable refinement to the theoretical discussion of resistance, it relies like so many previous studies upon only a small number of original sources, drawn entirely from the nineteenth century. Indeed, it is regrettable that so central an article belabors the misleading viewpoint (p. 324; cf. p. 319) that for considering Negro dissatisfactions "adequate records of personal slave response simply do not exist." Eugene D. Genovese, who has made important conceptual contributions in this area, rightly points out in private correspondence (Feb. 6, 1973) that interpretations of slave work habits must go beyond questions of inadequate incentives and modes of resistance to relate pre-industrial work patterns among Afro-Americans to those already being analyzed by E. P. Thompson and others among Europeans.

II

AFRICAN AWARENESS of plants and their powers has already been mentioned, and it was plain to white colonists from an early date that certain blacks were particularly knowledgeable in this regard. In 1733 the *Gazette* published the details of a medicine for yaws, dropsy, and other distempers "for the Discovery whereof, a Negroe Man in Virginia was freed by the Government, and had a Pension of Thirty Pounds Sterling settled on him during his Life."[11] Some of the Negroes listed by the name "Doctor" in colonial inventories had no doubt earned their titles. One South Carolina slave received his freedom and £100 per year for life from the Assembly for revealing his antidote to poison; "Caesar's Cure" was printed in the *Gazette* and appeared occasionally in local almanacs for more than thirty years.[12]

In West Africa, the obeah-men and others with the herbal knowledge to combat poisoning could inflict poison as well, and use for this negative capability was not diminished by enslavement. In Jamaica, poisoning was a commonplace means of black resistance in the eighteenth century,[13] and incidents were familiar on the mainland as well. At least twenty slaves were executed for poisoning in Virginia between 1772 and 1810.[14] In South Carolina, the Rev. Richard Ludlam mentioned "secret poisonings" as early as the 1720s.[15] The administering of poison by a slave was made a felony (alongside arson) in the colony's sweeping Negro Act of 1740.[16] No doubt in times of general unrest many poisoning incidents involved only exaggerated fear and paranoia on the part of whites, but what made the circle so vicious was the fact that the art of poisoning was undeniably used by certain Africans as one of the most logical and lethal methods of resistance.

The year 1751 was striking in this regard. The Rev. William

11 *SCG*, March 31, 1733.

12 *SCG*, May 9, 1750; Mabel L. Webber, comp., "South Carolina Almanacs, to 1800," *SCHGM*, XV (1914), 78. A collection of these almanacs is in the Library Society of Charleston.

13 Patterson, *The Sociology of Slavery*, pp. 265–66.

14 Jordan, *White Over Black*, p. 393. Cf. Mullin, "Patterns of Slave Behavior in Eighteenth Century Virginia," p. 426.

15 Klingberg, *Appraisal*, p. 46.

16 *Statutes*, VII, 402.

Cotes of Dorchester expressed discouragement about the slaves in St.
George's Parish, a "horrid practice of poisoning their Masters, or those
set over them, having lately prevailed among them. For this practice,
5 or 6 in our Parish have been condemned to die, altho 40 or 50 more
were privy to it."[17] In the same year the assemblymen attempted to
concoct a legal antidote of their own. They passed an addition to the
existing Negro Act, noting that "the detestable crime of poisoning
hath of late been frequently committed by many slaves in this Province, and notwithstanding the execution of several criminals for that
offence, yet it has not been sufficient to deter others from being guilty
of the same."[18] The legislation declared that any Negroes convicted
of procuring, conveying, or administering poison, and any others
privy to such acts, would suffer death. A £4 reward was offered to
any Negro informing on others who had poison in their possession,
and a strict clause was included against false informers.

Three additional clauses in the measure of 1751 suggest the
seriousness with which white legislators viewed the poisoning threat.
They attempted belatedly to root out longstanding Negro knowledge
about, access to, and administration of medicinal drugs. It was enacted "That in case any slave shall teach or instruct another slave in
the knowledge of any poisonous root, plant, herb, or other poison
whatever, he or she, so offending, shall, upon conviction thereof,
suffer death as a felon." The student was to receive a lesser punishment. "And to prevent, as much as may be, all slaves from attaining
the knowledge of any mineral or vegetable poison," the act went on,
"it shall not be lawful for any physician, apothecary or druggist, at any
time hereafter, to employ any slave or slaves in the shops or places
where they keep their medicines or drugs." Finally, the act provided
that "no negroes or other slaves (commonly called doctors,) shall
hereafter be suffered or permitted to administer any medicine, or
pretended medicine, to any other slave; but at the instance or by the
direction of some white person," and any Negro disobeying this clause
was subject to "corporal punishment, not exceeding fifty stripes." No
other law in the settlement's history imposed such a severe whipping
upon a Negro.[19]

A letter written five years later by Alexander Garden, the famous
Charlestown physician, sheds further light on the subject of poison-

[17] Cotes to Philip Bearcroft, Dec. 2, 1751, quoted in Klingberg, *Appraisal*, p. 89.
[18] *Statutes*, VII, 422–23.
[19] *Ibid.*

ings. The outspoken Garden was forthright in criticizing his own profession, observing to his former teacher in Edinburgh that among
South Carolina's whites, "some have been actually poisoned by their
slaves and hundreds [have] died by the unskilfulness of the practition-
ers in mismanaging acute disorders." He claimed that when local
doctors confronted cases

proving both too obstinate and complicated for them, they immediately call
them poisonous cases and so they screen their own ignorance, for the
Friends never blame the doctors neglect or ignorance when they think that
the case is poison, as they readily think that lies out of the powers of medicine. And thus the word *Poison* . . . has been as good a screen to ignorance
here as ever that of *Malignancy* was in Britain.[20]

Nevertheless, actual instances of poisoning intrigued Garden,
and he put forward a scheme "To examine the nature of vegetable
poisons in general." He took the association with Africa most seriously
and requested from his colleague "assistance in giving me what information you could about the African Poisons, as I greatly and do
still suspect that the Negroes bring their knowledge of the poisonous
plants, which they use here, with them from their own country."
Perhaps most conclusive of all is the fact that Garden listed explicitly
as part of his plan "To investigate the nature of particular poisons
(chiefly those indigenous in this province and Africa)."[21]

But apparently neither strict legislation nor scientific observation could be effective in suppressing such resistance, for in 1761 the
Gazette reported that "The negroes have again begun the hellish practice of poisoning."[22] Eight years later several more instances were detected, and although the apparent "instigator of these horrid crimes,"
a mulatto former slave named Dick, made good his escape, two other
Negroes were publicly burned at the stake. According to the account
in a special issue of the *Gazette*, Dolly, belonging to Mr. James Sands,
and a slave man named Liverpool were both burned alive on the
workhouse green, "the former for poisoning an infant of Mr. Sands's,
which died some time since, and attempting to put her master out of
the world the same way; and the latter (a Negro Doctor) for furnish-
ing the means." The woman was reported to have "made a free con-

[20] The letter from which these quotations are taken was written to Charles
Alston, Feb. 18, 1756, and is in the possession of the American Philosophical Society.
It is reprinted in Waring, *History of Medicine*, pp. 225–26.
[21] *Ibid.*
[22] *SCG*, Jan. 17, 1761.

fession, acknowledged the justice of her punishment, and died a penitant," but the man denied his guilt until the end.[23]

In 1770 the colony of Georgia passed a law similar to South Carolina's, but the practice was not curtailed. The Rev. Muhlenberg, living in the region in 1774, entered in his journal for October 1: "Visit from Mr. J[acob] M[ack], a neighbor of the Rev. Mr. Rabenhorst, who told me with sorrow that some time ago a household negress had given poison to Pastor Rabenhorst and his wife."[24] The next week Muhlenberg recorded (October 10):

He also told me the circumstances of the poisoning of Mr. Rabenhorst and his wife. One evening about six weeks ago an old, sullen house negress had taken some arsenic, which she had been using to kill rats, and put it into the coffee, seeking to kill her master and mistress. As soon as Mr. Rabenhorst drank the first cup of it he became dizzy and sick and had to vomit. Mrs. R, supposing it to be caused by something else, also drank a cup, whereupon she immediately suffered the same violent effects. When the contents of the coffee-pot were examined, the poison was discovered in the grounds. They were in extreme peril of death, but by God's grace were saved by the use of powerful medicines. The negress is said to have betrayed herself by saying to the other negress [an informer?], "I thought my master and mistress would get enough, but it was not sufficient." The negress fell into the hands of the authorities, was condemned, and after several weeks burned alive.[25]

III

THE ACT OF ARSON, highly destructive and difficult to detect, provided another peculiarly suitable means of subversion.[26] Early in the cen-

---

[23] *SCG*, "*Extraordinary*" issue, Tuesday, Aug. 1, 1769.

[24] *Muhlenberg*, II, 575.

[25] *Ibid.*, p. 585. Incidents from the northern colonies in which Negroes were accused of poisoning whites had been reprinted in the *Gazette*. Two of these illustrate not only the colonial preoccupation with this threat, but also the difficulty found in diagnosing arsenic poisoning from other kinds of sickness. *SCG*, Sept. 20, 1735; April 15, 1738.

[26] Despite the consideration given to arson by Aptheker in *Slave Revolts*, esp. pp. 144–49, and by others, there are still white texts which pretend "childlike" innocence about this matter. Cf. James B. Sellers, *Slavery in Alabama* (University of Alabama, 1950), p. 225:

> A few cases of arson committed by slaves are on record. This was regarded as a very serious crime, and it often brought the death penalty. It is hard to understand why Negroes should resort to this type of misdemeanor. Perhaps the impulse to burn was an expression of their childlike minds, their desire to "get even" with some one who had offended them, usually their master, mistress, or overseer. Seldom did a slave burn anything which was claimed by another slave.

tury, with considerable forced labor being used to produce naval
stores, the governor urged the Assembly "to make it ffelony without
beneffitt of Clergy, willfully to Sett ffire to any uncovered Tarrkiln or
Pitch and Tarr in Barrells, as in like cases, ffiring Houses and Barnes."[27]
In later decades arsonists also fired stores of rice, and the Negro Act of
1740 was explicit in declaring death for "any slave, free negro, mulat-
toe, Indian or mustizoe, [who] shall wilfully and maliciously burn or
destroy any stack of rice, corn or other grain."[28]

Indeed, as rice production intensified, the number of barns
which burned between the months of October and January (when the
majority of slaves were being pressed to clean and barrel the annual
crop) increased suspiciously. A telling letter to the *Gazette* in October
1732 reads:

SIR,

I Have taken Notice for Several Years past, that there has not one Winter
elapsed, without one or more Barns being burnt, and two Winters since,
there was no less than five. Whether it is owing to Accident, Carelessness,
or Severity, I will not pretend to determine; but am afraid, chiefly to the
two latter. I desire therefore, as a Friend to the Planters, that you'll insert
the following Account from Pon Pon, which, I hope, will forewarn the
Planters of their Danger, and make them for the future, more careful and
human.

*About 3 Weeks since, Mr. James Gray work'd his Negroes late in his Barn at
Night, and the next Morning before Day, hurried them out again, and when
they came to it, found it burnt down to the Ground, and all that was in it.*[29]

Several years later, just after Christmas, "the Barn of Mr. John Fair-
child at Wassamsaw, with all his Crop was burnt down to the Ground,"
and in November 1742, "a Barn, belonging to Mr. Hume, at Goose-
Creek, was burnt in the Night, and near 70 Barrels of Rice consumed."[30]

Undoubtedly Negroes were occasionally made the scapegoats
for fires which occurred by chance. The Rev. Le Jau relates vividly
how a woman being burned alive on the charge of setting fire to her
master's house in 1709 "protested her innocence . . . to the last."[31]

[27] *SCCHJ*, 1706, p. 11.

[28] *Statutes*, VII, 402.

[29] *SCG*, Oct. 14, 1732. (Italics in original.)

[30] *SCG*, Jan. 5, 1738; Dec. 2, 1742. It is conceivable that Hume (who was
Speaker of the Assembly) owed this misfortune to a runaway cooper for whom he
had advertised five weeks before. *SCG*, Oct. 28, 1742.

[31] *Le Jau*, p. 55.

But as with accusations of poisoning, numerous Negroes charged with burning their masters' homes had actually resorted to such sabotage. Moreover, arson could occur in conjunction with other offenses, serving to cover evidence or divert attention. Runaways sometimes resorted to setting fires, and arson was occasionally linked to crimes of violence as well.[32] The following news item from South Carolina appeared in Ireland's *Belfast News Letter*, May 10, 1763:

Charlestown, March 16. A most shocking murder was committed a few weeks ago, near Orangeburg by a Negro fellow belonging to one John Meyer, who happened to come to Charlestown; the cruel wretch murdered Mrs. Meyer, her daughter, about 16 years of age, and her sucking infant; he then dressed himself in his Master's best cloaths and set fire to the house, which was burnt to the ground; three other children of Mr. Meyers made their escape and alarmed the neighbors, some of whom did not live above half a mile distant. The murderer was taken up next day and by a Jury of Magistrates and Freeholders condemned to be burnt alive at a stake which was accordingly executed. The unfortunate husband and father, we are told, is almost, if not entirely distracted by his misfortunes; it is said both he and his wife used the barbarous destroyer of their family and substance with remarkable tenderness and lenity.[33]

It was fires within the town limits which aroused the greatest concern among white colonists, for not only were numerous lives and buildings endangered, but the prospect of subsequent disorder and vandalism by the city's enslaved residents was obvious. A fire engine was purchased by public subscription in the 1730s.[34] But it proved of little use in 1740, when the Carolina colony, having experienced several epidemics and a series of slave conspiracies in rapid succession, added a severe fire to its "Continued Series of misfortunes."[35] On the afternoon of Tuesday, November 18, flames broke out near the center of Charlestown, and, whipped by a northwest wind, burned out of control for six hours, consuming some three hundred houses, destroy-

---

[32] In the same week that Mr. Hume's barn burned (see previous paragraph), a news item from another colony illustrated how a "careless fire" might have been used to cancel out search efforts for a runaway slave: the grain-filled barn of a minister in Sudbury, Massachusetts, was consumed by fire, "supposed thro the Carelessness of his Negro Servant with his Pipe, who it is feared was asleep and perished in the Flames, as he has not been heard of since." *SCG*, Dec. 2, 1742. Slaves escaping during the Stono Rebellion may have used arson to slow their pursuers (see Chapter XII below).

[33] Belfast Newspapers Typescript, pp. 21–22, in the SCL.

[34] *SCG*, Sept. 14, 1734.

[35] BPRO Trans., XX, 329.

ing crucial new fortifications, and causing property losses estimated at
£250,000 sterling.[36]

Even though 2 P.M. seemed an unlikely hour for slave arson,
there were strong suspicions about the origin of the holocaust. Not
long before, in the strained atmosphere following the Stono Uprising,
a slave had been accused of setting fire to the home of Mr. Snow and
had been burned to death for the crime.[37] Officials suspected the Spanish of instigating arson by Negroes as one form of resistance, for an
act passed the previous April charged the Spaniards in St. Augustine
with, "encouraging thither the desertion of our Slaves and . . . exciting them to rise here in Rebellion and to commit Massacres and
Assassinations and the burning of Houses in divers parts of this Province of which practices there have of late been many proof[s]."[38]

Word of the November fire reaching northern ports was accompanied by rumors of arson and insurrection. In January a Boston paper
had to print a revised account of the fire, saying the story "that the
Negroes rose upon the Whites at the same Time, and that therefore it
was supposed to be done by them, turns out to be a Mistake, it hap-
pening by some Accident."[39] The story finally reaching London was
that the flames were "said to have begun among some Shavings in a
Saddler's Shop."[40]

Whatever the actual cause of the fire, the white minority feared
Negro violence in the aftermath of the blaze. "It is inexpressible to
relate to you the dismal Scheme [scene?] . . . ," Robert Pringle wrote
to his brother in London, "the best part of this Town being laid in
Ashes." He blamed his "Incorrect Confus'd Scrawl" on the fact that he
had hardly slept in the three days since the fire. He cited as an explanation "the great Risque we Run from an Insurrection of our Negroes which we were very apprehensive off but all as yet Quiet by
the strict Guards & watch we are oblig'd to keep Constantly night &
Day."[41] In a letter the next week he mentioned that much property
had been stolen and concealed, apparently by freemen and slaves
alike.[42] But large-scale disorder was prevented, and Negro labor was

---

[36] See Kenneth Scott, "Sufferers of the Charleston Fire of 1740," *SCHGM*,
LXIV (1963), p. 206.

[37] McCrady, *Royal Government*, p. 233.

[38] Parish Trans., S.C., Box I, folder 5, p. 23.

[39] *Boston Weekly News-Letter*, Jan. 22, 1741.

[40] *London Magazine* (1741), p. 48.

[41] Robert Pringle to Capt. Andrew Pringle, Nov. 22, 1740, Pringle Letterbook.

[42] Robert Pringle to John Erving, Nov. 29, 1740, Pringle Letterbook.

soon at work "pulling down the Ruins of Charles Town" and clearing away rubble for the arduous task of rebuilding.[43]

Regardless of its true origins, the November fire could only have confirmed to slaves the effectiveness of arson. Moreover, there was word the following spring of Negro incendiaries at work in the northern colonies, supposedly with Spanish connections. On July 30, 1741, the *Gazette* contained a front-page story about a rash of barn-burnings in Hackensack, New Jersey. The next page was given over to details of an arson plot in New York City, for which nine Negroes had already been burned at the stake. The conspiracy, stated the report from New York,

was calculated, not only to ruin and destroy this City, but the whole Province, and it appears that to effect this their Design was first to burn the Fort, and if Opportunity favoured to seize and carry away the Arms in store there, then to burn the whole Town, and kill and murder all the Male Inhabitants thereof (the Females they intended to reserve for their own Use) and this to be effected by seizing their Master's Arms and a general Rising, it appears also as we are informed, that these Designs were not only carried on in this City, but had also spread into the country. . . . And so far had they gone that the particular Places to be burnt were laid out, their Captains and other Officers appointed, and their places of general Rendezvous fixed, and the Number of Negroes concern'd is almost incredible, and their barbarous Designs still more so. . . .[44]

It may not be coincidence that within five days after these lurid reports appeared in Charlestown several slaves attempted to kindle another fire in the city. After dark a mulatto slave woman named Kate and a man named Boatswain entered Mrs. Snowden's house in Unity Alley, climbed to the roof, and placed a small bundle of straw on the shingles so that it rested under the gables of the adjoining house, belonging to Moses Mitchell and fronting on Union Street. They lit the tinder with a brand's end, and the fire they started might have been capable "of burning down the remaining Part of the Town," had not Mrs. Mitchell, walking in her yard, spotted the blaze so promptly that it could be dowsed with several pails of drinking water.[45]

[43] *SCCHJ*, *1739–1741*, pp. 458, 486.

[44] *SCG*, July 30, 1741. Other reports appeared in issues for April 9, July 23, and Oct. 10 of that year.

[45] *SCG*, Aug. 15, 1741.

An old Negro woman who heard one of the arsonists stumble descending the stairs testified against Kate, and within forty-eight hours she had been tried, convicted, and sentenced to die. At the eleventh hour, upon promise of pardon, Kate named Boatswain as a co-conspirator, and he in turn was sentenced to burn alive. According to the *Gazette*'s account, "On his Tryal after much Preverication and accusing many Negroes, who upon a strict Examination were found to be innocent, he confessed that none but he and *Kate* were concerned." Since Boatswain "looked upon every white Man he should meet as his declared Enemy," his prosecutors concluded that the incident stemmed from "his own sottish wicked Heart," and that there was probably no larger plot.[46] The same people may have been somewhat less sanguine several months later, when two slaves were found guilty of attempting to set fire to the city's powder magazine.[47]

Arson, real and suspected, remained a recurring feature in eighteenth-century South Carolina. In 1754, for example, a slave named Sacharisa was sentenced to burn at the stake for setting fire to her owner's house in Charlestown.[48] Two years later a suspicious fire started on a town wharf in the middle of the night.[49] In 1797 two slaves were deported and several others were hanged for conspiring to burn down the city.[50] In some ways the protracted Charleston Fire Scare of 1825 and 1826, which came four years after the Denmark Vesey Plot, was reminiscent of the concern for arson which followed in the wake of the Stono Uprising of 1739.[51]

[46] *SCG*, Aug. 15, 1741. Cf. *SCCHJ, 1741–1742*, pp. 344, 378, 394.

[47] Aptheker, *Slave Revolts*, p. 190. Aptheker cites SCCHJ, Jan. 13, 1741; he also quotes the following sentence from the *Boston Weekly News-Letter*, September 3, 1741: "By private letters from Charlestown in South-Carolina we are inform'd that the Town is in much Confusion, not only on account of the insolence of the Spaniards, but also from Apprehensions of Domestick Treachery, the Town having been several times alarm'd by Fire which too visibly appears to be wilfully occasion'd by their Blacks."

[48] MR "KK," p. 48.

[49] *SCG*, June 17, 1756:

Last Sunday Morning between 1 and 2 O'Clock, a Fire (which is supposed may have been maliciously kindled by some hellish Incendiary) broke out amongst a Parcel of Pitch that lay upon Colonel *Beale's* Wharf, and burnt with such Violence, that, although the Town Engins were there in a short Time, and played with great Judgement . . . , it consumed all the Stores on the said Wharf, with what was in them, before its Progress could be stopped.

[50] *City Gazette and Daily Advertiser* (Charleston), Nov. 22, 1797.

[51] Freehling, *Prelude to Civil War*, p. 61.

IV

WHILE POISONING and arson rarely involved more than one or two compatriots, organized forms of resistance, which involved greater numbers (and therefore higher risks), were not unknown in the royal colony. In fact uprisings appear to have been attempted or planned repeatedly by slaves. For obvious reasons, published sources are irregular on these matters—the *South Carolina Gazette* refrained from mentioning the Stono incident, which occurred within twenty miles of Charlestown—but a number of conspiracies were recorded. In these instances it is sometimes difficult to categorize the objectives of the insurgents, since often a will to overpower the Europeans and a desire to escape from the colony were intertwined in the same plot.[52] The province's first major conspiracy, uncovered in 1720, provides a case in point. "I am now to acquaint you," wrote a Carolina correspondent to the colony's London agent in June, "that very lately we have had a very wicked and barbarous plott of the designe of the negroes rising with a designe to destroy all the white people in the country and then to take the town in full body." He continued that through God's will "it was discovered and many of them taken prisoners and some burnt some hang'd and some banish'd." At least some participants in the scheme "thought to gett to Augustine" if they could convince a member of the Creek tribe to guide them, "but the Savanna garrison tooke the negroes up half starved and the Creeke Indians would not join them or be their pylott." A party of whites and Indians had been dispatched to "Savanna Towne," where fourteen captives were being held, and it was planned that these rebels would "be executed as soon as they came down."[53]

This incident, or perhaps another similar one, was mentioned in an official representation sent to the king late in 1721. His majesty was

[52] For a useful study which seeks to categorize numerous revolts, see Marion D. DeB. Kilson, "Towards Freedom: An Analysis of Slave Revolts in the United States," *Phylon*, XXV (1964), 175–87. The tendency of white sources to either minimize or exaggerate Negro conspiracies is discussed in Aptheker, *Slave Revolts*, Chapter VII.

[53] Letter to Mr. Boone, June 24, 1720, BPRO Trans., VIII, 24–27. The same letter appears in British Public Record Office, *Calendar of State Papers Colonial Series, American and West Indies, 1720–1721* (London, 1916), p. 57. One portion reads: "I think it proper for you to tell Mr. Percivall at home that his slaves was the principal rogues and 'tis my opinion his only way will be to sell them out singly or else I am doubtful his interest in slaves will come to little for want of strict management. Work does not agree with them."

informed that the "black slaves . . . have lately attempted and were very near succeeding in a new revolution, which would probably have been attended by the utter extirpation of all your Majesty's subjects in this province."[54] Not surprisingly, the Negro Act of the following year spelled out more fully than ever the punishments to be inflicted on any slaves attempting to rebel or conspiring together or gathering up "arms, powder, bullets, or offensive weapons in order to carry on such mutiny or insurrection."[55] A minister's letter from Goose Creek Parish in 1724 ascribed "secret poisonings and bloody insurrection" to certain Christian slaves.[56]

Another scantily documented incident occurred in mid-August 1730. A letter written five days after the episode and published in Boston conveyed the initial shock and fatalism felt by many whites. It mentioned the prominent causes of failure in such attempts—divided leadership, insufficient recruitment, and premature discovery.

I shall give an Account [the correspondent wrote from Charlestown] of a bloody Tragedy which was to have been executed here last Saturday night (the 15th Inst.) by the Negroes, who had conspired to Rise and destroy us, and had almost bro't it to pass: but it pleased God to appear for us, and confound their Councils. For some of them propos'd that the Negroes of every Plantation should destroy their own Masters; but others were for Rising in a Body, and giving the blow at once on surprise; and thus they differ'd. They soon made a great Body at the back of the Town, and had a great Dance, and expected the Country Negroes to come & join them; and had not an overruling Providence discovered their Intrigues, we had been all in Blood. . . . The Chief of them, with some others, is apprehended and in Irons, in order to a Tryal, and we are in Hopes to find out the whole Affair.[57]

What few details came to light may have been embroidered with time, for it seems likely that this foiled rebellion provided the basis for the tale told during the Revolution concerning a narrowly averted

---

[54] Representation of the Lords Commissioners for Trade and Plantations, to the King, Sept. 8, 1721, in *DRNY*, V, 610.

[55] *Statutes*, VII, 375. Since the financial loss from executing slaves was being borne locally at this time, which may have prompted those deciding such cases to restrict capital punishment, the act ordered that whenever the convicting judges sentenced some slaves to "suffer death as exemplary, and the rest to be returned to the owners," those owners were to share the cost of the executed slaves. *Ibid.*

[56] Richard Ludlam to David Humphreys, July 2, 1724, cited in Klingberg, *Appraisal*, p. 46.

[57] *Boston Weekly News-Letter*, Oct. 22, 1730. The letter from Charlestown is dated Aug. 20, 1730.

"Sicilian Vespers." Although the Hessian officer, named Hinrichs, who recorded the story mistakenly placed it in 1736, the scheme he described, like the one narrated in the Boston letter, unfolded in August and involved conflicting plans for plantation murders and an attack on Charlestown. Moreover, it took the form of a large gathering several miles outside the city two days before the intended coup and ended only "when fate was merciful and betrayed the horrible plot." Since all these details conform with the letter sent to Boston, there seems little doubt that Hinrichs was referring to the incident of 1730. There is probably substance to his concluding remark that "Through torture and punishment their leaders were found out . . . and . . . tortured to death, while many others were subjected to severe bodily punishment."[58]

Despite harsh reprisals, however, secret gatherings of slaves, sometimes exceeding one hundred people, were again reported within several years. In February 1733 the Assembly urged the slave patrols to special watchfulness and ordered a dozen slaves brought in for questioning, but there is no sign that any offence was uncovered.[59] Late in 1736 a white citizen appears to have sought a reward for uncovering a Negro plot. Early in the following year the provost marshal took up three Negroes "suspected to be concerned in some Conspiracy against the Peace of this Government," and although the Assembly cleared and released the most prominent suspect, it did not deny the existence of a plot.[60]

By September 1738 the government had completed "An Act for the further Security and better Defence of this Province" and given instructions that the two paragraphs relating to slaves were to be reprinted in the *Gazette*.[61] The paper complied several days later by publishing the section which ordered that within a month every slave-owner in the colony was to turn in to the militia captain of his local precinct "a true and faithful List, in Writing, of all the Slaves of such Persons, or which are under their Care or Management, from the Age

---

[58] "The Diary of Captain Johann Hinrichs," in Uhlendorf, *The Siege of Charleston*, p. 323. Hinrichs' journal is generally careful, and it is far more probable that he received the wrong year and certain traditional trimmings from his informant than that he recorded a totally fictitious event, as suggested by Jordan (*White Over Black*, p. 153) and Aptheker (*Slave Revolts*, p. 184). Cf. Chapter VIII, note 62, above.

[59] SCCHJ, Feb. 26, 1733, cited in Aptheker, *Slave Revolts*, p. 183.

[60] *SCCHJ, 1736–1739*, pp. 23, 28, 29, 245, 264.

[61] *Ibid.*, p. 586.

of 16 Years to the Age of Sixty Years." Each list was required to specify "the Names, Ages and Country of all such Slaves respectively, according to the best of the Knowledge and Belief of the Persons returning the same."[62]

The statute imposed a heavy fine of £ 100 upon any master who neglected or refused to comply, so that the required local lists (if collected and sent to the governor annually as authorized) must have constituted a thorough census of the colony's adult slaves. The unlikely reappearance of even a portion of these lists would be a remarkable boon to historians, in light of the unique request for the original country of all slaves. This detail appears to bear witness to the fact that masters were generally interested and informed as to the origins of the Negroes they owned. It may also reflect the belief, commonly accepted in the Carolinas as elsewhere, that new slaves from Africa posed the greatest threat to the security of the white settlers. John Brickell explained at this time, "The Negroes that most commonly rebel, are those brought from Guinea, and who have been inured to War and Hardship all their lives; few born here, or in the other Provinces have been guilty of these vile Practices." When country-born slaves did contemplate rebellion, Brickell claimed, it was because they were urged to it by newcomers "whose Designs they have sometimes discovered to the Christians" in order to be "rewarded with their Freedom for their good Services."[63]

V

THE THOUGHT that newcomers from Africa were the slaves most likely to rebel does not appear to have been idle speculation, for the late 1730s, a time of conspicuous unrest, was also a time of massive importation. In fact, at no earlier or later date did recently arrived Africans

[62] *SCG,* Sept. 21, 1738. The statute continued:

And to the End that the Number of able Slaves may be constantly known, the said Lists shall be renewed . . . once in every Year, on the first Muster Day after the 25th of March. And such Lists shall be return'd by the respective Captains to the Governor, Lieutenant Governor or President, within one Month after the same shall be given to the said Captains respectively.

[63] Brickell, *Natural History,* p. 274. (Compare this with nineteenth-century industrial lore concerning recent immigrants as the frequent originators of labor unrest.)

(whom we might arbitrarily define as all those slave immigrants who had been in the colony less than a decade) comprise such a large proportion of South Carolina's Negro population. By 1740 the black inhabitants of the colony numbered roughly 39,000. During the preceding decade more than 20,000 slaves had been imported from Africa. Since there is little evidence that mortality was disproportionately high among newcomers, this means that by the end of the 1730s fully half of the colony's Negroes had lived in the New World less than ten years. This proportion had been growing steadily. In 1720 fewer than 5 per cent of black adults had been there less than a decade (and many of these had spent time in the West Indies); by 1730 roughly 40 per cent were such recent arrivals. Heavy importation and low natural increase sent the figure over 50 per cent by 1740, but it dropped sharply during the nearly total embargo of the next decade, and after that point the established black population was large enough so that the percentage of newcomers never rose so high again.

Each of the lowland parishes must have reflected this shift in the same way. In St. Paul's, for example, where the Stono Uprising originated, there were only 1,634 slaves in 1720, the large majority of whom had been born in the province or brought there long before. By contrast, in 1742 the parish's new Anglican minister listed 3,829 "heathens and infidels" in his cure, well over 3,000 of whom must have been slaves. Of these, perhaps as many as 1,500 had been purchased in Charlestown since 1730.[64] A predominant number of the Africans reaching the colony between 1735 and 1739 have been shown to have come from Angola, so it is likely that at the time of the Stono Uprising there were close to 1,000 residents of St. Paul's Parish who had lived in the Congo–Angola region of Africa less than ten years before. While this figure is only an estimate, it lends support to the assertion in one contemporary source that most of the conspirators in the 1739 incident were Angolans.[65] The suggestion seems not only plausible, but even probable.

European settlers contemplating the prospects of rebellion, however, seem to have been more concerned with contacts the slaves

---

[64] William Orr, Sept. 30, 1742, cited in Klingberg, *Appraisal,* p. 81. Figures in this paragraph appear in the essay cited in Chapter V, note 1, above.

[65] "Account of the Negroe Insurrection," p. 233. The hypothesis that recently imported blacks were frequently troublesome due to group resistance based on a common African background was raised by Eugene D. Genovese in "Slave Revolts in the New World: A Comparative Analysis," a paper presented to the Southern Hist. Assoc., 1968. On arrivals from Angola, see Appendix C.

might establish in the future than with experience that came from their past. White colonists were already beginning to subscribe to the belief that most Negro unrest was necessarily traceable to outside agitators. Like most shibboleths of the slave culture, this idea contained a kernel of truth, and it is one of the difficult tasks in considering the records of the 1730s and 1740s to separate the unreasonable fears of white Carolinians from their very justifiable concerns.

Numerous anxieties were intertwined. It was all too clear, for example, that internal and external threats to white security were likely to coincide and reinforce each other, if for no other reason than that the militia with its dual responsibilities for defense and control was divided and thereby weakened in times of trouble. Even if not linked beforehand, hostile elements inside and outside the colony could be expected to join forces during any alarm, so Europeans were as anxious about foreign infiltration as domestic conspiracy. For this reason Indians often appeared to be the slaves' likeliest allies. For example, suspicion of a Negro plot had scarcely died in 1733, when an Indian slave was brought before the Assembly. He testified "that an Indian Woman had told him that all the Indians on the Continent design'd to rise and make War, against the English."[66] Had such word contained any substance it might have triggered slave impulses to rise against the English as well, but this particular rumor apparently lacked foundation, and the informant was dismissed.

The following spring the Assembly sent a memorial to the king, outlining the threats posed by the Indians, Spanish, and French and asking assistance in defense. This document from 1734 stressed that white colonists faced "many intestine Dangers from the great Number of Negroes" and went on to observe, "Insurrections against us have been often attempted, and would at any time prove very fatal if the French shoud instigate them by artfully giving them [the Negroes] an Expectation of Freedom."[67] The next ten years were filled with enough dangers—real and imagined—from these various quarters to keep the English in a constant state of agitation. In 1748 James Glen, thinking back to this period, summarized the sea of anxieties which had beset white Carolinians:

Sometime ago the People of this Province were Annually alarmed with accounts of intended Invasions, & even in time of profound Peace they were

[66] SCUHJ, May 30, 1733, Parish Trans., S.C., Box I, folder 4, p. 32a.
[67] April 9, 1734, BPRO Trans., XVI, 398–99.

made believe that the Spaniards had prepared Embarkations for that purpose at St. Augustine & the Havanna, or that the French were marching by Land from Louisiana with more Men than ever were in that Country to drive us into the Sea. Sometimes the Negroes were to rise & cut their Masters Throats at other times the Indians were confederating to destroy us.[68]

VI

OF THE VARIOUS SOURCES of outside agitation none seemed so continually threatening after 1720 as St. Augustine, for the abduction and provocation of slaves by the Spanish were issues of constant concern. While London and Madrid were reaching a peace settlement in 1713, Charlestown and St. Augustine had renewed their agreement concerning the mutual return of runaways, but Spanish depredations continued long after the conclusion of the Yamasee War. During the 1720s Spanish ships, "stiling themselves Guarda-Costas on Pretence of searching," plundered or captured English vessels bound for southern ports.[69] Often Africans were aboard these boats, as in the case of the sloop *Ann*, seized in 1721 coming from Barbados to South Carolina with a cargo of sugar, rum, and Negroes.[70] The disappearance to the southward of slaves owned in South Carolina continued also. In December 1722 a committee of both Houses concerned with the return of slaves from St. Augustine urged higher rewards for taking up runaways. To guard against infiltrators who might encourage such defections, the committee also suggested that "a Law be passed to Oblige all Persons possessing Spanish Indians and Negroes to transport them off the Country."[71] A mission sent to Florida in 1726 to confirm the agreement about returning fugitives seems to have accomplished little, for the Assembly soon received a petition from Thomas Elliott and several other planters near Stono seeking government action since they had "had fourteen Slaves Runaway to St. Augustine."[72]

In June 1728 Acting Gov. Arthur Middleton sent a formal complaint to authorities in London that not only were the Spanish

[68] Feb. 3, 1748, BPRO Trans., XXIII, 71.

[69] SCCHJ, July 1, 1741, p. 82, SCDAH.

[70] BPRO Trans., X, 38.

[71] SCUHJ, Dec. 12, 1722, mfm BMP/D 487, SCDAH. For other references to slaves escaping to St. Augustine at this time, see the same source, June 22, 23, and Dec. 6, 14, 1722.

[72] SCCHJ, Feb. 10, 1728, Parish Trans., S.C., Box I, folder 4, p. 20a.

"receivieing and harbouring all our Runaway Negroes," but also, "They have found out a New way of sending our own slaves against us, to Rob and Plunder us;—They are continually fitting out Partys of Indians from St. Augustine to Murder our White People, Rob our Plantations and carry off our slaves," Middleton stated, "soe that We are not only at a vast expence in Guarding our Southern Frontiers, but the Inhabitants are continually Allarmed, and have noe leizure to looke after theire Crops." The irate leader added that "The Indians they send against us are sent out in small Partys . . . and sometimes joined wth Negroes, and all the Mischeife they doe, is on a sudden and by surprize."[73]

These petty incursions soon subsided. Nevertheless, rumors reached South Carolina in 1737 from the West Indies of a full-scale Spanish invasion intended, in the words of Lt. Gov. Thomas Broughton, to "unsettle the colony of Georgia, and to excite an Insurrection of the Negroes of this Province." He reported to the Lords of Trade that the militia had been alerted, "and as our Negroes are very numerous An Act of the General Assembly is passed, to establish Patrols throughout the Country to keep the Negroes in order."[74]

The threatened assault never materialized, but in the meantime

---

[73] June 13, 1728, BPRO Trans., XIII, 61–67. Middleton reported that four Negroes carried off from an estate on the Combahee River near Port Royal in 1726 were later seen in St. Augustine and that the following summer two white captives were present when the Spanish governor sent out four dozen Yamasees, promising thirty pieces of eight for every English scalp and one hundred pieces "for every live Negro they should bring." The party murdered several border scouts and penetrated to a plantation within ten miles of Ponpon, where they took the scalps of two more whites named Micheau and Wood. A band of fifteen planters pursued them and recovered the ten slaves they were carrying away, but more successful raids followed. Middleton wrote that in September 1727 two pettiaugers "Manned with Six of our Runaway Slaves and the rest Indians" took eight white captives from French's Island. "The Indians would have murthered them all for the sake of their Scalps, but this time the Negroes would not agree to it." This was probably the same raid described to Carolina authorities by John Pearson, an English mariner. (Oct. 20, 1727, BPRO Trans., XIX, 127–28.) He reported that while he was in St. Augustine that month, "Two Canoes, one with Indians, and the other with Negroes returned from Hilton head," carrying eight English prisoners, one Negro man and a mulatto boy. He observed that there were "about Ten Negroes and fourteen Indians Commanded by those of their own Colour, without any Spaniards in Company with them." While Pearson was testifying in late October, a schooner manned by Spaniards and South Carolina runaways was preparing for a further raid. The vessel entered the North Edisto River, where its crew plundered the David Ferguson plantation and carried away seven Negroes. "It seems," concluded Middleton, "the Governor of Augustine Makes Merchandize of all our slaves, and ships them off to Havanah for his own Profit, as we are told by the Spaniards themselves at St. Augustine."

[74] Feb. 6, 1737, BPRO Trans., XVIII, 170.

a new element was added to the situation. Late in 1733 the Spanish king issued a royal *cédula* granting liberty to Negro fugitives reaching St. Augustine from the English colonies.[75] The edict was not immediately put into effect, and incoming slaves continued to be sold,[76] but in March 1738 a group of these former runaways appealed successfully to the new governor for their freedom and obtained it. Seignior Don Manuel de Montiano established them on land two and a half miles north of St. Augustine at a site called the Pueblo de Gracia Real de Santa Terese de Mose, which soon became known as "Moosa." With the approval of the Council of the Indies, the governor undertook to provision this settlement of several dozen families until its first harvest and arranged for a Catholic priest to offer them instruction.[77] He may also have urged other slaves to join them, for the captain of an English coasting schooner returning to Beaufort the following month testified that "he heard a Proclamation made at St Augustine, that all Negroes, who did, or should hereafter, run away from the English, should be made free." As a result, according to the captain, "several Negroes who ran away thither, and were sold there, were thereupon made free, and the Purchasers lost their Money."[78]

In November 1738 nineteen slaves belonging to Capt. Caleb Davis "and 50 other Slaves belonging to other Persons inhabiting about Port Royal ran away to the Castle of St. Augustine."[79] Those who made it joined the Negro settlement at Moosa. It was apparently at this time that the Catholic king's edict of 1733 was published (in the words of a South Carolina report)

by Beat of Drum round the Town of St. Augustine (where many Negroes belonging to English Vessels that carried thither Supplies of Provisions &c. had the Opportunity of hearing it) promising Liberty and Protection to all Slaves that should desert thither from any of the English Colonies but more especially from this. And lest that should not prove sufficient of itself, secret Measures were taken to make it known to our Slaves in general. In Consequence of which Numbers of Slaves did from Time to Time by Land and

[75] Wilber H. Siebert, "Slavery and White Servitude in East Florida, 1726–1776," *Fla. Hist. Soc. Quarterly*, X (1931), 3–4.

[76] SCCHJ, July 1, 1741, p. 83, SCDAH.

[77] Siebert, "Slavery and White Servitude in East Florida, 1726–1776," pp. 3–4. See also I. A. Wright, "Dispatches of Spanish Officials Bearing on the Free Negro Settlement of Gracia Real de Santa Teresa de Mose, Florida," *JNH*, IX (1924), 144–95.

[78] April 21, 1738, BPRO Trans., XIX, 76.

[79] *SCCHJ, 1736–1739*, Jan. 19, 1739, p. 596.

Water desert to St. Augustine; and the better to facilitate their Escape carried off their Master's Horses, Boats &c., some of them first committing Murder; and were accordingly received and declared free.[80]

When Capt. Davis went to St. Augustine to recover his slaves he was pointedly rebuffed, a sign for Carolina's legislature that this difficulty might grow worse in the coming year.[81] Any premonitions which colonial officials might have felt were to prove justifiable, for the year 1739 was a tumultuous and decisive one in the evolution of South Carolina. Only the merest twist of circumstances prevented it from being remembered as a fateful turning point in the social history of the early South.

[80] *SCCHJ, 1741–1742*, July 1, 1741, p. 83.

[81] *SCCHJ, 1736–1739*, Jan. 19, 1739, p. 596. Davis, a sugar trader familiar with the coast, reported to a Georgian (Dec. 15, 1738) that he had seen his slaves in St. Augustine and they had laughed at him. "The Journal of William Stephens," *CRSG*, IV, 247–48.

❧ XII ❧

The Stono Rebellion
and Its Consequences

I

IN September 1739 South Carolina was shaken by an incident which became known as the Stono Uprising. A group of slaves struck a violent but abortive blow for liberation which resulted in the deaths of more than sixty people. Fewer than twenty-five white lives were taken, and property damage was localized, but the episode represented a new dimension in overt resistance. Free colonists, whose anxieties about controlling slaves had been growing for some time, saw their fears of open violence realized, and this in turn generated new fears.

According to a report written several years later, the events at Stono "awakened the Attention of the most Unthinking" among the white minority; "Every one that had any Relation, any Tie of Nature; every one that had a Life to lose were in the most sensible Manner shocked at such Danger daily hanging over their Heads." The episode, if hardly major in its own right, seemed to symbolize the critical impasse in which Carolina's English colonists now found themselves. "With Regret we bewailed our peculiar Case," the same report continued, "that we could not enjoy the Benefits of Peace like the rest of Mankind and that our own Industry should be the Means of taking from us all the Sweets of Life and of rendering us Liable to the Loss of our Lives and Fortunes."[1]

The Stono Uprising can also be seen as a turning point in the history of South Carolina's black population. As the previous chapter made clear, this episode was preceded by a series of projected insur-

[1] *SCCHJ*, 1741–1742, July 1, 1741, p. 84.

rections, any one of which could have assumed significant proportions. Taken together, all these incidents represent a brief but serious groundswell of resistance to slavery, which had diverse and lasting repercussions. The slave system in the British mainland colonies withstood this tremor, and never again faced a period of such serious unrest. For Negroes in South Carolina the era represented the first time in which steady resistance to the system showed a prospect of becoming something more than random hostility. But the odds against successful assertion were overwhelming; it was slightly too late, or far too soon, for realistic thoughts of freedom among black Americans.

II

THE YEAR 1739 did not begin auspiciously for the settlement. The smallpox epidemic which had plagued the town in the previous autumn was still lingering on when the council and commons convened in Charlestown in January. Therefore, Lt. Gov. William Bull, in his opening remarks to the initial session, recommended that the legislature consider "only what is absolutely necessary to be dispatched for the Service of the Province."[2] The primary issue confronting them, Bull suggested, was the desertion of their slaves, who represented such a huge proportion of the investments of white colonists. The Assembly agreed that the matter was urgent,[3] and a committee was immediately established to consider what measures should be taken in response to "the Encouragement lately given by the Spaniards for the Desertion of Negroes from this Government to the Garrison of St. Augustine."[4]

Even as the legislators deliberated, the indications of unrest multiplied. In Georgia William Stephens, the secretary for the trustees

[2] *SCCHJ, 1736–1739*, Jan. 17, 1739, p. 590. Bull continued:

The Desertion of our Slaves is a Matter of so much Importance to this Province that I doubt not but you will readily concur in Opinion with me that the most effectual Means ought to be used to discourage and prevent it for the Future, and to render as secure as possible so valuable a Part of the Estates and Properties of his Majesty's Subjects.

[3] *SCG*, Jan. 25, 1739. Charles Pinckney, the Speaker of the Assembly, was reported as saying: "We consider the Desertion of our Slaves as a Matter of very ill Consequence to the Estates and Properties of the People of this Province; and if some speedy and effectual Care is not taken to prevent it before it becomes more general, it may in time prove of the utmost Disadvantage."

[4] *SCCHJ, 1736–1739*, Jan. 19, 1739, pp. 595–96.

of that colony, recorded on February 8, 1739, "what we heard told us by several newly come from Carolina, was not to be disregarded, viz. that a Conspiracy was formed by the Negroes in Carolina, to rise and forcibly make their Way out of the Province" in an effort to reach the protection of the Spanish. It had been learned, Stephens wrote in his journal, that this plot was first discovered in Winyaw in the northern part of the province, "from whence, as they were to bend their Course South, it argued, that the other Parts of the Province must be privy to it, and that the Rising was to be universal; whereupon the whole Province were all upon their Guard."[5] If there were rumblings in the northernmost counties, Granville County on the southern edge of the province probably faced a greater prospect of disorder. Stephens' journal for February 20 reports word of a conspiracy among the slaves on the Montaigut and de Beaufain plantations bordering on the Savannah River just below the town of Purrysburg.[6] Two days later the Upper House in Charlestown passed on to the Assembly a petition and several affidavits from "Inhabitants of Granville County relating to the Desertion of their Slaves to the Castle of St. Augustine."[7]

That same week the commons expressed its distress over information that several runaways heading for St. Augustine had been taken up but then suffered to go at large without questioning. An inquiry was ordered, but it was not until early April that the Assembly heard concrete recommendations upon the problem of desertions. The first suggestion was for a petition to the English king requesting relief and assistance in this matter. Secondly, since many felt that the dozens of slaves escaping in November had eluded authorities because of a lack of scout boats, it was voted to employ two boats of eight men each in patrolling the southern coastal passages for the next nine months. Finally, to cut off Negroes escaping by land, large bounties were recommended for slaves taken up in the all-white colony of Georgia. Men, women, and children under twelve were to bring £40, £25, and £10, respectively, if brought back from beyond the Savannah River, and each adult scalp "with the two Ears" would command £20.[8]

In the midst of these deliberations, four slaves, apparently good riders who knew the terrain through hunting stray cattle, stole some

[5] "The Journal of William Stephens," p. 275.
[6] *Ibid.*, pp. 283–84.
[7] *SCCHJ, 1736–1739*, pp. 631–32.
[8] *Ibid.*, pp. 628, 680, 681; cf. p. 707.

horses and headed for Florida, accompanied by an Irish Catholic servant. Since they killed one white and wounded another in making their escape, a large posse was organized which pursued them unsuccessfully. Indian allies succeeded in killing one of the runaways, but the rest reached St. Augustine, where they were warmly received.[9] Spurred by such an incident, the Assembly completed work April 11 on legislation undertaken the previous month to prevent slave insurrections. The next day a public display was made of the punishment of two captured runaways, convicted of attempting to leave the province in the company of several other Negroes. One man was whipped and the other, after a contrite speech before the assembled slaves, "was executed at the usual Place, and afterwards hung in Chains at Hangman's Point opposite to this Town, in sight of all Negroes passing and repassing by Water."[10]

The reactions of colonial officials mirrored the desperate feelings spreading among the white population. On May 18 the Rev. Lewis Jones observed in a letter that the desertion of more than a score of slaves from his parish of St. Helena the previous fall, in response to the Spanish proclamation, seemed to "Considerably Encrease the Prejudice of Planters agst the Negroes, and Occasion a Strict hand, to be kept over them by their Several Owners, those that Deserted having been Much Indulg'd."[11] But concern continued among English colonists as to whether even the harshest reprisals could protect their investments and preserve their safety.

A letter the same month from Lt. Gov. Bull to the Duke of Newcastle, summarizing the situation, reflected the anxiety of the white populace:

[9] "Account of the Negroe Insurrection," pp. 232–33. According to the account of this March escape:

> four or five who were Cattel-Hunters, and knew the Woods, some of whom belonged to Captain Macpherson, ran away with His Horses, wounded his Son and killed another Man. . . . They reached Augustine, one only being killed and another wounded by the Indians in their flight. They were received there with great honours, one of them had a Commission given to him, and a Coat faced with Velvet.

See also *SCCHJ, 1739–1741*, pp. 229–30; *SCCHJ, 1742–1744*, Feb. 23, 1743, p. 235.
[10] *SCG*, April 12, 1739. For the full description, see Chapter X, note 54, above.
[11] Quoted in Klingberg, *Appraisal*, p. 68. Klingberg mistakes this incident for the Stono Rebellion later in the year. He also appears to have mistaken the date of the letter, which was May 18. See S.P.G. Transcripts in the Library of Congress, series B, vol. 7, part 1, p. 233.

My Lord,

I beg leave to lay before Your Grace an Affair, which may greatly distress if not entirely ruin this His Majesty's Province of South Carolina.

His Catholick Majesty's Edict having been published at S^t. Augustine declaring Freedom to all Negroes, and other slaves, that shall Desert from the English Colonies, Has occasioned several Parties to desert from this Province both by Land and Water, which notwithstanding They were pursued by the People of Carolina as well as the Indians, & People in Georgia, by General Oglethorpes Directions, have been able to make their escape.[12]

Bull repeated the blunt refusal which the Spanish governor had given to deputies visiting St. Augustine to seek the return of fugitives, and he reported that "This Answer has occasioned great disatisfaction & Concern to the Inhabitants of this Province, to find their property now become so very precarious and uncertain." There was a growing awareness among whites, Bull concluded, "that their Negroes which were their chief support may in little time become their Enemies, if not their Masters, and that this Government is unable to withstand or prevent it."

III

DEVELOPMENTS DURING the summer months did little to lessen tensions. In July the *Gazette* printed an account from Jamaica of the truce which the English governor there had felt compelled to negotiate with an armed and independent force of runaways.[13] During the same month a Spanish Captain of the Horse from St. Augustine named Don Piedro sailed into Charlestown in a launch with twenty or thirty men, supposedly to deliver a letter to Gen. Oglethorpe. Since Oglethorpe was residing in Frederica far down the coast, the visit seemed suspicious, and it was later recalled, in the wake of the Stono incident, that there had been a Negro aboard who spoke excellent English and that the vessel had put into numerous inlets south of Charlestown while making its return. Whether men were sent ashore was unclear, but in September the Georgians took into custody a priest thought to be "employed by the Spaniards to procure a general Insurrection of the Negroes."[14]

Another enemy, yellow fever, reappeared in Charlestown during

---

12 BPRO Trans., XX, 40–41.
13 SCG, July 28, 1739.
14 SCCHJ, 1741–1742, July 1, 1741, pp. 83–84.

the late summer for the first time since 1732. The epidemic "destroyed many, who had got thro' the Small-pox" of the previous year, and as usual it was remarked to be "very fatal to Strangers & Europeans especially."[15] September proved a particularly sultry month. A series of philosophical lectures was discontinued "by Reason of the Sickness and Heat"; a school to teach embroidery, lacework, and French to young ladies was closed down; and the *Gazette* ceased publication for a month when the printer fell sick.[16] Lt. Gov. Bull, citing "the Sickness with which it hath pleased God to visit this Province," prorogued the Assembly which attempted to convene on September 12. The session was postponed again on October 18 and did not get under way until October 30.[17] By then cool weather had killed the mosquitoes which carried the disease, and the contagion had subsided, but it had taken the lives of the chief justice, the judge of the Vice-Admiralty Court, the surveyor of customs, the clerk of the Assembly, and the clerk of the Court of Admiralty, along with scores of other residents.[18]

The confusion created by this sickness in Charlestown, where residents were dying at a rate of more than half a dozen per day, may have been a factor in the timing of the Stono Rebellion,[19] but calculations might also have been influenced by the newspaper publication, in mid-August, of the Security Act which required all white men to carry firearms to church on Sunday or submit to a stiff fine, beginning on September 29.[20] It had long been recognized that the free hours at the end of the week afforded the slaves their best opportunity for cabals, particularly when whites were engaged in communal activities of their own. In 1724 Gov. Nicholson had expressed to the Lords of Trade his hope that new legislation would "Cause people to Travel better Armed in Times of Publick meetings when Negroes might take the better opportunity against Great Numbers of Unarmed men."[21] Later the same year the Assembly had complained that the recent statute

15 James Killpatrick, *An Essay on Inoculation*, p. 56; letter of Oct. 16, 1739, Pringle Letterbook.

16 *SCG*, Oct. 13, 1739; Dec. 1, 1739.

17 *SCG*, Sept. 15, 1739; Oct. 20, 1739.

18 Yates Snowden, *History of South Carolina*, 5 vols. (Chicago and New York, 1920), I, 231.

19 A letter from S.C., dated Sept. 28, was reprinted in the *Boston Weekly News-Letter*, Nov. 8, 1739: "A terrible Sickness has rag'd here, which the Doctors call a yellow billious Fever, of which we bury 8 or 10 in a Day; the like never known among us; but seems to abate as the cold Weather advances."

20 *SCG*, Aug. 18, 1739.

21 May 5, 1724, BPRO Trans., X, 111.

requiring white men "to ride Arm'd on every Sunday" had not been announced sufficiently to be effective, and in 1727 the Committee of Grievances had objected that "the Law w^{ch}: obliged people to go arm'd to Church &^{ca}: wants strengthening."[22] Ten years later the presentments of the Grand Jury in Charlestown stressed the fact that Negroes were still permitted to cabal together during the hours of divine service, "which if not timely prevented may be of fatal Consequence to this Province."[23] Since the Stono Uprising, which caught planters at church, occurred only weeks before the published statute of 1739 went into effect, slaves may have considered that within the near future their masters would be even more heavily armed on Sundays.[24]

One other factor seems to be more than coincidental to the timing of the insurrection. Official word of hostilities between England and Spain, which both whites and blacks in the colony had been anticipating for some time, appears to have reached Charlestown the very weekend that the uprising began.[25] Such news would have been a logical trigger for rebellion. If it did furnish the sudden spark, this would help explain how the Stono scheme, unlike so many others, was put into immediate execution without hesitancy or betrayal, and why the rebels marched southward toward Spanish St. Augustine with an air of particular confidence.

IV

DURING THE EARLY HOURS of Sunday, September 9, 1739, some twenty slaves gathered near the western branch of Stono River in St. Paul's Parish, within twenty miles of Charlestown. Many of the conspirators were Angolans, and their acknowledged leader was a slave named

[22] *SCCHJ, 1724*, June 4, 1724, pp. 7, 9; *SCCHJ, 1726–1727*, Jan. 13, 1727, p. 69.

[23] *SCG*, March 26, 1737. It is significant that the next set of presentments dealt with the other side of the coin. It was objected in October that the Sabbath laws were being violated "in several Parts of the Country by laying Negroes under a Necessity of Labouring on that Day, contrary to the Laws of God and Man." *SCG*, Nov. 5, 1737. Whether Sunday labor reduced or enhanced the prospects of rebellion would be debated repeatedly by whites in the next several years.

[24] A similar law, which made clearer provisions for the security of Charlestown, was passed in 1743. *Statutes*, VII, 417–19.

[25] "The Journal of William Stephens," p. 412. A confirmation that war had been declared and the first news of an insurrection at Stono reached Georgia before noon, Sept. 13, via the same "express" from Charlestown.

Jemmy.[26] The group proceeded to Stono Bridge and broke into Hutchenson's store, where small arms and powder were on sale. The storekeepers, Robert Bathurst and Mr. Gibbs, were executed and their heads left upon the front steps.

Equipped with guns, the band moved on to the house of Mr. Godfrey, which they plundered and burned, killing the owner and his son and daughter. They then turned southward along the main road to Georgia and St. Augustine and reached Wallace's Tavern before dawn. The innkeeper was spared, "for he was a good man and kind to his slaves,"[27] but a neighbor, Mr. Lemy, was killed with his wife and child and his house was sacked. "They burnt Colonel Hext's house and killed his Overseer and his Wife. They then burnt Mr Sprye's house, then Mr Sacheverell's, and then Mr Nash's house, all lying upon the Pons Pons Road, and killed all the white People they found in them."[28] A man named Bullock eluded the rebels, but they burned his house. When they advanced upon the home of Thomas Rose with the intention of killing him, several of his slaves succeeded in hiding him, for which they were later rewarded. But by now reluctant slaves were being forced to join the company to keep the alarm from being spread. Others were joining voluntarily, and as the numbers grew, confidence rose and discipline diminished. Two drums appeared; a standard was raised; and there were shouts of "Liberty!" from the marchers. The few whites whom they encountered were pursued and killed.

By extreme coincidence, Lt. Gov. Bull was returning northward from Granville County to Charlestown at this time for the beginning of the legislative session. At about eleven in the morning, riding in the company of four other men, Bull came directly in view of the rebel troop, which must have numbered more than fifty by then. Comprehending the situation, he wheeled about, "and with much

[26] U. B. Phillips (*American Negro Slavery*, p. 473) gives the leader's name as Jonny. Aptheker points out in *Slave Revolts*, p. 187 *n*, that Dr. Ramsey called the leader Cato and used the date 1740. (He could have been referring to a later incident mentioned below.) To avoid such confusions, I have bypassed derivative secondary sources and pieced together the following description of the Stono Uprising from the contemporary materials which survive.

[27] "Account of the Negroe Insurrection," p. 234. This would suggest that even in the midst of the most desperate revolt, slave violence was by no means haphazard. Such an instance of discretion was not unique. During Tacky's Rebellion in Jamaica in 1760, for example, slaves chose to spare one Abraham Fletcher while killing more than three dozen other whites. Robert Renny, *An History of Jamaica* (London, 1807), p. 66.

[28] "Account of the Negroe Insurrection," p. 234.

difficulty escaped & raised the Countrey." The same account states that Bull "was pursued," and it seems clear that if the lieutenant governor had not been on horseback he might never have escaped alive. Bull's death or capture would have had incalculable psychological and tactical significance. As it was, the rebels probably never knew the identity of the fleeing horseman or sensed the crucial nature of this chance encounter. Instead they proceeded through the Ponpon district, terrorizing and recruiting. According to a contemporary account, their numbers were being "increased every minute by new Negroes coming to them, so that they were above Sixty, some say a hundred, on which they halted in a field and set to dancing, Singing and beating Drums to draw more Negroes to them."[29]

The decision to halt came late on Sunday afternoon. Having marched more than ten miles without opposition, the troop drew up in a field on the north side of the road, not far from the site of the Jacksonburough ferry. Some of the recruits were undoubtedly tired or uncertain; others were said to be intoxicated on stolen liquor. Many must have felt unduly confident over the fact that they had already struck a more successful overt blow for resistance than any previous group of slaves in the colony, and as their ranks grew, the likelihood of a successful exodus increased. It has been suggested that the additional confidence needed to make such a large group of slaves pause in an open field in broad daylight may have been derived from the colors which they displayed before them.[30] Whatever the validity of this suggestion, the main reason for not crossing the Edisto River was probably the realistic expectation that by remaining stationary after such an initial show of force, enough other slaves could join them to make their troop nearly invincible by morning.

[29] *Ibid.*

[30] *Ibid.* Fisher, *Negro Slave Songs*, p. 70, points out that members of secret West African cults often claimed to derive invincible powers from the presence of a special banner (much as Roman legions or American marines have historically drawn inspiration from the sight of certain standards):

> Negro cultists in many instances acted as though they were invulnerable. A picture of one of their banners in Africa, drawn by a slave trader of the eighteenth century, shows the cultist carrying a large grigri bag. In it were charms to preserve one from hurt or harm. . . . Jemmy's insurrectionists in South Carolina in the eighteenth century and the Vesey plotters of that same area in the nineteenth century were reckless because of dependence upon their banners.

Cf. William C. Suttles, Jr., "African Religious Survivals as Factors in American Slave Revolts," *JNH* (1971), 97–104.

But such was not to be the case, for by Sunday noon some of the nearest white colonists had been alerted. Whether Bull himself was the first to raise the alarm is unclear. According to one tradition Rev. Stobo's Presbyterian congregation at Wiltown on the east bank of the Edisto was summoned directly from church, and since this would have been the first community which Bull and his fellow riders could reach, the detail is probably valid.[31] By about four in the afternoon a contingent of armed and mounted planters, variously numbered from twenty to one hundred, moved in upon the rebels' location (long after known as "the battlefield"[32]).

Caught off guard, the Negroes hesitated as to whether to attack or flee. Those with weapons fired two quick but ineffective rounds; they were described later in white reports as having "behaved boldly."[33] Seeing that some slaves were loading their guns and others were escaping, a number of whites dismounted and fired a volley into the group, killing or wounding at least fourteen. Other rebels were surrounded, questioned briefly, and then shot.

White sources considered it notable that the planters "did not torture one Negroe, but only put them to an easy death," and several slaves who proved they had been forced to join the band were actually released.[34] Those who sought to return to their plantations, hoping they had not yet been missed, were seized and shot, and one account claimed that the planters "Cutt off their heads and set them up at every Mile Post they came to."[35] Whether the riders used drink to fortify their courage or to celebrate their victory, a bill of more than £90 was drawn up the next day for "Liquors &c" which had been consumed by the local militia company.[36]

[31] Alexander Hewatt, *An Historical Account of the Rise and Progress of the Colonies of South Carolina and Georgia*, 2 vols. (London, 1779), rpt. in Carroll, ed., *Historical Collections of S.C.*, I, 332. The account in Edward McCrady, *South Carolina under the Royal Government*, which follows Hewatt, suggests that Bull went to Charlestown via John's Island while a companion named Golightly rode the eight miles to Wiltown church.

[32] *SCHGM*, X (1909), 28.

[33] "Account of the Negroe Insurrection," p. 235. One slave was said to have answered his owner's query as to whether he truly wished to kill his master by pulling the trigger on his pistol only to have the weapon misfire, at which the planter shot him through the head. "A Ranger's Report of Travels with General Oglethorpe, 1739–1742," in Mereness, ed., *Travels in the American Colonies*, p. 223.

[34] "Account of the Negroe Insurrection," p. 235.

[35] "A Ranger's Report," p. 223.

[36] *SCCHJ*, 1739–1741, p. 158.

V

ALTHOUGH SECONDARY ACCOUNTS have suggested that the Stono Uprising was suppressed by nightfall,[37] contemporary sources reveal a decidedly different story. By Sunday evening more than twenty white settlers had already been killed. Initial messages from the area put the number twice as high and reported "the Country thereabout was full of Flames."[38] The fact that black deaths scarcely exceeded white during the first twenty-four hours was not likely to reassure the planters or intimidate the slave majority. Moreover, at least thirty Negroes (or roughly one third of the rebel force) were known to have escaped from Sunday's skirmish in several groups, and their presence in the countryside provided an invitation to wider rebellion. Roughly as many more had scattered individually, hoping to rejoin the rebels or return to their plantations as conditions dictated.

During the ensuing days, therefore, a desperate and intensive manhunt was staged. The entire white colony was ordered under arms, and guards were posted at key ferry passages. The Ashley River militia company, its ranks thinned by yellow fever, set out from Charlestown in pursuit. Some of the militia captains turned out Indian recruits as well, who, if paid in cash, were willing to serve as slave-catchers. A white resident wrote several weeks later that within the first two days these forces "kill'd twenty odd more, and took about 40; who were immediately some shot, some hang'd, and some Gibbeted alive. A Number came in and were seized and discharged."[39] Even if these executions were as numerous, rapid, and brutal as claimed, the prospect of a sustained insurrection continued. It was not until the following Saturday, almost a week after the initial violence, that a white militia company caught up with the largest remnant of the rebel force. This band, undoubtedly short on provisions and arms, had made its way thirty miles closer to the colony's southern border. A pitched

[37] This version is repeated in Sirmans, *Colonial S.C.*, pp. 207–8, and it has recently been echoed again in Richard Hofstadter, *America at 1750, A Social Portrait* (New York, 1971), p. 129.

[38] "The Journal of William Stephens," p. 412; cf. "A Ranger's Report," p. 222, which says "about forty White People" died.

[39] *Boston Weekly News-Letter*, Nov. 8, 1739, extract of a letter from S.C. dated Sept. 28.

battle ensued, and at length (according to a note sent the following January) "yᵉ Rebels [were] So entirely defeated & dispersed yᵗ there never were Seen above 6 or 7 together Since."[40]

It was not until a full month later, however, that a correspondent in South Carolina could report that "the Rebellious Negros are quite stopt from doing any further Mischief, many of them having been put to the most cruel Death."[41] And even then, white fears were by no means allayed. The Purrysburg militia company had remained on guard at the southern edge of the colony, and in Georgia Gen. Ogle-thorpe, upon receiving Lt. Gov. Bull's report of the insurrection, had called out rangers and Indians and issued a proclamation, "cautioning all Persons in this Province, to have a watchful Eye upon any Negroes, who might attempt to set a Foot in it."[42] He had also garrisoned soldiers at Palachicolas, the abandoned fort which guarded the only point for almost one hundred miles where horses could swim the Savannah River and where Negro fugitives had previously crossed.[43] Security in South Carolina itself was made tight enough, however, so that few if any rebels reached Georgia. But this only increased the anxiety of whites in the neighborhood of the uprising.

In November several planters around Stono deserted their homes and moved their wives and children in with other families, "at particular Places, for their better Security and Defence against those Negroes which were concerned in that Insurrection who were not yet taken."[44] And in January the minister of St. Paul's Parish protested that some of his leading parishioners, "being apprehensive of Danger from yᵉ Rebels Still outstanding," had "carried their Families to Town for Safety, & if y Humour of moving continues a little longer, I shall have but a Small Congregation at Church."[45] The Assembly placed a special patrol on duty along the Stono River and expended more than £1,500 on rewards for Negroes and Indians who had acted in the white interest during the insurrection. Outlying fugitives were still

---

[40] Andrew Leslie to Philip Bearcroft, St. Paul's Parish, S.C., Jan. 7, 1740, quoted in Klingberg, *Appraisal*, p. 80.

[41] *Boston Weekly News-Letter*, Nov. 30, 1739. Although the printer put Aug. 18, the date on the letter from S.C. must have been Oct. 18 or thereabouts. The correspondent added: "The Yellow Fever is abated, but has been very mortal."

[42] "The Journal of William Stephens," p. 427; cf. "A Ranger's Report," p. 222.

[43] "Account of the Negroe Insurrection," p. 236.

[44] *SCCHJ, 1739–1741,* Nov. 21, 1739, p. 37.

[45] Letter of Andrew Leslie cited in note 40 above.

being brought in for execution the following spring,[46] and one ring-leader remained at large for three full years. He was finally taken up in a swamp by two Negro runaways hopeful of a reward, tried by authorities at Stono, and immediately hanged.[47]

VI

It is possible to emphasize the small scale and ultimate failure of the uprising at Stono or to stress, on the other hand, its large potential and near success. Either approach means little except in the wider context of slave resistance during these years. Certain elements of the insurrection—total surprise, ruthless killing, considerable property damage, armed engagements, protracted aftermath—are singular in South Carolina's early history. Yet it remains only one swell in the tide of rebellious schemes which characterize these years. In retrospect, its initial success appears a high-water mark, and its ruthless suppression represents a significant turning of the tide. But the troubled waters of resistance did not subside any more abruptly than they had risen. For several years after the outbreak in St. Paul's Parish, the safety of the white minority, and the viability of their entire plantation system, hung in serious doubt for the first time since the Yamasee War.

Rebels from Stono were still at large in late November 1739 when rumors of new threats began. The Assembly requested of Bull that special precautions be taken for the upcoming Christmas holidays,[48] and on December 7 Assemblyman Joseph Izard departed for a week in order to raise the local militia and pursue "several runaway Negroes belonging to Mrs. Middleton that kept about Dorchester who

[46] *SCCHJ, 1739–1741,* pp. 341, 528–29.
[47] *SCG,* Dec. 27, 1742; *SCCHJ, 1742–1744,* p. 263.
[48] *SCCHJ, 1739–1741,* p. 69:

May it please your Honour,

The late Insurrection and Rebellion of the Slaves at Stono, is a sufficient Precaution to us, to take all the Care in our Power, to guard against any further wicked Designs they may have in Agitation; and as the Christmas Holy Days are drawing near (which being a Time of general Liberty to the Slaves throughout the Province) it is to be feared, if they have any such Intention, they will put it in Execution; we therefore desire your Honour will be pleased to give Directions to the proper Officers of the several Regiments in this Province to order the Captains and other Officers under their Command, to draw out of their respective Companies a Number of Men sufficient to patrol in the Christmas Holy Days; pursuant to the Directions of the Act for establishing and regulating of Patrols.

had committed a great many Robberies in those Parts."[49] Four days later the council, in a message outlining the critical situation of the white inhabitants, explained that "we have already felt the unhappy Effects of an Insurrection of our Slaves . . . (an intestine Enemy the most dreadful of Enemies) which we have just Grounds to imagine will be repeated." The council continued, "it is well known to us, that . . . if the present Session of Assembly be determined with the same unhappy Conclusion as the last," then "many of our [white] Inhabitants are determined to remove themselves and their Effects, out of this Province; insomuch, that upon the whole the Country seemed to be at Stake."[50]

Such fears were apparently well founded. Two days after Christmas Robert Pringle, the Charlestown merchant, wrote to his brother:

We have been fatigued for this Week past keeping Guard in Town, on acco^t of a Conspiracy that has been detected to have been Carrying on by some of our Negroes in Town but has been discovered before it came to any maturity. We shall Live very Uneasie with our Negroes, while the Spaniards continue to keep Possession of St. Augustine & it is pity our Goverm^t at home did not incourage the disslodging of them from thence.[51]

In response to a special order of the lieutenant governor and council, the attorney general "spent a great Deal of Time" on an investigation and trial, but the Assembly had to be reminded in May that it had forgotten to repay this officer for "his Trouble and Attendance in prosecuting the Negroes concerned in the intended Insurrection last Christmass."[52] In March, Assembly members had rejected a £60 bill from the five constables of Charlestown for their attendance at the six-day examination of "certain Negroes who were apprehended on Suspicion of a Conspiracy,"[53] probably the same one investigated by the attorney general.

The legislature had scarcely adjourned when another potential uprising was revealed during the first week of June 1740. According

[49] *SCCHJ, 1739–1741,* p. 84.

[50] *Ibid.,* p. 97. The previous session of the Assembly had ended without passage of a new Negro act.

[51] Robert Pringle to Capt. Andrew Pringle, Dec. 27, 1739, Pringle Letterbook.

[52] *SCCHJ, 1739–1741,* May 6, 1740, p. 332. This message from the Upper House was dated May 5. Attorney General James Abercromby had previously submitted to the Assembly (Feb. 6, p. 182) a bill for £308 "for Prosecutions of Felons and other Offenders at March Sessions 1739 and October Sessions 1739, and for Prosecutions of Negro Offenders by special Directions of the Government."

[53] *Ibid.,* March 3, 1740, p. 225.

to first reports among whites, this conspiracy had "the Appearance of greater Danger than any of the former."[54] It originated somewhere between the Ashley and Cooper rivers "in the very Heart of the Settlements."[55] Its focus was apparently on the western edge of St. John's Parish, Berkeley County, near the rice-growing district of Goose Creek. This time between 150 and 200 slaves "got together in defiance."[56] These rebels lacked weapons, and they must also have had the failure of the Stono scheme fresh in their minds. For these reasons, nearby Charlestown, rather than the southern border, became their immediate objective. "As they had no prospect of escaping through the Province of Georgia, their design was to break open a store-house, and supply themselves, and those who would join them, with arms."[57]

How carefully such a strike had been planned and how close it came to execution cannot be determined. It appears that the conspirators' large numbers, which must have provided the confidence for so direct and desperate a plan as the seizure of Charlestown, also proved the source of their undoing. The hope for secrecy was destroyed, in this instance by a slave of Maj. Cordes named Peter, and white forces had time to prepare a suitable ambush for the rebels. Therefore, according to an account reaching Georgia, "when they appeared the next day fifty of them were seized, and these were hanged, ten in a day, to intimidate the other negroes."[58] All told, some sixty-seven slaves were brought to trial, and their betrayer, Peter, appeared personally before the legislature to receive thanks in the form of a new wardrobe and £20 in cash.[59] Robert Pringle summarized the incident in a letter to his wife in Boston at the end of the summer: "We had a Report in June last of some Negroes Intending to make an Insurrection, but [it] was timely Discovered and the Ring Leaders punished."[60]

[54] "The Journal of William Stephens," p. 592.
[55] *SCCHJ, 1739–1741*, p. 364.
[56] "The Journal of William Stephens," p. 592.
[57] [Martyn], *An Impartial Inquiry*, p. 173.
[58] *Ibid.*
[59] *SCCHJ, 1739–1741*, p. 480. Under "Insurrections" in the index for this volume (p. 586), there is confusion as to whether this plot occurred in St. John's Colleton or St. John's Berkeley. But since Maj. Cordes, whose slave revealed the plan, was the representative from the latter parish, it seems certain that the incident centered in St. John's Berkeley.
[60] Robert Pringle to Jane Pringle, Aug. 30, 1740, *SCHGM*, L (1949), 93. New Englanders already had word of the incident, for the *Boston Weekly News-Letter*, July 10, 1740, carried a notice datelined Philadelphia, June 26: "We hear from South Carolina, that a new Negro Plot is just discovered there, but two Days before it was to be put in Execution."

Further hints of slave resistance would follow. Acts of arson were suspected, and the great Charlestown fire that November did little to ease tensions. The spring of 1741 brought lurid tales of slave resistance in northern colonies,[61] and during the winter of 1742 the Assembly was obliged to investigate reports of "frequent Meetings of great Numbers of Slaves in the Parish of St. Helena" which were still striking "Terror" into local Europeans.[62] But by 1740 the implications of growing rebelliousness among slaves had already become unavoidable for the white minority. One Englishman, reflecting back upon Stono and other incidents, wrote:

Such dreadful Work, it is to be feared, we may hear more of in Time, in case they come to breaking open Stores to find Arms, as they did the last Year; and are able to keep the Field, with Plenty of Corn and Potatoes every where; and above all, if it is considered how vastly disproportionate the Number of white Men is to theirs: So that at best, the Inhabitants cannot live without perpetually guarding their own Safety, now become so precarious.[63]

The Europeans' response to this "precarious" situation was desperate and effectual. Confronting at last the actual possibility of widespread revolution, bickering factions were able to cooperate in ways which maintained the English slave colony and determined many aspects of Negro existence for generations to come. Their actions constitute the beginning of a new chapter in the history of South Carolina and therefore lie outside the scope of this study, but they also signify the end of an era for the Negro in the colony, so it is fitting to cite them briefly in conclusion.

VII

ONE THRUST of the white response involved efforts to reduce provocations for rebellion. Besides waging war on the Spanish in St. Augustine, whose proximity was considered a perpetual incitement, the colonial government laid down penalties for masters who imposed such excessive work or such brutal punishments that the likelihood of revolt was enhanced. Efforts to extend Negro dependence were also

[61] See Chapter XI above.
[62] *SCCHJ, 1741–1742*, Feb. 17, 1742, p. 388; cf. pp. 381–82.
[63] "The Journal of William Stephens," p. 592.

undertaken: it was at this time that a Negro school was started in
Charlestown on the assumption that a few slaves might be trained to
teach other slaves certain carefully selected doctrines of the Christian
faith, such as submissiveness and obedience. (The school persisted for
several decades, though its impact on the total Negro population was
negligible.)[64]

These gestures of calculated benevolence were overshadowed
by far more intensive efforts to control and to divide the slaves. The
comprehensive Negro Act, which had been in the works for several
years but about which white legislators had been unable to agree in
less threatening times, was passed into law and stringently enforced.
This elaborate statute, which would serve as the core of South Carolina's slave code for more than a century to come, rested firmly upon
prior enactments. At the same time, however, it did more than any
other single piece of legislation in the colony's history to curtail *de
facto* personal liberties, which slaves had been able to cling to against
formidable odds during the first three generations of settlement. Freedom of movement and freedom of assembly, freedom to raise food, to
earn money, to learn to read English—none of these rights had ever
been assured to Negroes and most had already been legislated against,
but always the open conditions of life in a young and struggling colony
had kept vestiges of these meager liberties alive. Now the noose was
being tightened: there would be heavier surveillance of Negro activity
and stiffer fines for masters who failed to keep their slaves in line.[65]
Even more than before, slaves were rewarded for informing against
each other in ways which were considered "loyal" by the white minority (and "disloyal" by many blacks). The ultimate reward of manumission was now taken out of the hands of individual planters and
turned over to the legislature, and further steps were taken to discourage the presence of free Negroes.[66]

Finally, and most significantly, authorities took concrete steps to
alter the uneven ratio between blacks and whites which was seen to
underlie the colony's problems as well as its prosperity. Since the economy by now was highly dependent upon rice exports, and since the
Europeans in South Carolina were dependent upon African labor at
every stage of rice production, there was talk of developing labor-

saving machinery and of importing white hands to take on some of the jobs which could not be mechanized. A law was passed reiterating the requirement for at least one white man to be present for every ten blacks on any plantation, and the fines collected from violators were to be used to strengthen the patrols.[67] The most dramatic move was the imposition of a prohibitive duty upon new slaves arriving from Africa and the West Indies. While Negroes had arrived at a rate of well over one thousand per year during the 1730s, slave importations were cut to nearly one tenth this size during the 1740s, and the duties collected were used toward encouraging immigration from Europe. Before 1750 the slave trade was resuming its previous proportions, but this interim of nearly a decade meant that newly imported slaves would never again constitute so high a proportion of the colony's total population as they had in the late 1730s.

Among all these simultaneous efforts by whites to reassert their hold over black Carolinians, no single tactic was entirely successful. There is little to suggest that treatment became notably less brutal among masters or that doctrines of submissive Christianity were accepted rapidly among slaves. Despite the Negro Act of 1740, slaves continued to exercise clandestinely and at great cost the freedoms which the white minority sought to suppress. Those who wished to travel or to congregate, those who wished to grow food, hunt game, practice a trade, or study a newspaper learned increasingly to do these things secretly, and since informants were well rewarded, it was necessary to be as covert among other blacks as among whites. The result was not stricter obedience but deeper mistrust; a shroud of secrecy was being drawn over an increasing portion of Negro life.

Nor could white dependency on Negro workers be effectively reduced. The technique of periodically flooding the rice fields to remove weeds without the use of slave labor (which came into practice sometime around mid-century) may have originated in part to serve this end. But machines which could supplant the slaves who pounded rice every autumn made little headway until after the Revolution. Moreover, the recruitment of European settlers never burgeoned, despite offers of free land on the frontier. Therefore, in spite of the reduced import of slaves in the 1740s, the black–white ratio in the colony did not alter markedly.

[67] For example, in May 1744 Peter Taylor was fined £10 "for keeping Slaves without a white Person." *SCCHJ, 1744–1745,* p. 147.

If no one of these efforts succeeded fully enough to alter the nature of the colony, the combined effects were nevertheless clearly felt. The Negro majority, through persistent and varied resistance to the constraints of the slave system, brought South Carolina closer to the edge of upheaval than historians have been willing to concede. But in the process the slaves inspired a concerted counterattack from their anxious and outnumbered masters. The new social equilibrium which emerged in the generation before the Revolution was based upon a heightened degree of white repression and a reduced amount of black autonomy. By the time Europeans in America were prepared to throw off the yoke of slavery under which they felt themselves laboring as the subjects of the English king, the enslaved Negroes in South Carolina were in no position to take advantage of the libertarian rhetoric. Though they still constituted the bulk of South Carolina's population, too many had been reduced too soon into too thorough a state of submission. Had the earlier pervasive efforts at black resistance in South Carolina been less abortive, the subsequent history of the new nation might well have followed an unpredictably different path.

What we call the beginning is often the end
And to make an end is to make a beginning.
The end is where we start from.

We die with the dying:
See, they depart, and bring us with them.
We are born with the dead:
See, they return, and bring us with them.

We shall not cease from exploration
And the end of all our exploring
Will be to arrive where we started
And know the place for the first time.

—T. S. ELIOT, *Four Quartets*

*Appendixes, Bibliography
and Index*

Appendix A

Excerpts concerning labor from a letter written by Edmund White in London to Joseph Morton in South Carolina, February 29, 1688:[1]

Lord Cardross told me negroes were more desirable than English servants & such you may have enough of from Barbadoes: or if you desire to be concerned in a small vessell from hence to Ginny & your port the Royal [African] Comp^a now gives leave upon the allowance of 20 pr. cent? or thereabouts for any vessell to trade to any of their ports & they furnish the cargo cheaper than others can buy. . . . If you approve not of this way or can have none to joyne wth you, then write to Coll John Johnson at Barbados . . . that he would do you the kindness, when any bargaine of negroes is to be had, he would buy them for you and keep them upon his plantation till he can send them [to] you & this he can doe with much care & the negroes will be the better after they have been ashore for sometime and their work will be worth their keeping & he may draw upon me & I doubt not but he will buy of masters of ships for bills of exchange at 11 or 12 lb [£] a head & that will certainly be the most profitable for you & you need not trouble your friends for servants from hence: you still fill up yr letters with the bad conditions of the Milkmayd I sent. I shall endeavour the next ship to gett another haveing lately heard of one that was willing to goe uppon wages, and the same party I hope will supply me when I want one. But as to all other serv^ts let y^r negroes be taught to be smiths shoemakers & carpenters & bricklayers: they are capable of learning anything & I find when they are kindly used & have their belly full of victualls and clothes, they are the truest servants.

[1] The full text is published in *SCHGM*, XXX (1929), 1–5.

Appendix B

"Inventory . . . of John Smyth late of this province. . . ."[1]

	£ s d
Two white servants by name Thomas pindar Samuell hermitage haveing nineteene months to serve	08–00–00
One serv[t] by name Morgan Jones for ditto time being sicke	02–00–00
Three Negroe men Sambo: Smart & Tony	52–00–00
One Negroe womean by name Doll	16–00–00
One Mallatta by name Marea & four pickaninys[2] nanny, Will, theata [?], & pegge	26–00–00
three Indian Girles Named Betty Giny & Sarah	15–00–00
One Indian boy named Hercules	02–00–00
[Several dozen head of livestock	75–00–00]
Thirty head of Cattle of Severall sorts run wild in the woods	37–10–09
Six hogs wild in the woods	01–00–00
[Assorted linen and household items as well as the following supplies and implements: 240 bushels of corn, 20 bushels of peas, 6 shovels, 7 broad hoes, 2 narrow hoes, 3 grubbing hoes, 4 pitching axes, 1 old crosscut saw, 7 old guns, 1 old plow, 1 harrow, 1 mortar and pestle[3]	49–07–03]
	283–18–00

Carolina ffeb[ry] 13th 168⅔

[1] RSP (1675–95), pp. 21–22; cf. Chapter II, note 76, above. Smyth, or Smith, apparently died during the previous fall, for by Dec. 7, 1682, the prosperous Arthur Middleton had already contracted to marry his widow. Middleton assured Mary Smyth her entire inheritance from her husband, "Late of Booshoo in Ashley river," and set aside an additional 1,780 acres for her along with ten Negroes: "Samson, Will, Prince, Quaminy, Hanson, Guy, Santoe men, Cassander a woman and her two Children by Name Dyana Girlie, and, Pompy Boy." RRP-RSP (1696–1703), pp. 92–94.

[2] Such early and formal use of the term "pickaniny" is notable. See Chapter VI, note 17, above.

[3] It is unclear whether this mortar and pestle set (valued at five shillings) is a small household item or the large wooden device later used to clean rice.

Appendix C

THE FOLLOWING TABLE has been compiled from the Treasury Records in the SCDAH and from evidence in the *South Carolina Gazette*.[1] It covers slave imports into Charlestown between March 1735 and March 1740. Arrivals for each of the five years (from March to March) are grouped separately, and a summary of the data is presented in Table X. For a few entries the dates of arrival and sale are unknown and the names of the captain, the importer, and the vessel itself have not been determined and remain blank. Where I have found general and specific listings for the origin of a shipment (implying the vessel stopped at more than one port), I have given the specific name, accompanied by an asterisk, which indicates that another source lists the shipment as originating in "Africa." The point of origin for two shipments and the numerical data for several others have been arrived at indirectly; these have been enclosed in parentheses.

Certain slaves are missing from this tabulation. First of all, Negroes who had spent more than six months in other colonies were subject to a £50 duty designed to prevent the transportation of miscreants from the Caribbean to Carolina.[2] Although the *SCG* of November 8, 1735, listed the arrival of 236 slaves from the West Indies in the previous year, the Treasury Records for the year ending the following March show only seventy-two slaves incurring the higher rate, and all but two were re-exported with a remission of duty. Almost no slaves were taxed at the £50 rate and almost none were re-exported during the remainder of the decade. These two small categories of slaves imported from or shipped to other colonies tended to cancel each other out in these years and can therefore be ignored.

Several of the most valuable Negroes aboard each ship were designated "privilege slaves," since it was the captain's privilege to sell them for his own profit. No doubt the importer often paid the duty and handled the sale of these slaves, but there were instances when

---

[1] Useful but much less complete compilations are available in Donnan, *Documents*, IV, 279–80 (Table 152), 296 *ff.* (Table 158). The Treasury Records themselves are available on microfilm from the SCDAH.

[2] *Statutes*, III, 160–61.

the captain paid the duty himself.[3] Some commanders may have avoided paying the duty altogether, and the same could apply to the occasional "ventures" allowed other ships' officers. At any rate, the number of privilege slaves is small enough to be ignored statistically, even in calculating the average size of shipments. Besides these slaves, the Treasury Records omit a few babes-in-arms who entered untaxed and also those Africans (perhaps several hundred) who arrived at Georgetown and Port Royal. No slaves smuggled into the colony

[3] It appears from the Treasury Records that this applies to items 20, 31, 36, 51, 56, and 62 in Table IX and perhaps to items 9, 34, 45, 58, 60, 63, 78, and 79 as well.

TABLE IX   *Africans Arriving in Charlestou*

	NOTICE GAZETTE	DATE OF SALE	VESSEL	CAPTAIN
	1735			
1.	Apr. 19	Apr. 29	*Morning Star*	W. Hamley
2.	May 10	May 14	*Rainbow*	R. Morgan
3.	May 17	May 28	*London,* Frigate	J. Sutherland
4.	June 28	July 2	*Dove*	R. Fothergill
5.	July 12	July 16	*Amoretta*	D. Jones
6.	July 26	July 31	*Diana*	J. Malone
7.	Aug. 2	Aug. 6	*Faulcon*	S. Sanders
8.	Aug. 30	Sept. 10	*Molly*	J. Carruthers
9.				
10.	Sept. 13	Sept. 24	*Happy Couple*	Mr. Hill
	1736			
11.	Jan. 17	Jan. 21	*Berkley*	P. Stockdale
12.				
13.				
14.				
15.	June 26	June 30	*Amoretta*	D. Jones
16.	June 26	June 30	*Scipio,* Galley	R. Smith
17.	Aug. 7	Aug. 11	*Bonetta,* Pink	P. Comyn
18.	Aug. 21	Aug. 25	*Garlington*	H. Watts

duty-free would appear, but there is little evidence of such activity in the 1730s.

The most striking aspect of the compilation is that during this specific five-year period 70 per cent of all incoming slaves appear to have been drawn from Africa's Angola region. The implications of this fact for the Stono Rebellion and other disturbances of the period are touched on briefly in Chapter IX, section V, above. A fuller discussion of these tables occurs in the author's essay for *Race and Slavery in the Western Hemisphere: Quantitative Studies*, edited by Engerman and Genovese, and cited in note 1 of Chapter V above.

uth Carolina, Between March 1735 and March 1740

SOURCE OF SHIPMENT	DUTY IN £	SLAVES	ADULTS	CHIL-DREN	IMPORTER
Angola	2,965	324	269	55	B. Savage & Co.
Africa	1,450	153	137	16	J. Wragg & Co.
Angola	3,510	378	324	54	Cleland & Wallace
Angola	2,060	208	204	4	J. Wragg & Co.
Africa	(2,280)	(233)	(223)	(10)	B. Savage & Co.
Windward & Gold Coast	(670)	(68)	(66)	(2)	B. Savage & Co.
Angola°	3,610	363	359	4	Jenys & Baker
Angola	3,820	398	366	32	B. Godin
Africa	400	40	40	0	R. Hill
Coast of Guinea°	1,105	118	103	15	J. Wragg & Co.
Angola°	3,470	358	336	22	Jenys & Baker
Barbados	20	4	0	4	James Crokatt
Providence	40	5	3	2	J. Wragg & Co.
Jamaica	10	1	1	0	J. Frasier
Africa	2,100	224	196	28	B. Savage & Co.
Angola°	2,330	262	204	58	Jenys & Baker
Angola	3,610	382	340	42	J. Wragg & Co.
Gold Coast & Angola	2,740	289	259	30	Jenys & Baker

Appendix C

T A B L E I X *Africans Arriving in Charlesto*

	GAZETTE NOTICE	DATE OF SALE	VESSEL	CAPTAIN
19.	Aug. 21	Aug. 25	*Princess Caroline*	J. Coe
20.				
21.	Sept. 18	Sept. 22	*London*	J. Sutherland
22.	Sept. 18	Sept. 25	*Dorothy*	W. Douglas
23.				
24.				
25.				
26.				
27.	Oct. 16	Oct. 27	*Speaker*	H. Flower
28.	Oct. 30	Nov. 2	*Sheperd*	M. Power
29.	Nov. 6	Nov. 10	*Phoenix*	D. Arthur
	1737			
30.	Jan. 8	Jan. 19	*Loango*	T. Dolman
31.				
32.	Feb. 5	Feb. 9	*Mary*	R. Pollixsen
33.				
34.				
35.	May 28	June 1	*Amoretta*	D. Jones
36.				
37.	July 23	July 27	*Pine-Apple*	D. Hallowe
38.	July 30	Aug. 3	*Pearl,* Galley	E. Hardwick
39.				
40.				
41.				
	1738			
42.				
43.			*Susannah,* Snow	
44.				
45.				
46.				
47.	Mar. 2	Mar. 15	*Shepherd*	M. Power
48.	Apr. 6	Apr. 12	*London Merchant*	J. Thomas

South Carolina, Between March 1735 and March 1740   (*continued*)

SOURCE OF SHIPMENT	DUTY IN £	SLAVES	ADULTS	CHIL- DREN	IMPORTER
Gambia	1,390	148	130	18	Hill & Guerard
Gambia°	50	5	5	0	J. Coe
Angola	2,960	319	273	46	Cleland & Wallace
Antigua	30	3	3	0	"To be sold at Publick Ven- due at the usual place"
Barbados	190	19	19	0	S. Haven
Angola	420	44	40	4	B. Savage & Co.
Gambia	315	35	28	7	J. Wragg & Co.
N. Carolina	5	1	0	1	A. Scharmahorn
(Angola)	(3,225)	(356)	(289)	(67)	J. Wragg & Co.
Angola	(3,205)	(350)	(291)	(59)	J. Wragg & Co.
Angola	(2,745)	(300)	(249)	(51)	J. Wragg & Co.
Angola	3,170	337	297	40	B. Savage & Co.
Angola	190	19	19	0	T. Dolman
(Angola)	(960)	(101)	(91)	(10)	J. Wragg & Co.
Angola	1,230	128	118	10	P. Jenys
Angola	40	4	4	0	H. Powell
Africa	2,040	221	187	34	B. Savage & Co.
Africa	70	7	7	0	D. Jones
Angola	1,470	157	137	20	J. Wragg & Co.
Angola	2,415	247	236	11	Hill & Guerard
Montserrat	10	1	1	0	R. Austin
London	10	1	1	0	A. Sutton
Mobile	40	4	4	0	R. Lampton
Angola	815	83	80	3	Montaigut & Curry
Angola	770	79	75	4	Cattell & Austin
Angola	2,600	260	260	0	Hill & Guerard
Angola	10	1	1	0	B. Cross
London	10	1	1	0	T. Shubrick
Angola°	2,665	354	179	175	J. Wragg & Co.
Angola	2,680	292	244	48	J. Wragg & Co.

TABLE IX *Africans Arriving in Charlestow*

	GAZETTE NOTICE	DATE OF SALE	VESSEL	CAPTAIN
49.	Apr. 15	Apr. 19	*London,* Frigate	J. Pickett
50.	Apr. 27	May 3	*Amoretta*	J. Crode
51.				
52.	May 18	May 24	*Bettsey*	A. Duncomb
53.	June 29	July 6	*Speaker*	H. Flower
54.	July 27	Aug. 2	*Mary*	J. Coe
55.	July 27	Aug. 9	*Princess Caroline*	W. Johnson
56.				
57.	Aug. 17	Aug. 23	*Seaflower*	J. Ebsworthy
58.				
59.				
60.				
61.	Oct. 12	Oct. 25	*Maremaid*	W. Wilson
62.				
63.				
64.	Nov. 16	Nov. 22	*Squirrel*	J. Dyke
65.				
	1739			
66.	Mar. 24	Mar. 28	*Hiscox*	S. Saunders
67.	June 9	June 13		
68.	June 9		*Amoretta*	J. Crode
69.	June 9	June 20	*Shepherd*	M. Power
70.				
71.				
72.				
73.				
74.				
75.	Nov. 24	Dec. 5	*Mary*	N. Roberts
76.	Dec. 1	Dec. 5	*Levant,* Galley	Mr. Packer
77.				
78.				
79.				
80.				
	(March, 1740)			

outh Carolina, Between March 1735 and March 1740 (*continued*)

SOURCE OF SHIPMENT	DUTY IN £	SLAVES	ADULTS	CHIL- DREN	IMPORTER
Angola	2,265	254	199	55	Cleland & Wallace
Africa	1,720	208	136	72	B. Savage & Co.
Africa	60	7	5	2	J. Crode
Angola	2,145	223	206	17	Cleland & Wallace
Angola/St. Christophers	2,880	306	290	16	J. Wragg & Co.
Gambia	995	101	98	3	J. Wragg & Co.
Gambia	1,595	169	150	19	Hill & Guerard
Gambia	155	16	15	1	W. Johnson
Africa/St. Christophers	1,450	149	141	8	J. Wragg & Co.
Angola	10	1	1	0	W. Mathews
Gambia	230	23	23	0	Yoemans & Escott
Gambia	40	4	4	0	John Thomson
Angola	1,605	170	151	19	Hill & Guerard
Angola	60	6	6	0	W. Wilson
Gambia	10	1	1	0	J. Dalrymple
Africa	1,910	211	171	40	B. Savage & Co.
Antigua	120	12	12	0	Hill & Guerard
Angola	3,650	374	356	18	Hill & Guerard
Gambia	1,120	118	106	12	Hill & Guerard
Africa	1,875	206	169	37	B. Savage & Co.
Angola	2,760	318	234	84	J. Wragg & Co.
Antigua	50	5	5	0	R. Ellis
St. Kitts	275	30	25	5	Hill & Guerard
Africa	1,865	205	168	37	B. Savage & Co.
Calabar	2,045	227	182	45	J. Wragg & Co.
Antigua	45	6	3	3	Pringle & Reid
Gambia	785	85	72	13	J. Wragg & Co.
Bonny°	3,550	382	328	54	J. Wragg & Co.
Africa	465	53	40	13	F. Holmes
Africa	10	1	1	0	J. Grill
Africa	10	1	1	0	E. Malbone
Africa	50	5	5	0	F. Holmes

Appendix C

TABLE X *Africans Arriving in Charlestown, South Carolin*

TREASURY YR. MARCH–MARCH	FROM ANGOLA				FROM GAMBIA				FROM	
	SHIPMENTS	OVER AGE TEN	UNDER AGE TEN	TOTAL	SHIPMENTS	OVER AGE TEN	UNDER AGE TEN	TOTAL	SHIPMENTS	OVER AGE TEN
1735–1736	6	1,858	171	2,029	—	—	—	—	4	569
1736–1737	12	2,474	417	2,891	2	163	25	188	1	196
1737–1738	5	789	38	827	—	—	—	—	1	194
1738–1739	6	1,276	330	1,606	3	291	23	314	3	453
1739–1740	2	590	102	692	2	178	25	203	5	894
5-Yr. Total	31	6,987	1,058	8,045	7	632	73	705	14	2,306

% of Total Slaves	69.6				6.1				23.5	
Average Size of Shipment	260				101				194	
% Over Age Ten	86.9				89.7				84.8	
% Under Age Ten	13.1				10.3				15.2	

Aarch 1735–March 1740), by Year and by Origin of Shipment

SEWHERE IN AFRICA		FROM WEST INDIES, ETC.				TOTALS			
UNDER AGE TEN	TOTAL	SHIPMENTS	OVER AGE TEN	UNDER AGE TEN	TOTAL	EST. NO. OF SHIPMENTS	SLAVES OVER AGE TEN	SLAVES UNDER AGE TEN	TOTAL NO. OF SLAVES
43	612	3	4	6	10	13	2,431	220	2,651
28	224	3	22	1	23	18	2,855	471	3,326
34	228	4	7	0	7	10	990	72	1,062
122	575	1	12	0	12	13	2,032	475	2,507
186	1,080	3	33	8	41	12	1,695	321	2,016
413	2,719	14	78	15	93	66	10,003	1,559	11,562

	0.8		100
	7		175
	83.9		86.5
	16.1		13.5

Appendix D

THE FOLLOWING DESCRIPTION, printed in the *South Carolina Gazette* for September 17, 1772, is worth reprinting in full even though it falls outside the chronological limits of this study. It was one of a series of essays on South Carolina by an author who signed himself "Stranger" and who expressed concern over the lax enforcement of the Negro Act of 1740, particularly the clauses regulating the unauthorized comings and goings of slaves:

The *Stranger* had once an opportunity of seeing a Country-Dance, Rout, or Cabal of *Negroes*, within 5 miles distance of this town, on a Saturday night; and it may not be improper here to give a description of that assembly. It consisted of about 60 people, 5–6th from Town, every one of whom carried something, in the manner just described; as, bottled liquors of all sorts, Rum, Tongues, Hams, Beef, Geese, Turkies and Fowls, both drest and raw, with many luxuries of the table, as sweetmeats, pickles &c. (which some did not scruple to acknowledge they obtained by means of false keys, procured from a Negro in Town, who could make any Key, whenever the impression of the true one was brought to him in wax) besides other articles, which, without doubt, were stolen, and brought thither, in order to be used on the present occasion, or to be concealed and disposed of by such of the gang as might have the best opportunities for this purpose: Moreover, they were provided with Music, Cards, Dice, &c. The entertainment was opened, by the men copying (or *taking off*) the manners of their masters, and the women those of their mistresses, and relating some highly curious anecdotes, to the inexpressible diversion of that company. Then they *danced, betted, gamed, swore, quarrelled, fought,* and did *everything* that the *most modern* accomplished gentlemen are *not ashamed of;* except *breaking of lamps, abusing the watch,* and what is commonly called *beating up of quarters,* which would have endangered their own safety. They had also their private committees; whose deliberations were carried on in too low a voice, and with so much caution, as not to be overheard by the others; much less by the *Stranger,* who was concealed in a deserted adjacent hut, where the humanity of a well-disposed grey headed Negro man had placed him, pitying his *seeming* indigence and distress. The members of this *secret council,* had much the appearance of Doctors, in deep and solemn consultation upon life or *death;* which indeed might have been the scope of their meditations at that time. Not less than 12 fugitive slaves joined this respectable company before midnight, 8 of whom were mounted on good horses; these, after delivering a good quantity of Mutton, Lamb, and Veal, which they brought with them, directly associated with one or other of the private consultators; and went off about an hour before day, being supplied with liquor, &c. and perhaps having also received some instructions.—The *Stranger* is informed, that such assemblies *have been* very common, and that the company has sometimes amounted to 200 persons, even within one mile's distance of this place: Nay, he has been told, that intriguing meetings of this sort *are* frequent even in Town, either at the houses of *free Negroes,* apartments *hired to slaves,* or the *kitchens* of such Gentlemen as frequently retire, with their families, into the country, for a few days; and that, at these assemblies, there are seldom fewer than 20 or 30 people, who commit all kinds of excesses. Whenever or wherever such nocturnal rendezvouses are made, may it not be concluded, that their deliberations are never intended for the advantage of the white people?

Bibliographical Note

THE FEW BOOKS LISTED BELOW, in addition to those included in "Notes on the Text," have been cited in an abbreviated form throughout the volume. All other sources have received a full reference in the first footnote in which they appear. Most of these sources, and a number of others, are grouped together in the bibliography which appears in Wood, "Black Majority," pp. 608–21. Rather than reproduce that listing here, it seems sensible to urge interested readers toward useful existing guides on the one hand and toward the primary resources on the other.

Printed sources for South Carolina history are surveyed in J. H. Easterby, ed., *Guide to the Study and Reading of South Carolina History, A General Classified Bibliography* (Columbia, S.C., 1950) and in Robert J. Turnbull, *Bibliography of South Carolina, 1563–1950,* 6 vols. (Charlottesville, Va., 1956–60). The best essay describing colonial materials is by the late Gene Sirmans; it can be supplemented with the more recent and specialized notes of Converse Clowse. (Both books are listed below.) All those interested in any aspect of Afro-American history and culture should know and own the book edited by James M. McPherson, Laurence B. Holland, James M. Banner, Nancy J. Weiss, and Michael D. Bell: *Blacks in America, Bibliographical Essays* (Garden City, N.Y., 1971).

South Carolina's archival resources are best approached through John Hammond Moore, ed., *Research Materials in South Carolina, A Guide Compiled and Edited for the South Carolina State Library Board* (Columbia, 1967). The *South Carolina Historical and Genealogical Magazine,* which began in 1900 and which became the *South Carolina Historical Magazine* in 1952, contains relevant subject matter in almost every volume. Three articles in that journal by Charles E. Lee and Ruth S. Greene (vols. LXVII-LXVIII, 1966–67) provide a useful guide to the legislative journals of the colony. Hennig Cohen's volume, *The South Carolina Gazette, 1732–1775* (Columbia, S.C., 1953), serves as an introduction to that newspaper. Most public documents which survive from the colonial period are in the South Carolina Department of Archives and History in Columbia. Useful collections of private papers are contained in the South Carolina Historical Society and the South Caroliniana Library. In these excellent archives, as well as at others inside and outside the state, it continues to be rewarding to draw advice from knowledgeable individuals as well as printed guides.

Finally, although there is no substitute for the direct examination of documentary sources, it is worth remembering that written records represent only one avenue of access to the past. North American historians have yet to consider fully what new contributions can be made by archaeology, anthropology, and other less obvious disciplines in reinterpreting the continent's cultural heritage.

Aptheker, Herbert. *American Negro Slave Revolts.* 2nd edn. New York, 1969.

Brickell, John. *The Natural History of North-Carolina.* Dublin, 1737. Republished, Raleigh, N.C., 1911.

Childs, St. Julien Ravenel. *Malaria and Colonization in the Carolina Low Country, 1526–1696.* (*Johns Hopkins University Studies in Historical and Political Science,* Series 58). Baltimore, 1940.

Clowse, Converse D. *Economic Beginnings in Colonial South Carolina, 1670–1730.* Columbia, S.C., 1971.

Donnan, Elizabeth, ed. *Documents Illustrative of the History of the Slave Trade to America.* 4 vols. Washington, D.C., 1930–35.

Equiano, Olaudah. *The Interesting Narrative of the Life of Olaudah Equiano, or Gustavus Vassa, the African.* London, 1789. Republished as "The Life of Olaudah Equiano, or Gustavus Vassa, the African, Written by Himself." Arna Bontemps, ed., *Great Slave Narratives.* Boston, 1969.

Force, Peter, ed. *Tracts and Other Papers Relating Principally to the Origin, Settlement, and Progress of the Colonies in North America, from the Discovery of the Country to the Year 1776.* 5 vols. Washington, D.C., 1836–46.

Gascoyne, Joel. *A True Description of Carolina.* London, 1674.

Glen, James. *A Description of South Carolina.* London, 1761. Republished in Chapman J. Milling, ed., *Colonial South Carolina: Two Contemporary Descriptions.* Columbia, S.C., 1951.

Gray, Lewis Cecil. *History of Agriculture in the Southern United States to 1860.* 2 vols. Washington, D.C., 1933.

Johnston, Gideon. *Carolina Chronicle, The Papers of Commissary Gideon Johnston, 1707–1716.* Frank J. Klingberg, ed. Berkeley, Calif., 1946.

Jordan, Winthrop D. *White Over Black, American Attitudes Toward the Negro, 1550–1812*. Chapel Hill, N.C., 1968.

Klingberg, Frank J. *An Appraisal of the Negro in Colonial South Carolina, A Study in Americanization*. Washington, D.C., 1941.

Laurens, Henry. *The Papers of Henry Laurens*. Philip M. Hamer and George C. Rogers, eds. 3 vols. Columbia, S.C., 1968–.

Lawson, John. *A New Voyage to Carolina*. London, 1709. Republished with introduction and notes by Hugh Talmage Lefler. Chapel Hill, N.C., 1967.

Le Jau, Francis. *The Carolina Chronicle of Dr. Francis Le Jau*. Frank J. Klingberg, ed. Berkeley, Calif., 1956.

McCrady, Edward. *The History of South Carolina under the Proprietary Government, 1670–1719*. New York, 1897.

Milligen, George. *A Short Description of the Province of South-Carolina . . . Written in the Year 1763*. London, 1770. Republished in Chapman J. Milling, ed., *Colonial South Carolina: Two Contemporary Descriptions*. Columbia, S.C., 1951.

Muhlenberg, Henry M. *The Journals of Henry Melchior Muhlenberg*. Theodore G. Tappert and John W. Doberstein, trans. and eds. 3 vols. Philadelphia, 1942–58.

Nairne, Thomas. *A Letter from South Carolina*. London, 1710.

Rivers, William J. *A Sketch of the History of South Carolina to the Close of the Proprietary Government, 1719*. Charleston, S.C., 1856.

Salley, Alexander S. *Narratives of Early Carolina, 1650–1708*. (J. Franklin Jamison, ed., *Original Narratives of Early American History* series.) New York, 1911.

Sirmans, M. Eugene. *Colonial South Carolina, A Political History, 1663–1763*. Chapel Hill, N.C., 1966.

Weston, Plowden Charles Jennett, ed. *Documents Connected with the History of South Carolina*. London, 1856.

NOTE: The attention of researchers is called to John Donald Duncan, "Servitude and Slavery in Colonial South Carolina, 1670–1776," unpublished Ph.D. dissertation, Emory University, Atlanta, Georgia, 1971.

Index

COLONIAL AND REVOLUTIONARY AMERICAN HISTORY IN NORTON PAPERBACK